Representing Shakespeare

Representing Shakespeare

New Psychoanalytic Essays

edited by Murray M. Schwartz
and Coppélia Kahn

The Johns Hopkins University Press
Baltimore and London

Copyright © 1980 by The Johns Hopkins University Press
All rights reserved
Printed in the United States of America

The Johns Hopkins University Press, Baltimore, Maryland 21218
The Johns Hopkins Press Ltd., London

Originally published, 1980

Johns Hopkins Paperbacks edition, 1982

Library of Congress Cataloging in Publication Data

Main entry under title:

Representing Shakespeare.

Bibliography: p. 264.
1. Shakespeare, William 1564-1616—Criticism
and interpretation—Addresses, essays, lectures.
2. Psychoanalysis and literature—Addresses,
essays, lectures.   I. *Schwartz,* Murray M.
II. *Kahn,* Coppélia.
PR2976.R4   822.3'3   79-3682
ISBN 0-8018-2302-1
ISBN 0-8018-2825-2 (pbk)

For Judd and Peggy, and in memory of
C. L. Barber, who fostered so much of this work

Contents

Acknowledgments

We wish to express our gratitude to William P. Sisler and Joyce Latham of The Johns Hopkins University Press and to Kevin Bowen and Laura Simpson for their cooperation in the preparation of the manuscript for publication. Coppélia Kahn wishes to thank Wesleyan University for research funds in support of her writing. Murray M. Schwartz wishes to thank his colleagues at the Center for the Psychological Study of the Arts, especially Norman N. Holland and David Willbern, for their intellectual support and criticism. They are a constant reminder of the value of friendship in the creation of new relations between psychoanalysis and literature.

Introduction

Murray M. Schwartz
and Coppélia Kahn

The essays in this book can be seen to represent an emerging consensus on the recurrent, defining features of Shakespeare's art as it is reflected through contemporary psychoanalytic concepts. The essays were not written to achieve a consensus, nor have they been revised to advocate one. Instead, they show a confluence of critical views made possible by the interaction of individual sensibility and broad agreement in theoretical emphasis. The encounters between Shakespeare and psychoanalysis that began in Freud's work continue to yield critical rereadings of Shakespeare's personal and artistic representations; these essays constitute a new phase in this evolutionary process. The consensus we see in them is, in a sense, always "emerging."

To view this anthology as a contribution to a larger process may seem an odd way to announce its value for Shakespeareans or literary critics (including, perhaps, some of the contributors) who are interested in exploring the relations of psychoanalysis and art. Freudians have been more used to programmatic schemes for applying psychoanalysis to texts, more comfortable with so-called applied scientific values in a supposedly impersonal critical practice, and so they have been perceived by Shakespeareans and critics in general. But for both literary critics and psychoanalytic theorists, this position (the scientific virtue of the nineteenth century) is becoming untenable, the more so as we realize the implications of psychoanalysis in the study of language and, alternatively, the implications of its language for the structure of psychoanalytic methods. "I do not think illnesses have changed," writes psychoanalyst M. Masud R. Khan, "but our ways and means of reading and meeting these illnesses continue to change, and that constitutes the true function of theory in our practice."[1] Altered theoretical formulations of psychic illness have been matched by new ways of conceiving the entire range of human development and activity.

The literary counterpart of this self-consciousness can be seen in the variety of uses to which theory is put in these essays. In each instance, theoretical commitment informs a way of "reading and meeting" the resonant complexities of Shakespeare's art so as to create significance that is not reducible to some exterior and prior biography or principle. The orthodox distinctions among art, criticism, and biography can thus vary into freer relationships among text, author, and reader. Critics are implicated in the text they write as fully as in the text they write about. Their interpretations are both inventive and interventive, not merely a discovery but also a formation of meaning. To realize this is to practice a psychoanalytic method of interpretation at once richer and more problematic than the stance of the applied scientist allows. The emerging we see here is intimately bound to this flexible interplay of theory and practice.

Before we turn to the representations of Shakespeare in these essays, therefore, their most common psychoanalytic commitments deserve to be sketched. The works of Erik H. Erikson, G. S. Klein, R. D. Laing, Heinz Lichtenstein, Margaret Mahler, D. W. Winnicott, and others assimilated in these essays share an effort to articulate root issues in human development. In differing ways, they view development as an individuating of subjectivity in an interaction of the infant with the mother and other persons. This interaction results gradually in the assimilation and inscription of idioms of representation we call identity. The human subject, in this view, is reducible neither to what is given (innate drives, autonomous ego functions, maturational capacities) nor to what is imposed from without (the determining power of symbol systems, including language) but is a result of the relationship of those two factors in specific times and places. The relationship between the given and the imposed is never, by the very definition of its terms, completed, except by death.

Although the ratio of given and imposed varies according to constantly evolving circumstances, it always involves continuities as well as changes. In recent years, as the active contribution of the infant to this ratio has been accorded increasing prominence because of systematic observation of child development, the dialogic structure of individuation has become clearer. Development occurs within a process of mutual reflection that binds the infant's incipient subjectivity to the parenting response it provokes. (As Brutus says, "The eye sees not itself/But by reflection, by some other things.") The continuity that results from this always-changing interaction is enmeshed in the interactive matrix, so that the child's identity should not be imagined as a self-sufficient unit independent of relationship, but a structuring of relationship, an internalization of the repeated aspects of the first dialogue.

Especially in connection with Shakespeare, two dimensions of this developmental process deserve emphasis: the *representative* role of the parent and the *dramatic* nature of the process itself. In the first dialogue, the parent communicates a preverbal representation of the child's emotional and bodily condition as the parent experiences it. This representation to the child is partly determined by the parent's representation to himself or herself of the child's condition, which is itself partly determined by the parent's own experience as a child. Thus we see an open series of representations, each involving the interplay of at least three terms: the child responds to the parent's response to it; the latter response is informed both by the relation to the child, as shaped by the present environment, and by the parent's past response to parents, who responded to him or her in an earlier variation of a complex and open-ended process. The continuity of relation between self and other that the child gradually identifies as "myself" is always a representation of his subjectivity in relation to another. The process is circular, and development is the broadening of the circle of possible representations.

The dramatic aspect of development is bound to its temporal dimension. From the beginning, the timing of parental response is crucial for the child's experience of continuity and transformation. In the course of development, the interactions of parent and child will involve both gradual and critical periods, both smooth and opposing contours. The stages of development that psychoanalysis has gradually delineated generalize the encounters in time between biological maturation and the broadening field of cultural representation. Development is a staging of stages.

A crucial graduation in development takes place in the movement from preverbal representations to the acquisition of language. Language both preserves and transforms preverbal modes of representation. It preserves them by the stabilization of image or mood, by the association of bodily processes with the rhythms of speech, and by the power of words to re-create absent objects and relationships. It transforms preverbal representations by bringing them into play with structures of meaning inherited through language, in its formal characteristics and in the history of the meanings of words. The decisive encounter for subsequent cultural life between what is given and what is imposed is staged through the acquisition of language. Therefore, any psychoanalytic understanding must enter into detailed relation with the subject's representation of himself through a verbal idiom. Reading through metaphor, image, phrase and the design of sound, psychoanalytic interpretation seeks to re-create the structure of mediation that language embodies and conceals.

To summarize, what we call identity is the representation of a subject for another subject, and this entails for each participant not only what Freud called the person's "conditions for loving," but his conditions for meaning as well.

It follows that in representing the other we represent ourselves. Just as the dialogue of analyst and analysand creates meanings in the present that can be felt as continuous with meanings in the analysand's past, so the critical dialogue represents the other—Shakespeare in his world—in terms of the individual and collective *present* concerns of the authors of these essays. The reader will discover whether and to what extent the critic present in each chapter and the Shakespeare created in the critic's representation of him can be made to fit the reader's own dialogue with Shakespeare. Criticism grounded in contemporary psychoanalysis offers no more certainty and no less promise than this.

To say this, however, is not to relegate the critical act to solipsism or subjectivity, but to complicate the relation between a primary text and its perpetuation. Michel Foucault has said that the very notion of an author, once it is understood historically, leads us to question the ways in which we individuate the originators of various works. An author can be seen as "the principle of a certain unity of writing" and as "the principle of thrift in the proliferation of meaning." To accept this idea is not to license all interpretations or to deny the possibility of consensus, but to recognize that we are always in a dialogic relation to both the author we describe and the audience we address. Foucault writes that "The author is not an indefinite source of significations which fill a work; the author does not preceed (*sic*) the works, he is a certain functional principle by which, in our culture, one limits, excludes, and chooses; in short, by which one impedes the free circulation, the free manipulation, the free composition, decomposition, and recomposition of fiction."[2]

To achieve a consensus is thus to share in the "authorization" of an author, and this process always has both imaginative and ideological dimensions. What we see in the design of Shakespeare's works that seems to point beyond them to the personal existence of their originator is a representation, a convergence of what we reveal with what we form through our language. To read, to interpret, is not only to speak *about*, but to speak *for*.

The essays in this book speak for a Shakespeare who imagined the world in extreme terms, and who was fascinated by the ways in which extremes meet. He was therefore perpetually exploring the relation of opposites, the ways they mask and generate identities, the ways they create gaps between self and self, class and class, action and speech, men and women, parents and children. Being a dramatist of opposites, gaps and identities, he seems to have made his identity of the question of identity, and so, paradoxically, he seems an absent author himself, the poet Keats imagined without identity. But the obverse of this seeming absence is the negative capability that Keats saw as the style of the poet.

Taken to its extreme, Shakespeare's central subject is the formation and contexts of the very identity he seems at once to lack and to exemplify. If he returns again and again to the ways in which individuation is disrupted by violence, he returns equally to the ways in which the potential for violence is mediated by the interplay of individual desire and hierarchic power. The author of extremities was also "Temp'ring extremities with extreme sweet" (*Romeo and Juliet*).

Very often the relation of opposites takes the form of splittings or separations. Parents are separated from children, or whole families from each other. Twins are divided, brothers displaced by geographical or ideological differences, husband and wife psychically divorced. Shakespeare's preoccupation with the family leads him to interweave the definition of theatrical space with the vicissitudes of family bonds, so that plot becomes at once a material and imaginative reality; the splitting of families becomes the plot of a play, and the recognition of one's "place" coincides with the return of the family to its land. To split the family is thus to structure the play, to land the family at the edge of the sea, which always remains a possibility and a threat.

But to split is also to multiply. The most extreme negation of order becomes for Shakespeare a generative strategy. "The multiplying villanies of nature" fill the gaps opened in the absence or murder of kingly authority. The figure of authority (degree, law) is for him the symbol of a union always beyond final realization, for in the very act of imagining the integration of masculine and feminine, control and nurturance, Shakespeare also imagines its destruction. To kill or mask the presence of the King is thus to set in motion a series of doubling relations that make Shakespeare's plays seem to resonate with internal parallels and repetitions. He makes of negation, violence, and dismemberment a multiplication of characters and meanings, a celebration of creative possibilities.

Even the most destructive action thus becomes part of a dialectic of contraries, an alternation within extremes. "As I multiply, so I halve; as I generate relationships and meanings, so I divide wholes, split unities": this might be a way of transcribing the Shakespearean idiom of identity. Stated thus formally, Shakespeare's style may seem the apotheosis of unresolved ambivalence, or the very opposite, continual openness to dramatic interplay at many levels. Depending on specific contexts, this style of construing reality reflects and structures different central themes in different plays and is not confined to one mode of representation. Shakespeare's dramatic power derives as much from the concrete interpersonal ramifications of his vision as from its formal design. His plays and poems do not merely illustrate his identity but are in each instance a dynamic expression of the struggle to re-create and explore its origins and consequences. Within the recurrent features of his self-representations, we see patterns of self-reflection that vary from work to work and impart to his work as a whole an apparently unlimited capacity for variation.

To display this recurrence and variation most fully, we have organized the essays in pairs or groups that focus on common issues of interpretation. We begin with two essays to illustrate psychoanalytic methods. Norman Holland recapitulates the history of psychoanalytic criticism in the form of three overlapping interpretations of Hermia's dream in *A Midsummer Night's Dream*. The first takes the literary dream as an actual dream, inferring associations to it which imply the standard oral, anal, phallic, and genital phases of development. The next interpretation gives a context to the dream in the play, to illustrate how the actual and literary dreams share configurations of defense and wish, threat and anxiety. The third encompasses the other two within the concept of identity, defined as a theme and variations. Ambivalence is the theme, and Shakespeare plays it through love and hate, trust and betrayal, fusion and separateness. Holland, in representing this alternation, discovers Shakespeare's design by playing it through his own consciousness of fidelity and possession. His essay thus illustrates *de jure* what most of the others illustrate *de facto* about psychoanalytic interpretation.

In a comparable illustration of interpretive methodology, Murray M. Schwartz locates the reader in the intermediate space between subjective and objective perception. What D. W. Winnicott called "potential space" —the realm of spontaneity in relating, of which the prototype is the mother-child dialogue—has an analogue for the interpreter in the representation of the reading experience as a confluence of inner and outer realities. Making a further analogy between the potential space of interpretation and that of relationships between characters in the plays from *Hamlet* through the romances, Schwartz then states some themes central to many of the following essays.

Shakespeare, he says, enacts in tragedy the rupture of potential space and reconstitutes that space in romance. He portrays the deepest source of this rupture as the hero's experience of betrayal by or violent separation from the mother, a breach that separates him from all women and from part of himself as well. Trapped between dependency and rage, the hero then embarks on a vain and self-destructive quest to reestablish what was ruptured, either by denying his separateness from others or by violently rejecting dependency on them. In his quest, he projects his anger onto women: Gertrude, Desdemona, Cordelia. Beginning with *Antony and Cleopatra*, however, Schwartz finds Shakespeare reopening potential space through restored trust in women, renewed hope in generational continuity, and validation of the paternal structures that link men and women.

These paternal structures are the subject of David Sundelson's essay on *The Tempest*. Sundelson centers on Shakespeare's drive toward an affirmative representation of fatherhood, and he sees the play as a study in paternal narcissism that depicts the father as the sole authority whose dominion shelters, nurtures, and even creates (in the numerous rebirths Prospero sponsors) everyone in the play. Yet, anxieties about fatherhood and authority persist: in Prospero's obsessive need for Miranda's submission and attention, in the way the despised Caliban personifies the sexual and appetitive desires Prospero would deny, and in Ferdinand's sexual threat and Prospero's rigorous subjugation of him. Nonetheless, the hero masters them through "altruistic surrender." He embodies his own gratification in Ferdinand, and in the wedding masque he restores both Ceres, the nurturing mother absent from the rest of the play and whose place he had tried to fill, and a socially patterned sexuality in the form of the concluding dance. Thus is his fatherhood enacted in designing the artifice of gratification for others.

We then turn from paternal to fraternal relationships, from hierarchy and authority to parity and rivalry. Both Leonard Tennenhouse and Joel Fineman focus on the way bonds with women conflict with bonds between men in many Shakespearean plays. Tennenhouse explores this conflict in the intersection of two deeply held cultural ideals in *The Merchant of Venice*: friendship and marriage. He suggests that Shakespeare's culture stresses these ideals in order to contain or deny the tensions they arouse. The masculine competition in venture capitalism, for example, is muted by affirming the Christian-humanistic ideal of masculine friendship. Though the comic action moves toward the usual happy pairing of male and female, marriage comes about at the expense of friendship, friendship delays the consummation of marriage, and, in the ring plot, friendship appears a betrayal of marriage. Moreover, though marriage loosens the narcissistic bond between the men, it does not completely undo it, as evidenced in the sense of dissatisfaction and guilt that lingers about the isolated Antonio, an excessively generous narcissist whose bonding with the hero echoes that of speaker and friend in the sonnets.

Joel Fineman's paradigm of fratricidal rivalry, the enmity of identical equals, is also rooted in a notion of culture—culture as ordered by violence. Interpreting Shakespeare's use of hostile doubles in several plays, but focusing on *Hamlet*, Fineman follows René Girard in arguing that these doubles "act out the myth of Difference" to ward off the catastrophe of "no difference," the loss of all distinction. In the comedies,

Fineman says, the denial of difference takes two forms, both benign: women disguised as men, and the narcissistic affinity of same-sex siblings. But in *Hamlet*, fratricide becomes enmeshed with betrayal by women when Gertrude sleeps with two brothers and abolishes difference, which must be reestablished by revenge. In *Troilus and Cressida*, violence itself is the only order, in an action of incessant and fruitless rivalry between equals that only generates more violence. Similarly, the only constancy is inconstancy.

Fineman extends his anatomy of Shakespearean doubles into a redefinition of Freud's oedipally based conception of masculinity. He suggests that since the male's first sense of self is implicated in femininity, during the preoedipal phase, his masculinity must then be conditional on establishing a self differentiated from femininity. But the price of this achievement is an internal division that Shakespeare recurrently depicts.

Similar insights into the driving need of Shakespearean men to repudiate femininity outside and within themselves inform the essays by David Leverenz on *Hamlet*, by Janet Adelman on *Coriolanus*, and by Richard Wheeler on patterns of merger and autonomy in the tragedies. Leverenz relates Hamlet's radical confusion to historical assumptions that make manliness dependent on the repression and denigration of feeling (the assigned province of women). These same assumptions link reason and patriarchal order, represented by the Ghost. He emphasizes the mind's suspicion of Claudius while denying expression of the heart's outrage at Gertrude. Burdened by his father's destructive expectations and mixed communications, Hamlet delays revenge because he wants at the same time to restore his mother's validation of his feelings. In the last act, Leverenz argues, Hamlet succeeds in revenge but fails to affirm what his world calls the woman in himself—"everything denied by reasonable men." This view opposes the notion of the Oedipus complex as the product of innate drives, and following Sullivan, Laing, and Winnicott, represents Hamlet's matricidal and parricidal desires as responses to precariously internalized and contradictory expectations of his society.

Janet Adelman's close reading of *Coriolanus*, on the other hand, portrays a pervasive and coherent preoedipal dynamic in its action. She shows how the hero's masculine identity is based on turning his dependency and vulnerability (which in Rome are exclusively associated with femininity) into phallic aggression. The rigid masculinity he displays as a warrior enables him to think he is self-sufficient, but this character is in fact a false one, a role that his mother has written and directed for him. In a tragic paradox, he actually remains "a boy of tears," inwardly dependent on the mother who thrust him from dependency into an excessive and narrow masculinity. When Coriolanus turns against Rome, Adelman says, he is retaliating against this dependency on Volumnia and is trying to establish a separate existence. This attempt is destined to fail, because his deepest desire, to stand alone and be author of himself, is self-contradictory.

Between *Hamlet* and *The Tempest*, Richard Wheeler finds the same kind of polarity that Adelman shows within *Coriolanus*: the oscillation between a longing for merger and a drive toward autonomy. In the "trust-merger" group of plays, *Hamlet, Othello, King Lear,* and *Antony and Cleopatra*, the effort to establish autonomy is in tension with the stronger need for a lost or jeopardized mutuality. In the "autonomy-isolation" group, an overinvestment of self in others or a denial of psychic separateness leads to estrangement and isolation. Like Schwartz, Wheeler believes the romances reconstruct what was destroyed in the tragedies. Using Winnicott's understanding of the role of aggression in the formation of the self, he distinguishes between the destruction of objects in the attempt to control them omnipotently in the tragedies (Lear's relation to Cordelia, for example) and the ability to use, that is, to have a creative relationship with, objects in the romances.

Writing as a feminist critic who wishes to "de-center" the structures of dominance and submission underlying Shakespeare's tragedies, Madelon Gohlke finds that heterosexual union or the prospect of it tends to unleash violence against women in his heroes. The language of prostitution, rape, and murder that men use toward women, she argues, has two layers. While it seems to portray women as weak and despicable in betraying men, it springs from a sense that ultimately women, not men, are powerful, because their betrayals humiliate and thus feminize men. It is this subtext that provides a rationale for the manifest patriarchal text of dominance over and violence against women. Gohlke's conclusions cohere with those of Schwartz, Leverenz, Wheeler, and Adelman when she writes that "Shakespeare's tragedies may be viewed as a vast commentary on the absurdity and destructiveness of this defensive posture." Finally, she contends that Freud's conception of women as castrated males participates in the prevailing cultural metaphors that reinforce such a defensive posture, and she urges us to recognize the historicity of psychoanalysis in this respect.

Our final group of essays places this masculine identity crisis in a filial context. In his meditation on the centrality of the family in the Shakespearean canon, C. L. Barber claims that Shakespeare evades the problem of manliness in his early works. In the sonnets, he does so by identifying himself with the cherishing parent; in the histories, by avoiding conflict between sons and fathers; in the comedies, by dramatizing release from family ties in festive actions benignly supervised by women. When Shakespeare does confront this problem in the tragedies, he depicts "versions of the Oedipus complex tragically unresolved"— failures to identify positively with adult male authority. Indeed, the tragedies swerve back to the deepest family ties, investing in the human family the expectations and values formerly entrusted only to the Holy Family now banished by Protestantism.

Exploring some of these expectations and values in *Cymbeline*, Meredith Skura begins by noting that families in the romances navigate between two dangers: holding onto their children too tightly (as in *Pericles'* incest plot) or expelling them too violently (as in Leontes' rejection of Perdita). In generational terms, the romances portray the perennial conflict between family inheritance and personal individuality, often through symbolic reenactments in adult life of original family situations. Posthumus' movement from son to husband in the context of several families is such a reenactment. He goes from Cymbeline's family, which holds on too tightly, to Belarius' family, which makes room for a stranger, to an imaginative experience of his own family in the dream vision. In Skura's representation, Shakespeare joins and transforms two literary traditions through Posthumus' dream, the divine epiphany, and the family recognition scene. Thus he presents the family both "from above" as a sacred revelation, and "from below" as the memory of infantile experiences.

The problem of passage from emotional residence within the family to independence and adulthood spans Shakespeare's career, from *The Comedy of Errors* to *The Tempest*. Coppélia Kahn discusses a group of plays as imaginative strategies for dealing with a version of this problem: the ambivalent desire to retain one's position within the oedipal triangle, with parents as sexual objects, and to break away from the family, transferring affections to others outside of it. Forms of doubling are the means of expressing this ambivalence, she finds. In *Errors* and *Twelfth Night*, the twin is a double through whom the protagonist retains ties with the filial past, but who also enables him (or her) to find a mate and break with that past. In three of the late romances, daughters are doubles for their fathers; they repeat but reverse their fathers' experience, lifting them decisively out of the oedipal families of their pasts. Finally, in *The Tempest*, doubling takes the form of revenge: repeating what was done to you, but reversing it onto the other. And the renunciation of revenge becomes the way to gain final independence and authority—to become, so to speak, one's own father.

Since the anthology re-creates in the Shakespearean canon the ramifications of a primary ambivalence toward parental authority, it is appropriate to end it with an essay by David Willbern on circles that contain everything and nothing. In Willbern's formulations of Shakespearean meanings, the extremes within which the other essays work are made to meet. His richly textured study evokes and analyzes the paradoxically positive generativity of Shakespeare's sense of "nothing" as sign, ·sound, and symbol. Drawing on psychoanalytic ideas of the origin of language in absence, separation, and loss (which create a desire to fill a void with signification), he meditates on the ideas of nothing in its sexual and bodily senses and in its linguistic and metatheatrical senses. He finds in Shakespeare's images of female enclosures the same ambivalence toward creation and destruction that many other authors in this collection find, but he also sees them as the basis for the poet's conception of theatrical space as generative and destructive female interiority. The tragedies exemplify this paradox. Depicting the extremes of dissolution and nihilism, their image-making power counterbalances their images of negation. The play *signifies* nothing, awards meaning to destruction.

But to *signify* nothing is a particularly Shakespearean way to give playing an identity and thus to name Shakespeare's own most significant strategy of self-representation. Willbern's essay returns us to the general formulation that began our summary of the Shakespearean idiom of dramatic expression. Whatever the specific familial content, whatever the developmental analogue of the action, Shakespeare plays within extremes so as to generate dialogues of unity in division: "two distincts/Division none." We could say that his dilemma and his achievement, as they are seen through contemporary psychoanalysis, are that he represents his identity as the dilemma of identity itself. If the essays in this collection are read as variations on this theme, they too can be seen as a unity.

Notes

1. M. Masud R. Khan, *The Privacy of the Self* (New York: International Univ. Press, 1974), pp. 93-98.
2. "What Is an Author?" in *Language, Counter-Memory, Practice: Selected Essays and Interviews*, ed. Donald F. Bouchard (Ithaca: Cornell Univ. Press, 1977), pp. 113-38.

Representing Shakespeare

1 ❀ Hermia's Dream

Norman N. Holland

> Literature is a dream dreamed for us.
> —*The Dynamics of Literary Response* (1968)

What could be more imaginary than a dream of a dream of a dream? Yet Hermia's dream is just that in *A Midsummer Night's Dream*. She dreams but later decides she was dreaming that she dreamed. Then, at the very end of the play, we, the audience, are told: "You have but slumb'red here"; we dreamed that she dreamed that she dreamed.

A dream of a dream of a dream—surely this is what the comedy means when it tells how:

> . . .as imagination bodies forth
> The forms of things unknown, the poet's pen
> Turns them to shapes, and gives to aery nothing
> A local habitation and a name.
>
> (V.i.14–17)[1]

The psychoanalyst and the literary critic do the same. In our effort to give imaginary dreams a local habitation and a name, those of us who use psychoanalysis to talk about literature have historically used several different approaches. The first is typical of the first phase of psychoanalysis: we would use Hermia's dream as an illustration of someone's unconscious made conscious. In the second phase, we would place her dream within a system of ego functions. Finally—today—we would use this airy nothing to symbolize ourselves to ourselves.

For the moment, though, let me go back to the circumstances that lead up to Hermia's dream. At the opening of the play, Duke Theseus hears a plea from Hermia's father, Egeus. Egeus wants the Duke to force Hermia to marry Demetrius, who loves Hermia and has the approval

This chapter first appeared in *The Annual of Psychoanalysis,* 7 (1979). Reprinted by permission of the journal.

of Egeus. Hermia, however, loves Lysander, and he loves Hermia. Theseus nevertheless agrees with Egeus and promises to enforce the law of Athens, which provides that Hermia must either marry the man her father has chosen, or die, or vow to live the rest of her life as a nun, abjuring forever the society of men. This was a dreadful fate for a young lady even in Elizabethan times, but perhaps not so bad a fate when you see what men were available.

Hermia and Lysander decide that the best way to cope with this decree is to run away from Athens. They do so, but Lysander gets lost and Hermia becomes exhausted from wandering in the wood. They sleep and Hermia has her dream.

When we first hear the dream, it is still going on. That is, I think she is still dreaming when she first speaks about it. As with so many nightmares, she is having trouble waking:

> Help me, Lysander, help me! do thy best
> To pluck this crawling serpent from my breast!
> Ay me, for pity!

And only now, I think, is she beginning to come out of it:

> Ay me, for pity! what a dream was here!
> Lysander, look how I do quake with fear.
> Methought a serpent eat my heart away,
> And you sate smiling at his cruel prey.
> Lysander! what, remov'd? Lysander! lord!
> What, out of hearing gone? No sound, no word?
> Alack, where are you? Speak, and if you hear!
> Speak, of all loves! I swoon almost with fear.
> No? Then I well perceive you are not nigh.
> Either death, or you, I'll find immediately.

(II.ii.145-56)

In effect, as Hermia tells the dream, she splits it into two parts. In the first, we hear the dream actually taking place. In the second, Hermia reports the dream to us after it is over. In the first part she makes a plea for help, but in the second we learn that Lysander wasn't interested in helping at all—he was just smiling and watching the serpent eat Hermia. Further, if we take the most obvious Freudian meaning for that serpent—a penis or phallus—the masculinity in the dream is split between the attacking, crawling serpent and her lover Lysander, smiling at a distance.

Among the fifty-one topics Erikson suggests considering in a full dream analysis, let me be merciful and select just one: "methods of defense, denial, and distortion," which might be considered a variation on another topic, "mechanisms of defense," itself a subtopic of "ego identity and lifeplan."[2] I see in this dream something I think is fundamental to Hermia's character.

If I go back to the first things Hermia says and look just at her speeches as an actor would, I see a recurring pattern.[3] After hearing her father, Theseus admonishes her, "Demetrius is a worthy gentleman," and Hermia replies with her first words in the play, "So is Lysander" (an alternative). But, replies Theseus, since Demetrius has your father's approval, he "must be held the worthier." "I would my father look'd but with my eyes," answers Hermia. Next she begins a long speech by begging Theseus' pardon, wondering why she is bold, and worrying lest, by revealing her thoughts, she impeach her modesty. But, she says:

> . . . I beseech your Grace that I may know
> The worst that may befall me in this case,
> If I refuse to wed Demetrius.

> (I.i.62–64)

I hear in all these speeches a distinct, recurring pattern. Call it a concern for alternatives, for other possibilities, or for an elsewhere: Lysander as alternative to Demetrius, her judgment as an alternative to her father's, her boldness contrasted with her modesty, or the alternatives the law allows her. We could say that Hermia's personal style or character consists (in the theoretical language of Heinz Kohut) of creating self-objects.[4] Thus, after her dialogue with Theseus, the lovers are left alone, and Hermia uses a variety of examples and legends from the elsewhere of classical mythology to illustrate and buttress their love. Then, to Helena, who loves Demetrius, she describes how she and Lysander will run away, again looking for an elsewhere, an alternative to Athens: "To seek new friends and stranger companies." I would phrase Hermia's personal style as the seeking of some alternative in order to amend something closer to herself.

Her last speeches as well as her first show this sense of alternatives. Theseus, Egeus, and the rest have come upon the lovers and wakened them. However, the lovers are not sure they aren't still dreaming. Says Hermia:

> Methinks I see these things with parted eye,
> When every thing seems double.

> (IV.i.189–90)

Demetrius starts checking reality and asks: "Do you not think/The Duke was here, and bid us follow him?" And Hermia, for her last word in the play, offers one final alternative: "Yea, and my father."[5]

Her dream dramatizes her "parted eye" in all its divisions, in the double telling, in the here and there of Lysander and the serpent, and in the very content of the dream—her effort to save herself by getting the serpent away and bringing Lysander closer. I think I could show the same theme of amendment by alternative if I were to trace through the dream the various levels of this adolescent girl's development: oedipal, phallic, anal, and oral.

Following the symbols (like that snake) and the libidinal levels of Hermia's dream would be the first and classical way of analyzing the dream, provided we ground the analysis on the free associations of the dreamer. Alas, however, this being a literary dream, we do not have associations in the way they usually float up from the couch. Nevertheless, we can analyze the dream in the classic way by inferring Hermia's associations.

I

We can begin by guessing at the day residue of Hermia's dream—a conversation she has with Lysander just before they lie down to go to sleep:

> *Enter Lysander and Hermia.*
> *Lysander.* Fair love, you faint with wand'ring in the wood;
>   And to speak troth I have forgot our way.
>   We'll rest us, Hermia, if you think it good,
>   And tarry for the comfort of the day.
> *Hermia.* Be't so, Lysander. Find you out a bed;
>   For I upon this bank will rest my head.
> *Lysander.* One turf shall serve as pillow for us both,
>   One heart, one bed, two bosoms, and one troth.
> *Hermia.* Nay, good Lysander. For my sake, my dear,
>   Lie further off yet. Do not lie so near.
> *Lysander.* O, take the sense, sweet, of my innocence!
>   Love takes the meaning in love's conference.
>   I mean that my heart unto yours is knit
>   So that but one heart we can make of it;
>   Two bosoms interchained with an oath,
>   So then two bosoms and a single troth.
>   Then by your side no bed-room me deny;
>   For lying so, Hermia, I do not lie.
> *Hermia.* Lysander riddles very prettily.
>   Now much beshrew my manners and my pride,
>   If Hermia meant to say Lysander lied.
>   But, gentle friend, for love and courtesy,
>   Lie further off, in humane modesty;
>   Such separation as may well be said
>   Becomes a virtuous bachelor and a maid,
>   So far be distant; and good night, sweet friend.
>   Thy love ne'er alter till thy sweet life end!
> *Lysander.* Amen, amen, to that fair prayer, say I,

And then end life when I end loyalty.
Here is my bed; sleep give thee all his rest!
Hermia. With half that wish the wisher's eyes be pressed!
[*They sleep.*]

(II.ii.35–65)

(Notice how she closes by alternating Lysander's wish.)

Their conversation concerns just exactly the question of separation, as in "lie further off," and the danger of union, Hermia's fear for her maidenly modesty if Lysander comes too close. If I think about Hermia's dream in the general framework of an adolescent girl's oedipal fears and wishes about the opposite sex, particularly in the light of this conversation, I see her imagining Lysander in two aspects. First, there is the Lysander who is physically close to her, and in the conversation they had before sleeping this is a sexual Lysander, one whom she feels is a threat to her maidenly virtue. The other is a Lysander at a distance, and him she associates with love, courtesy, humane modesty, and loyalty. In the dream, she will image this distant Lysander as smiling. Not so the nearer. In the day residue, the Lysander trying to get close proclaims that "my heart unto yours is knit, / So that but one heart we can make of it." In the dream, this sexual union of hearts becomes a snake eating her heart away. The dream separates these two aspects of Lysander, the sexual and the affectionate, but has images of both as hostile. By her waking cry for Lysander to help her, Hermia tries to put them back together in a more benevolent, pitying way, but reality fails her in this. While she dreamed, Lysander left her for Helena.

The next time we see Hermia, she has managed to track down the missing Lysander by his voice. Lysander has been following Helena because, while he and Hermia were briefly asleep, Puck dropped on his eyes the "love-juice" or "this flower's force in stirring love," which made Lysander fall in love with the next being he saw. While Hermia was sleeping, Helena came in and woke Lysander. He promptly fell madly in love with her and followed her off into the forest. Thus when Hermia woke from her nightmare, she could not find him.

We have no way of knowing how much Hermia has heard through her sleep of Puck's talk about the charm for Lysander's eyes or of the ensuing dialogue between Helena and Lysander, but I am willing to assume that some of this talk has percolated into her dream. In particular I think she may have heard Puck speaking about the charm and may have drawn on the idea of a special fluid in representing the oedipal Lysander as a snake with its venom. She may also have heard Lysander declare his love for Helena, and that is why she shows him in the dream as hurting her and as a double person, that is, one who lies. This is a key word not only because his name is "Lies-ander," but also because he made all those puns on "lie" during the dialogue before their nap. As he said, "for lying so [close to you], Hermia, I do not lie." Puns and lies, in which one word carries two meanings, might have helped Hermia to split and so double her representation of Lysander, especially Lysander as a snake.

In a true free association, the next time we see Hermia, she misunderstands Demetrius and thinks he has killed Lysander while he was sleeping. She promptly compares Demetrius to a snake:

> O brave touch!
> Could not a worm, an adder, do so much?
> An adder did it! for with doubler tongue
> Than thine, thou serpent, never adder stung.

(III.ii.70–73)

In other words, Hermia's free association for falseness while sleeping is a snake, and her free association to the snake is the doubleness of its tongue. As one of the fairies had sung earlier, "you spotted snakes with double tongue" (II.ii.9).

Both in the doubleness and in the tonguiness, the snake says what Hermia might well want to say about her now false Lysander. Moreover, the serpent fits Hermia's thoughts in another curious way. Twice in Shakespeare's works (although not, as it happens, in *A Midsummer Night's Dream*) we are told that the adder is deaf. So in Hermia's dream, Lysander does not seem to hear her cries for help.

In yet another way, then, Hermia applies her characteristic personal style to the sexual problems imaged in her dream. She separates the oedipal Lysander into two aspects: a sexual, hostile, intrusive being right on top of her and a milder but also hostile man at some distance. In the same way, her dream shifts its sensory mode (to return to another of Erikson's topics for dream analysis). She begins with something touching her—the serpent crawling on her breast. She shifts to looking: "Lysander, look how I do quake with fear." Then she looks for Lysander and does not find him: "What, remov'd?" Then she calls to him, but he does not answer: "What, out of hearing gone?" She has moved from the immediate sense of touch to the more distant senses of sight and hearing. Interestingly, Hermia comments on—or if you will, associates to—just this shift when next we see her. The very words she speaks when she finds her lost Lysander are:

> Dark night, that from the eye his function takes,
> The ear more quick of apprehension makes.
> Wherein it [night] doth impair the seeing sense,
> It pays the hearing double recompense.
> Thou art not by mine eye, Lysander, found;
> Mine ear, I thank it, brought me to thy sound.

(III.ii.177–82)

Again, with her doubling and with the ear gaining what the eye loses at night, she shows her characteristic concern with alternatives, particularly one alternative compensating for another.

Sight takes on still more importance if we can imagine that Hermia has unconsciously overheard Lysander falling in love with Helena. Puck has just dropped the love-juice into Lysander's eyes. Further, when Helena comes upon the sleeping Hermia and Lysander right after Puck leaves, she is complaining that her eyes will not attract Demetrius the way Hermia's eyes do. Then, almost the first thing Lysander says when he awakes and falls in love with Helena is:

> Transparent Helena, nature shows art,
> That through thy bosom makes me see thy heart.

> (II.ii.104-05)

Hermia seems to me to take this image of complete truth or candor and dream it into a snake eating her own heart, an emblem of doubleness, treachery, and hostility.

If we were to limit ourselves to the old, rigid, one-to-one symbolism of early psychoanalysis, we would say simply that the snake is a symbol for a penis or a phallus. Rather than call it simply phallic, though, I would like to go beyond the symbolic code to a more human meaning for that stinging, biting snake. I can find it in Erikson's modal terms *intrusive* or *penetrating*. Hermia expresses that intrusion into her body as eating. In other words, she has built into the oedipal or phallic levels of the dream (the dream considered as an expression of an adolescent girl's attitude toward male sexuality) a regression to earlier levels of development. In yet another way, Hermia has provided an alternative— namely, anal and oral significances—to her own oedipal and phallic sexuality.

For example, one of the issues raised by the serpent in Hermia's dream is possession in contrast to true love. The serpent proposes to eat Hermia's heart, to make it a prey—in other words, to possess it. Earlier that day Hermia's father, Egeus, had accused Lysander: "With cunning hast thou filch'd my daughter's heart" (I.i.36), just as he had given her bracelets and rings, knickknacks and nosegays. Lysander partly replies by insisting that he has just as much money and land as Demetrius. Finally, when Hermia sees that Lysander has fallen in love with Helena, she cries:

> What, have you come by night
> And stol'n my love's heart from him?

> (III.ii.283-84)

False love is treating a heart like a possession that can be stolen. In true love, by contrast, hearts fuse and become one, as in Lysander's plea for Hermia to lie down by him: "My heart unto yours is knit,/So that but one heart we can make of it." Similarly, Helena recalls that she and Hermia were such close friends they had "two seeming bodies, but one heart" (III.ii.212).

Yet it is precisely this fusion of hearts that Hermia refused when she would not let Lysander lie down with her. She left herself open to the other, possessive kind of love. Now, after her dream, she pleads to Lysander: "Do thy best/To pluck this crawling serpent from my breast!" In other words, make an effort to get this repellent, crawling thing away—and I hear the faintest trace of an excremental metaphor here: make an effort to push this disgusting thing out of you or me.

"Crawling" she calls it, a word she uses only one other time in the play, much later, when Puck has thoroughly befuddled all four lovers, leading them on a wild goose chase through the woods. Finally, each collapses, with Hermia saying:

> I can no further crawl, no further go;
> My legs can keep no pace with my desires.
>
> (III.ii.444–45)

Legless crawling is something less than fully human. Crawling suggests a desire for possession almost disembodied from the human, a desire that in life she has kept within "humane modesty" but which in her dream she feels as overpowering.

At the deepest level of the dream, that desire for possession becomes eating and thus both fusing with and taking away a person's essence: "Methought a serpent eat my heart *away*." Phallic intrusion and possession become a hostile, consuming oral possession. The dominant image of the dream seems to me to be the mouth: the serpent's eating and Lysander's smiling. Hermia's thought moves in the direction of sublimation from the eating to the smiling, from her being the serpent's "prey," to "pray" in the other sense, her prayer to Lysander to help her. Similarly, in the dream she moves from being eaten to being looked at: "Lysander, *look* how I do quake. . . ." The day before, she had parted from Lysander by saying that, "we must starve our sight/From lovers' food till morrow deep midnight" (I.i.222-23). The sight of the beloved is lovers' food. We should perhaps hear a pun in Hermia's exclamation during her dream: "Ay me, for pity!" "Ay me" includes "Eye me," look at me, as well as "I—me," a blurting out of her dual self. Again, Hermia has defended by setting up alternatives. She deals with the nightmare by saying she is both in the dream and out of it.

In the same way, when she cannot find Lysander, she cries "alack," and I hear the word in its original sense—just that, a lack: something is missing, taken away, dissociated. Her characteristic defense of providing an alternative can lead to a tragic separation—here it is Lysander's going off after the alternative, Helena.

Doubleness thus takes on a special charge for Hermia because it plays into her characteristic mode of defenses and adaptation: the providing of alternatives. Now, finally, I can surmise why out of all the materials that might have been important to her—her meeting with the Duke, the argument with her father, her flight by night—she dreams about the conversation she has with Lysander before they lie down to go to sleep. That conversation hinges on precisely the key issue for Hermia: one and two. Lysander wants them to have "one turf . . ./One heart, one bed, two bosoms, and one troth," but this idea Hermia finds threatening, not only for the ordinary reasons a young girl of the gentry in the English Renaissance would, but because such a fantasy would deprive her of her customary mode of adaptation. At all levels of her dream, she is working out a theme of love within her characteristic way of dealing with inner and outer reality, namely, by finding alternatives. Union in love is one possibility, but she dreams about her fear of it as a deadly possession that would prey upon and eat away her very being. However, the other alternative, separation, leads to another kind of cruelty through distance and indifference and—alack!—a loss.

The sexual symbolism of her dream thus rests upon a far deeper doubleness, her wish and her fear that alternatives won't work, that she will have to settle for just one thing: one intrusive, penetrating, possessive lover. In a psychoanalytic context, we can guess that the adolescent Hermia is working out with Lysander a much earlier, more formative relationship with a figure never seen, never even mentioned, in this comedy: her mother.

II

When we come to mother, we come to both the beginning and the end of this kind of dream analysis. What you have just read is an analysis of this fictitious dream as if I were doing it ten years ago. I have been thinking about Hermia's dream mostly as though it were an event "out there" in a play "out there," wholly separate from me. I have been tracing her associations through deeper and earlier phases of her development.

In the earliest years of psychoanalysis, when people turned to invented dreams like Hermia's, they did so for two reasons. Either they were going to use the insight of the poet to confirm the views of the scientist, or they were going to use the ideas of the scientist to understand what the poet had done. One could use Hermia's dream to confirm various ideas about dreaming: that associations explain dreams, that dreams express character structure, that dreams work at a variety of developmental levels, and so on. Then one could say: "See, Shakespeare knew this intuitively. Now psychoanalysis has shown it scientifically." Alternatively, the psychoanalytic literary critic might say, "Here is all this scientific knowledge about dreams. If we apply it to Hermia's dream, we shall see what an extraordinarily rich and complex thing it is." In effect, the Shakespearean critic got a boost from psychoanalysis, and the psychoanalyst got a lift from Shakespeare.

Both these approaches, however, rest on the assumption that we can treat the dream Shakespeare invented for Hermia like a real dream. We are assuming that a play is an exact representation of reality, which obeys the same laws as reality and to which we can apply the same rules for interpretation that we would apply in real life. We can have free associations and symbols and oedipal, phallic, anal, and oral levels in Hermia's dream just as in any real adolescent girl's dream.

Such an assumption is, of course, one way of relating to a play, and some psychoanalytic criticism is still written this way, but few indeed are the literary critics who would settle for this one way. For some four decades now, literary people have been insisting that literary works are not meant to be looked through so as to discover some other, imagined reality they portray. Rather, they are to be looked at as ends in themselves. They are artifacts, just like paintings or sculpture, but made of words instead. This nonrepresentational attitude, furthermore, is part and parcel of the whole twentieth-century concept of art. As Matisse replied to a lady who complained that the arm of a woman in one of his paintings was too long: "Madame, you are mistaken. That is not a woman, that is a picture." So here Hermia is not an adolescent girl—she is a character in a remarkably artificial comedy, so artificial, in fact, that she states her dream in rhymed couplets. How many patients in real life do *that*?

Some ten or twenty years ago, we psychoanalytic literary critics shifted our objective. No longer did we want to treat Hermia like a literal adolescent. Instead, we wanted to understand her as one part fitted into the total play, as the arm fits into Matisse's painting. Both the character and the play are sequences of words that we understand by giving them meaning. Treating Hermia as a real person leads, of course, to one possible meaning, but a very closely limited one, and literary critics prefer to find a larger, more general meaning through themes.

For example, most literary critics treat Hermia's dream as simply "an accurate, if symbolic, account of what has just happened."[6] In that sense, the dream fits into the play's major theme: revelations through

vision, like watching plays or seeing fairies or falling in love with someone you look at.

At least two Shakespeareans, however, have found their way to larger
themes by treating Hermia's dream more dreamily. Marjorie Garber
analyzes this dream as part of her study of all Shakespeare's dreams and
dream imagery.[7] She sees Hermia as afraid of the doubleness she represents in the snake. Hermia separates Lysander as beloved from the
sexuality and violation she associates with the serpent. Yet, in the context of the play as a whole, says Garber, Hermia should not be afraid of
ambiguity or double meanings, for that is what this play is. She should
take doubleness rather as a form of creativity, for in this play the
dream—and that includes the whole play—is truer than reality.

Melvin D. Faber has analyzed this dream, too. The strength of his
analysis lies in the thoroughness with which he has followed out every
symbolic and associative possibility. The limitation comes from resting
the analysis on the overly simple one-to-one symbolic equations so popular in the first exuberant years of applying psychoanalytic symbolism.
Thus the snake is Lysander's penis, dissociated from Lysander, thereby
making him less sexual, and therefore less dangerous. Hermia's heart
stands for her genitals, and the serpent's eating symbolizes (but regres-
sively disguises) genital sex. Thus, concludes Faber, the dream fulfills
Hermia's wish for sex with Lysander, and Lysander's smiling expresses
his satisfied desire and Hermia's as well.

Faber sees in the play as a whole Shakespeare's effort to establish
masculine control over unruly impulses associated with the lack of proper boundaries between male and female. The play establishes control
by dissociating the conscious, social part of the mind from the unconscious, sexual, and dreamlike part—as, says Faber, Hermia does in
miniature in her dream.[8]

As for my own themes for this comedy, I see the questions of separation and fusion that appear in Hermia's dream permeating the play.
That is, _A Midsummer Night's Dream_ begins with the separation of lovers. Theseus and Hippolyta have to wait out the four days till their
wedding, the fairy King and Queen, Oberon and Titania, have quar-
reled, and, of course, the lovers have tangled up their affections and
drawn down the threats of the Duke and the father.

The end of the comedy brings all these lovers together and in between, what has happened is _our_ dream. Puck says in the epilogue:

> Think . . .
> That you have but slumb'red here
> While these visions did appear.
> And this weak and idle theme,
> No more yielding but a dream . . .   (V.i.424–28)

Hermia's dream is, as we have seen, a dream within a dream, a wish therefore that what she dreams of were a wish like the dream around it, therefore the truest part of the play. What, then, is the truth she dreams? She dreams of the doubleness of lovers and the separation of the two aspects of her own lover. As in our word *duplicity*, this doubleness connotes his falseness, as perhaps his name also does: "Lie-sander." One part of him wishes to fuse sexually with her, and she turns to a more separate part of him for help. But, divided this way, both parts of Lysander are cruel, one more physically so than the other.

Cruelty pervades this comedy. As Theseus says to his fiancée in the opening lines:

> Hippolyta, I woo'd thee with my sword,
> And won thy love doing thee injuries.

(I.i.16–17)

You could say the same of Oberon, who humiliates Titania, or of either of our two young men, each of whom deserts and reviles and threatens his future wife. Throughout the play, the ruler, the father, the lovers, the King of the fairies, the amateur actors, and even the audience at the play within the play—all proclaim love, but they also threaten violence or humiliation. The play within the play focuses this ambivalence: it is a "very tragical mirth" (V.i.55), and "the most lamentable comedy and most cruel death of Pyramus and Thisby" (I.ii.11–12) is both the funniest and the bloodiest part of the play.

This comical tragedy within the comedy comes about because the lover Pyramus, separated from his love Thisby and confused in the dark (like our four lovers), believes a lion has eaten her. That lion in Renaissance symbology provides the opposite to Hermia's snake.[9] The royal beast takes his prey in the open, by force and grandeur. The low serpent sneaks his prey by stealth and cunning. Thus the lion in the clowns' broad farce causes right before your eyes a bloody fusion of lovers as Pyramus stabs himself over Thisby's bloody mantle and Thisby stabs herself over Pyramus' bloody body. By contrast, the snake in Hermia's dream images a much subtler cruelty, the desertion and indifference of these not-so-courtly lovers.

This is a second way, then, to read Hermia's dream. The first way is as a clinical study of an adolescent girl. This second, larger reading sets Hermia's dream in the whole atmosphere and development of ambivalence in the comedy. We move beyond the nineteenth and early twentieth-century concern with realism toward a more contemporary interest in theme. Instead of treating the various levels (oedipal, phallic, anal, and oral) as aspects of some particular adolescent girl, I would see them all as variations on the comedy's theme of ambivalence, separations that are both loving and cruel.

Yet both these methods treat Hermia or her dream or her play as though they were "out there," as though I were distant and indifferent to them except for a coolly intellectual curiosity. Both readings pretend the dream and the play are not connected to any me "in here" who shapes and re-creates both the dream and the comedy to fit my own character or, as I prefer to say, my identity. Rather, an abstractly skilled interpreter finds "the" meaning of the dream and fits it to "the" meaning of the play.

III

In the ten years since I wrote such externalized dream analyses, most of us in literature and psychology have come to feel that same new interest in the self that has quickened psychoanalytic theory throughout the world: in Paris through the writings of Lacan, in London in the object-relations theory of Milner and Winnicott and others, or in Chicago in the remarkable technical and theoretical studies of Heinz Kohut. Rather than simply look for an abstract theme "out there" in *A Midsummer Night's Dream*, we have become more interested in how a self— my self, for example—uses the text of the play or the dream as an object to establish a self-structuring relation.

Clearly, the kind of level-by-level exegesis you have just read makes up part of that relation: working out the implications of the dream through such schemes as Erikson's for analyzing the interaction of manifest and latent content or the classic psychoanalytic scheme of developmental levels. But this kind of analysis leaves out a great deal. It ignores, for example, my feelings as I hear this dream. It ignores the personal quality of my reading, which makes it different from Professor Faber's or Professor Garber's.

Ten years ago, psychoanalytic literary critics cared little about the personal qualities that set one interpretation off from another, partly because we believed there was a best reading (a "the" reading) that would rise to the top as we refined our literary ideas, and the other readings left in the pot simply wouldn't matter very much. Partly, too, we ignored the personal element because we had no way of talking about it. Now, however, we are less confident that there is some best reading, and we have a way of talking about the personal quality of a response.

That is, we have identity theory. We have a way of conceptualizing each new thing someone does as new, yet stamped with the same personal style as all the other actions chosen by that person. Each of us is a mixture of sameness and difference. We detect the sameness by seeing what persists within the constant change of our lives. We detect the difference by seeing what has changed against the background of sameness.

The most powerful way I know to think of that dialectic of sameness and difference is the one suggested by Heinz Lichtenstein: to see identity as a theme and variations like a musical theme and variations. Think of the sameness as a theme, an "identity theme." Think of the differences as variations on that identity theme. That is the way I have read Hermia's character, for example. She creates an alternative that will amend the original possibility. That is her identity theme, and we have seen her work out variations on it in her opening plea to Theseus, in her witty dialogue with Lysander before they lie down to sleep, and, above all, in her dream. These are all various ways by which she tries to amend through an alternative.

Now, just as Hermia develops a variation on her identity theme when she dreams, so you and I develop variations on our identity themes when we read her dream. Thus we arrive at a new kind of psychoanalytic method with literature. Our group at Buffalo calls it "transactive criticism." We actively create, we transact—for example, Hermia's dream and A Midsummer Night's Dream. As critics, it is our job to articulate the relation of those two explicitly.

For me, the two images of Hermia's dream, the eating snake and the smiling lover, evoke large questions of fidelity and possession between men and women that I find puzzling and troubling as I watch my students struggling to find and maintain stable relationships or as I see in my own generation yet another friend's marriage break up. That is, Hermia's dream, her very presence in the forest with Lysander, builds on the mutual promises she and Lysander made, a contract sealed by a dangerous elopement, a pledge of faith that her lover, at the very moment of her dream, has abandoned. Her dream begins from his infidelity.

As I visualize the dream, I see a small snake at a distance—yes, like a penis in the classic Freudian symbolism—but I also remember a picture from a book of nature photographs of a snake's wide open mouth with long, curved fangs under a pink, arched palate, one demonic eye showing behind the furious jaws. The head is all mouth, really, there is so little else besides that act of biting. Hermia describes the snake as "crawling," and we have already guessed at her associations. Mine are to a baby who is all helpless, inarticulate demand. For me, then, Hermia's image of the snake sets up the idea of possession, the way a lover or a penis can make a total demand as an animal or a baby demands food.

Curiously, food comes up again when Shakespeare has the two men explain why they switched partners. When Demetrius announces he is back in love with Helena, he says:

> . . . like a sickness did I loathe this food [Helena],
> But, as in health, come to my natural taste,
> Now I do wish it, love it, long for it,
> And will forevermore be true to it.

(IV.i.173–76)

The first time Shakespeare explains the switching of affections, it is Lysander who has suddenly fallen in love with Helena just before Hermia's dream. He looks at the sleeping Hermia and says:

> For as a surfeit of the sweetest things
> The deepest loathing to the stomach brings,
>
>   *   *   *
>
> So thou, my surfeit and my heresy,
> Of all be hated, but most of me!

(II.ii.137–42)

Both times Shakespeare has his lovers refer emotional love to oral appetite, and an appetite of total desire or total rejection, fidelity to one girl meaning disgust at all others—at least for a time.

As we have seen, mouths appear twice in Hermia's dream, once in the serpent's eating and once when Hermia says of Lysander, "You sate smiling." For me, there is a great cruelty in that smile, just as there is in his radical rejection of Hermia as a "surfeit" that brings "deepest loathing to the stomach." I feel hatred in that smile and in that imagery of disgust, a hatred that psychoanalysis, in one of its hardest truths, asks us to believe tinges every human relationship. As the tough-minded La Rochefoucauld put it once and for all, "In the misfortune of our best friends we always find something that is not entirely displeasing."[10]

In other words, if I bring my own associations to Hermia's dream and its context, I begin to read the comedy of which it is a part as a rather uncomfortable hovering between different views of love. In one view, love is a total, consuming desire like a baby's for food. In the other, the relation is less demanding: it admits a change of heart or appetite. Yet so cool a lover may be hateful in his very smiling, just as hateful as the snake is in his eating.

Nowadays, people reject the idea that love entitles you to possess another person. I too reject that kind of possessiveness—at least I consciously do. Yet the opposite possibility, a cool, distant love, does not satisfy me as a solution. I believe in a fidelity of mutual trust, an exchange of promises that I will be true to you and you will be true to me. I realize that contemporary patterns of marriage and sex deeply question this style of relationship. Many people believe they can and do love more than one person passionately and sexually at the same time.

No matter how contemporary I like to think myself in sexual matters, however, I have to admit that, deep down, I do not feel that the mutual pledge of loving or of sexual promises is the kind of contract one can negotiate like a lease on an apartment, with provisions for termination, renegotiation, or repairs. Nor do I believe one can hold several such leases at once. To be intimate is to risk oneself with another, and it is difficult, for me at least, to feel free to open myself up to another person without being able to feel that that opening up will be one-to-one, that neither of us will compromise our intimacy by sharing it with some third person. Somewhere inside me I deeply fear that I would be made small and ridiculous, like a child, were my lover to share our one-to-oneness with another lover. Hence I perceive Lysander's smiling as a cruel ridicule.

The comedy, however, like today's lovers, rejects possessiveness. Hermia's father states the theme: "As she is mine, I may dispose of her." The comedy as a whole moves away from this dehumanizing possessiveness, when what the play will substitute is not exactly clear. At the end, Duke Theseus rules:

> Egeus, I will overbear your will;
> For in the temple, by and by, with us
> These couples shall eternally be knit.

(IV.i.179–81)

They will be married, and the power of the Duke will knit them together as couples and as his subjects.

Paradoxically, though, the comedy arrives at this knitting by a system of separations and infidelities. At first Demetrius had been in love with Helena, but at the opening of the play he has fallen in love with Hermia. Then, when Lysander's eyes are charmed, *he* falls in love with Helena. Later, the same thing happens to Demetrius: his eyes are drugged and he too falls in love with Helena. Finally, Puck uncharms Lysander, and the lovers fall into their natural pairs. The Polish critic, Jan Kott, urges us to think of this part of the comedy as a drunken switch party on a hot night, in which all the scantily clad lovers are interchangeable objects of desire who exchange with one another, finally waking up the next morning hung over, exhausted, and ashamed.[11]

Perhaps Kott takes too extreme a view, but the comedy does seem to say the lovers learn fidelity through their infidelities. Yet very little is said about how this union comes about. After they all wake up, Demetrius says of the events of the night before: "These things seem small and indistinguishable" (IV.i.187). And once they are reunited with their proper lovers, the two girls say not another word for the whole long last scene of the comedy.

In other words, the comedy is silent just at the point where I, with my puzzling about fidelity, am most curious. How do these lovers, who now pledge to be true to one another, derive fidelity from their previous infidelity? The play doesn't say. I feel it is up to us as readers and critics to find a solution. One distinguished Shakespearean, Norman Rabkin, writes:

> In *A Midsummer Night's Dream* Shakespeare opposes reason to the folly of lovers whose choices are often magically induced and always willful, only to make us realize that those choices are ultimately right and of the same order as that anti-rational illusion-mongering, the performing and watching of plays, which, depending on the charitable suspension of disbelief . . . nevertheless tells us truths of which reason is incapable.[12]

Rabkin suggests a parallel between the lovers falling in love and the way the rest of us give ourselves to plays. Illusions, fancies, fictions—if we can tolerate them, even lies—can lead us to a higher truth, a loving experience beyond reason. In psychoanalytic terms, I think this transcending corresponds to the basic trust we must all have developed in translating an imagining of a mother's nurturing presence into a confidence that she would really be there when needed. By not being there, she is unfaithful, but out of that first infidelity, most of us made the most basic of fidelities.

Thus I read Hermia's dream as having three parts. First, the snake preys on a passive Hermia's heart in an act of total, painful, destructive possession—hard on Hermia, but satisfying to that masculine snake. That possessiveness is one possibility open to me in relating to a woman or a play.

Second, Lysander smilingly watches the woman he so recently loved being possessed by another. His smile signals to me another kind of cruelty—dispassion, distance, indifference—another way of relating to a play or a lover. The snake is fantastic and symbolic, whereas Lysander presents a far more realistic lover whom I can interpret all too well through our century's alternatives to romantic commitment.

Then there is a third aspect to the dream, as I view it. It is a nightmare. The dream has aroused anxieties too great for Hermia to sleep through. She wakes, and we never learn how she might have dreamed that a loving Lysander plucked away a possessive snake. Instead, we are left with his deserting her for another woman.

For me, the sense of incompleteness is particularly strong, because I very much need to see a coherence and unity in human relations. I want a happy ending for this comedy. I want these couples married at the end, but I don't see—I don't trust, really—the way the comedy gets them together. Out of infidelity comes fidelity—but how? Hermia trusts Lysander, but he is unfaithful and leaves her alone and terrified: "I swoon almost with fear." It is hard for me to trust that there will be a happy outcome despite his cruel and contemptuous abandonment.

When I confess my uneasiness because the dream is incomplete and the play is silent on the creation of trust, I am working through something about myself I have faced many times before. It's hard for me simply to trust and to tolerate uncertainty or absence or silence. I question both Hermia's dream and the sexual revolution of our own time because I need to *know* things, particularly about human relations. I need to feel certain.

None of this, of course, do Lysander or the other lovers say. They talk about feelings of love and jealousy we can all share, but they do so within the conventions of Renaissance marriage. You and I, however, read what they say from a perch in our own culture, with its many marital and nonmarital and extramarital possibilities, all challenging the traditional limits on relations between the sexes. Where Shakespeare's lovers proceeded in their own day to a sure and socially structured Renaissance conclusion, now I feel they are opening up all kinds of twentieth-century uncertainties without, naturally, saying much about them. In particular, Hermia's dream images the tension between possessiveness and distance and the—to me at least—unknown way trust will resolve that tension.

Often, I think, we Shakespeareans teach Shakespeare as though we were ourselves unaffected by any of the changes in the relations between men and women that have happened since the days of Queen Elizabeth or A. C. Bradley. We are reading Shakespeare's romantic comedies in the middle of a sexual revolution. It would make sense to come to grips with the way our own feelings about that revolution shape our perception of episodes like Hermia's dream (or, even more drastically, Kate's antifeminist speech at the end of *The Taming of the Shrew*). That assertion of our selves is the new direction psychoanalytic literary criticism has begun to take.[13]

In acknowledging my role in bringing these twentieth-century issues to this comedy of 1594, I am discovering through Hermia's dream how I am unconsciously or half-consciously possessive, even though I consciously aspire to an ethic of mutual trust. More generally, I am discovering that Hermia's dream takes its life not from some fictitious dreamer, but from my own concern with relations between men and women in my own time and my own hopes for those relations. I read Hermia's dream as an emblem of two human problems. One is an American problem of the 1970's and 1980's. Can one separate love from trust? The other is a universal human question: how can we establish trust with another being whom we partly trust and partly mistrust? Reading Hermia's dream this way, I—or you and I, if you will go along with me—can go beyond the earlier relationships with literature that psychoanalysis made possible.

At first we treated the unconscious processes in literary characters as though they were fact, not fiction, happening "out there," separate from us dispassionate observers. Then we set the character into an ego process embodied in the play as a whole. We began to acknowledge that we were included in that process, too, as we lent ourselves to the play. Now we have begun to make explicit the self-discovery that was only implicit and silent in those two earlier methods.

We can learn how each of us gives life to Shakespeare's imaginings "out there" through our own times and lives, our wishes and fears and defenses "in here." Through psychoanalytic identity theory, we can understand how we are able to talk about the words of another through ourselves and, in doing so, talk about ourselves through the words of another—even if they are as airy a nothing as dream of dream of dream. When we do, we each continue Shakespeare's achievement in and through ourselves. Just as self and object constitute each other in human development, so in the literary transaction the reader constitutes text so that text may constitute its reader. In this mutuality, Hermia's dream is not simply a dream dreamed for us. Rather, we dream her dream for ourselves, and as we know ourselves so we know the dream, until its local habitation is here and its name is us.

Notes

1. Throughout, I am relying on the text of *The Riverside Shakespeare*, ed. G. Blakemore Evans et al. (Boston: Houghton Mifflin, 1974), although I occasionally repunctuate it.

2. Erik H. Erikson, "The Dream Specimen of Psychoanalysis," in *Psychoanalytic Psychiatry and Psychology: Clinical and Theoretical Papers, Austen Riggs Center*, ed. Robert P. Knight and Cyrus R. Friedman (New York: International Univ. Press, 1954), pp. 131–70, 144–45.

3. For a more elaborate example of this method, see Norman N. Holland, "A Touching of Literary and Psychiatric Education," *Seminars in Psychiatry*, 5 (1973), 287–99.

4. Heinz Kohut, *The Analysis of the Self: A Systematic Approach to the Psychoanalytic Treatment of Narcissistic Personality Disorders* (New York: International Univ. Press, 1971), pp. xiv–xv and passim.

5. Most Shakespeareans regard Hermia and Helena as interchangeable, except for height and hair color (III.ii.290ff. and II.ii.114). Reading their "sides," though, as an actress would (see n. 3 above), I detect a characterological difference. As in the text, Hermia speaks and acts through "amendment by alternative" (to compress her identity into a theme). Helena tries to cope (I think) by establishing a contradiction or opposition and then seeking to become that opposite. See, for example, her speeches in I.i.: "Call you me fair? That fair again unsay," and "O that your frowns would teach my smiles such skill." She would give everything, she tells her rival Hermia, "to be to you translated." And she adds: "How happy some o'er other some can be." All these lead to her explication of the emblem of Cupid in

terms of reversals and her decision at the end of the scene to convert Demetrius' pursuit of Hermia in the wood to his presence with herself. Compare her last words in the play, "And Hippolyta" (Theseus' opposite) to Hermia's, "and my father" (Theseus' parallel).

6. David P. Young, *Something of Great Constancy: The Art of "A Midsummer Night's Dream"* (New Haven, Conn.: Yale Univ. Press, 1966), p. 120.

7. Marjorie B. Garber, *Dream in Shakespeare: From Metaphor to Metamorphosis* (New Haven, Conn.: Yale Univ. Press, 1974), pp. 72-74.

8. Melvin D. Faber, "Hermia's Dream: Royal Road to *A Midsummer Night's Dream*," *Literature and Psychology*, 22 (1972), 179-90.

9. See the similar juxtaposition of lion and snake threatening a sleeper in *As You Like It* (IV.iii.106-18).

10. La Rochefoucauld, *Maximes*, ed. F. C. Green (Cambridge: At the Univ. Press, 1946), maxime 583, p. 138 (my translation).

11. Jan Kott, *Shakespeare Our Contemporary*, trans. Boleslaw Taborski (Garden City, N.Y.: Doubleday, 1964), pp. 210-16.

12. Norman Rabkin, *Shakespeare and the Common Understanding* (New York: Free Press, 1967), p. 74; see also pp. 201-05 and 234n.

13. For a particularly fine example of this new mode, applied to a number of Shakespearean plays, see Murray M. Schwartz, "Shakespeare through Contemporary Psychoanalysis" (Chapter 2 in this book).

2 ❖ Shakespeare through Contemporary Psychoanalysis

Murray M. Schwartz

Seventy-six years after *The Interpretation of Dreams*, the frame of theory that defines the boundaries of psychoanalysis has undergone drastic expansions and revisions. Psychoanalytic ways of reading and meeting basic data of human expression—free associations—have been reformed in every dimension to include the earliest developmental relationships, cognitive as well as libidinal capacities and failures, and the social world in the very definition of human identity. Without too severely simplifying their complex, multinational history, I think we can say that psychoanalytic modes of interpretation have been developed in these directions: (1) from readings downward and backward, toward unconscious and infantile actions, also toward reading the significance of manifest relations in the life of the whole person; (2) from the language of libidinal forces to the language of relationships between persons or parts of persons; (3) from preoccupation with the consequences of trauma and frustration to concern also with the consequences of correspondence between inner and outer realities. But these evolutions of the body of psychoanalytic theory are developments of earlier theoretical forms and remain continuous with the tradition Freud initiated when he began a psychology of human intentionality. I know of no better summary statement of the nature of this inclusive evolution than the late George Klein's:

> Psychoanalysis is a psychology of the *meanings and syntheses arising out of crises in an individual's lifetime.* Freud's central contribution was not merely the discovery of sexuality or aggressive determinants of behavior, though these were also fundamental. It was of understanding behavior as *syntheses* that evolve from *conflict*—as modes of *resolution of conflict.* . . . The key,

This chapter first appeared in *Hebrew University Studies in Literature*, 5 (Autumn 1977). Reprinted by permission of the journal.

21

then, to the profundity of Freud's insights is the effort to look at life as a problem-solving venture, involving a constant adjudication of incompatible polarities, actual or fantasized, in which structures are the products of a synthesis of opposing tendencies, with symptoms viewed as solutions carried to pathological extremes.[1]

We can see in Klein's formulation a complete transcendence of the reductive, dismissive attitude toward manifest expression that so frequently characterized psychoanalytic interpretation, especially interpretation of literature, in the flush of exposures of unconscious, repudiated meanings. Contemporary psychoanalysis is not only a "school of suspicion," in Paul Ricoeur's phrase,[2] but a school of trust that remains open to suspicion. The new perspective encompasses its predecessors in a way analogous to organic evolution, but not analogous to a linear, "scientific" progress that approaches closer and closer to some external, unchanging truth. Earlier concepts are not left behind but assimilated to later ones. Trust, in this broader perspective, does not mean disavowal of the inhibiting processes Freud named repression, resistance, infantile fixation, regression, repetition compulsion, and the like. It implies seeing these processes in the context of a "dialectic of contrariety,"[3] an interplay of protective and adaptive actions that begins with birth (or even before birth) and continues throughout life.

Also fundamental to contemporary psychoanalysis is a radical shift in the relation of the interpreter to the person or text interpreted. Freud may have provided the basis for an introspective psychology that could systematically answer "why?" questions about human action, but he also clung to nineteenth-century physical and biological models of explanation that he indirectly demonstrated were inadequate to meet the nature of human creations of meanings, of symbolic discourse. He thought the answers to his questions could be unveiled, penetrated "out there," in the mind or body of the object of his study, even if that object were himself. Here is Freud, the archeologist of the psyche, at his most scientifically optimistic:

If his work is crowned with success, the discoveries are self-explanatory: the ruined walls are part of the ramparts of a palace or a treasure-house; the fragments of columns can be filled out into a temple; numerous inscriptions, which by good luck may be bilingual, reveal an alphabet and a language, and, even when they have been deciphered and translated, yield undreamed-of information about the events of the remote past, to commemorate which the monuments were built. *Saxa loquuntur.*[4]

Nowhere in this image of the interpreter as the reconstructor of the past can I find a statement of Freud's own interpretive activity. When he succeeds, "the discoveries are self-explanatory." *Saxa loquuntur*, not Freud. The world "out there" is opened up to him (by whom?) as by magic, as if the crown of success were bestowed by a god imminent in the interpretive process, independent of himself. For me, this image and process feels exhilarating, but I suspect that the project of reconstruction involves Freud's ignoring of his role in the process. The voice of the interpreter speaks in the object of interpretation. The project involves a projection.

Freud also recognized that perception is a normal *constructive* activity, but he could not (or would not) assimilate this insight into his epistemology of interpretation:

> The projection outwards of internal perceptions is a primitive mechanism, to which, for instance, our sense perceptions are subject, and which therefore *normally* play a very large part in *determining the form taken by our external world.* Under conditions whose nature has not yet been sufficiently established, internal perceptions of emotional and intellective processes can be projected outwards in the same way as sense perceptions; *they are thus employed for building up the external world, though they should by rights remain part of the internal world.*[5] (Italics mine)

For me, this passage is as frustrating as the other was exhilarating. I see Freud passing judgment on a revolutionary insight, one that goes right to the center of the psychoanalytic challenge to so-called scientific thought as he knew and used it. A *normal* process of perceiving the external world, *by constructing it through the process of perception itself, should,* he tells us, remain internal. Freud's "should," it seems to me, closes a door he has just opened and marks his retreat from his own insight into the process of interpretation. In closing the door he left himself with a logical contradiction: what is normal has no right to occur. And he left psychoanalytic interpreters with the comfort of an objective model of science and the unsolved riddle of their own activity, which is subjective, personal, and all-too-humanly pervasive.

The door Freud opened and then closed has been reopened by several psychoanalytic theorists in recent years.[6] In fact, Freud himself remained equivocal and ambiguous on the issue of constructing meanings and interpretations, sometimes sounding his note of absolute confidence, and at other times announcing his frustration at not being able to conquer the territory of the unconscious for science. Those who have followed him have frequently adopted the language of natural science and the depersonalization of the interpreter that it seemed to require, while simultaneously constructing interpretations that, ironically, grant the patient or text interpreted a greater freedom than they grant themselves. If the dream, the symptom, the adaptive act can all be viewed as overdetermined constructs that create meaning even as they delimit awareness, then why not include the choices of the interpreter in this process?

I can put this question positively. Given a more inclusive theoretical framework that does not grant infantile fantasies sole determining status in the creation of meanings, and relinquishes the privileged status of the interpreter as a mirror, a receiver rather than an actor, how does contemporary psychoanalytic retelling of life history happen?

An answer is provided by D. W. Winnicott, and it enables us not only to clarify the nature of a psychoanalytic reading of Shakespeare but to inquire of Shakespeare's dramatic worlds and his projections of human relationships in new ways.

Winnicott defines an area of experience that is both "inside" and "outside," neither subjective nor objective, both assimilation of the world to the structure of our minds and accommodation of our minds to the structure of the world. He calls this area a "potential space," the space of relationship and interplay:

> The potential space between baby and mother, between child and family, between individual and society or the world, depends on the experience which leads to trust. It can be looked upon as sacred to the individual in that it is here that the individual experiences creative living.
>
> By contrast, exploitation of this area leads to a pathological condition in which the individual is cluttered up with persecutory elements of which he has no means of ridding himself.[7]

In potential space we do not ask whether our experience is real or illusory, for the need to distinguish dissolves in the activity of relating inner and outer actualities. We do not ask whether our perceptions or actions create their objects or whether the world external to ourselves determines our perceptions; interplay means that each creates the other. Potential space is between the opposites Freud thought of as alternatives between which we must choose. "He retained the concept of immaculate perception," Jean Schimek writes, "rather than assuming that perception always involves the interaction between the 'objective' features of the external stimuli and the 'subjective' drive or schemata of the individual which selectively organize and give meaning to immediate experience.[8]

Potential space begins with the first interplaying of mother and child and can be actual for the individual throughout life whenever trust is possible. In this transitional area, the modes of action we learn to categorize as mutually exclusive—work and play, knowing and feeling—are not distinguished; we frequently denigrate one mode when we elevate the other, but in this area we are *homo ludens*, and what is real for us is the "dialectic of contrariety" itself.

Imagine a psychoanalyst and a patient, or a person at a play. The analyst or the member of the audience knows what is occurring in the other, the person or play, by responding, by observing the affective relationship that he or she establishes with the other. He or she cannot claim that this knowledge is in the play, or the other person, or that his or her knowing has a reality independent of the other. We know the other person or the play by experiencing in the transitional area between us. The other person or the play becomes a "transitional object," in Winnicott's phrase.

The meaning we establish with the other relies on this process of knowing by yielding the difference between self and other. But this yielding is never complete, since we cannot totally abandon our defensive strategies, which are usually unconscious ways of protecting the very difference between self and other that we relax in the process. Each of us, then, will construct a meaning that depends on who we are, how fully and in what way we establish and use the potential space between us and the object of our knowledge. Even when the stones seem to speak, they speak differently to each of us, because each of us speaks differently to them.

But not entirely. The interplay between ourselves and others, in or out of the analytic setting, may be an experience unique to the individual (one can play with oneself), but when we communicate that experience we use another transitional object—language. In the analytic setting, the verbal interpretation of the patient's actions is an interpolation that "outers" the patient's reality by giving voice to the relationship between the analyst's experience and the patient's experience. In interpreting, the analyst makes a difference in the patient's consciousness by having first allowed himself to experience an identification as fully as he can. The interpretive words, then, make a difference in a double sense, by changing the relationship between self and other for both self and other. This is why an effective analyst "cannot merely employ the idea 'Oedipus complex.' He must use *what it feels like in terms of the actual experiences* of a child."[9] In this context, language bridges the gap between subjective and objective realities by symbolizing their relationship. And in this function of symbolization, the analytic setting can be seen as a prototype of continuous social relationships in general, as a cultural world in miniature.

Interpretation, then, is a symbolizing activity that happens on the overlap between dualities, the very overlap that can lead to endless violence when it is ruptured, unchanging repetition when it is closed off, spontaneity and social well-being when it is flexible—when the individual can freely open and close it. If we try to destroy potential space, we make the other merely an object of aggressive or libidinal actions. If we cannot re-create this space, we endlessly repeat the past. If we can both re-create and use the potential spaces available to us, we create meanings that did not exist before the interplay of dualities occurred. The interpretive process, when we succeed in enacting it, is a form of intercourse, with all the risks and possibilities that we may wish or fear in bodily intercourse. As we love and hate, so we interpret.[10]

Shakespeare first and foremost enabled us to create potential spaces, and he played from the beginning of his dramatic life until the end with forms of play and the consequences of the failures of play. I want to offer some broad formulations of the Shakespearean use of play space in tragic and comic modes during the so-called mature period, starting about 1600.

As I experience the transitional area of the theatre, the Shakespearean play space, I imagine Shakespeare enacting the rupture of just this area *within* the worlds of the great tragedies, and enacting his reconstitution of it in the projects of his final plays. For my Shakespeare, the great work of drama—comparable to the dream work, but happening within a sharable cultural space—was the reconstitution of symbolic (cultural) continuity after he had seen through his own defensive actions (false autonomy, untested idealization, hierarchy as enforced power) in the mature tragedies. I mean that he saw through these illusions in a double sense: he used them as ways of structuring motives (he saw by means of them), and he saw them through, exhausted their possibilities in love and aggression. He wanted, as I see his development, a reformation of potential space in which he would not deny or abandon the insights into the failures of symbolic action his characters had enacted at least from the turn of the century onward.

In *Hamlet*, I experience a world structured by multiple splittings and reduplication of family relationships that cannot lead to generational continuity or shared significance for the characters in the play. I hear Hamlet interrogating the sources of his own identity in an attempt to integrate words and sharable meanings, language and action, masculine and feminine. But I also see him reenacting these polarized realities by using words to obscure meanings, language as a substitute for action, degraded femininity as a projected location for his frustrated desires. The Hamlet I re-create meets his doubles everywhere, because his divided perceptions of the world seem to me to mirror his divided self. Within the potential space of the theatre, I find myself searching for uninterrupted relationships, and I fail, as Hamlet fails.

Instead of continuities, I experience the aggressive manipulation of playing space in a war of masculine wills, as Hamlet, Polonius, Claudius, and the Ghost of Hamlet's father each use the others as actors in their plays, as each seeks to author the script of the others. Hamlet envies the player's ability to "Make mad the guilty and appal the free,/Confound the ignorant, and amaze indeed/The very faculties of eyes and ears" (II.ii.537-39).[11] He would live through the actor's imagined capacity to define the experience of others, but in the rush of action, he comes to see himself as an actor in a play he has not written: "Being thus be-netted round with villanies,—/Ere I could make a prologue to my brains,/They had begun the play" (V.ii.29-31). My experience of the rivalry that leads to mutual persecution in *Hamlet* is the very opposite of the mutual trust Winnicott defines as the ground of cultural existence.

In *Hamlet*, as throughout the tragedies (I except *Antony and Cleopatra* here), the degradation of the feminine is coincident with the rupture of ceremonial order by men. The more demonic, sexualized, defining, and consequential the feminine characters and actions seem to my (masculine) self, and to the masculine characters in the plays, the more precarious the potential space between masculine and feminine aspects of the self and masculine and feminine relations between characters become. Hamlet "Must, like a whore, unpack [his] heart with words" (II. ii.561), must, as I see it, play with and in words because he cannot unite the feminine and masculine aspects of himself, cannot integrate speech and action. To speak is to be a whore; to be silent is to court disaster at the hands of men; to act without speech is to deny his feminine self, however degraded. In this catastrophe of exclusive alternatives, I experience the space of the drama anxiously, warily. I want a union of action and meaning, a story that will not lead from words to violence, but this story can only be promised by Horatio at the end.

In *King Lear,* I experience the splitting of a symbolic order, away from the power to enforce its structure. For me, the center of the play is Lear's refusal to mourn the loss of maternal provision, a refusal that leads him into a persecutory universe within which the breakdown of psychic and social boundaries reaches its most devastatingly powerful Shakespearean form. He becomes his own double in a universe of subjective, painful realities:

> *Lear:* Who is it that can tell me who I am?
> *Fool:* Lear's shadow.

(I.iv.230-31)

The Fool's brutally honest response names the kind of reality I perceive throughout the central action of the play. I find Lear in the shadows his reflectors cast, in the Fool's words, in Kent's surrogate royalty, in his daughter's opposite and opposing relations to him. He becomes in my mind what others do to him and for him, and he is utterly powerless to restore the ceremonies of words, the mediations of language and symbol, even at the end, when the play comes full circle in Lear's desire to find, and his failure to find, symbolic nurturance from Cordelia's mouth.

Instead of witnessing an experience that leads to trust, I witness a usurpation of others in Lear's initial ceremony. The Lear I re-create wants to assimilate the existence of his daughters to his own desires, wants them to be only for him: "Which of you shall *we say* doth love us most?" (I.i.50, italics mine). Instead of interplay, I experience Lear dictating the script. Like a dramatist whose need for love is so total that it destroys its object and itself, Lear puts words in his daughters' mouths and demands that they feed the words back to him—a narcissistic circuit that forecloses the space between self and other. When this strategy fails with Cordelia's attempt to reoccupy an autonomous position in relation to her father, Lear's response is, again, total: "Cornwall and Albany,/With my two daughters' dowers digest this third" (I.i.126–27). For me, as I imagine for those on the stage, Lear has reduced the structure of relationships to a model of infantile feeding. If he cannot make "his generation messes/To gorge his appetite" (I.i.116–17), then others will digest his daughters.

As a consequence of Lear's foreclosure of potential space, I experience a world that devours itself. Whatever cannot be assimilated to Lear's dependency becomes "new adopted to our hate" (I.i.203), and I see him bound by malignant symbiosis rather than nurturant provision, with all the attendant dread of annihilation that Shakespeare associates with feminine enclosure. Goneril and Regan drain the symbolic space between Lear's desires and Lear's power, allowing him no trusted substitutes for original provision. I experience the main action, until Lear's reunions with Cordelia, as a zero-sum game in which separate existence itself is at issue. If the King exists, others are nothing but his instruments; if others exist he is nothing but the locus of their power. Nothing exists for me to pull with against these extremes except the Fool's mad therapy and Kent's invocations of traditional hierarchic obligations, both of which fail to be my resources for imagining psychic and interpersonal continuity in the world of the play when they are no longer there. I feel trapped between dependency and rage. I imagine Lear trapped between dependency and rage, his suffering relieved only temporarily in the short spaces of communion between himself and Cordelia that Shakespeare interrupts with her death. At the end, as always in Shakespearean tragedy, the feminine sources of masculine identity are dead or powerless, and the final lines express to me the very possibility that I have experienced as absent in the course of the play: "Speak what we feel, not what we ought to say" (V.iii.324).

The rupture of potential space in Shakespearean tragedy has its focal point for me in Lady Macbeth's lines:

> I have given suck, and know
> How tender 'tis to love the babe that milks me.
> I would, while it was smiling in my face,

Have pluck'd my nipple from his boneless gums
And dashed the brains out, had I so sworn as you
Have done to this.

(I.vii.54–59)

When I read these lines, I have the uncanny sensation that I am hearing and seeing the prototypical moment in Shakespeare's use of theatrical space in tragedy to enact the violent interruption of ceremonial order. In the first two lines, I see a relationship of mutuality, a loving mother, a nursing child. Then this moment is violently interrupted "while it was smiling in my face," precisely when the interplay between the two is most intensely happening. I feel this violent interruption of a nurturant, communal interplay as a source of Shakespeare's recurrent preoccupation with betrayal and with feminine powers to create and destroy *suddenly,* and in the repeated desire of his male characters both to be that all-powerful woman and to control the means of nurturance themselves, to the exclusion of the otherness of others. In Macbeth's response to Lady Macbeth's verbal violence—"If *we* should fail?" (I.vii.59, italics mine)—I hear him identifying with the woman he fears would annihilate him. They are no longer separate psychologically: they have become a "we" who will murder Duncan, and live isolated from each other for the rest of the play.

What is interrupted in Lady Macbeth's violence is the first location of potential space, and I sense the repetition of this violence again and again in the interruption of communal order in this and other plays. Macbeth disrupts the feast with his delusion of Banquo. Lear shatters his own ceremony in his rage at receiving less than total symbolic response from his daughters. Timon rails against a world he cannot control by feeding. Coriolanus attacks the maternal source of his own masculine rigidity. In all these actions, I recognize a common theme: Shakespeare's mistrust of femininity within and without that results, for these tragic heroes, either in their denial of separateness from others or their violent rejection of dependency on others. It is as if Shakespeare's heroes achieve their identities in the ways they attempt to adapt to the inner reality of Lady Macbeth's threat of violence. In the mature tragedies, the breakdown of play space I experience within the play space of the theatre seems to me to imitate Shakespeare's deepest fear (and wish), that all the symbolic, illusory, shared interplay of creative living will be destroyed like Lady Macbeth's child.

But, with *Antony and Cleopatra,* I begin to experience a new design, as Shakespeare brings the interplay of differences back inside the play. As I have the illusion of moving from Egypt to Rome, from Rome to Egypt, I experience a "dialectic of contrariety" almost impossible in the earlier tragedies. For me, Antony acts out an intensely ambivalent struggle between masculine hardness and feminine fluidity, finally choosing both and neither, a new synthesis. He seems no less a man for having broken out of his soldierly space and into the realm of Cleopatra:

> O, cleave, my sides!
> Heart, once be stronger than thy continent,
> Crack thy frail case! Apace, Eros, apace.—
> No more a soldier. Bruised pieces, go;
> You have been nobly borne.

(IV.xiv.39–43)

I hear Antony in these lines addressing himself with the steady authority he seems to his Roman soldiers to have abandoned. His choice of Cleopatra, as I know it, is not purchased at the price of splitting himself. Rather, his imagery of cleavage and fragmentation seems to me to reveal his emergent acceptance of the feminine aspect of himself, from which the Roman armor defended him.

The interplay of contraries I experience within Antony I also experience in the movement of the play itself. I find myself gradually merging the space of the theatre with the illusory play space created by Antony and Cleopatra, so that by the last act, when I know that Antony is dead, he seems, in Cleopatra's fantasy, more alive than before, and Cleopatra seems more vital, erotic, and seriously playful as she re-creates Antony and dies herself than she seemed earlier, when I felt a need to choose between opposites. For me, it is the interpenetration of opposites, self and other, male and female, that transcends the dilemma of the other tragedies, in which men's desire for separateness masks a failure of differentiation. The interplay allows for metamorphosis, active transformation of the self. This new vision would not be possible, I think, if Shakespeare had not achieved a new degree of mastery of the ambivalent desire for omnipotence that derives from, and then leads to, the distrust of women as "other."

But in *Antony and Cleopatra,* Shakespeare keeps the play space of the lovers separate from the "real" world of masculine political power. Caesar does inherit the earth, however dry and stony. Only in the late romances does Shakespeare bring playing into the play, along with the possibility of generational continuity. As I read them, the re-creation of masculine identity and cultural continuity in the romances depends on restored trust in feminine capacities *and* the restoration of paternal design of the relationships within which women exist.

Even where feminine power is most pervasive, in *The Winter's Tale,* Camillo invents the plot that leads to the reunions, and Leontes does have the last words. But by the time these actions take place, I have experienced both a loss of masculine control and a transformation of

Leontes' madness in the self-conscious playing that the pastoral festival enables me to share. I pass through the world of Sicily, in which playing is delusory—"Thy mother plays, and I/Play too; but so disgrac'd a part whose issue/Will hiss me to my grave" (I.ii.187–89)—to the world of Bohemia, in which playing is sanctioned by the cultural (that is to say, shared) form of the festival—"our feasts/In every mess have folly, and the feeders/Digest it with a custom . . . (IV.iv.10–12)—and back to Sicily, where I imagine Shakespeare playing with me as well as with his characters.

I feel both taken in by the final illusion of Hermione's living statue—"If this be magic, let it be an art/Lawful as eating" (V.iii.110–11)—and aware of the illusion as theatre. I feel that I am participating in the creation of a potential space within a potential space, that the illusion *of* the drama is both merged with and differentiated from the illusion *in* the drama (a doubleness that defines my experience of the world of *The Tempest*), and I feel that this is true both for myself as audience and for the characters on the stage, who are both audience and participants. I perceive an interplay of subjective and objective realities in the characters' responses to the statue, and it seems to me no accident that the visual focus of the scene is a maternal woman who is both an object and a person (as mothers first are for children when they enter the transitional area of play). Shakespeare seems to me to be playing with his rediscovery of potential space, and involving me in the play, which opens out, at the end, into a future that continues and transforms the characters' lives in time. At the end, I feel that I have experienced a reunion of childhood and cultural realities, "infancy and grace" (V.iii.27), as Leontes says.

I cannot imagine my double re-creation without imagining Shakespeare both inside and outside his creation, both masculine and feminine, both self and other. He seems to me to have accepted these differences and to have merged them into identities, and into his own identity, after he had enacted his own struggle with archaic rage over archaic dependency. I am asserting that Shakespeare, as I read him, learned something that psychoanalysis has just recently learned, the interwovenness of his cultural world and the earliest forms of trust in femininity, which is reenacted by each of us in the movement from absolute dependence to the potential space of playing. My Shakespeare learned, having used the space of the theatre to enact the failure of cultural order, the absolute necessity of playing seriously. His world is not only a metaphorical stage. And his stage is not only a metaphorical world. In the interplay between a metaphorical world and the perception of reality as other and alien, between ceremonial order and the rage that followed its collapse, I imagine his creative space, and mine in his as well.

Notes

1. George S. Klein, *Psychoanalytic Theory: An Exploration of Essentials* (New York: International Univ. Press, 1967), p. 54.

2. Paul Ricoeur, *Freud and Philosophy: An Essay on Interpretation,* trans. Denis Savage (New Haven, Conn.: Yale Univ. Press, 1970), p. 32.

3. Klein, p. 39.

4. Sigmund Freud, *The Aetiology of Hysteria,* in *The Standard Edition of the Complete Psychological Works of Sigmund Freud,* ed. and trans. James Strachey et al., 24 vols. (London: Hogarth Press, 1953-74), 3, p. 192.

5. Freud, *Totem and Taboo, Standard Edition,* 13, p. 64.

6. See, for examples, Marion Milner, "The Role of Illusion In Symbol Formation," in *New Directions in Psycho-Analysis,* ed. Melanie Klein, Paula Heimann, and R. E. Money-Kyrle (New York: Basic Books, 1957), pp. 82-107; M. Masud R. Khan, *The Privacy of the Self* (New York: International Univ. Press, 1974), pp. 251-69; and Norman N. Holland, "The New Paradigm: Subjective or Transactive?" *New Literary History,* 7 (1976), 335-46.

7. D. W. Winnicott, *Playing and Reality* (New York: Basic Books, 1971), p. 103.

8. Jean Schimek, "A Critical Re-Examination of Freud's Concept of Unconscious Mental Representation," *International Review of Psycho-Analysis,* 2 (1975), 180.

9. Emanuel Peterfreund, "How Does the Analyst Listen?" *Psychoanalysis and Contemporary Science,* 4 (1975), 78.

10. The wording of these ideas follows suggestions by Norman N. Holland and David Willbern.

11. All quotations from Shakespeare follow the text of *The Riverside Shakespeare,* ed. G. Blakemore Evans et al. (Boston: Houghton Mifflin, 1974).

3 ⚙ So Rare a Wonder'd Father: Prospero's *Tempest*

David Sundelson

◯ Dramatic conflict is strikingly absent from *The Tempest*. Brothers try to kill brothers, servants stalk their masters, and the union of attractive young lovers is delayed by an old man's whim, but none of these things creates suspense. Once we have seen Prospero calm the raging waters with a wave of his arm, danger and difficulty cease to be more than prelude to an inevitable harmony. The movement of the plot toward fulfillment is the most serene and secure in Shakespeare.

This tranquility requires the sacrifice of some characteristic Shakespearean complexity. One can be either master or servant in *The Tempest*, either parent or child; middle ground scarcely exists. Antonio supplanted Prospero because "my brother's servants/Were then my fellows; now they are my men" (II.i.268-69).[1] Antonio's new mastery is a delusion, however; his plot against Prospero only puts him in debt to the King of Naples/ just as Caliban's later plot makes him Stephano's slave. Ferdinand and Miranda are wiser: they outdo each other in their eagerness to serve/ Ferdinand is a "patient log-man" (III.i.67) for Miranda and will be "thus humble ever" (III.i.87), while the princess who once had "four or five women" (I.ii.47) to attend her insists:

> to be your fellow
> You may deny me; but I'll be your servant,
> Whether you will or no.
>
> (III.i.84–86)

Real fellowship, so common in Shakespeare, is elusive in *The Tempest*, and certainly less important than finding a good master. Without one, as the opening scene shows, all is chaos. Prospero's storm mocks and destroys the hierarchy on Alonso's ship: "What cares these roarers for the name of King?" (I.i.16-17). Great lords become snarling children who distract the sailors from their desperate work, and King, Captain, and Boatswain are equals in their utter vulnerability. The central, repeated

33

cry in the scene is "Where's the master?" (ll.9,12)—the absent authority who might bring safety to all.

"Where's the master?" is the question that echoes across the battlefield of Shrewsbury in *Henry IV, Part I,* where many men are dressed like the King but true authority is absent. Hamlet never finds an answer, and Angelo must wait for one until the final moments of *Measure for Measure. The Tempest* answers the question almost as soon as it is posed, however, for the first scene's brevity matches the ferocity of its threats. The movement from this scene to the next is from nightmare to waking relief, from a plunge toward death to the comfort of a father's reassurance: "No more amazement: tell your piteous heart/There's no harm done" (I.ii.14-15). Long before Prospero calls himself "master" (I.ii.20) or Ariel addresses him as "great master" (I.ii.189), it is clear that he is the ordering power whose absence released such terrors in the preceding scene and whose very presence restores the world to harmony. The tempest is the only one of Prospero's shows that the audience experiences at first as "real," so the opening sequence prompts in us sentiments expressed later by the Boatswain and eventually shared by nearly all the *dramatis personae:* "The best news is, that we have safely found/Our King" (V.i.221-22). In *The Tempest,* every man is Prospero's fortunate subject.

Indeed, the play belongs to Prospero in a way that seems downright un-Shakespearean. Duke Vincentio must contend with Lucio and Pompey, Rosalind with the melancholy Jaques, Henry V with the stubborn soldier, Williams—even the sonnets are marked by dialectic. In *The Tempest,* however, there are no discordant voices with enough wit or dignity to command attention. Dissent is confined to the discredited, to Caliban, to Antonio and Sebastian, and even they bow at last to "a most high miracle" (V.i.177). A number of critics have commented on Prospero's undisputed preeminence in the play and the unusual thinness of the other characters. G. Wilson Knight, for example, concludes that "except for Prospero, Ariel, and Caliban, the people scarcely exist in their own right."[2] Rather than treating this disparity as a given, I want to ask what makes it necessary. Why does Shakespeare endow Prospero with such extraordinary dominion? Over what anxieties does it triumph, and what conflicts does it resolve?

The calm and homage that surround Prospero on his island have little place in the story he tells Miranda. Like Duke Vincentio in *Measure for Measure,*[3] Prospero yielded to a strong ambivalence about power and withdrew from active rule, ceding real authority to his brother Antonio:

> he whom next thyself
> Of all the world I lov'd, and to him put
> The manage of my state; as at that time

> Through all the signories it was the first,
> And Prospero the prime duke, being so reputed
> In dignity, and for the liberal Arts
> Without a parallel; those being all my study,
> The government I cast upon my brother,
> And to my state grew stranger, being transported
> And rapt in secret studies.
>
> (I.ii.68-77)

The broken sentences may reflect excitement, as Frank Kermode suggests,[4] or conflict, since Prospero asserts both the prominence of his state and his indifference to such public considerations. He wants to be "prime duke" without any responsibilities, and the narrative goes on to reveal similar contradictions. Prospero poses to Miranda as an injured ascetic who wanted very little and was denied even that: "Me, poor man, my library/Was dukedom large enough" (I.ii.109-10). Only fifteen lines later he complains about the loss of "all the honours" and "fair Milan." In "casting the government" upon his brother, Prospero behaves like a child abdicating responsibility to an adult.[5] Nonetheless, he accuses Antonio of usurping a father's prerogative when he "new created/The creatures that were mine" (I.ii.81-82). Like Lear, Prospero wants both the status of a father and the security and ease of a child.

The language hints at sexual uncertainties that underlie the conflict about power, at a fantasy that Duke Prospero was both mother and father, but doubly vulnerable rather than doubly strong. Antonio was "the ivy which had hid my princely trunk/And suck'd my verdure out on't" (I.ii.86-87). The metaphor makes Prospero androgynous: the second clause suggests a mother drained by an insatiable child, while the hidden "princely trunk" is an image of male strength defeated or replaced. This is not the only hint of impotence. Prospero complains that Antonio thought him "incapable" of "temporal royalties" (I.ii. 110-11) and projects this anxiety onto his state. The new Duke had to:

> bend
> The dukedom, yet unbow'd,—alas, poor Milan!—
> To most ignoble stooping.
>
> (I.ii.114-16)

Even fatherhood, the keystone of Prospero's island identity, seems to have been doubtful in Milan:

> *Miranda.*   Sir, are not you my father?
> *Prospero.* Thy mother was a piece of virtue, and
>   She said thou wast my daughter; and thy father
>   Was Duke of Milan; and his only heir
>   And princess, no worse issued.
>
> (I.ii.55-59)

The question itself is surprising, and the answer is oddly evasive and ambiguous; the shift from first to third person and the disjunctive syntax separate Prospero from both daughter and dukedom. Just as his own anxiety about impotence is projected onto a personified Milan, these half-suppressed doubts of his wife's chastity are related to the imagery of his expulsion from the city. His "fair Milan" rejects him violently; he was, he says later, "thrust forth of Milan" (V.i.160), and Gonzalo echoes the phrase: "was Milan thrust from Milan" (V.i.205). Milan is like a rejecting woman, and the "thrusting" suggests a traumatic birth that Prospero shared with Miranda:

> one midnight
> Fated to th' purpose, did Antonio open
> The gates of Milan; and, i' th' dead of darkness,
> The ministers for th' purpose hurried thence
> Me and thy crying self.
>
> (I.ii.128-32)

The departure from Milan is an escape from shame and weakness as much as an expulsion. The Duke flees from the fearful demands of office; the father and daughter flee together from a rejecting wife and mother.[6]

For Prospero, the defeat is a happy one. In *The Tempest*, it is the absence of a daughter, not a wife or mother, that leaves a man truly vulnerable. Thus when Antonio tries to enlist Sebastian in a plot to murder Alonso, his main argument is that Alonso's daughter Claribel "dwells/ Ten leagues beyond man's life" (III.i.241-42). Prospero is in no such danger. Though only an infant, on their voyage Miranda provided a substitute for the lost maternal protection: "a cherubin/Thou wast that did preserve me" (I.ii.152-53). In one sense their exile is an ordeal to be endured, but in more important ways it is a delicious idyll on an island which, to borrow Lear's description, unites them "like birds i' th' cage."

Prospero is anxious because Miranda knows him only as "master of a full poor cell,/And thy no greater father" (I.ii.19-20)—the last phrase hesitates between shame and vanity—but she can imagine no greater eminence: "More to know/Did never meddle with my thoughts" (I.ii. 21-22). Throughout his long narration, Miranda is the ideal listener; she has no critical faculty of her own, and her responses are invariably just what her father wants. She weeps when appropriate, and when Prospero reflects smugly on his success as her "schoolmaster," she promptly cries: "Heavens thank you for it" (I.ii.175). This heroine has neither Perdita's liveliness nor Imogen's dignity. Coleridge remarks that "the moral feeling called forth by the sweet words of Miranda, 'Alack, what trouble/Was I then to you!,' in which she considered only the sufferings and sorrows of her father, puts the reader in a frame of mind to exert his imagination in favor of an object so innocent and interesting."[7] Perhaps—but Miranda's "sweet words" also cater to Prospero's need for admiration, indeed for reverence, and they mold the audience's sense that other relationships ought to do the same. Consider the undercurrent as Prospero recounts their history:

Prospero. Obey, and be attentive.   (I.ii.38)

Prospero. Dost thou attend me?
Miranda.   Sir, most heedfully.   (I.ii.78)

Prospero. Thou attend'st not?
Miranda. O, good sir, I do.
Prospero.   I pray thee, mark me.   (I.ii.87–88)

Prospero. Dost thou hear?
Miranda.   Your tale, sir, would cure deafness.   (I.ii.106)

Shakespeare shows us a pattern of doubt and reassurance, of a father's obsessive need for attention and a daughter who fulfills it, and also of a man preparing to relinquish something precious by clutching it more passionately than ever.[8]

For the question remains: a mothering daughter of perfect, unceasing devotion and an omnipotent father who basks in her affection—why does Prospero accept her approaching marriage so willingly?

So glad of this as they I cannot be,
Who are surpris'd with all, but my rejoicing
At nothing can be more.

                                                            (III.i.93–95)

Understatement makes the first line poignant, balancing the surprising claim that follows—surprising because the play as a whole equates a daughter's marriage with her death. "Would I had never married my daughter there," Alonso cries:

                    for, coming thence,
My son is lost, and, in my rate, she too,
Who is so far from Italy removed
I ne'er again shall see her.

                                                            (II.i.103–07)

Prospero himself, when Alonso grieves over Ferdinand's supposed death, replies that he has suffered "the like loss" (V.i.142) and is less able to console himself.[9] What is such a major defeat doing at the very center of a play that otherwise tends to grant Prospero's every wish? How does Shakespeare reconcile the loss with his hero's ongoing mastery?

Miranda makes a major contribution to what I want to call Prospero's—and the play's—paternal narcissism: the prevailing sense that there is no worthiness like a father's, no accomplishment or power, and that Prospero is the father *par excellence.* Praise of Miranda—even a lover's—has a way of rebounding to her father:

> for several virtues
> Have I lik'd several women; never any
> With so full soul, but some defect in her
> Did quarrel with the noblest grace she ow'd,
> And put it to the foil: but you, O you,
> So perfect and so peerless, are created
> Of every creature's best!

(III.i.42–48)

"Created" and "creature" (an echo of "new created/The creatures that were mine") draw our attention to Prospero's marvelous powers of nurture—of design, one might say. Ordinary, imperfect women are merely born; only his art can produce a paragon.

Much in the play that might pass for dissent only adds to Prospero's stature—the brief quarrel with Ariel, for example. "What is't thou canst demand?" (I.ii.245), Prospero asks; the master fails to imagine that serving him could leave anyone other than perfectly contented. In general, Shakespeare seems to share his point of view: Ariel begs pardon for his momentary rebellion. Even the cynicism of Sebastian and Antonio promotes our reverence for Prospero. Another man's grief is merely the grindstone for their wit, and they turn the encounters between Alonso and Gonzalo into music hall entertainment:

> *Antonio.* (Aside to Seb.) The visitor will not give him o'er so.
> *Sebastian.* (Aside to Ant.) Look, he's winding up the watch of
>   his wit; by and by it will strike.
> *Gonzalo.* Sir,—
> *Sebastian.* (Aside to Ant.) One: tell.
> *Gonzalo.* When every grief is entertain'd that's offer'd,
>   Comes to th' entertainer—
> *Sebastian.* A dollar.
> *Gonzalo.* Dolour comes to him, indeed: you have spoken truer
>   than you purpos'd.
> *Sebastian.* You have taken it wiselier than I meant you
>   should.

(II.i.11–21)

Why should an audience not prefer this flippancy to Gonzalo's ponderous earnestness and sense of wonder? We know, after all, that the tempest is part of Prospero's plan, that Ferdinand is alive and safe, that the island holds no real dangers; we might well identify with the spectator-like detachment of the two "wits." But Shakespeare makes them so callous and sneering that we are forced to adopt a contrasting attitude, to acknowledge the seriousness of the events we witness. Their smug posturing, a caricature of self-regard, makes us susceptible to a romance perspective and to the grander, sanctioned narcissism of Prospero.

This reverence for father Prospero does not extend to mothers. Whatever ambivalence toward them is hidden in Prospero's tale of his expulsion, the one mother in the play is unmistakably demonic: Sycorax. She is a "foul witch" (I.ii.257), a "damned witch" (I.ii.263), banished for "mischiefs manifold, and sorceries terrible/To enter human hearing" (I.ii.264-65). Unlike Prospero's, her commands were so "earthy and abhorr'd" (I.ii.273) that the delicate Ariel refused to obey them. Sycorax imprisoned Ariel in a cloven pine for twelve years:

> it was a torment
> To lay upon the damn'd, which Sycorax
> Could not again undo; it was mine Art,
> When I arriv'd and heard thee, that made gape
> The pine, and let thee out.
>
> (I.ii.289-93)

This demon mother's rage is "unmitigable" (I.ii.276); only a father could end the torture. The passage (with its overtones of castration) lets us imagine a mother whose ultimate punishment is permanent imprisonment in a constricting womb.

By contrast, Prospero becomes a midwife whose art enables him to implement Ariel's rebirth. Rebirth is a staple of romance, including Shakespeare's,[10] but *The Tempest* gives Prospero the power to direct processes that elsewhere defy even understanding, not to speak of control. Thus he arranges a rebirth for Ferdinand and Alonso after each has believed the other dead, and also for the Captain and crew of Alonso's ship. During the play, Ariel keeps "the mariners all under hatches stow'd" (I.ii.230); the ship is like a body holding many children, whose birth takes place in Act V with appropriate accompanying sounds. Vulnerable in Milan, on his island Prospero is both strong father and mother, or a father whose life-giving power defeats the vindictive mother, Sycorax.

The conflict between Prospero and Caliban, who claims the island "by Sycorax my mother" (I.ii.334), extends the struggle between maternal and paternal forces. Caliban invokes his mother's power repeatedly:

> As wicked dew as e'er my mother brush'd
> With raven's feather from unwholesome fen
> Drop on you both!   (I.ii.322-24)

> All the charms
> Of Sycorax, toads, beetles, bats, light on you.
>
> (I.ii.341-42)

Such prayers always fail, because command of maternal responses in the play has been given to Prospero. In good humor he calls for heavenly nurture: "Heavens rain grace/On that which breeds between 'em" (III.i.75-76); in a graver mood he threatens to withhold it: "No sweet aspersion shall the heavens let fall/To make this contract grow" (IV.i. 18-19). These might seem like empty gestures were it not for his manifest power over food, a more effective means of control than any pinches and cramps. "I must eat my dinner" (I.ii.333), Caliban admits. His cruelly interrupted dream of riches about to drop on him[11] —"when I wak'd,/I cried to dream again" (III.ii.139-41)—is dramatized in the humiliation of Alonso and his company at the magic banquet that vanishes when they go to eat. Prospero himself was thrust from Milan and its nourishment; here he subjects his enemies to symbolic versions of his own ordeal.

Fortune sends Caliban a new master who can strut more boldly than Prospero and provides an unlimited supply of food. Stephano's bottle is a mother accessible to all, a parody of Prospero's maternal powers, and he is fully aware of its advantages: "He shall taste of my bottle; if he have never drunk wine afore, it will go near to remove his fit. If I can recover him, and keep him tame, I will not take too much for him . . ." (II.ii.76-79). Those who have starved leap at the chance to deprive someone else. Caliban would like to punish Trinculo as Prospero has punished him—"I do beseech thy greatness, give him blows,/And take his bottle from him" (III.ii.63-64)—but Stephano's dominion is brief:

> Trinculo. Ay, but to lose our bottles in the pool,—
> Stephano. There is not only disgrace and dishonour in
>   that, monster, but an infinite loss.

> (IV.i.208-10)

Prospero's punishment demonstrates once again the utter vulnerability of those who are children rather than fathers.

Throughout the play, Prospero's references to Caliban stress his own failure to transform the "mis-shapen knave" (V.i.268) and Caliban's resistance to "any print of goodness" (I.ii.354). The monster is an affront to his pride as a shaper of character, a pride that unites the artist and the father:

> A devil, a born devil, on whose nature
> Nurture can never stick; on whom my pains
> Humanely taken, all, all lost, quite lost;
> And as with age his body uglier grows,
> So his mind cankers.

> (IV.i.188-92)

The tone here combines self-pity and self-congratulation, and the speech ends with an assertion that projects onto the totally demonized

Caliban the anxieties about age and weakness that are Prospero's own. Caliban is Prospero's servant and carries wood for him, but the real reason why "as 'tis,/We cannot miss him" (I.ii.312) is that he carries the greater burden of Prospero's projected anxieties and wishes: "This thing of darkness I/Acknowledge mine" (V.i.275-76).

Caliban's complex symbolic value is most apparent when he meets Trinculo, mistaking him at first for one of his master's agents. He has learned how to propitiate Prospero by minimizing his ominous erectness:[12] "I'll fall flat;/Perchance he will not mind me" (II.ii.16-17). Expecting another tempest and believing Caliban to be dead, Trinculo crawls under his "gaberdine." When Stephano comes upon the pair, it looks to him like some version of Iago's "beast with two backs," an incarnation of the monstrous in lovemaking: "I have not scap'd drowning, to be afeard now of your four legs" (II.ii.60-61). "Afeard" or not, Stephano betrays a certain nervousness about female demands and his own ability to satisfy them: "Doth thy other mouth call me? Mercy, mercy! . . . I have no long spoon" (II.ii.98-100). The monstrous form suddenly divides: Caliban "vents" Trinculo, and for a moment, the scene becomes a parody of childbirth. "Vent" also suggests defecation, however, as if the two acts were conflated in Shakespeare's imagination. This second fantasy becomes explicit when Stephano calls Trinculo "the siege of this moon-calf" (II.ii.107)—Kermode glosses "siege" as "excrement"[13]—an identity later confirmed by his immersion in the "filthy-mantled pool" (IV.i.182) and its "horse-piss" (IV.i.199). With its dreamlike fusion of the surreal and the antic, the sequence is what psychoanalysis calls highly overdetermined. Much of what Shakespeare finds disquieting or repulsive about women and sexuality—indeed, about nature, as compared to Prospero's cleaner art—is filtered through the bizarre humor and given unexpected shape.

Caliban himself also takes a plunge in the cesspool, a fitting punishment for his greatest crime:

> I have us'd thee,
> Filth as thou art, with human care; and lodg'd thee
> In mine own cell, till thou didst seek to violate
> The honour of my child.

(I.ii.347-50)

The final euphemism in this speech is a defense against contemplating the rape that Caliban attempted, and his reply confirms Prospero's fears:

> O ho, O ho! would't had been done!
> Thou didst prevent me; I had peopled else
> This isle with Calibans.

(I.ii.351-52)

Paternity for Caliban is an infinite multiplication of himself. By comparison, Prospero's pride in his fathering seems reasonable and attractive.

Prospero tries to fend off all that Caliban represents, but his attempts to polarize his world are posed against a fear that opposites may be only too similar. Caliban, after all, can master the courtly language that belongs to his betters: "I thank my noble lord. Wilt thou be pleas'd to hearken once again to the suit I made to thee?" (II.ii.36–37). His "I never saw a woman, / But only Sycorax my dam and she" (III.ii.98–99) sounds startlingly like Miranda's confession:

> nor have I seen
> More that I may call men than you, good friend,
> And my dear father.
>
> (III.i.51–53)

Nature and nurture do not always diverge, and at times the island resembles England as Trinculo describes it: "Were I in England now . . . there would this monster make a man" (II.ii.28–31). We may laugh when Caliban asserts that, without his books, Prospero is "but a sot, as I am, nor hath not / One spirit to command" (III.ii.91–92), but the parallel is less outrageous than it seems. The proximity of man and monster is a subversive motif in *The Tempest*, but it remains subordinate to the overriding concern for security and order.

Caliban serves because he must; Ariel does so willingly, even lovingly: "All hail, great master! grave sir, hail! I come / To answer thy best pleasure" (I.ii.189–90). Caliban embodies impulses that Prospero must avoid or master; Ariel gratifies Prospero's sense of his own importance and fulfills his wish for superhuman powers:

> I boarded the king's ship; now on the beak,
> Now in the waist, the deck, in every cabin,
> I flam'd amazement: sometime I'd divide,
> And burn in many places; on the topmast,
> The yards and boresprit, would I flame distinctly,
> Then meet and join.
>
> (I.ii.196–201)

Prospero is a guardian, not a lover; he gives Miranda to Ferdinand and warns them both against "th' fire in th' blood" (IV.i.53). As a ruler, he would rather forgive than punish. Ariel allows him to burn by proxy, to burn like an avenger and like a lover too, for the language ("boarded," "now in the waist") confirms Prospero's own association of fire and sexuality. Caliban is grotesquely united with Trinculo in the four-legged monster; Ariel can "meet and join" delightfully without any partner at all. Separated from Caliban's explicit sadism—"thou mayst knock a nail into his head" (III.ii.60), the slave tells Stephano—Prospero is not just master but "potent master" (IV.i.34) with Ariel at his command.

Whatever sexuality Ariel represents is completely stripped of physical grossness,[14] leaving only his delicacy and airiness:

> Where the bee sucks, there suck I:
> In a cowslip's bell I lie;
> There I couch when owls do cry.
> On the bat's back I do fly
> After summer merrily.

(V.i.88–92)

This song suggests the perfect child, perfect not only in grace and charm but in independence. This is a child who needs nourishment but not a mother, since he can suck "where the bee sucks," who needs protection but not a father, since he can hide in a flower from the predators of the night. Ariel is a child who recognizes the absoluteness of Prospero's paternal authority, who both embodies the father's power and makes no demands whatsoever on his attention and care. It is no wonder that Prospero seems more relaxed with him than with Miranda, more in his element. Ariel brings him satisfactions that a real child cannot, even one as compliant as his daughter. The sprite's very longing for freedom is, by comparison, gratifying to Prospero; Ariel has no interest in a younger, more virile rival, but wants freedom simply for its own sake.

The only one of Ariel's talents that Prospero has as well is invisibility. Unlike the lovers, who have "chang'd eyes" (I.ii.444) at their first meeting, Prospero likes to see without being seen, to supervise instead of gazing candidly. His voyeurism seems to be a substitute for other, more direct modes of gratification, and he has a complementary urge to exhibit himself:[15] "I will discase me, and myself present / As I was sometime Milan" (V.i.85–86). It is a measure of his dominion that he both reserves certain choice spectacles for himself (the courtship of Miranda and Ferdinand) and controls the seeing done by others—sometimes in an oddly literal way. "The fringed curtains of thine eye advance, / And say what thou seest yond" (I.ii.411–12), he tells Miranda, directing her initial sight of Ferdinand. Shakespeare gives Prospero an air of mastery here over the very process that is sure to wound him, the one that most comedy treats as inevitable, just as he lets Alonso believe that Claribel married only to please her father. The curtain metaphor connects this moment with Prospero's more explicitly artful shows:[16] the masque, the false banquet, the final revelation of the lovers playing chess. Such displays master his audiences, reducing them to a wondering passivity. "No tongue! All eyes!" (IV.i.59), he commands Miranda and Ferdinand as the masque begins.

When Prospero does not direct it, the act of seeing can become the "open-ey'd conspiracy" (II.i.296) of Antonio and Sebastian, but it seems curious when he puts Ferdinand in the same class: "thou . . . hast put thyself/Upon the island as a spy" (I.ii.456-58). The irony may be at Prospero's expense, since he accuses Ferdinand of what is in fact his own kind of watching, but his anger is easy to understand: Ferdinand's arrival threatens the rule of fathers:

> *Ferdinand.*   My language! heavens!
>   I am the best of them that speak this speech,
>   Were I but where 'tis spoken.
> *Prospero.*   How? the best?
>   What wert thou, if the King of Naples heard thee?
>
> (I.ii.431-34)

His identification with the King makes Prospero take offense at Ferdinand's readiness to succeed him. "Best of them" slights the dignity of fathers, and Prospero is quick to elicit a show of filial grief:

>   myself am Naples,
>   Who with mine eyes, never since at ebb, beheld
>   The King my father wrack'd.
>
> (I.ii.437-39)

The piety mollifies Prospero, as does the unwitting confession of faulty seeing, but only for a moment: Ferdinand is "a traitor" (I.ii.464), he insists.

In addition to Prospero's anger, the threat to paternal dominance provokes a counterwish, expressed by Alonso's belief that Ferdinand is drowned. This belief waxes and wanes in accordance with Alonso's hostility or guilt. Just after Francisco's impressive description of Ferdinand swimming to safety, Alonso asserts doggedly, "No, no, he's gone" (II.i. 118). But his vindictive thought leads to an abrupt change of heart: "Let's make further search for my poor son" (II.i.318-19). The arduous search soon seems a sufficient show of love, however, and Alonso gives it up rather easily:

>   Even here I will put off my hope, and keep it
>   No longer for my flatterer: he is drown'd
>   Whom thus we stray to find; and the sea mocks
>   Our frustrate search on land. Well, let him go.
>
> (II.iii.7-10)

In *The Tempest*, the word "hope" can connect apparently altruistic thoughts to selfish ones. Here the murderous impulse emerges not in Alonso's own voice but in Antonio's : "I am right glad that he's so out of hope" (II.iii.11). This echoes Antonio's attempt to engage Sebastian in his plot:

> *Sebastian.*   I have no hope
>   That he's undrown'd.

> *Antonio.*   O, out of that "no hope"
> What great hope have you!

> (II.i.233–35)

In Antonio and Sebastian, the sorts of wishes that are more unconscious in Alonso lie on or near the surface, and even in Alonso they surface persistently. When at last he sees his son playing chess with Miranda,
the King exclaims:

> If this prove
> A vision of the island, one dear son
> Shall I twice lose.

> (V.i.175–77)

One might argue that such caution is only reasonable in Prospero's confusing realm, but Ferdinand has had similar lessons and says nothing of
the kind.

Ferdinand must be cleansed of whatever hostility he has toward
fathers, since Prospero is eventually to accept him as his "son" (IV.i.
146), and Ariel's song does the crucial work:

> Full fadom five thy father lies;
>   Of his bones are coral made;
> Those are pearls that were his eyes:
>   Nothing of him that doth fade,
> But doth suffer a sea-change
> Into something rich and strange.
> Sea-nymphs hourly ring his knell: . . .

> (I.ii.399–405)

Here magical transformation makes the father's death acceptable. The
song denies that death brings decay or oblivion; instead, it offers an escape from mutability, a watery Byzantium. A father's bones—and, more
important, his eyes—become beautiful, permanent, and precious; even
after death he receives the homage of attractive sea nymphs, as if in
tribute to his gorgeously preserved authority. The song allows Ferdinand to accept Alonso's death without undue grief or guilt, and its cool
grace reflects the fact that the dead father is not Prospero.[17]

Ferdinand's most serious threat to paternal dominance is his love for
Miranda, however. The Prince has gentler manners than Caliban, of
course, but is less likely to make a permanent servant; Francisco portrays him as one of nature's rulers:

> I saw him beat the surges under him,
> And ride upon their backs; he trod the water,
> Whose enmity he flung aside, and breasted
> The surge most swoln that met him; his bold head
> 'Bove the contentious waves he kept, and oared
> Himself with his good arms in lusty stroke
> To th' shore . . .

> (II.i.110–16)

Ariel and his coworkers enable Prospero to humble even "the most mighty Neptune" (I.ii.204), but this young man, whose entire body seems vigorously phallic, needs no magic to master the waves. At first Prospero presents him as "a goodly person" (I.ii.419), but the hostility beneath his colorless phrase soon emerges. "To th' most of men this is a Caliban" (I.ii.483), he warns, and Ariel's first song addresses this very fear.

> Come unto these yellow sands,
>   And then take hands:
> Courtsied when you have and kiss'd
>   The wild waves whist:
> Foot it featly here and there,
>   And sweet sprites bear
> The burthen, Hark, hark.

(I.ii.377–83)

Here sexuality is subordinated to decorum and courtesy in the formal ordering of a dance. The song provides an alternative to Caliban's threat of rape, for the lovers content themselves with taking hands and kissing. Only "footing" is ambiguous,[18] and "the wild waves whist" (a long-standing textual problem) suggests the containment of passion. The animal-noise refrain, however, reveals the cruder sexuality that the song barely suppresses: "I hear/The strain of strutting chanticleer" (I.ii.387–88). The rooster's assertive maleness underlines Prospero's warning.

Prospero responds to the approaching marriage with a threefold defense. Ferdinand's awe of Miranda must harness his desire, first of all, and the father must have a symbolic victory over the younger man's confident sexuality. Even though Ferdinand, unlike Miranda, has been in the world and knows what women look like, he reacts just as Prospero wants him to: he addresses her as a goddess and asks humbly for "some good instruction" (I.ii.427). Such reverence is not enough to pacify Prospero, however:

> I'll manacle thy neck and feet together:
> Sea-water shalt thou drink; thy food shall be
> The fresh-brook mussels, wither'd roots, and husks
> Wherein the acorn cradled. Follow.

(I.ii.464–67)

The striking image of neck and feet manacled together echoes the description of Sycorax "grown into a hoop" (I.ii.259). Becoming circular seems to be a form of castration, an imposed impotence—in any case, the opposite of Ferdinand the thrusting swimmer. The food Prospero mentions confirms such a reading: "wither'd roots" recall the withering Prospero himself expects and fears; "husks/Wherein the acorn cradled" suggest what Prospero will be after he has lost the child he cradles now.

Prospero is forcing on Ferdinand the food of impotence and loneliness that will soon enough be his own.

Ferdinand draws his sword, determined to resist such enslavement until his "enemy has more power" (I.ii.469), but while *The Tempest* continues Prospero has all the power he needs:

> Put thy sword up, traitor;
> Who mak'st a show, but dar'st not strike, thy conscience
> Is so possess'd with guilt: come from thy ward;
> For I can here disarm thee with this stick
> And make thy weapon drop.
>
> (I.ii.472–76)

Similar victories of stick over sword occur elsewhere. When Antonio and Sebastian prepare to stab Alonso and Gonzalo, Ariel thwarts their plan, and when they draw following the false banquet, the sprite derides their sudden, nightmarish impotence: "Your swords are now too massy for your strengths,/And will not be uplifted" (III.iii.67–68). Ariel merely repeats Prospero's mockery of Ferdinand: "Thy nerves are in their infancy again,/And have no vigour in them" (I.ii.487–88). For a brief time, the sexual rival is reduced to the impotence of a child and the political heir to the ignominy of a servant.

If the play ended with this triumph, we would have another version of *Measure for Measure*, in which the older man reserves the maiden for himself. But Ferdinand's ordeal is only temporary, a ritualistic endurance of the father's hostility. He is eventually to marry Miranda, and it is not sufficient, nor is it necessary, to conclude that many trivial gratifications compensate for one major loss. The explanation is rather that Prospero transforms a loss into a gratification, a piece of magic at least as pretty as raising a tempest. Again *Measure for Measure* provides a helpful parallel. When the disguised Duke asks Escalus to describe his character, the old counselor gives a reply that is more astute than he knows: "Rather rejoicing to see another merry, than merry at anything which professed to make him rejoice" (III.ii.238–40). Anna Freud has analyzed just this psychological pattern: "This normal and less conspicuous form of projection might be described as 'altruistic surrender' of our own instinctual impulses in favour of other people."[19] *Measure for Measure* is an unsatisfying play precisely because the altruistic surrender does not really function: the Duke cannot give up Isabella as Prospero does Miranda. But like Anna Freud's patient, who "gratified her instincts by sharing in the gratification of others,"[20] Prospero identifies with Ferdinand and surrenders to him the pleasure of possessing Miranda.[21] The success of this surrender accounts in part for the deep harmony that distinguishes *The Tempest*.

Even after this resolution, Prospero elicits a vow of premarital chastity from Ferdinand, although not from Miranda; her sexuality is not consciously acknowledged. Heartfelt as it is, the young man's promise leaves room for concern:

> As I hope
> For quiet days, fair issue and long life,
> With such love as 'tis now, the murkiest den,
> The most opportune place, the strong'st suggestion
> Our worser genius can, shall never melt
> Mine honour into lust, to take away
> The edge of that day's celebration
> When I shall think, or Phoebus' steeds are founder'd,
> Or Night kept chain'd below.
>
> (IV.i.23–31)

Ferdinand protests too much: his words suggest fantasies of rape and reveal a disturbing contradiction. He feels no lust now—"The white cold virgin snow upon my heart / Abates the ardour of my liver" (IV.i.55–56) —but he will, once the vows are spoken. When Miranda has been possessed, however, she will no longer be desirable; Ferdinand will lose the "edge" of his interest, and she may be abandoned like the "widow Dido" (II.i.75) who turns up so mysteriously in the chatter of Antonio and Sebastian.[22]

Ferdinand's oaths cannot resolve the play's anxieties about sex any more than his temporary incapacity. The somber undercurrent persists, but the "potent Art" (V.i.50) of Prospero's masque succeeds, however briefly, in containing both threats to women and the dangers of their malice. Ceres recalls how, with the help of Venus, "dusky Dis my daughter got" (IV.i.89)—an echo of Caliban's attempted rape and Alonso's lamented decision to "loose" his daughter "to an African" (II.i.121)—but now, although she and Cupid had planned "some wanton charm" (IV.i.95) against the lovers, Venus is defeated:

> Mars's hot minion is return'd again;
> Her waspish-headed son has broke his arrows,
> Swears he will shoot no more, but play with sparrows,
> And be a boy right out.
>
> (IV.i.98–101)

This retreat from menacing potency to the reassuring innocence of boyhood reenacts in myth Ferdinand's passage from threat to dependent infant in Act I and Caliban's comparable transformation in Act II.

Instead of Venus and her threats of sexual corruption, the masque gives us Iris, with the "refreshing showers" (IV.i.79) that fulfill the new couple's hope of sweet aspersion from the heavens, and Ceres, the nurturing mother so painfully absent throughout the play. She is "a most bounteous lady" (IV.i.60) who brings to the lovers "Earth's increase, foison plenty, / Barns and garners never empty" (IV.i.110–11)—the abundant food denied Alonso and his men when Prospero's banquet vanished. The landscape that Ceres leaves is a setting for "cold nymphs" (IV.i.66) and "the dismissed bachelor" (IV.i.67), but the masque moves away from this sterility. Iris summons two sets of dancers: "naiads" and "sunburn'd sicklemen." The former have "ever-harmless looks" (IV.i.129)—no Sycorax here—and the men are robust, attractive, and well-protected by their sickles. The final lines echo Ariel's earlier command to "foot it featly here and there": "And these fresh nymphs encounter every one/In country footing" (IV.i.137-38). The playwright who has Hamlet ask sarcastically about "country matters" is surely aware of the sexual puns contained in "encounter" and "country." Both sexuality and the nurturing mother are restored to the play by Prospero's magic and are subject to his reassuring control.

Caught up earlier in the glory of his own lesser vision, Gonzalo asserts that he "would with such perfection govern, sir,/T'excel the Golden Age" (II.i.163-64). Sebastian and Antonio meet this claim with their customary derision.

> *Sebastian.* No marrying among his subjects?
> *Antonio.* None, man; all idle; whores and knaves. . . .
> *Sebastian.*   'Save his majesty!
> *Antonio.* Long live Gonzalo!
>
> (II.i.161-65)

In the "real" world, nymphs and sicklemen may still become whores and knaves. But since Gonzalo's vision precedes Prospero's, it absorbs the hostile mockery that might otherwise undermine the masque and frees the audience to share Ferdinand's absolute reverence:

> Let me live here ever;
> So rare a wonder'd father and a wise
> Makes this place Paradise.
>
> (IV.i.122-24)

Paradise is made, the line emphasizes, not found. This supreme validation of the father's creating power is the central wish fulfillment of the play.

Outside of the masque, brute aggression persists: the "foul conspiracy/Of the beast Caliban and his confederates" (IV.i.139-40). Just as he reduces Ferdinand's powers to their infancy, Prospero meets the more primitive sexual and political threat by turning his foes into foolish children who follow the malicious "mother" Ariel: "calf-like, they my lowing follow'd, through/Tooth'd briars, sharp furzes, pricking goss, and thorns" (IV.i.179-80). Caliban now sees the folly of worshipping anyone other than the supreme father: "I'll be wise hereafter,/And seek for grace" (V.i.294-95).

Caliban can hope for pardon, but Prospero's treatment of Antonio is more equivocal:

> For you, most wicked sir, whom to call brother
> Would even infect my mouth, I do forgive
> Thy rankest fault,—all of them.
>
> (V.i.130-32)

This is forgiveness in name only. Prospero still insists on separating his own goodness from the evil of his enemies, like Isabella in *Measure for Measure*, with her distinction between her own "chaste body" and her tormentor's "concupiscible intemperate lust" (V.i.97-98). But while Isabella learns that at times the chaste must plead for the concupiscible, very little in *The Tempest* modifies Prospero's belief in radical opposites. Because Antonio has "expelled remorse and nature" (V.i.76), Prospero suspends a threat of punishment over him and Sebastian:

> But you, my brace of lords, were I so minded,
> I here could pluck his highness' frown upon you,
> And justify you traitors: at this time
> I will tell no tales.
>
> (V.i.126-29)

Earlier, Ariel condemns Alonso to "ling'ring perdition" (III.iii.77) but withdraws the sentence if the criminal will promise "heart-sorrow/And a clear life ensuing" (III.iii.81-82), and the pattern is repeated: Prospero brandishes the rod but enjoys his own magnanimity.

Only Ariel obtains complete freedom at the end of the play, and Prospero calls attention to his own generosity in granting it: "Why that's my dainty Ariel! I shall miss thee;/But yet you shall have freedom" (V.i.95-96). Freedom is Ariel's right, of course, just as it is Miranda's, Ferdinand's, or Caliban's. But the play manipulates us into feeling that if Ariel were truly wise he would remain with Prospero—where else could he find such a perfect master? His final song about the life he will lead, "Merrily, merrily shall I live now/Under the blossom that hangs on the bough" (V.i.93-94), only adds to our sympathy for his master, who anticipates no merriment, only a lonely life in which "every third thought shall be my grave" (V.i.311).

Freedom, finally, is unimaginable in *The Tempest*—Ariel will enjoy it only after the play is over—and even dominion is an illusion. "The great globe itself,/Yea, all which it inherit, shall dissolve" (IV.i.153-54). The word "inherit" reminds us that the speech is directed at Ferdinand, the "heir/Of Naples and of Milan" (II.i.107-08). Prospero gives him an old man's warning: only fools like Stephano think that "the King and all our company else being drown'd, we will inherit here" (II.ii.174-75). The most one can do is choose one's heirs, and this Prospero has done quite successfully. Prospero completes his altruistic surrender;

he can contemplate his own death calmly because Ferdinand has "received a second life" (V.i.195) from him.

So he breaks his staff, after using "every possible resource to enforce the potency of his powers"[23] in a farewell to the elves and spirits who have served him. As his other charms dissolve, Prospero retains the skills of an actor and playwright—his final entrance before the assembled company is especially well timed—and a kind of sublimated potency through story telling. Alonso would wear himself out trying to pierce the maze, while for Prospero it is no maze at all:

> Do not infest your mind with beating on
> The strangeness of this business; at pick'd leisure
> Which shall be shortly single, I'll resolve you . . .

(V.i.246–48)

The magician becomes a poet whose only magic is to make the night "go quick away" (V.i.305). One can hardly help but conclude that the celebration of Prospero's paternal power is Shakespeare's celebration of himself,[24] qualified by irony but never seriously undermined. When Alonso asks for his son's forgiveness, Prospero stops him abruptly; no one else is to dispense pardons, and fathers are not to humble themselves before children.

The epilogue draws the audience into the psychological structure of the play by making it feel the power of a father and the vulnerability of a child. Prospero now has only his own strength, which he admits is "most faint" (l. 3), but we have for the moment gained his special powers. With them goes the choice either to imprison or to liberate. Just as in the final act Prospero releases Miranda, Ferdinand, Alonso, and finally Ariel, now we must do the same for him: "But release me from my bands/With the help of your good hands" (ll. 9–10). He promised Alonso a good wind for the voyage back to Italy; now "Gentle breath of yours my sails/Must fill, or else my project fails" (ll. 11–12). And what was Prospero's project? In a word: "to please." Denied the real gratification that Ferdinand will enjoy, Prospero must share in the pleasure of others. As his last piece of magic, he forestalls any criticism by proving to us that we too find pleasure and security in liberating rather than possessing. The play's final couplet reminds us that, although Prospero is returning to Milan, the Heavenly Father with whom he identifies can never be evaded: "As you from crimes would pardon'd be/Let your indulgence set me free."

Notes

1. Quotations from *The Tempest* follow the new Arden edition, ed. Frank Kermode (London: Methuen, 1954).

2. G. Wilson Knight, *The Crown of Life* (New York and London: Methuen, 1947), p. 220. See also Bonamy Dobrée, *"The Tempest,"* in *Essays and Studies*, New Series Collected for the English Association by Arundell Esdaile, 5 (London: John Murray, 1952), pp. 13–25. Reprinted in *Twentieth Century Interpretations of "The Tempest,"* ed. Hallett Smith (Englewood Cliffs, N. J.: Prentice-Hall, 1969).

3. One of the most interesting critics who compare Prospero and Vincentio is Harry Berger, Jr., "Miraculous Harp: A Reading of Shakespeare's *Tempest*," *Shakespeare Studies*, 5 (1970).

4. In the new Arden edition, p. 13 n, Kermode notes that Prospero has "some difficulty with this exposition."

5. Karl M. Abenheimer makes the same point in his Jungian analysis of the play: "Shakespeare's *Tempest*, A Psychological Analysis," *Psychoanalytic Review*, 33 (1946), 401.

6. Cf. Alfred Freiherr von Winterstein, "Zur Psychoanalyse des Reisens," *Imago*, 1 (1912), 497. Norman N. Holland summarizes the article in *Psychoanalysis and Shakespeare* (New York: McGraw-Hill, 1964), p. 213.

7. *Coleridge's Writings on Shakespeare*, ed. Terence Hawkes (New York: Capricorn Books, 1959), p. 213.

8. Joseph Summers opens his persuasive reading of the play with a discussion of this passage: "Prospero, like most fathers standing before their children awaiting judgment, feels anxious, vulnerable, tempted to assert his authority." See "The Anger of Prospero," *Michigan Quarterly Review*, 12 (1973), 118.

9. According to Holland *(Psychoanalysis and Shakespeare)*, Otto Rank is the first to discuss Prospero as a jealous father. See *Das Inzest-Motiv in Dichtung und Sage*, 2nd ed. (Leipzig: Franz Deuticke, 1926), p. 352 n.

10. See, for example, Knight, *The Crown of Life*, and Northrop Frye, "The Mythos of Summer: Romance," in Frye, *Anatomy of Criticism* (New York: Atheneum Publishers, 1965).

11. "The clouds methought would open, and show riches/Ready to drop upon me" (III.ii.139–40). As Norman Holland notes, perhaps too literal-mindedly, "it is not too difficult to see in the clouds a breast symbol and in the 'riches' the longed-for, nurturing milk." See "Caliban's Dream," in *The Design Within*, ed. M. D. Faber (New York: Science House, 1970), p. 523.

12. Cf. the Boatswain's command during the tempest: "Down with the topmast! yare! lower, lower!" (I.i.34).

13. Kermode, new Arden edition, p. 65 n. The Oxford English Dictionary also gives this meaning.

14. Knight sees him as a boy, "with a boy's silvery voice," talking "pert, pretty, inconsequential boy-talk" (pp. 234–35).

15. Cf. Berger, who notes Prospero's fondness for "the one-way window relationship in which he may observe without being observed" as well as his "love of the limelight" (p. 275). Cf. also Otto Fenichel: "The counterpart to scoptophilia is exhibitionism, which usually appears together with scoptophilia. . . . Its erogenous pleasure is always connected with an increase in self-esteem, anticipated or actually gained through the fact that others look at the subject." See *The Psychoanalytic Theory of Neurosis* (New York: W. W. Norton, 1945), p. 72.

16. Cf. Olivia in *Twelfth Night* when she removes her veil: "But we will draw the curtain and show you the picture" (I.v.233–34).

17. W. H. Auden calls the song "a magic spell, the effect of which is, not to lessen his feeling of loss, but to change his attitude towards his grief from one of rebellion—'How could this bereavement happen to me?'—to one of awe and reverent

acceptance." See *The Dyer's Hand* (New York: Random House, 1968), p. 525.

18. According to Eric Partridge, "foot" can mean "to copulate." See *Shakespeare's Bawdy* (New York: Dutton, 1969), p. 108.

19. Anna Freud, *The Ego and the Mechanisms of Defense* (New York: International Univ. Press, 1946), p. 133.

20. Anna Freud, p. 136.

21. Cf. Sonnet 37, where the poet speaks as "a decrepit father" and outlines the same mechanism: "Look what is best, that best I wish in thee./This wish I have; then ten times happy me!"

22. Kermode notes the "series of apparently trivial allusions to the theme of Dido and Aeneas which has never been properly explained" (new Arden edition, p. 46 n).

23. Kermode, new Arden edition, p. 115 n.

24. Cf. Knight: "Prospero, who controls this comprehensive Shakespearean world, automatically reflects Shakespeare himself" (p. 220). Stanley Edgar Hyman also makes the comparison, and traces its history from Coleridge through the nineteenth century to the work of Hans Sachs and Norman Holland. See "Portraits of the Artist: Iago and Prospero," *Shenandoah*, 21 (1970), 18–42. There is an opposing tradition, which includes Lytton Strachey, *Books and Characters* (New York: Harcourt Brace, 1922); E. E. Stoll, *Shakespeare and Other Masters* (Cambridge: Harvard Univ. Press, 1940); and Harold C. Goddard, *The Meaning of Shakespeare* (Chicago: Univ. of Chicago Press, 1951).

4 ❧ The Counterfeit Order of
The Merchant of Venice

Leonard Tennenhouse

The Merchant of Venice has always been susceptible to a variety of approaches and methodologies because its surface—the linguistic patterns, the themes, the ideational content, the relationships of its characters—seems to invite attempts to unify and complete the coherence of its design. It is in this respect a very accessible text, appealing to quite a diverse audience. At the same time, it is a deeply disturbing play. The sheer bulk of criticism, the intensity of critical arguments, and the variety of critical discussions clearly indicate that the play is not uniformly perceived by its readers. Indeed, the argument over what it is really "about" is a permanent feature of *Merchant* criticism, as Norman Rabkin observed when he examined what had been written about the play.[1] Shakespeare criticism was in trouble, he said, because many readings of the play attend to the surface coherence of the text, but few acknowledge its disturbing qualities. Although the play appears to be held in balance by sets of economic, moral, theological, and geographical oppositions, they create an inadequate basis of order.[2] For we can read the play in terms of such themes without ever confronting the evocative and disruptive features of the play that point to its hidden order.[3]

A psychoanalytic description of literature seeks the subject's own vantage point in discovering the configuration of what is avowed, repressed, and defended. Psychoanalytic criticism thus has as its provenance the disturbing or seemingly incoherent features of a text. Such an approach, however, loses credibility with competent readers when it focuses exclusively on the subject and ignores the rules, languages, or codes of the author's culture. The fact is that we never encounter the speech of an individual free from history. Not only does the culture lay down the preconditions for intelligibility that an author must observe in communicating with an audience or readership, but the culture also provides each individual with a set of choices and limitations for personal fantasies. These cultural rules are what offer possible coherence or relationship among symbols, institutions, social forms, professed values, and approved norms and thus enable us to identify a culture's paradigms.[4] These rules undoubtedly exist, or are insisted upon, precisely because each culture has its characteristic stresses and contradictions, and it is invariably the case that such stresses and contradictions emerge in literary works.

Conflicts in matters of economics, religion, government, and relations between the sexes can clearly be seen in the various ways Elizabethans tended to insist upon those aspects of their cultural self-image that most contradicted historical fact. The rivalrous and competitive relations among men, which dominated politics and economics, could be countered at times by the celebration of a Christian-humanistic ideal of friendship, just as the distrust of women could be denied by the complex language of courtship.[5] The quest for office could be presented as selfless service to monarch and state and the motive of personal ambition denied.[6] Political enemies, of course, could always charge the office seeker with ambition and deny in turn the ideal of service. Hatton, Leicester, Ralegh, Cecil, and Essex were all interpreted in this way at one time or another. Frustration in the pursuit of office could be denied in such a way as Sidney chose when, out of favor with Elizabeth following his second diplomatic mission, he retired from court to indulge himself in a pastoral fiction, much to the consternation of Languet.[7] The tensions thus reflected in the paradigm of civic humanism could find literary expression in the dramatic conflict between public duty and private desire or the poetic conflict of competition among males or the pursuit of love.

In contrast with such cultural myths and ideologies, however, the meanings of literary texts do not derive exclusively from conflict within the codes of a culture. In literature, we never encounter the culture free of an author's personal history. That this is so is most apparent at points of incoherence in a text where the formal and ideological problems and resolutions do not convey a corresponding affect, that is, where the affect strikes us as excessive or insufficient for the matter at hand. At such points of conflict between personal style and cultural code, meaning appears to have a dual basis. The terms by which Shakespeare set up his play, the characters he created, the needs he had them express, and the network of relationships he established for them reflect not only the contradictions in his culture but also the ambivalence of his own desires. The author's personal manipulation of his culture's materials produces the disturbances and discontinuities that tend to confound most kinds of criticism but locate for literary criticism the proper territory for psychoanalytic work.

In *The Merchant of Venice*, those values identified by the ostensible opposition of Venice and Belmont reveal contradictory cultural paradigms. This suggests that the specific values expressed in the codes and languages of Shakespeare's England, far from stabilizing its cultural order and beliefs, only highlight its cultural tensions and contradictions.[8] This, of course, is true of every culture.[9] By composing the play in terms of geographical, moral, and economic oppositions, Shakespeare obviously sought to make from his material a dramatic world that was finally whole, social, and stable. These oppositions are not simply ideological, however, but reflect psychological tensions as well. The use of two locales, Jessica's betrayal of Shylock, the androgynous characteristics of Portia, the idealization of patronage, the relationship between love and wealth, the ring plot, and the bawdry in the fifth act are all means of resolving oppositions within Shakespeare's culture. At the same time, all signal disturbance, conflict, and anxiety.

I

Shakespeare's use of two locales characterizes the design of many of his plays in which emotionally different areas of action are marked off by means of geographical boundaries.[10] In *The Merchant of Venice*, however, the two locales are associated with sexual identifications and diametrically opposed in a way characteristic of no other play—except perhaps *Antony and Cleopatra*. Venice seems masculine, competitive, and commercial, operating according to harsh laws that create and perpetuate a scarcity economy and threaten strict punishment for anyone who endangers the economic life of the city.[11] Presented initially as a romance world that promises love and money, Belmont seems contrastingly maternal, bountiful, and generous. To enter and exit Venice, women must disguise themselves as men. Men come to Belmont either as adventurers in search of marriage and wealth, or, in the case of Lorenzo, as a Christian privateer in quest of a safe harbor and a sympathetic monarch.

At the end of the play, Shakespeare does not return or even promise to return his major characters to the world of social and economic reality. In one sense, of course, he cannot change Venice as he changes other closed worlds. Certainly Venice is associated with Shylock and the emotional reverberations he arouses, but there is another, equally important, reason Shakespeare abandons Venice for the resolution of the play. The city, as he presents it, is so firmly rooted in mercantilism that no amount of artistry can wish these economic realities away. Thus, by ending the play in Belmont, Shakespeare distances us from the harsh facts of economic life in Venice. Nonetheless, something seems to have gone wrong with the ending, even after we justify the setting. The translation of the meaning of the bond, the humor of the ring plot resolution, and the isolation of Antonio are disturbing. The fact that some critics have argued that the fifth act is unified with the rest of the play, that the setting is appropriate, and that the business of the rings is good-natured fun, suggests (to me at least) that the resolution is in fact an uncomfortable one.[12] Despite its contrast to Venice, as established in the first four acts, Belmont becomes in the fifth act a less lyrical, less benevolent world—a world of sexual contest, threatened betrayals, and rivalrous competition.[13] To understand the problem we need to examine the social order of Venice more closely.

With its sad and benevolent merchant and his coterie of solicitous friends who express their concern for him, Venice as presented at the opening of the play is an idealized Elizabethan version of a masculine world. We never learn the exact cause of Antonio's melancholia, but either in spite of it or because of it he is willing, for the love of Bassanio, to unlock his purse, his person, his extremest means and finance Bassanio's venture. Bassanio is an idealized portrait of a courtier, perhaps like one of those young gentlemen who participated in the raid on Cadiz where the "wealthy Andrew" (I.i.27) was seized.[14] He is handsome, wasteful, manipulative, Jason-like, a lord of love in desperate need of capital that will allow him to compete for Portia and her wealth, or as he says, "to hold a rival place" (I.i.174) with other suitors. The image of rival suitors, the competition they threaten, the language of venturing and hazarding, and the specific situation of the caskets by which Portia exists as a ward of her dead father—all reflect Shakespeare's condensation into one complex metaphor of the different, culture-specific ways in which young men of the gentry and the aristocracy hoped to make their fortunes.[15] By so conceiving the object of the quest, Shakespeare gives voice to a very powerful cultural fantasy.

An equally powerful fantasy revolves around the wealthy merchant who will finance such a venture out of love for the needy courtier. From what we know of such men as Horatio Palavacino, Lionel Cranfield, or any of the other London merchants of the period, the benevolent merchant-patron of this play, though desperately desired, existed only in fiction.[16] Unlike *Il Pecorone*, where the merchant is godfather to the young man, *The Merchant of Venice* stresses that the relationship is one of friendship in which the ideal of male-male bonding is at stake.[17] Thus Antonio freely chooses to feed Bassanio's needs by risking himself in a bond with Shylock. Significantly, the issues of the venture and the bond arise in a Venice at whose center is a figure of paternal nurturance and whose love is given in the form of wealth. By entrusting his body to Shylock, Antonio makes it the source of his show of love. The network of relationships thus established is based solely on forms of dependence and trust and hence is constantly subject to the threat of betrayal.[18]

The first real betrayal in the play, however, is Jessica's betrayal of Shylock. But it is presented in such a way as to *deny* that it is in fact a betrayal, an illusion that those who are disturbed by Jessica's behavior find reassuring to accept. And yet the justifications that Shakespeare has built into this plot seem to reflect a real ambivalence on his part.[19] We know that Shylock treats his daughter like his money, locking her up and preventing contact with suitors; in these respects he is like some other fathers in Shakespeare's comedies. Although to be unfaithful to this Jewish father is to be gentle (with a pun on gentile), the theft of the jewels is marked by shame. Preferring the shadows to the light of Lorenzo's torch, Jessica flees at night, disguised as a boy. Like the other fathers in Shakespeare's plays who discover their daughters have betrayed them, Shylock rages and wishes his daughter dead. Usually in the comedies, betraying daughters are finally not punished, either because their fathers are appeased or the paternal antiromantic dictates are overruled. In *The Merchant of Venice*, however, the additional information that Shakespeare provides about the couple's flight indicates that something has gone wrong with the expected comedic formula.

Shylock hears that Jessica and Lorenzo were seen in Genoa, where they spent eighty ducats in one night and Jessica used a turquoise ring to purchase a monkey. This ring Shylock identifies: ". . . it was my turquoise, I had it of Leah when I was a bachelor . . ." (III.i.110–11). The sudden reality of his pain and the significance of the ring shock many readers, precisely because the ring makes Shylock seem so humanly vulnerable. Although the flight of the daughter and the theft of money and jewels are in one sense a comic retaliation felt as castration by Shylock (who equates money and offspring and who argues that metal breeds like living things), Jessica's prodigal spending is also a way of figuratively undoing the parents' marriage and denying the mother's token of love and fidelity.[20] Thus Jessica's flight is not only the first instance of betrayal, but it also establishes the emotionally complex association of betrayal with the spending of a ring, an undoing of a marriage, and a denial of love. The violation of the bond between father and daughter becomes the occasion for the testing of other bonds and the enactment of other betrayals.[21]

Shakespeare has so arranged the material that the news of the lovers' extravagance is interspersed with the news of Antonio's failed argosies. Shylock's decision to enforce the terms of the contract thus seems to be conceived by Shakespeare as a way of retaliating for the loss of the daughter. The loss and what that loss symbolizes are to be acted out upon Antonio's body, as if he were not just an economic rival and a spiritual enemy but also a surrogate for Jessica. For the loss of his daughter, his ducats, his two bags, his two stones, Shylock determines that the literal terms of the contract be fulfilled and the flesh cut *off* from Antonio's body.

The rules that operate in Venice not only encourage the conversion and flight of Jessica from Shylock but also require the punishment of Antonio for the well-being of the city. In Belmont, Gobbo can joke that "this making of Christians will raise the price of hogs" (III.v.21–22). In Venice, the economic life of the city literally starves on inflation; the law invoked by the angry and betrayed father must be observed because it protects the flow of capital into the city:

> *Antonio.* The Duke cannot deny the course of law:
>   For the commodity that strangers have
>   With us in Venice, if it be denied,
>   Will much impeach the justice of the state,
>   Since that the trade and profit of the city
>   Consisteth of all nations.
>
> (III.iii.26–31)

Given such a law, Portia's bountiful supply of money is useless in Venice, and given such a plaintiff, her call for mercy goes unheeded. It is only when she acts as sternly as her father might have that she is effective.[22]

Yet, even after we acknowledge that her decision is legally just, there remains something that continues to disturb readers about Shylock's punishment and Portia's role in that punishment. Unlike Rosalind or Viola, Portia does not go into disguise either for protection or for the purpose of wooing. In fact, Shakespeare gives no reason for the disguising except that it allows women to play at being men. Portia explains to Nerissa that Bassanio and Gratiano will not even recognize their wives, for the husbands "shall think we are accomplished/With that we lack" (III.iv.61–62). As a man without a penis, as a dutiful daughter released from the will of her father, as a source of paternal wealth and maternal love, as a married woman who is still a virgin, Portia can come into Venice, where the males are helpless to act, and can free Antonio. But when she leaves Venice, she is, like Shylock, the victim of a betrayal. Moreover, her repossession of the ring not only signals that the betrothal vows have been violated, but it also implies, as the joking in the last act makes clear, that she has just cuckolded her husband, even as he has betrayed her. It is in her deeply complicated self-possession that she becomes such a disturbing presence in the play.

II

Aside from *The Taming of the Shrew,* perhaps, *The Merchant of Venice* is the only comedy in which marriage is not the goal of the action or the signal for the comic closure.[23] The marriage takes place in the middle of the play. It is the consummation of the marriage, the actualization of the union, that is deferred. If we ask what it is that bars consummation, we have to look at the needs that bind and threaten the various relationships in the play. It was, after all, Shakespeare's choice to interrupt the celebration of the doubling of love and to prevent the multiple consummations with the news of Antonio's misfortunes. Moreover, it was Shakespeare's choice to depart from his source in conceiving of the relationship between courtier and patron.

Bassanio explains to Portia what his relationship to Antonio is and what binds them together:

> I have engag'd myself to a dear friend,
> Engag'd my friend to his mere enemy
> To feed my means.
>
> (III.ii.260–62)

This betrothal of self to friend and friend to enemy characterizes the Bassanio-Antonio-Shylock bond in the first half of the play. The enemy is absolute ("mere") in that he is murderous and his hostility is total.[24] At the end of the play, Portia will have replaced Shylock in the triangle, and the enemy will be "merely" a rival in love.[25] The former relationship is essentially an oral one. Antonio feeds Bassanio's needs by signing his body over to Shylock, and Shylock, of course, is presented throughout the play as orally threatening.[26] He is the one who will not eat with others and who allegedly denies food to that huge feeder, Gobbo.[27] He releases Gobbo into Bassanio's service so that the servant might feed on the prodigal. When Shylock first meets Antonio at the beginning of the play, the Jew says: "Your worship was the last man in our mouths" (I. iii.54). Later in the play, Shylock's desires are described as "wolvish, bloody, starv'd, and ravenous" (IV.i.138). Even Bassanio's description of Antonio's letter indicates this devouring quality of Shylock:

> Here is a letter, lady,
> The paper as the body of my friend,
> And every word in it a gaping wound
> Issuing life-blood.
>
> (III.ii.262–65)

It is as if Shylock has already begun to feed on Antonio. Indeed, it is the differing oral styles of Shylock and Antonio that characterize their economic practices as well. Shylock always takes back more than he gives, and Antonio risks being emptied on the chance of enjoying a huge return.

As the one whose show of love is in his generosity, his willingness to offer money and self, Antonio is an idealized version of the Renaissance patron. Although his conduct comes close to the description of Timon's activities, Antonio's excesses are so slight compared to Timon's that they appear as virtues. Yet just as Antonio is almost too generous to Bassanio, he is almost too passive, too willing to submit his body to the law. He sees himself too easily as "a tainted wether of the flock,/Meetest for death" (IV.i.114-15), yielding to Shylock's retaliatory rage. Moreover, when he cancels Bassanio's debt, his request of Bassanio is suspiciously self-indulgent.[28] He writes that the debt is cleared "if I might but see you at my death" (III.ii.318). Later he repeats this wish: ". . . pray God Bassanio come/To see me pay his debt, and then I care not" (III.iii.34-35). His insistence that Bassanio's debt is cleared by witnessing the death is excessive, as is his desire to see Bassanio and be seen by him as he fulfills the bond. He is too exhibitionistic in his suffering, and denies with too much facility that he is competing for Bassanio's love, initially by giving his money, and subsequently by yielding his body.

The excesses of Antonio's virtues, his oral dependency, his isolation and loneliness are characteristic of a kind of narcissistic behavior that is particularly disturbing because his apparent selflessness consists of denying those very needs and dependencies upon which he acts. Implicit in that style of behavior is the denial that he is either competing with Portia for the love of Bassanio or that he is at all envious of their relationship. By attributing envy to her, however, he reveals the nature of his competition with her. This can be seen when Antonio turns to Bassanio just before the judgment is rendered and says:

> Commend me to your honourable wife,
> Tell her the process of Antonio's end,
> Say how I lov'd you, speak me fair in death:
> And when the tale is told, bid her be judge
> Whether Bassanio had not once a love. . . .

> (IV.i.269-73)

Here Antonio presents himself as bonded to Bassanio, while he places Portia in the position of admiring the love between the two men. Bassanio responds to Antonio by saying that although his wife is as dear to him as life, he would sacrifice life, wife, and the world to Shylock in order to save Antonio. Gratiano echoes the same sentiments. Needless to say, the two women, who are standing by disguised as judge and clerk, are not particularly taken with these professions of love. Shakespeare has so arranged the material that the women are present to overhear their husbands deny them. Moreover the situation is so managed that Bassanio's newly acquired wealth is of no use in Venice, and all the men are impotent to save Antonio from Shylock's narcissistic rage. In effect, Shakespeare has it both ways. He can indulge in the idealization of male love and he can so determine the course of events that it is Portia who "delivers" Antonio, then turns the delivery into a test of Bassanio's love when she asks for the gloves and the ring. This test of Bassanio's fidelity to Portia becomes, *at Antonio's insistence*, a test of Bassanio's love for Antonio.

The set of relationships presented here at the end of the fourth act is essentially the same as that portrayed in the sonnets. Unlike the situation in the sonnets, however, where the older man is the client competing for the love of the younger patron, in *Merchant* it is the patron who is competing for the love of the client. Leslie Fiedler has already pointed to the general correspondence between Sonnet 20 and *The Merchant of Venice*, but the last six lines of that sonnet deserve closer consideration:[29]

> And for a woman wert thou first created,
> Till Nature as she wrought thee fell a-doting,
> And by addition me of thee defeated,
> By adding one thing, to my purpose nothing.
>   But since she prick'd thee out for women's pleasure,
>   Mine be thy love, and thy love's use their treasure.[30]

The poet here as deprived lover is in the position of Antonio; the young man, separated from the poet by his masculinity, is in that of Bassanio, and Portia is like the women of the sonnet, who might take the young man's body but not his love. The play, however, does not end with the characters in this configuration, in which self and masculine "other" are in a dyadic love relationship on a moral level above the degraded woman. The characters of *The Merchant of Venice* form various triadic relationships in which the male-male bond is loosened (slightly) and the woman assumes a position of authority. The dilemma of Antonio is the emotionally complex situation Shakespeare would have in the sonnets if the poet were to conceive of himself as the patron and, as such, the victim of two conflicting ideals of love and of the social orders those ideals determine.

On the one hand, the romantic-comedic design of the play promises a happy pairing of male and female. On the other hand, such a configuration threatens the male-male bond. Both configurations are deeply held cultural ideals, and each contradicts the other. At the center of this conflict between two social orders is Antonio, the title figure of the play. Bassanio, after all, negotiates both sets of relationships by submitting separately to the demands of either Antonio or Portia, depending on whom he is with.[31] Portia wins her contests and is clearly in control of events from the fourth act on. It is Antonio, however, whose needs cannot successfully be accommodated. Even for those readers who are untroubled by the other elements of the fifth act, it is Antonio's isolation that seems most disturbing in what would otherwise be a festive conclusion. Moreover, Shakespeare chose not to follow his source in providing a wife for the patron figure.

This contrast to the source indicates the degree to which Shakespeare personally formulated the dramatic problem and worked through a solution. The disturbances that Antonio's dilemma and Shylock's punishment create reflect the fantasy material that embodies the implicit contradictions of the cultural code. The belief that selfless charity triumphs over selfish need and the assumption that venture capitalism is more natural than usury are cast in the form of the idealized patron-client relationship, which the play presents at its most favorable as the mutual exchange of love between males. The idealization of male love serves to deny the competition between males, and it masks the particular needs being satisfied.

Shylock, the figure of the father as selfish usurer and oral aggressor, would seem to be the chief threat to the humanistic, theological, and economic values represented in the relationship between Antonio and Bassanio. Because of Shakespeare's attribution of particular male and female, paternal and maternal characteristics to Portia, she can control Shylock, and in that sense she preserves the values he threatens. She not only controls Shylock, however, she also replaces him as the threat to the Antonio-Bassanio bond because of the test of fidelity she arranges.[32] Since she, like Antonio, is a source of wealth and love, she exposes the extent to which the men are subject to the needs of the patron. With her, however, Shakespeare does not resolve the problem of oral dependency that binds the men because she creates her own set of such relationships.

In this play the conversion of wealth into love is the fantasy that binds people together in forms of oral dependency.[33] Nowhere is that fantasy more apparent than when Bassanio correctly chooses the lead casket. As Portia declares him her lord, her governor, and her king she places her ring on his finger. Bassanio's response signals that this submission of the woman to the man is the moment of oral fusion and bliss:

> Madam, you have bereft me of all words,
> Only my blood speaks to you in my veins,
> And there is such confusion in my powers,
> As after some oration fairly spoke
> By a beloved prince, there doth appear

Among the buzzing pleased multitude,
Where every something being blent together,
Turns to a wild of nothing, save of joy
Express'd, and not express'd. . . .

(III.ii.175–83)

The political metaphor he uses reciprocates her offer of fealty. The language Shakespeare employs equates that political moment when a populace has heard a monarch with what Bassanio feels at his betrothal: he is parts, "every something," now merging, fusing, "being blent together," turning into nothing "save of joy." The excesses of his speech emphasize that life is present only at the moment of fusion, which he then equates with the union of finger and ring:

. . . but when this ring
Parts from this finger, then parts life from hence,—
O then be bold to say Bassanio's dead!

(II.ii.183–85)

Metaphorically, this speech suggests, separation is death; the spending of the ring would be a betrayal which would threaten to undo the marriage and violate the bond of fealty. Portia's love, however, was acquired by means of Antonio's wealth; her wealth was won because of Antonio's love. To reciprocate that show of love, not to pay off the investment, Antonio asks that the ring be spent.

III

The fifth act concerns betrothals, bonds, and betrayals. It begins appropriately enough with Jessica and Lorenzo in a lyrical celebration of the night and their love, a celebration curiously undercut by the situations of the famous lovers they cite. On just such a night, they say, Troilus looked across the lines to the Grecian camp where Cressida was, Thisby ran from the lion, Dido had just seen Aeneas depart, Medea was in the act of betraying her father, and Jessica fled from Shylock. Each event they mention consists of a betrayal marked by separation. Moreover, the language of this last act is saturated with metaphors of cuckoldry, treachery, and disguise. Shakespeare's elaborate trick with which the wives outface their husbands centers on the wives' accusation of marital treachery, their threat of cuckoldry, and the revelation of their disguises. Since Portia's ring has replaced Shylock's contract as the principal object of contention and the ring has acquired multiple associations through the play, possession of the ring powerfully expresses ambivalence about the idealized woman who has been implicit throughout the play.

Gratiano brusquely explains his loss of the ring: "I gave it to the judge's clerk/Would he were gelt that had it . . ." (V.i.143-44). This joke that Shakespeare has with the audience turns on a common male fantasy about women. It implies, however, that possession of the ring warrants gelding. When Portia reproaches Gratiano for taking the vow of betrothal too lightly, Bassanio's aside carries the implication further: "Why I were best to cut my left hand off,/And swear I lost the ring defending it" (ll.177-78). The intent of these lines signals the disintegrative consequences of the loss of the ring, but the lines suggest as well that the qualities of the ring are such that the male who defends his possession of it invites castration. This ambivalent attitude toward the ring as associated with female sexuality can even be seen in the quip that concludes the play. Gratiano looks forward to couching with Nerissa not as wife but as the doctor's clerk, even as he declares that he'll fear "no other thing/So sore as keeping safe Nerissa's ring" (V.i.306-07).

The husbands' insistence that they have given their rings to other men rather than to women reveals their naïveté in making the foolish distinction between betrayal and infidelity. It leaves them open to the threat of cuckoldry when Portia says she will sleep with the judge who has her ring. Since we know that, like Nerissa, Portia has her own ring literally and metaphorically, the joke is on Bassanio. Although Portia successfully outfaces her husband, implicit in the good-natured gaming is the not-so-good-natured threat (and fear) that if a man betrays his wife's love for the love of another man, the woman in turn will betray her husband for a narcissistic object who is the woman herself. The joke, then, wittily emphasizes the importance of the bond on the one hand, but on the other hand it reveals the anxiety-arousing fantasy that Portia is sexually enclosed, simultaneously male and female. Indeed, there is behind all of the joking and bawdry something as dangerous in the ring as there is in the caskets with which Portia is also associated.[34]

It is only when Antonio volunteers himself as a bond to guarantee Bassanio's fidelity, that is when he relinquishes his claims and yields to Portia, that Portia produces her ring for Antonio to give to her husband. She restores Bassanio as her husband by figuratively placing Antonio, the man whom she "delivered" and to whom he says she gave life, in the position of offspring; his loyalty to the tie he has established with her will guarantee the bond between Bassanio and Portia. Moreover, only after Antonio has admitted her claim does she give him the news that his ships are safe. Throughout the play, the value of Bassanio's love is equated with Antonio's argosy; in the second half of the play, the value of Antonio's love is equated with Portia's ring. By her mysterious possession of the information she gives Antonio, she in effect becomes the source by which his fortunes are restored.

By replacing Shylock with Portia in the triangular relationship with Bassanio and Antonio, Shakespeare has substituted for an orally destructive father a nurturing mother. Fidelity to wife in turn replaces loyalty to patron-friend. The narcissistic bond between males has been loosened, but Antonio's isolation, like Shylock's punishment—regardless of how we understand either of them morally or thematically—still disturbs the resolution. Moreover, Portia's successful mediation of the crisis in Venice and her triumphant outfacing in Belmont require that she be an androgyne. She is most successful either when she is dressed like a man and acting like her father, or when she is sexually self-enclosed and threatening to cuckold her husband hermaphroditically. Finally, while the theology of the play may be correct and the morality just, the economics are suspect and, like Portia's sexuality, most effective when counterfeit. For that reason, the play ends in Belmont, where marriage substitutes for patronage and love is wealth.

Notes

1. Norman Rabkin, "Meaning and Shakespeare," in *Shakespeare 1971: Proceedings of the World Shakespeare Congress*, ed. Clifford Leech and J.M.R. Margeson (Toronto: Univ. of Toronto Press, 1972), pp. 89–106.

2. Rabkin, pp. 103–04. See also D. J. Palmer, "'The Merchant of Venice' or The Importance of Being Earnest," in *Shakespearian Comedy*, ed. Malcolm Bradbury and David Palmer (London: Edwin Arnold, 1972), pp. 97–102. Palmer says: "Our attention is often held by moral arguments of one kind or another while a different order of awareness and response is being solicited by other . . . means" (p. 98).

3. For a discussion of this communication model, see Anton Ehrenzweig, *The Hidden Order of Art: A Study in the Psychology of Artistic Imagination* (Berkeley: Univ. of California Press, 1971), and Arthur F. Marotti, "Countertransference, the Communication Process and the Dimensions of Psychoanalytic Criticism," *Critical Inquiry*, 4 (1978), 471–89.

4. On this point, see Fred Weinstein and Gerald M. Platt, *Psychoanalytic Sociology: An Essay on the Interpretation of Historical Data and the Phenomena of Collective Behavior* (Baltimore: Johns Hopkins Univ. Press, 1973), pp. 92–94.

5. The distrust of women was a corresponding way of denying their idealization. Expressing such distrust is a common feature of the pamphlets of advice to sons written by such fathers as Burghley, Ralegh, Henry Sidney, and Henry Percy.

6. Lawrence Stone, *The Crisis of the Aristocracy, 1558–1641* (Oxford: Clarendon Press, 1965), pp. 398–504, discusses the change in the idea of service in the sixteenth century, the reward for service, and the personal cost of pursuing office. See also Wallace T. MacCaffrey, "Place and Patronage," in *Elizabethan Government and Society*, ed. S. T. Bindoff, J. Hurstfield, and C. H. Williams (London: Athlone Press, 1961), pp. 95–126.

7. James M. Osborne, *Young Philip Sidney, 1572–1577* (New Haven, Conn.:

Yale Univ. Press, 1972), p. 504; *The Correspondence of Sir Philip Sidney and Hubert Languet*, trans. Steuart A. Pears (London: William Pickering, 1845), p. 182.

8. See George Devereux, *From Anxiety to Method in the Behavioral Sciences* (The Hague: Mouton, 1971), p. 215, for a discussion of the irrational, equivocal nature of cultural patterns, values, and beliefs.

9. Devereux, p. 212.

10. Sherman H. Hawkins, "The Two Worlds of Shakespearean Comedy," *Shakespeare Studies*, 3 (1968), 62–80.

11. For a discussion of the two worlds in this play, see Norman N. Holland, *The Shakespearean Imagination* (Bloomington, Ind.: Indiana Univ. Press, 1964), pp. 94–100.

12. John Russell Brown, "The Realization of Shylock: A Theatrical Criticism," in *Early Shakespeare*, ed. John Russell Brown and Bernard Harris (London: Edwin Arnold, 1961), pp. 208–09; Herbert S. Donow, "Shakespeare's Caskets: Unity in *Merchant of Venice*," *Shakespeare Studies*, 4 (1969), 93; James E. Siemons, "*The Merchant of Venice*: Act V as Ritual Reiteration," *Studies in Philology*, 67 (1970), 207. C. L. Barber stresses the lighthearted comedy of the last act, but he admits that on reflection there are elements in the play, and particularly its resolution, that disturb him. See *Shakespeare's Festive Comedy* (Princeton, N.J.: Princeton Univ. Press, 1959), pp. 189–90.

13. Two readings that emphasize the less lyrical aspect of the last act are Marilyn Williamson, "The Ring Episode in *The Merchant of Venice*," *South Atlantic Quarterly*, 71 (1972), 587–94, and Marvin Felheim, "The Merchant of Venice," *Shakespeare Studies*, 4 (1969), 94–108.

14. My text here is the new Arden edition, ed. John Russell Brown (London: Methuen, 1955).

15. It is important not to misconstrue this imagery or literalize the metaphor and assume that Bassanio's quest is simply either a calculating business venture or an erotic enchantment. The metaphor works because it is part of the symbolic code of the culture and reflects an inherent tension between two goals.

16. Lawrence Stone, *An Elizabethan: Sir Horatio Palvacino* (Oxford: Clarendon Press, 1956). See also R. H. Tawney, *Business and Politics Under James I: Lionel Cranfield as Merchant and Minister* (Cambridge: At the Univ. Press, 1958).

17. In *Il Pecorone*, the Bassanio figure is the youngest of three sons and, like many younger sons in the Renaissance, he does not receive any of his father's legacy. His godfather in Venice is literally a substitute father. Shakespeare's alteration of the source highlights the issue of patronage and idealizes the client-patron relationship.

18. Psychoanalysis habitually locates the deepest crises of trust and dependence in the early oral relationship between infant and mother. See, for example, Erik H. Erikson, *Childhood and Society* (New York: W. W. Norton, 1963), pp. 72–80, 247–51.

19. I think his ambivalence is communicated and can be seen in the various ways that readers try to control the event by imposing meaning on it or, failing that, by simply expressing anger at Jessica. For a sample of such varied responses, see Rabkin, pp. 97–98; Barber, p. 165; Barbara K. Lewalski, "Biblical Allusion and Allegory in *The Merchant of Venice*," *Shakespeare Quarterly*, 13 (1962), 335–36; and René E. Fortin, "Launcelot and the Uses of Allegory in *The Merchant of Venice*," *Studies in English Literature*, 14 (1974), 263–65. One of the angrier responses to Jessica's flight is Sigurd Burkhardt, *Shakespearean Meanings* (Princeton, N.J.: Princeton Univ. Press, 1968), pp. 219–27.

20. E. Pearlman, "Shakespeare, Freud, and the Two Usuries, or, Money's a Meddler," *English Literary Renaissance*, 2 (1972), 217–36, discusses the psychodynamics of the equation of money and offspring in *Merchant*.

21. The fantasy of a daughter betraying a father has the same dynamics as the fantasy of a mother betraying a son. *King Lear* offers a good example of such a reversal.

22. Leo Rockas, "'A Dish of Doves': *The Merchant of Venice*," *ELH*, 40 (1973), 339–51. He says that if we look for an appropriate "character to play the judge it might more likely be the father who devised the judicial lottery . . ." (p. 344).

23. Leo Salingar, *Shakespeare and the Traditions of Comedy* (Cambridge: At the Univ. Press, 1974), 301–03. Salingar points out that there are three other plays in which the wedding itself is postponed. *Merchant* is unique in that the ceremony is not delayed, but the celebration and the consummation are.

24. "Mere" is one of those primal words with antithetical meanings that Freud discussed in "The Antithetical Sense of Primal Words," in *The Standard Edition of The Complete Psychological Works of Sigmund Freud*, ed. and trans. James Strachey et al., 24 vols. (London: Hogarth Press, 1953–74), 11, pp. 153–61.

25. Lawrence W. Hyman, "The Rival Lovers in *The Merchant of Venice*," *Shakespeare Quarterly*, 21 (1970), 109–16. My notion of the rivalry differs considerably from Hyman's. Hyman does not see any reason for Bassanio to need Antonio's money except as a counterpart to Portia's wealth.

26. This type of excessive oral aggression is usually projected onto a distorted maternal image (Erikson, pp. 74–79). The absence of mothers in Shakespeare's comedies should not blind us to the presence of maternal features in various characters. Thus, just as Portia has benevolent paternal qualities, so Shylock has malevolent maternal qualities. Of greater interest is this kind of "contamination" of parental imagoes, coupled with the interruption of the marriage celebration and the dangers associated with keeping and losing the ring. On the interrelationship of these qualities, see Otto Kernberg, *Borderline Conditions and Pathological Narcissism* (New York: Jason Aronson, 1975), pp. 40–44.

27. Attempts to identify Gobbo with Sir Robert Cecil have failed because readers have mistakenly assumed that the joke in the name was the Italian meaning of Gobbo as hunchback. See Geoffrey Bullough, ed. *Narrative and Dramatic Sources of Shakespeare* (London: Routledge and Kegan Paul, 1966), 1, p. 445. It would seem, however, that the joke is an Italianate version of the English word "gob," meaning mouth.

28. J. A. Bryant, "*The Merchant of Venice* and the Common Flaw," *Sewanee Review*, 81 (1973), 614–16.

29. Leslie Fiedler, *The Stranger in Shakespeare* (New York: Stein and Day, 1972), p. 89. See also Rockas, p. 346.

30. My text here is G. L. Kittredge's *Complete Works* (Boston: Ginn, 1936).

31. Robert Hapgood, "Portia and *The Merchant of Venice*: 'The Gentle Bond,'" *Modern Language Quarterly*, 28 (1967), 28.

32. In the source, Portia's counterpart twice empties the ship of the young prodigal after she has lured him into her chamber and made him fall asleep with the help of generous portions of wine. In the source, then, she poses the same kind of oral threat as Shylock does in the play.

33. Such a fantasy is structured around the wish that love might convert into wealth and wealth might convert into love. This formulation is different from a statement such as John Russell Brown's that the play is "informed by Shakespeare's

ideal of love's wealth." See *Shakespeare and His Comedies* (London: Methuen, 1957), p. 62.

34. Freud, "The Theme of Three Caskets," *Standard Edition*, 12, pp. 289-301.

5 ❀ Fratricide and Cuckoldry: Shakespeare's Doubles

Joel Fineman

> I love Shakespeare's clowns—they have a lot of humour,
> but nevertheless they express hate, they are not from God.
> —*Vaslav Nijinsky*

> If others have their will Ann hath a way.
> —*Stephen Dedalus*

Throughout his career, Shakespeare worked with symmetrical patterns, with pairs of doubles, with relationships of edged and ironically reciprocal equipoise. These structures of opposition are often placed in an explicit familial frame—*The Comedy of Errors*, for example, with which Shakespeare began his experiments in comic form, is purely a farce of twins, and a mechanical farce at that—but just as often a familial context is merely suggested, unspoken but presupposed. Think, for example, of Hermia and Helena, who "grew together,/Like to a double cherry, seeming parted,/But yet an union in partition—/Two lovely berries molded on one stem" (*A Midsummer Night's Dream*, III.ii.208-11), or of Leontes and Polixenes, who call each other "brother" because, "They were train'd together in the childhoods; and there rooted betwixt them then, such an affection, which cannot choose but branch now" (*The Winter's Tale*, I.i.21-23).

These branching pairs of siblings, real or virtual, male and female, rooted together in synonymous rivalry, are significant not only because the example of brothers and sisters poised against each other calls up and somehow jeopardizes a delicate paradox at the center of Shakespeare's erotic imagination—"Two distincts, division none"[2]—but also

This chapter first appeared in *The Psychoanalytic Review*, 64 (Fall 1977), Copyright © 1977 by Human Sciences Press, 72 Fifth Ave., New York, N.Y. 10011. Reprinted by permission of the press.

because the opposition itself, an opposition of equals, sororicidal, fratricidal, is embedded and employed in the very dramatic economy of the plays. Sometimes, as though the story did not hold together for him unless tied by bloodlines, Shakespeare would manufacture fraternal relations nonexistent in his source, as in *As You Like It* or, again, *The Comedy of Errors* with its extra pair of twins. At other times Shakespeare rewrote history itself so as to develop suitable fraternal and therefore violent relationships of foils, as in *Henry IV, Part I*, where Hotspur is reduced to rivaling coeval with Hal. But even when their fraternity is confirmed only by imagery, Shakespeare's doubles are always imagined, whether they are in love or at war, as two of a "kind"—their familiarity, their similarity, giving dramatic point either to their romance or to their enmity.

In the early comedies, especially the romance comedies, this symmetry of reciprocally opposed figures turns almost into choreography, whence the grace with which the implausible plots develop. An exit from one side of the stage is answered by an entrance from the other. The course of true love runs through a binary series of contrived mixups in which permutations are as mathematical as they are romantic. In these comedies the witty proprieties, almost geometries, of stylized, antiphonic action spell a mood in which fate is not so much acted as danced out—just the sort of morosco or jig with which the players, several in theatrical drag, did in fact signal the end of a day's performance. As a result, as though to fit abstractly structural requirements, the figures of the comedies typically receive minimal characterization. They mistake each other for each other, they are equally adept at repartee, they each speak the *same* language. Because the differences between them are accidental (for example, with Hermia and Helena, one is tall and the other short, a difference that signifies nothing, which is why the audience accepts the fact that the one is so easily taken for the other), they share the same essential nature, a sameness that in turn contributes to the atmosphere of comic domesticity. Being *specially* connected, as members of the same family, their coupling, the marriage of Shakespearean comic doubles—when it occurs or when it is deflected to a bifurcated mirror object—is incestuous in tone if not in fact, yet happily so, being the benign interpretation of a desire that links equals each to each. This is certainly the comic, but by no means the only, Shakespearean response to patterns of equivalent desire. In the comedies Shakespeare's wit untangles the very webs of erotic homology that in the tragedies generate catastrophe. Perhaps, then, it would be better to say that in the comedies Shakespeare encapsulates those webs within a comic form, distancing them with rhythms that defuse the danger rather than resolve the tensions of family romance.

These are preliminary generalizations that, to be useful, must be refined by reference to specific plays. Nevertheless, as a whole, the love
portrayed in the intelligently elegant comedies stands in marked contrast to the eroticism of the tragedies, where desire is too nostalgically
narcissistic, too homosexually paranoiac, to resolve itself in romance.
In them fraternity concludes with murder, not union, as fratricide and
sororicide, not incest. Correspondingly, as a structural corollary reflecting the difference between comic and tragic motivation, characterization in the tragedies becomes increasingly specific and individuating—
this despite the fact that the comic is usually supposed to feature particular humors. To be set off as especial, unique, alone, is precisely the
point of a world where violence is the medium of desire and where envy
is the natural, or at least the most appropriately dramatic, substitute for
love.

But while the splits of the middle tragedies are neither so obviously
nor so rigorously reciprocal as those of the early comedies, the two
dramatic modes nevertheless depend upon the same doubling structure.
In the former it is a given that "ourselves we see in ladies' eyes" (*Love's
Labor's Lost,* IV.iii.311), a formula that establishes the romantic reso-
nance of a kind of comic narcissism. In the latter, more viciously, there
is a cancellation, a repression, of erotic mediation: "Two stars keep not
their motion in one sphere" (*Henry IV, Part I,* V.v.64—and here I quote
from a play that may be a transitional node between the two modes).
The difference defines the gap between the two genres, but for our
present purpose what is important is that in both cases dramatic personality is a function of duplicitous self-regard, the product of the
dialectical interplay between what Freudians of a certain odor call primary and secondary narcissism. This is a dynamic visibly at work in the
earliest plays and in the sonnets as well, where, however, the conven-
tionally reflexive mirror imagery of Renaissance love poetry—e.g., Sidney looking into his own heart and finding his beloved's image engrafted
upon it—is frequently employed by Shakespeare to surprisingly ironic
but not precisely amorous effect.

A doubling structure, a constant dichotomizing multiple, is built into
the Elizabethan theater. As David Bevington,[3] among others, has pointed out, the limited casting pool of the early popular drama obliged
playwrights to design striated plays in which each actor might play several roles. The development of the Elizabethan playing company, while
it regularized and expanded the size of this pool, did not do away with
the splitting traditions established by the early troupe theater. Bevington describes three techniques by which casting possibilities were sup-
plemented through doubling movements.[4] Scenes would alternate so as
to allow time for costume changes. Characters would be suppressed

while the men or boys who played them appeared in some other guise. Finally, several characters would be compressed into one role—for example, seven vices collapsing into one vice figure. We should note that these three dramatic tactics correspond to the three central procedures of dreamwork: displacement, repression, and condensation. This is a meaningful correspondence, for it suggests that a playwright such as Shakespeare, whose psyche assembled around and responded to polarities, doubling negations, structures of distributive reciprocity, had available to him a theater whose forms and conventions gave flesh to just such structures.

Like dreamwork, though, plays are not only a means of representative expression but as such constitute strategies of psychological defense, defending, that is, against the very fantasies they represent. Moreover, certain kinds of fantasies go along with certain particular kinds of defense, just as they go along with particular kinds of emotional experience. As a result, because the Elizabethan theater is ordered by the principle of doubles to which Bevington refers, there emerge definite patterns, repeated organizational forms, that contain and envelop characteristically problematic themes—themes, that is, which are affectively appropriate to the forms that contain them. This is obvious but worth mentioning. For if the Elizabethan theater begins with a split that it tends to resolve with yet further divisions, then we must recognize in this a psychological fact as well as a theatrical convention. Literary critics of Renaissance drama, noting a dialectical form and responding also to the apparent moral material of the plays, generally call this order reconciliatory, sacerdotal, fecund. We may postpone such evaluations for the moment and remark only that splitting is a typically oral modality and tactic, a means of defense characteristic of the earliest stages of boundary formation and of self and object discrimination.[5] Moreover, and more appropriate to dramas of heroic distinction, this dialectical pattern, joining horizontal oppositions by means of vertical syntheses, resolving oppositions by raising them by design one degree, recapitulates what we understand to be the internal psychic procedures by means of which self-consciousness develops.

Shakespeare, as we have said, generally manipulates these divisive patterns dexterously. As we have observed, doubles were for him both a congenial form and, almost obsessively, a suggestive content. But at one troubled moment in his career we can watch this defensive strategy begin not so much to fail him as itself to raise dramatic problems for him. *Twelfth Night, Hamlet,* and *Troilus and Cressida* are the plays in which Shakespeare begins to question duplicity. What is remarkable is that of these three plays, two of them at least still manage to be "popular," by which I mean not only that they are well received but that they are received on common assumptions. *Troilus and Cressida* is a special case in which scurrility, misogyny, "unanaled" anality, and, of course, homosexuality, reveal the idiosyncratic, the unsocialized Shakespeare—a Shakespeare whom so far only the twentieth century has either performed or enjoyed. We will talk about *Troilus and Cressida* later. For now we need only point out that these three plays mark the transition from Shakespeare's comedies to his high tragedies; they set the stage, as it were, for Shakespeare's maturity, when he no longer complains about growing old (Feste's "Youth's a stuff will not endure") but begins, rather, to worry about dying (Laertes', but not only his, "The canker galls the infants of the spring").

The two plays surely written between 1599 and 1601, *As You Like It* and *Hamlet*, both depend upon explicit fratricidal rivalry. *As You Like It* has no less than two pairs of enemy brothers: the exiled Duke Senior and the usurper, Duke Frederick, plus Oliver and Orlando. So too and famously, *Hamlet* is the drama of *Der Bestrafte Brudermord*.[6] By suggestive contrast, *Twelfth Night*, which either immediately precedes or follows *Hamlet*, begins with a reclusive Olivia mourning her dead brother and concludes, symmetrically enough, with that same Olivia grown more expansive, disabused of solitude, and married to Sebastian, Viola's temporarily dead brother. Olivia-Viola: the names are Shakespeare's, and, as the transposition of letters and sounds suggests, we are meant to understand them as a pair, each an incomplete rebus of the other, a system, as it were, of sisterly regret just the reverse of the organized fraternal rancor to be found in the two other plays.[7]

In all three of these plays, *As You Like It, Hamlet,* and *Twelfth Night,* such structural reciprocities appear on vertical as well as horizontal planes. In *As You Like It*, not only are the brothers paired, and their fiancées too (Celia and Rosalind "being ever from their cradles bred together," I.i.101), but the subplots too—Touchstone's wooing of Audrey, Silvius' of Phebe—constitute ironic comments upon, and form thematically a mirror image of, the more elegant romance of the principals. The only unmatched figure in *As You Like It*'s world of epicyclical dichotomy is Jaques, cut off, appended in his melancholy. And Jaques, while he may be meant to function in the first part of the satire as a counterpoise to Touchstone, is nonetheless sent off at the end to join Duke Frederick in the hermitage, dispatched to where his cynicism, like the Duke's capacity for violence, can no longer intrude upon the world of pastoral romance. Like Malvolio in *Twelfth Night*, Jaques plays the role of the outsider whose unhappiness is the measure of comic spirit, the alternative to comedy who makes us value the comic all the more. As such, his structural aloofness, his very loneliness, affirms in a formal way the integrity of comic symmetry.

In *Hamlet*, where we have much the same, this merry, comedic symmetry is turned inside out. Here too the subplots mirror the main action. Laertes, Fortinbras, even Ophelia—even, for that matter, Polonius —all act out destinies in reference to which Hamlet can say: "By the image of my cause I see / The portraiture of his" (V.ii.78–79). But in *Hamlet*, in contrast to the affirmative recursiveness of *As You Like It* and the other comedies, the plot parallels bespeak a malignancy in which all the principals share. *Hamlet's* subplots are more carefully, more linearly, integrated into the main action than are those of *As You Like It*. Perhaps because in this respect Hamlet is his own Jaques, just as he is his own Orlando, it therefore makes more sense that the heartsick, melancholy skepticism of the hero is built not only into his own end but into the end of his world. But so too, at the end, Hamlet, like Jaques, is sent to a sacred resting place where for all his heroism he can do no further harm. In the course of his play Hamlet thus *becomes an outsider*, an exile whose singularity is the measure of his own world's frustrations. With such "greatness thrust upon him," Hamlet completes as tragic scapegoat a movement that begins (or ends, for we cannot decide which) with Malvolio as comic butt.[8] In structural terms, then, *Hamlet*, true to its images of centripetal claustrophilia, sacrifices the focus of its symmetries, its hero, in order to resolve the tensions symmetry has bred. But the result, even with a negative sign placed before it, is nonetheless even homeostatic.

Looking at these three plays together, we have a sense of the parameters of Shakespearean fraternity, at least as the theme presented itself to Shakespeare around the turn of the century. *As You Like It* is comic by virtue of its refusal to investigate the source of fraternal enmity. Oliver in private address to the audience explains that he *cannot* explain why he hates his brother so: "For my soul, yet I know not why, hates nothing more than he" (I.i.151–53). Here fratricidal animosity is a dramatic given and because what is given can easily be taken away by fortuitous dramatic accident—a chance encounter with a lion or a hermit—it is something the author can wish, we might almost say hallucinate, away. By tragic contrast, *Hamlet* insists upon the origin, the originality, of fraternal opposition, displaying it as a violence in which motives, though they are repressed, immediately reappear in other, ostentatiously equivalent, forms. As a result, *bruder-mord* is much more central to, inherent in, the rottenness of Denmark than it is to or in the pastoral woods of Arden. In *Hamlet* fratricide is not merely a cause but is elevated into a fundamental paradigm of all the ensuing dramatic action, functioning as the play's myth, the simple story by reference to which the larger story is organized. The gap between these two narrative levels is important, for Shakespeare exploits to theatrical purpose the difference between *Hamlet* and its myth.

Let us consider the fraternity of *Hamlet* in more detail. Claudius is another Cain, just such a lecherous twin as the apocryphal elaborations of the Bible story describe. He kills his brother in order to gain his brother's kingdom and woman, just as (and Shakespeare stresses the importance of this first battle, in the first scene of the first act, when Horatio points to this as the cause and "the chief head/Of this post-haste and romage in the land," I.i.81–107) in the original Amleth myth the prototype of the elder Hamlet kills the prototype of the elder Fortinbras for a piece of his kingdom and the victory prize of a wife. From this repetition, a kind of cybernetic redundancy, comes the quality of reenactment in Claudius' crime, our sense that whatever it is *Hamlet* is showing us it is something perpetual. Claudius simply does again in domestic terms what his brother had before accomplished in epic terms of tournament violence; it is a violence that in the cycles of revenge-myth necessarily precedes any particular narrative beginning. Claudius' "primal curse" is thus presented and dramatically received as the declension of a violence larger than its own, as the familial version of heroic contest. Yet the consequence of the homology, the similarity between regal heroism and domestic villainy, is that fratricide —at least as theatrically realized by Shakespeare in *Hamlet*, precisely because it locates an origin—can be no more original than its revenge; it is "primal" because it is "common," the perversion of a norm rather than the inflorescence of an eccentricity.

It was to this universal, normative dimension that Freud and Jones responded with their "psychological" reading: Claudius with his villainy acts out Hamlet's oedipal desire and in doing so both stimulates and frustrates Hamlet's oedipal will. What was intended as specific character analysis carried with it a structural insight that neither Freud nor Jones made much of but that can help us relate *Hamlet* to the plays that surround it in the canon. For when we extend the logic of transpositional identification upon which the oedipal reading depends, a logic that unarguably coordinates the psychodynamics of the play, we see that by raising himself to the place of Hamlet's father, Claudius at the same time raises Hamlet to what formerly was Claudius' own place. In other words, for the characters in the play, as for the audience that perceives them, Hamlet becomes Claudius' brother when Claudius becomes Hamlet's father, which is what makes them, as Hamlet defines their relation in his first words, "A little more than kin, and less than kind!" (I.ii.65), and which explains the inverted self-regard with which uncle and nephew measure each other by reference to the ambiguity of "our sometime sister, now our queen" (I.ii.8).[9]

This link between father and brother, the projection of duality onto oedipal triangularity (a conflating equation that we can follow out at many levels) is the gloss Shakespeare gives to "the primal eldest curse"; it is his explanation of the symmetrical violence of fratricide. Moreover, this familial "explanation" of fratricidal violence, which for all its incisiveness we might more accurately categorize as an obfuscation, a defense, reconstitutes whatever remained of the mythic quality of the tale after Saxo and Belleforest were finished rationalizing the legend they received. For it is the Shakespearean theory of fratricide, if such we may call Shakespeare's organization and manipulation of the theme—his effort, only partially successful, to comprehend fratricide as a matter of mediated jealousy and related psychological affect—that defines the cosmogonic intention of the tragedy. To Shakespeare, fratricide is always linked to envy and revenge, and these emotions in turn are images for him—metatheatrical and cannibalistic images, we might point out— of social and cosmic chaos. Northumberland's vow in *Henry IV, Part II* is a pertinent example:

> Let order die!
> And let this world no longer be a stage
> To feed contention in a lingering act.
> But let one spirit of the first-born Cain
> Reign in all bosoms, that each heart being set
> On bloody courses, the rude scene may end,
> And darkness be the burier of the dead!

(I.i.154–60)

This is the way a Shakespearean father regrets the death of a son slain by that son's equivalent rival. This is patriarchy lamenting fraternity. Reverse it and you have both Hamlet's burden as "minister and scourge" and also his accompanying stagey unhappiness. Further, I think Northumberland's vow shows us how Shakespeare's personal fantasies served his theatrical sensibility. As a motif, fratricide on the Elizabethan stage was as old as Cambises' murder of Smirdis, or older if we recall the mysteries' representations of the Cain story. But the authors of those earlier pageants could rely, as Shakespeare could not (or could not so comfortably), upon a mythic superstructure whose imperatives immediately informed fratricide with supernatural significance, with inevitably fatal consequence. As a result, there was no need for the villains of these earlier melodramas to signify more than the crimes they committed; as the plays describe them, their dramatic density is composed of spectacular gesture only.

By Shakespeare's time, the stage had grown too sophisticated for such didactically cosmological figures, the *Ur-Hamlet* and *The Spanish Tragedy* having already appropriated the immediate responses of common sense. Shakespeare, then, was obliged to realize his drama so as to outpace the tired or, rather, the conventional expectations of an audience already accustomed to the determinants of a genre. The dramatic revival of the topos required that fratricide be supplied with a new meaning equivalent to the old, one which reversed the explanatory direction of myth. Where the myth instanced universal chaos, political disorder, themes of metaphysical eschatology, with particular fratricides, Shakespeare instead defined the domestic catastrophe in cosmological terms—hence the hyperbolic scope of his rhetoric. Between the myth and Shakespeare's play, the same correlations are maintained, but Shakespeare inverts the affective movements of the myth, beginning with what heretofore the story had concluded. Oedipus finds out what he has done; Hamlet discovers what he must do.

It is a significant reversal, tailored to the requirements of a recognizably modern theater. And to accomplish his rereading, Shakespeare is forced to situate fratricide within a system of familial plausibility wherein its motives can be perceived, if only at an unconscious level, and wherein its familial consequence might revivify, by replacing, the cosmogonic values of the old myths. Otherwise, as Shakespeare intuitively recognized, an equally dramatic development of the tables of revenge could derive only from a denial similar to the model proposed by *As You Like It*. Quite apart from the evolution of the Elizabethan stage, by the time of *Hamlet* such a direct negation, though it may have been desired, was no longer feasible, since pleading ignorance—"For my soul, yet I know not why, hates nothing more than he"—or the sudden removal of enmity—the fortunate hermit—purposefully explains "nothing," and, as we will see, "nothing" is precisely what Shakespeare was now using fratricide to deny.

Thus the equation of father-brother that Claudius announces in his discourse on the death of fathers represents something new in Shakespeare, a stipulatory revision of the dramatic formulas of familial authority. The whole speech is a kind of continuous stumbling of the tongue that reveals Claudius' character. But more than that, it presents a proposition that the play will address itself to verifying:

> Fie, 'tis a fault to heaven,
> A fault against the dead, a fault to nature,
> To reason most absurd, whose common theme
> Is death of fathers, and who still hath cried,
> From the first corse till he that died today,
> 'This must be so.'

(I.ii.101–06)

The first corpse was Abel's, just as the first murderer was Cain. To Shakespeare, at least at this point in his career, parricide gains meaning, and thereby loses its horror, when it is reunderstood as fratricide. Death then becomes something that happens to brothers and the rest, defensively, is a structured silence within which Horatio can report Hamlet's cause aright.

Whatever we may think of Hamlet's thus "authorized" story—and many critics have seen in this a kind of oblique defense of a strangely aesthetic Shakespearean sensibility, whereby the hero is a poet who recites his own aftermath—it is worth noting that *Twelfth Night* gives us just the inverse of this resituated "primal" sin. In *Twelfth Night*, *bruder-mord* is no more than the condition of sorority, Olivia and Viola being sisters not only to their brothers but, by virtue of their mourning, to each other as well. Where *Hamlet* begins with a dead brother whose death must be revenged, the crime being done away with when it is done again, *Twelfth Night* instead begins with a dead brother whose death must be undone by substitution—negated, we might say, by displacement rather than by repetition. Olivia's lost brother is neatly replaced by Sebastian, a found brother, who, having first drowned in a typically tempestuous Shakespearean sea, is then, equally typically, miraculously brought to life. In *Twelfth Night*, then, the paradoxes of fraternal identification explored by *Hamlet* receive a comic resolution, sealed rather than exacerbated by incestuous marriage. As in *As You Like It*, they are transferred elsewhere, away from a battle between equivalent brothers and onto themes of misplaced sexual desire, a desire for an "other" who is simultaneously the "same" and "not-the-same" as one's own self. Hence the immediate appropriateness of Viola's male disguise, the disguise by means of which Viola, like Rosalind, becomes "brother" to herself.

This sister-brother transformation upon which both plays repeatedly comment is the comically erotic formulation of Hamletian confusion. By means of a fusion of familial and sexual distinctions, theatrical transvestitism—even as distanced by comic necessity—reduces to one fragile androgynous image all the polarities inherent in symmetrical equipoise. As the projection of a divided subject, this androgyny is a significant image because its evocative wholeness negates division. But at the same time, this is necessarily a suspect wholeness, only a hypothetical image, its negativity secure only to the extent that it is comic. We will come back to this point later when we have clarified the connection between androgyny and fratricide. But we can say in advance that an apparent paradox conditions Shakespeare's dramatic tone. Somehow explicit androgyny is comic because it is false. By contrast, clearly defined sex roles evoke tragedy because their definitions, being unstable, must be supported by violence.

Man-woman disguise, we must quickly say, is a staple of Elizabethan comedy, and simply to note its presence gives us no particular insight into Shakespeare's dramatic imagination. At the simplest level it is a device that gives mobility to the plot, since it allows the dramatist to have his well-bred women move about by themselves (as the sources indicate, a woman alone was a woman to be raped). As such, it was a piquantly utilitarian complication for a theater in which the female parts were played by boys (though we should be careful not to make too much of this, since the same disguise mechanism frequently appears in contemporary prose romance). For all these reasons, though, Shakespeare had often and confidently relied before on playfully androgynous girl-boy figures: Julia in *The Two Gentlemen of Verona*, Jessica and Portia in *The Merchant of Venice*, Rosalind in *As You Like It*. But in all these previous examples, none of which are purely conventional, disguise was used by Shakespeare as part of the solution to complications engendered otherwise by the plot. In this context, *Twelfth Night* is unusual in that its disguise by itself constitutes the play's problem. And *Hamlet* is thus exceptionally unusual in that in it we see the comic procedures of *Twelfth Night* inverted to tragic purpose.

There is then, if we trace it, and quite apart from traditional stage business, a progressive focalization of the use of girl-as-boy disguise in the three plays we are here considering. In *As You Like It* Rosalind, the girl-as-boy, teaches Orlando, the lover, how to win a girl. She is half a kind of mysterious goddess of the woods who finally gives herself as prize to her most faithful votary, and half an eager young woman, her femininity oozing out of her disguise, who behaves very much as though she believed in the Petrarchan sentiments she mocks. Viola, by contrast, is both teacher and student of love, essentially feminine, but with no mystery beyond her mask. Moreover, unlike vigorous Rosalind, who can rid herself of disguise whenever she so chooses, Viola, as critics have remarked, is fundamentally passive, obliged to trust to time and its great whirligig for the unraveling of the tangles of the plot (II.ii.39–40).

In *Hamlet*, to complete the triad and to follow out the declension of these important Shakespearean themes, both time and disguise grow more macabre and less trustworthy, for there not only "time is out of joint," but the only disguise, if it is such, is Hamlet's "antic disposition," which by the end of the play turns into Hamlet's self-declared madness (V.ii.220–26). The transvestite disguise of the comedies thus becomes something disturbingly more than disguise in *Hamlet*, where the confusion between men and women, allied to Hamlet's trickster role, emerges at the level of imagery as androgynous metamorphosis. When, for example, Polonius says of Hamlet's amorous vows: "They are brokers,/Not of that dye which their investments show,/But mere implorators of unholy suits,/Breathing like sanctified and pious bawds, /The better to beguile" (I.iii.127–31),[10] he merely gives first voice to a systematic reversal of sex roles in the play that is later confirmed by Hamlet himself: "This is most brave,/That I . . . Must like a whore unpack my heart with words/And fall a-cursing like a very drab,/A stallion" (i.e., a male prostitute, II.ii.569–73). By themselves these images simply define Halmet's impotence in much the same way that a captive Hamlet sarcastically calls Claudius his "mother" (IV.iii.48–52). In the play as a whole, though, they establish the limits of Shakespearean sexual identity.

In *Hamlet* all women are prostitutes, and they are Hamlet-like to the extent that all of them are by nature in disguise. Because it is axiomatic that beauty transforms honesty into a bawd (III.i.110–13), it follows as a logical consequence that Hamlet, who is "indifferent honest," goes mad when confronted with the spectacle of dissembling woman: "God hath given you one face, and you make yourselves another . . . it hath made me mad" (III.i.143–46). This connection between alternately shifting sex roles, male and female disguise, madness, and androgyny— a connection that we can see growing ever more ominous in the progression: *As You Like It, Twelfth Night, Hamlet*—seems, then, whatever else it implies, to depend upon a consistent language of misogyny whose grammar inexorably links female unfaithfulness to fratricidal violence. To some extent, such an association is part of the culture (cf. Donne's "The Expostulation," whose theme is that "no woman's true" and which uses Cain as the representative for the cuckolding rival). But Shakespeare, I think, in both the comedies and the tragedies, separates and combines these codes of reviling regret in a uniquely theatrical fashion.

The constant joke of the comedies is cuckoldry, the wit of which is inspired by disguise. When Viola receives Olivia's ring, proof that the virginal gentlelady is in love with her suitor's page, Viola says of this infatuation:

> Poor lady, she were better love a dream.
> Disguise, I see thou art a wickedness
> Wherein the pregnant enemy does much.
> How easy it is for the proper false
> In women's waxen hearts to set their forms!
> Alas, our frailty is the cause, not we,
> For such as we are made of, such we be.

(II.ii.25–31)

In the comedies women's "frailty" breeds both wit and the answer to the thrust of wit. Female unfaithfulness suggests a complication that comic transvestitism turns into a joke.[11] Viola's soliloquy, depending as it does upon a long tradition that flytes women as incorrigible Cressidas, is sententious, purposefully so. But because the boys, some of them, are girls, this expresses a proverbial wisdom that is no longer grounded in common sense and, therefore, no longer threatening. After all, if Viola were in fact a boy, it would not take much to turn Orsino into Othello. By the same token, if Rosalind had no "sister," Oliver and Orlando would soon enough be rivals in love. Such symmetrical desire, a structure of homosexual jealousy that is resolved in the comedies by apportioning out to each pair of rivals a matching pair of beloveds, is precisely what we have unresolved in *Hamlet* where, correspondingly, disguise is the imaginary aspect of female unfaithfulness and where, we might say, woman herself, as woman, because her name is "frailty"—is the image of androgyny. In the comedies, jealousy is suggested but then immediately forestalled by a punned sexuality. In *Hamlet* the ambiguity of woman has only one, and a disgusting, significance. As a result, in *Hamlet* fratricide and frailty present themselves as complements, not alternatives, each evoking a fractured duality that can only be joined by violence. The "union" that was temporary in the comedies, and therefore fortunate, is permanent in the tragedy, a fixed poison, and therefore inescapable.

In his excellent essay on *Twelfth Night*, C. L. Barber speaks to just this aspect of Shakespeare's comic imagination, Shakespeare's use of exaggerated duplicity as a defense against unsettling ambiguities.[12] The fun of *Twelfth Night*, says Barber, comes from the way the play plays with the distinction between what is mad and what is not, while at the same time reassuring us that the difference between the two is ultimately secure. The contrast here, of course, is *Hamlet*, where, because nothing is as it seems, all distinctions have broken down absolutely: the funeral baked meats having coldly furnished the marriage tables with the same impious indifference to the natural categories of difference that has made "the night joint-laborer with the day." Barber is right to see *Twelfth Night* as a play about difference, and he is even more incisive when he notes that its particular theme, the issue from which the play with madness derives, is the pleasure that comes from confirming, despite the premise of temporary confusion, the reality of sexual difference. It is not that the difference between men and women is ever fundamentally lost in the comedy, but rather that by forcing the protagonists to win through to its realization, their and their audience's appreciation of the difference is refreshed. Barber's point is that Shakespearean difference is valued only in the imagination of its loss. As with madness, though, such playfully designed chaos is only possible because the sex difference, the "little thing" Viola lacks (III.iv.282–83), is secure, acknowledged, presumed—something that is by no means the case in *Hamlet*, where it is an insult, not a sacrament, that "man and wife is one flesh" (IV.iii.51).

Barber's comments on *Twelfth Night* apply with equal force to *As You Like It*, another play that develops a dialectic of differences rooted in the temporary dissolution of sex difference. In *As You Like It*, the main theme is not the distinction between madness and sanity but rather that between realistic and idealized love. Rosalind's sex disguise is central to this in that it provides the merry matter for the debate between pastoral and antipastoral sentiment that the play argues out for the most part with metaphoric instances of fidelity and fidelity's opposite, cuckoldry. Thus *As You Like It* is semantically as well as structurally related to *Twelfth Night*. Both plays draw out the relationship between the sexes by comparing the relative infidelities of men and women (cf. Orsino's and Viola's counterclaims for their own sex's "giddiness" in love, II.iv.14-40). The psychological constant, then, the axis upon which both comedies turn, is neither a theme nor a structure but a relationship between theme and structure—namely, that the idea of androgyny goes with the idea of cuckoldry in the same strange, complex ratio that says we are, comically, what we are by virtue of reciprocal betrayal ("As horns are odious, they are necessary," *AYL*, III.iii.51-52 —again, a perception whose permutations are worked out in the sonnets) and, tragically, like Hamlet, that we are undone by sexual duplicity. The possibilities for paradox here are obviously enormous. To be cuckolded is to be castrated by the whoring phallic mother, with the result that men are effeminized by what, from their male point of view, is an exquisitely female lust for maleness. That this is a threatening world of endless and ironic mirror reflections should be clear. Yet, however dizzying the infinite regress, all these confusions bred by inverted similitude point to but one single phallocentric determination, since this is a scheme, like Freud's, in which for male and female alike there is only one libido (a male one) and only one sexual organ (the phallus) that always emerges in the register of loss. The genre difference between comedy and tragedy derives from the way that loss is recorded: in *Hamlet* cuckoldry is not a joke, just as its androgyny is not a disguise.

All this cuckoldry and infidelity humor that we find in *Twelfth Night* and *As You Like It* (as also the play with gender) appears so frequently on the Elizabethan stage as to define a comic convention. The wit, we need hardly say, is primarily developed from a masculine point of view—there being no such thing, at least no *fun* in such a thing, as a "horned" woman. Yet even in their use of the convention, both *Twelfth Night* and *As You Like It* represent the elaboration of a characteristically Shakespearean principle of plot construction, one with which Shakespeare organized his comedies from the very beginning.

In *The Comedy of Errors*, an appeal to a kind of Pauline subjugation of women was the reconciliatory condition that linked Shakespeare's first pairs of male twins within an inclusive pact of social brotherhood. So too, in *The Comedy of Errors* we have the same world of happenstance, madness, infidelity, prostitutes, and doubled confusion that reappears less grossly and with more sophistication in the imagery of both *Twelfth Night* and *As You Like It*.

In *The Taming of the Shrew*, another relatively early double play, we have Shakespeare's most vividly imagined instance of dominant, though worried, masculinity. But even there, we must remember, Shakespeare tames the taming by making us see it through the drunken, cozened eyes of a Christopher Sly, upon whom the joke is not only that he is not a lord, but also that his supposed wife is a page boy in drag disguise. The fantasy of powerful men manipulating even more powerful women is thus attenuated in *The Taming of the Shrew* by being placed within a deflationary metatheatrical perspective that values Kate not only as Sly's entertainment but as part of his lunacy, too. This suggests that Shakespeare's essentially conventional expression of male dominance, something which he seems able to imagine only within an atmosphere compact of lunacy and transvestite disguise, is the other side of a more defensive and threatened masculinity. And indeed, in his less guarded comedies, such as *The Merchant of Venice* or *Much Ado about Nothing*, Shakespeare typically shows us masculine women whose virtue it is to manage—we might better say, mother—their somewhat childish men. Many psychoanalytic critics have pointed to this aspect of Shakespeare's attitude toward his female characters; i.e., that Shakespeare frequently exhibits a not uncommon defensive gynophobia. I will argue later that in fact Shakespeare achieves his masculinity, secures it, by reconciling himself to what he perceives to be its feminine weakness: Shakespearean man becomes such by comparing himself to Shakespearean woman and then finding himself wanting. In Lacanian terms, man's desire is always a desire of the "other" which is always the desire of the mother for the phallus that is not there. But the critical point for now is not that Shakespeare perceived his masculinity as fragile, but rather that he associates that fragility with the particular dialectical clusters of *Hamlet, Twelfth Night,* and *As You Like It*.

I am here trying, though no doubt in too summary a fashion, to evoke in a few words the ensemble of Shakespearean themes that later develop into the ambiguously misogynist jealousy of such plays as *Othello, Cymbeline,* and *The Winter's Tale*. In *As You Like It* we have, I think, a play where those themes are employed only to the extent that their resonating ambiguities can be stabilized by comic dissociation: *As You Like It* is comedy that contains its divisive jests (hence the distancing balance of its resolution). So too does *Twelfth Night*, but there we have the first hint that those themes possessed for Shakespeare, and in a way that was suddenly controlling, a more vicious and dangerous aspect. To be sure, in *Twelfth Night* the difference between men and women still survives, reassuring us at the same time of the difference between brother and sister. So too, *Twelfth Night's* women are lovely (though perhaps only because they are girlish) and its conclusion celebratory (though perhaps only because the play is relieved to have so tidily concluded its confusions). Yet in *Twelfth Night*, as critics have remarked, the tone begins to darken. This is comedy, but comedy that knows worse than itself, since no manner of undisguised disguises will revive the dead brother with whom the play begins. In *As You Like It*, when Jaques left the stage, his exit was the last we could expect to see or hear of him. When the same thing happens in *Twelfth Night*, when Malvolio goes off swearing his revenge, we suddenly discover that the good captain who preserved Viola's life is in prison at Malvolio's suit (V.i.266–69). In the unfolding of the play, this is absolutely gratuitous but for that very reason disturbing. Why must the celebrants "entreat" the killjoy "to a peace" (V.i.368) before they can conclude their celebration? Though we can no doubt propose some pious formula of Christian humanism to explain why they ought, the play remains in form an anomalous Shakespearean comedy. So, too, Feste's final song is gay and lyrical, but its rehearsal of the move from silly youth to drunken senility is not, after all, so very different from Jaques' deflationary account of the ages of man. There is, then, much wit and a fully established comic form in *Twelfth Night*, but it is hard and knowing wit, more charged than the settled lyricism of *As You Like It*, and while the play is by no means a "problem play," still it does not quite resolve all the issues it so delicately raises.

If we locate the roots of *Twelfth Night's* vaguely inappropriate melancholy in a persuasively more obsessive elaboration of a felt and represented connection between androgyny and female unfaithfulness, we can then readily relate the play to the contaminated world of *Hamlet* and then to the lusting, syphilitic, leprous world of *Troilus and Cressida*. Further, we can continue through the canon, through the "unsexing" plots of the tragedies—*Macbeth, Coriolanus, King Lear*—so as finally to draw a straight line to the painfully reconciliatory world of the late jealousy plays. But the question still remains, if *As You Like It* and *Twelfth Night* together with *Hamlet* define a turning point in the canon, as to why brothers, fratricidally opposed, play so crucial a role in the transition from comic to tragic Shakespearean sensibility. This is an important canonical question, for the same brothers, or at least their reciprocal violences, survive into the late plays.

In our effort to answer this question, I take a clue from the world of myths, the same sort of myths out of which many of these plays develop. René Girard has recently argued that at bottom all myths are fratricide myths, for they all address themselves to a fundamental need to distinguish hero from villain, good from bad, in such a way that social value is itself corroborated.[13] To Girard, the perennial myth motif of the enemy twins supplies a family name for the different kinds of binary analysis employed by sociologists and anthropologists such as Durkheim, Lévi-Strauss, Radcliffe-Brown, Mary Douglas, and Edmund Leach, each of whom derives generic classification systems from a somehow extraordinary reconciliation of original dualities. The rival brothers, says Girard, echoing Barber's less phenomenological comments on *Twelfth Night*'s androgyny, act out the myth of Difference, a story—always a story—by means of which societies resolve and ward off a catastrophe of order that Girard labels the crisis of "No Difference" and defines as a loss of cultural distinctions so profound as to spell cultural suicide. The storied twins thus fight not so much to settle the differences between them (which, of course, can only barely exist, since equivalent brothers fight because they are the "same"), but instead to establish through violence a definitive difference—victor-vanquished—by means of which they can be distinguished each from each.

The decisions wrought by mythic violence are arbitrary, necessarily so, but once sealed by blood they are themselves the sign of their own differentiating validity. The king wins the battle and his kingdom by ordained faith, by God's grace, and by virtue of other such transcendental confirmations. The villain receives a punishment *equal* to the hero's reward. Fratricide, then, as a social fact—and it is only as a social artifact that it can be a myth—is necessarily a story once removed from reality, for only a narrative with poles polarized by scheme can formalize violence within a moral order. Or, to say the same thing from the point of view of one of the twins, only such a narrative can moralize violence by referring it to a cultural order. The point is not that this is the inevitable history of any society, but rather that this is the way each society must necessarily reimagine its history. So "Difference," too, is itself always a myth, the end of an imaginary story, just as fraternity is always an exaggeration, the grounds for a groundless quarrel.

Girard points out that society can tell itself this same story in different ways, as law, as ritual, as taboo, or as novel transformations of the original myth. In a communal extrapolation of the fratricide scheme, for example, we watch society expel a differentiated scapegoat, a violently designated "other," denying thereby the "sameness," a kind of repulsive cultural equality, that his presence within society reveals. This is a familiar, almost sentimental, literary theory of tragedy, but the proclaimed particularity of the "unique" scapegoat merely disguises the fact that anybody can play his role. Substitution is the economy of both fratricide and sacrifice. Oedipus is cast out of Thebes; later, repeating the basis of the theme, Etiocles and Polynices, Oedipus' sons, fight for the right to do unto each other what Thebes has already done to Oedipus. With the decisiveness of fatal necessity, a unilateral act of violence thus appropriates to itself the authority with which to conclude the chain of reciprocal, equipoised violation, at least so the retrospective story goes. Finally, by pointing to its discriminating results, violence shadows its nondiscriminatory motives. In the darkness created by myth, the sacred then withdraws from a now sacramentally structured world in which Oedipus rises from Colonus as much a god as he is a sacrifice.

Difference depends upon the sacred.[14] So too do the myths of difference that exist as machines from whose recesses—as in classic drama, where the process is more concretely enacted—the sacred issues forth into society. The sphinx-like, monstrous combination of differences by which in myth the sacred manifests itself corroborates, with the unspeakable horror of its occasional presence, both the social validity of social differentiation and the personal validity of individual, individuated identity. More precisely, in its immanence the sacred violently precipitates itself as the structure of reality. If chaos is the opposite of the cultural order, so too is it the opposite of the sacred, a series of oppositions from which logicians in a polarized world can conclude that the sacred and the cultural order are themselves the same, the latter a diffusive, analytic discrimination of the synthetic holiness of the former. It is this dynamic reciprocity, a mutually reverent loathing, linking the categories of the cultural order to those of the sacred mixture (a linking further shadowed by the negatively reciprocal engagement of each to the chaotic) that determines the procedure by which myths and the rituals attached to them solve by obfuscation the crisis of No Difference that calls them up. The "miracle" consists of a sacrificial epiphany whose polarizing violence makes *all* the difference. This is the "secret" of the sacred just as it is the "secret" of fratricide, a categorical secret, a scandal of "names."[15]

This is complicated and involves more, much more, than we can here discuss. But we can see that Girard's theory of myth as the solution to cultural synonymity certainly applies to *Hamlet*, which begins, as we have said, with a paradigmatic violence between equals, the elder Hamlet and the elder Fortinbras, a violence that is then both emulated and perverted by Claudius' fratricide. Horatio's description of this original violence stresses the legalistic, ceremonial, tournament-like atmosphere of this first royal battle. So too, Horatio emphasizes the balance, the equi-valence of the issues at stake: the defeated king

> Did forfeit, with his life, all those his lands
> Which he stood seized of to the conqueror;
> Against the which a moiety competent
> Was gaged by our king, which had returned
> To the inheritance of Fortinbras
> Had he been vanquisher, as by the same comart
> And carriage of the article designed,
> His fell to Hamlet.
>
> (I.i.88-95)

Claudius, though he imitates this first, legitimizing violence, frustrates its differentiating intention when he murders an equal who lives within his own realm. Where the elder Hamlet killed a brother outside his kingdom, an outsider, Claudius instead kills a brother within, with the result that his violence necessarily rebounds back upon his own head—"so that my arrows . . ./Would have reverted to my bow again,/ And not where I had aimed them" (IV.vii.22-25). This geometry of violence, a system whose laws Shakespeare always obeys, explains why border imagery and the establishment of boundaries is so important in *Hamlet*. To kill a brother who is unalterably the same, one who resides within the same moral universe, undercuts both the phenomenological and the psychological rationale of the murdering brother's own life, just as at the social level it negates the differences of cultural distinction. Fratricide, thus constrained, thus organized and socialized, necessarily translates itself into suicide, an equation that is as decisive for Hamlet as it is for Claudius, since Hamlet, brother to the perverted brother, can with his revenge merely repeat the equivalent of his brother's crime— "That I have shot my arrow o'er the house/And hurt my brother" (V. ii.231-32).

Hamlet's performance, then, of what constitutes a second internal fratricide, his burden as Denmark's "scourge and minister," gives society what it needs, a new villain and a new hero, the old difference newly re-established by symmetrical violence. So too, it negates the disorder generated by Claudius' disruption of the scheme—the sickness imagery in the play, its atmosphere of sullied rottenness, corresponds to *Oedipus'* plague. But at the same time, the structure of doubles, the inexorable imperatives of fratricidal myth, render even the unilateral violence of the hero reflexive and reciprocal. Hence Hamlet's suicidal meditations and his eventual death (at the hands of his most immediate opposite, in a duel made equal "at the odds"). But hence, too, in deference to the cultural function he has performed (and lest the arbitrary value of that function be perceived), the sacralized nature of Hamlet's death: the flight of angels singing him to his half Catholic, half Protestant "rest." When the play is over, what remains is Hamlet's "story," another myth that, like the battle between the elder Hamlet and the elder Fortinbras, orator-Horatio can (as Hamlet with his last words directs him to) tell the world.

Yet *Hamlet*, if only because Shakespeare's hero sees through the myth his tragedy exposes, is more complicated than this mythic formula, were we to apply it, implies. Hamlet's soliloquies reflect a consciousness (or an unconsciousness) aware of the motives of its rivalry. They define a hero, then, who struggles against, regrets, the myth he is forced to enact. It was with this dissatisfaction, the essence of Hamlet's famous skepticism, that Shakespeare found a way to reachieve the purposes of the myth. For just as the allegorized, generic vice figure turned into a secular, realistic villain when he no longer functioned as tempter in a moral psychomachia, so Shakespeare, in order to dramatize his hero—in order, that is, to motivate his action—was obliged to articulate the polarities at stake in the tragedy once its mythic form was revealed. Having personalized his hero, Shakespeare had to personalize his hero's motives so as to render the mythic material of the legend accessible to the postmythic world of the Renaissance theater. A drama of psychological individuation thus replaces a myth of generative community. The mythic alternatives are phrased in terms of psychologically plausible desires. The dialectic of Difference and No Difference contained by the original fratricide structure is transferred by Shakespeare to another formula of mirroring reciprocity, to themes of women and their "frailty," to a kind of masculine misogyny that finds in the ambiguity of woman its own self-divided self-consciousness, its own vulnerability, its mortality.

In the myth, fraternal violence is built into a world of doubles; the battle between the enemy twins is its own cause and its own explanation. In *Hamlet*, though all violence is doubled, reflexive, fratricidal, Shakespeare immediately reunderstands that violence in terms of, and makes it seem the consequence of, erotic duplicity. This still measures a world of doubles, but now Difference is built into a divided nature, the prey as opposed to the achievement of an "unnatural villain." Parricide is indeed reread as fratricide, but fratricide in turn is reread as incest. Thus Gertrude, the "imperial jointress" on account of whom "the time is out of joint," represents far more than the simple point of difference between the two brothers. For it is her sensuality that has abolished Difference in Denmark. By sleeping first with one brother and then with the second—by sleeping, that is, both with Hamlet's father and with Hamlet's brother—Gertrude makes it finally apparent that there is in Denmark No Difference at all, at least no difference around which a secure, a sacrally corroborated, masculine identity can be organized. Hamlet says as much when he shows his mother the two pictures of the two brothers:

> Look here upon this picture, and on this,
> The counterfeit presentment of two brothers.
> See what a grace was seated on this brow:
> Hyperion's curls, the front of Jove himself,
> An eye like Mars, to threaten and command,
> A station like the herald Mercury
> New lighted on a heaven-kissing hill—
> A combination and a form indeed
> Where every god did seem to set his seal
> To give the world assurance of a man.
> This was your husband. Look you now what follows.
> Here is your husband, like a mildewed ear
> Blasting his wholesome brother. Have you eyes?
> Could you on this fair mountain leave to feed,
> And batten on this moor? Ha! have you eyes?
> You cannot call it love, for at your age
> The heyday in the blood is tame, it's humble,
> And waits upon the judgement, and what judgement
> Would step from this to this? Sense sure you have,
> Else could you not have motion, but sure that sense
> Is apoplexed, for madness would not err,
> Nor sense to ecstasy was ne'er so thralled
> But it reserved some quantity of choice
> To serve in such a difference.

(III.iv.54–77)

Hamlet thus talks sense to his sensuous mother, verbally raping her with all the resonant imagery of the play, in an effort to refashion in her the Difference her discovered sexuality, not Claudius' fratricide, has destroyed.[16] All the rhetoric of hyperbolic distinction in the play—"Hyperion to a satyr", "I to Hercules"—is thus linked to the loss of difference imaged in Gertrude's incest. It is a failure of the sacred as much as it is a catastrophe of the familial order. Hence the debasement of the brothel-nunnery, the ambiguous resting house of both divine and perverted female sexuality.[17]

The ambiguity of woman is the complement of the loss of difference that comes when the enemy twins of the myth no longer constitute a useful "story." At an oral level, the funeral meats become marriage meats, a point that rapidly blends into a language of reciprocating, non-differentiating, anal violence when Hamlet observes that the same fish-mongering Polonius whom we can "nose" in the lobby is no longer an eater but an eaten: "Your fat king and your lean beggar is but variable service—two dishes but to one table. That's the end . . . a man may fish with the worm that hath eat of a king, and eat of the fish that hath fed of that worm . . . a king may go a progress through the guts of a beggar" (IV.iii.23–31). The same holds true, most importantly, at the phallic level upon which final gender identifications depend, but to discuss this fully we would need to consider both *Hamlet*'s castration themes (a trauma that, as Freud pointed out, quite frequently produces doubling defenses and systems of frustrating repetition)[18] and its primal scenes, and for such a discussion we unfortunately have no time here. But at an oedipal level, it is surely apparent that we must read the play fraternally, as the description of a maturational threshold in which one dares to kill the father only when he is recognized as an equal, a rival, a brother. So too, we must relate the preoedipal thematics of the play to the structure of fraternal reciprocity, reading it as an account of two mothers, good and bad, Niobe and her incestuous opposite,[19] who are discovered to be a complete and single object, a divided being whom, after the collapse of original splitting mechanisms, we must take whole. Furthermore, though Shakespeare's dramatic development of these themes proceeds at the level of individual desire, the themes themselves have a social content. This too we cannot discuss here, since we are focusing on psychological, not sociological, values. But because those individual themes are themselves attached to cultural attitudes—relationships between men and women, mother and father, wife and husband, structures of political authority, issues of religious division—the integrative resolution of the play, its psychological coherence, reachieves the generic differentiations of the myth. This social dimension is the nonidiosyncratic "moral" of Hamlet's "story." So too does it constitute the affirmation in the play to which critics like to point.

Again, more should be said about *Hamlet*, but we have said enough to recognize the thematic parallels and structural connections between *Hamlet* and the two comedies that are most closely associated with it chronologically. In a formula, we can say that the symmetrical mechanics of fratricide correspond to the androgynous disguisings of the comedies. But where Shakespeare's tragic form disguises incestuous No Difference with violence, his comedies uncover Difference with incestuous desire.

Both *As You Like It* and *Twelfth Night* are festive comedies in C. L. Barber's sense of the term. Both plays depend upon a kind of holiday misrule in which disorder is allowed, a time of Saturnalian chaos wherein the customary uses of "degree" are momentarily set aside. In *As You Like It*, this mood takes an explicit pastoral form, the "holiday humor" (IV.i.62) to which Rosalind refers being physically translated to a special, quasi-magical world outside the every-day of the court, similar to *A Midsummer-Night's Dream*'s woods or *The Merchant of Venice*'s Belmont. Such a pastoral form is closely allied to holiday extravagance, but, as critics have remarked, *As You Like It* is satiric pastoral, self-conscious pastoral, in a way that separates it from its source and from its genre. It achieves its effect by mocking pastoral ideals, by admitting the cold of the winter weather so as to strike a balance between, on the one hand, the hard, real world where "Men have died from time to time, and worms have eaten them, but not for love" (IV.i.106–08), and, on the other, the antithetical opposite of that world, the world of Petrarchan sentiment and Renaissance idealism that the play continually undercuts: Touchstone's wit, which mocks the "country copulatives"; Phebe's response to Silvius' complaints; Rosalind's cuckolding jokes; even simple Audrey, who does not know what "poetical" is. The play repeatedly makes fun of the exaggerated sentiments of romance, but does so only thereby to reaffirm them.

"If," says the actor playing Rosalind, in an epilogue soliciting applause, "I were a woman, I would kiss as many of you as had beards that pleased me, complexions that liked me, and breaths that I defied not" (V.iv.16–18). This is Touchstone's "if," the "if" that consummates the "degrees" of the lie, and that forestalls fraternal violence:

> I knew when seven justices could not take up a
> quarrel, but when the parties were met themselves,
> one of them thought but of an If: as, 'If you said
> so, then I said so'; and they shook hands and swore
> brothers. Your If is the only peacemaker.
>
> (V.iv.92–97)

When Rosalind takes off her male disguise, she resolves thereby all the cross-sworn vows of the misprisioning lovers in Arden; she manages, as she says, "To make these doubts all even" (V.iv.25). When, therefore, in the epilogue the actor who *plays* Rosalind shows himself a boy, he accomplishes with the nakedness of his masculinity a final unmasking, pointing thereby to the play's last disguise and to the conditional that is the premise of the play itself. By translating fantasy into an ostentatious hypothetical, by candidly admitting to its own unreality, the play transforms, in C. L. Barber's phrase, its own ritual magic into imagination. Doing so, it becomes something the audience can provisionally accept, a fiction as a fiction, a substitute for holiday that points to itself as the justification for the lyric world of controlled release, which it both describes and endeavors to have the audience participate in. The duplicity of irony is thus the last formal "double" of Shakespeare's comedy—the result of a devious procedure of secondary revision by means of which the play makes itself real by mirroring itself with mockery and confessing to its own exaggerations. But, as we have seen, the hinge around which the play manages to accomplish this circular turn upon or into itself is precisely the "unreal" androgyny that counterbalances the play's discovery of the polarity of the sexes.

This, we may say, is the model of the way Shakespeare handled all the dangerous themes that he manipulates in his comic mood. It is because the differences are secure, because the plays know what *is* mad and what *is not*, that Shakespeare can dissolve those differences within the transitional space of the theater. With the boundaries established, he can "play" within them—"play" in Marion Milner's or Winnicott's sense of the term, as the *purposefully* unreal acting out of unconscious fantasy.[20] When Rosalind, for example, dresses as a boy, the phallic imagery of her disguise—"A gallant curtle-axe upon my thigh,/A boar-spear in my hand" (I.iii.113-114)—is an admission of the "little thing" Viola lacks. As a result, the "edge," as Hamlet says, is taken off all the associated themes that go with androgyny. Thus, while *As You Like It* is filled with cuckoldry imagery, with intimations of inevitably coarsened lust, with all the antipastoral sentiments of a "libertine" Jaques, this is all nonetheless undercut and undone by the wit with which confusion is resolved and Jaques rebuffed. In psychoanalytical terms, Shakespeare develops a modality to express and to deny both his desires and his fears; he accomplishes, that is, the communicational economy that Freud identified as the basis of wit.

Twelfth Night is much the same. It too alternates between lyric fantasy and realistic deflation. So too, as its title implies, its tone depends upon the holiday spirit of disorder. But the point is not so much that Sir Toby is a licensed fool, but rather that the confusions of *Twelfth Night* are appropriate to a holiday mood wherein differences are safely, though only momentarily, forgotten. Like *As You Like It, Twelfth Night* passes through mix-up to a musical disposition of sets of married pairs. So too, both plays measure their merry world against the jaundiced eyes of melancholy outsiders. But in *Twelfth Night*, as we have said, the wit, like the disguise, is just at the edge, almost as though Shakespeare were now making fun of something about which he cared too much to joke. It is as though the protective, psychological boundaries surrounding his play were beginning to crumble and, as a result, the differences summed up for him both by fratricide and the ensemble of themes attached to androgyny—incest, castration, female unfaithfulness, cuckoldry—began therefore to join, each denying with its own divisions the distinctions predicated by the other. In *Hamlet*, where theater turns definitively into metatheater, where play itself is more than play, Shakespeare no longer faces off fratricide and frailty as comic alternatives; instead he defines each as both an explanation and a version of the other. And so Feste's wit becomes Hamlet's skepticism, Viola's disguise turns into Gertrude's incest, Olivia's mourning for a brother becomes Hamlet's melancholy brooding for a ghostly father-brother, and even the good captain Antonio turns back into a pirate. Taken together, regardless of which is prior, *Hamlet* and *Twelfth Night* show how unstable was the compact of fratricide and frailty that Shakespeare had developed around the turn of the century. The slightest disturbance (the death of his *twin* son Hamnet? the death of his father—we are not really free to speculate) might unsettle the delicate equilibrium upon which the coordination of violence and desire between equals depends.

Admittedly, I am treating all three of these plays very quickly, and we would have to look carefully at each in order to corroborate the progression I am sketching out here. There is no space to do that now, but the castration wit of both *Twelfth Night* and *As You Like It*, the unspeakable *c*'s, *u*'s, *'n*'s, and *t*'s by which Malvolio salaciously identifies the signs of women, the corresponding image clusters surrounding the cuckoldry thematic in all three plays, the reciprocal inflation and debasement of female eroticism, the complicated familial relations of *Hamlet* where Hamlet alternately identifies with everyone in the play, including (and especially) his mother—all this and more besides will bear out, I think, the lines of argument to which so far I have merely pointed. I can here only suggest that the plays be reread with that argument in mind. For what I want to do now, having adumbrated the main structural themes of the plays that immediately precede it, is suggest that *Troilus and Cressida* shows us the shape that Shakespeare's more mature organization of those themes would later assume. Moreover, *Troilus and Cressida* shows us in retrospect what those earlier plays were daring to accomplish.

For *Troilus and Cressida* presents Denmark as it would be were it unrelieved by revenge. The whole battle, as the debate between the Trojan brothers makes clear (II.ii), is for name and repute, for what Troilus calls "a theme of honor and renown" (II.ii.199), and what Thersites, more faithful to the atmospherics of the play, summarizes as: "All the argument is a whore and a cuckold, a good quarrel to draw emulous factions and bleed to death upon" (II.iii.68-70). "Emulous" is a key word in *Troilus and Cressida*, directly appearing some eight times, but, more important, always appearing as the explanatory center of the play's images of sullied violence. For example, the riot of the Greek camp is the consequence of "an envious fever/Of pale and bloodless emulation" (I.iii.133-34); Hector, in accord with the logic of inviolable familial boundaries, refuses to fight his german-cousin Ajax because: "The obligation of our blood forbids/A gory emulation 'twixt us twain" (IV.v.121-22).

As that paradoxical labor of envy that seeks to find difference in imitation, "emulation" is the emotional modality appropriate to the scheme of differentiating violence between equals that we described before.[21] Thus, in *As You Like It*, Oliver maligns his brother as "an

envious emulator of every man's good parts, a secret and villainous con-
triver against me his natural brother" (I.i.132-34). Similarly, in *Hamlet*
it is young Fortinbras' imitation of his father's "emulate pride" (I.i.83)
that leads him to reenact the myth of oppositional contest first enacted
by his father in the fatal battle with the elder Hamlet. Once this structure is thus clarified, it is dramatically plausible that young Fortinbras
becomes in turn an object of imitation for young Hamlet (IV.iv.32-66),
thereby recreating the play's originally pristine structure of heroic
duality. At the end, with young Fortinbras' triumphant reentry as substitute hero, the myth completes itself by presenting Fortinbras as a
new and appropriately military prince of a revived and reestablished
social order.

In *Troilus and Cressida*, though, we have young Fortinbras' martial
spirit, his violence, without an accompanying heroicizing frame. There
the myth of dual contest, the fratricide structure, is present only so as
to be reduced by Thersitean reduction—e.g., a coward Achilles killing
Hector in a sneak's attack. In *Troilus and Cressida* no violence is heroic
and, therefore, no violence is conclusive. The war continues beyond the
play with Troilus, like a frustrated Malvolio, swearing his revenge and,
unlike the *Iliad*, with no definitive conclusion formally foreseen. Shakespeare's satiric undoing of Homer's mythic universe (of which, of course,
he had no direct literary experience) thus displays one limited version
of a society wherein "emulation" is the order of things, a world, then,
which is an almost too perfect instance of Girard's crisis of cultural synonymity—"One touch of nature makes the whole world kin" (III.iii.
174). Thus too, *Troilus and Cressida* repeatedly charts the trajectory of
a differentiating violence that frustrates itself with its own reflexiveness. It is a world where, to take a few examples, "The raven chides
blackness" (II.iii.205); where "He that is proud eats up himself" (II.iii.
150), and, too, "Lechery eats itself" (V.iv.34); where "Pride hath no
other glass/To show itself but pride" (III.iii.47-48); and where man
"Cannot make boast to have that which he hath,/Nor feels not what he
owes but by reflection" (III.iii.98-99)—a world, then, to take a final
example whose metatheatrical resonances suggest what is going on for
the audience in its response to the play as a whole, where "imitation"
is the exercise of a homosexual Patroclus whose "scurril" mockery of
his peers "serves . . . to make paradoxes" (I.iii.184).

This absence of an organizing myth to control violence between
equals accounts for the principle of contagious infection in the play, its
expansion of *Hamlet*'s disease imagery into a pregnant, syphilitic infection. But again, it is important to recognize that Shakespeare roots
these themes in a psychology of desire rather than a phenomenology of
"degree." Shakespeare does not really see through the myth so much as

he discovers what he associates with its structure. Ulysses' famous speech about degree summons up the values of order, discretion, difference that the myth of fratricidal violence is intended to uphold. But note, now it is difference itself rather than femininity that is in disguise:

> Degree being vizarded,
> Th' unworthiest shows as fairly in the mask.

(I.iii.83–84)

When we take degree away, not only does chaos come again, but with it come the plots of Shakespeare's middle and late plays:

> The heavens themselves . . .
> Observe degree, priority, and place . . .
> But when the planets
> In evil mixture to disorder wander,
> What plagues, and what portents, what mutiny,
> What raging of the sea . . .
> Divert and crack, rend and deracinate
> The unity and married calm of states
> . . . How could communities,
> Degrees in schools, and brotherhoods in cities,
> Peaceful commerce from dividable shores,
> The primogenity and due of birth,
> Prerogative of age, crowns, sceptres, laurels,
> But by degree, stand in authentic place?
> Take but degree away, untune that string,
> And hark what discord follows. Each thing meets
> In mere oppugnancy . . .
> . . . the rude son should strike his father dead
> And appetite, an universal wolf, . . .
> Must make perforce an universal prey
> And last eat up himself.

(I.iii.85–124)[22]

Yet the culminating instance of this anthology piece, which by itself is merely a medieval topos—by now only a bourgeois Elizabethan's world picture—comes not in the play's images of debased violence but in a tableau of feminine infidelity. Shakespeare makes the war, the "argument for a whore and a cuckold," into the social correlative, a background context, of Troilus' cuckolding. Ulysses' vision of emulative chaos finds its final expression in Troilus' response to Cressida's wanton sexuality:

> The bonds of heaven are slipped, dissolved, and loosed;
> And with another knot, five-finger tied,
> The fractions of her faith, orts of her love,
> The fragments, scraps, the bits and greasy relics
> Of her o'er-eaten faith, are bound to Diomed.

(V.ii.152–56)

As a result, the play acts out one of those Russellian paradoxes in which a class of classes classifies itself. The only constant is inconstancy. Fate herself becomes the system of Cressida's betrayal of Troilus. Where, in *As You Like It*, Fortune was a good housewife who, despite temporary confusion, ultimately disposed of an ordered, balanced world ("Let us sit and mock the good housewife Fortune from her wheel, that her gifts may henceforth be bestowed equally," I.ii.29–31),[23] where in *Hamlet* Fortune had become a prostitute whose genitality is the sign of asymmetrical fracture (Rosencrantz and Guildenstern, one of *Hamlet*'s many formal pairs, live as the "indifferent children of the earth" in the "secret," "private" parts of a "strumpet Fortune" who gives her favors indiscriminately, II.ii.224–233), in *Troilus and Cressida* it is Difference itself that is subject to Fortune's erotic vagaries, as is brought home in the irony of Agamemnon's

> The fineness of . . . metal is not found
> In Fortune's love; for then the bold and coward,
> The wise and fool, the artist and unread,
> The hard and soft, seem all affined and kin.
> But in the wind and tempest of her frown,
> Distinction, with a broad and powerful fan,
> Puffing at all, winnows the light away.

> (I.iii.22–28)

Correspondingly, complementing the developing transformation of a nurturing mother into a whoring arbitrariness, we find in *Troilus and Cressida* that the "If," the conditional upon which Shakespeare predicates the fantastic status of his comedies, is articulated only as an indictment of its own hypotheticals. In *As You Like It*, the admission of "if" placed mixed differences, male and female, within protected imaginary space. Even in *Hamlet*, where the "if" is itself imaginary, placed within the frame of a play within the play (the player queen's "Each opposite that blanks the face of joy/Meet what I would have well and it destroy,/Both here and hence pursue me lasting strife,/If, once a widow, ever I be wife!" III.ii.212–15), there is still an almost formulaic reserve about the expression of maternal guilt—witness all the nineteenth-century debates about the extent of Gertrude's complicity in Claudius' crime. In *Troilus and Cressida*, though, "if" is used only to point to the inherent frustration of subjunctive desire. Troilus and Cressida both speak part-sung vows, each to be true to the other, concluding with Cressida's rhetorical: "If I be false or swerve a hair from truth . . . Yea let them say, to stick the heart of falsehood,/'As false as Cressid'" (III.ii.176–88). Pandarus immediately repeats the proposition in memorably sententious cadence:

> If ever you be false to one another, since I
> have taken such pains to bring you together, let
> all pitiful goers-between be called to the world's

end after my name; call them all Pandars; let all
constant men be Troiluses, all false women Cressids.

(III.ii.190–95)

In one critical vocabulary, I suppose, this would be called the "tenor" of Fortune's "vehicle," but in psychoanalytical terms what we see here is a defense of the mechanisms of defense. For, since Shakespeare works in a medieval tradition in which Cressida was the proverbial and despicable instance of female inconstancy, since Cressida's faithlessness is already built into language, these speeches are charged even as they are spoken with a sarcasm that goes beyond irony. It is as though *Troilus and Cressida* were designed to show us not only the fact but the determining structure that informs the destructive negations of the player queen's vow: "Each opposite that blanks the face of joy/Meet what I would have well and it destroy." In *Troilus and Cressida* opposites meet with morbid fecundity: "As near as the extremest ends/Of parallels, as like as Vulcan and his wife" (I.iii.167–68). Vulcan and his wife are mentioned here not only to evoke figures of beauty and the beast, but because they are Shakespeare's mythological instance of Olympian cuckoldry (cf. "Vulcan's badge," *Titus Andronicus* II.i.89). Vulcan and his faithless wife define a controlling, cosmological infidelity built into the marriage of Shakespearean opposites: "two distincts, division none." Astrologically, the play takes place under their sign, unfolding along the ecliptic of their paradoxical conjunction.

There is much more that can be said to point up the way in which *Troilus and Cressida*, beginning with an assumption of perverted difference, unravels with its cuckoldry the same structures of determined differences that support the symmetrical organization of both *Hamlet* and the preceding festive comedies. Touchstone becomes Feste, becomes, perhaps, Hamlet or Yorick, but concludes as Thersites who, as a "privileged man" (i.e., a licensed fool), rephrases as scatological invective the same ensemble of themes that the earlier fools had before broached only as outrageous wit. Jaques, the libertine malcontent, becomes Ajax, a jakes, the "monstrous fool," an "ass," an "asinico," whose anal reference balances the poisoned food imagery with which the play abounds. Orsino's oral universe of contentment ("If music be the food of love, play on," I.i.1) turns into Troilus' "appetite," a lust more effete even than Orsino's delicacy, and an "appetite" whose "relish is so sweet" that Troilus fears he will "lose distinction in my joys" (III.ii.25). Even the ceremonial formulas of heroic, oppositional violence are transformed in this reduction of mythic and lyric values into the sleazily legalistic terms of Pandarus' "contract": "In witness whereof the parties interchangeably . . ." (III.ii.54–55).

All this contributes to the bleak and ultimately disquieting tone of the play, to what is usually called its darkness. Betrayed by Difference, having lost "degree," *Troilus and Cressida* substitutes for a belief in order a disgust for chaos, framing its hero in a labyrinth of delusions that present him as an unframed Christopher Sly. Thus Troilus, in an ironic echo of Rosalind's "if" and taking refuge in an omnipotently solipsistic madness wherein both his differences and his beloved still hold true, refuses to believe the "deceptions" of his eyes and ears. Now it is not, as in *Hamlet*, the woman's eye that refuses to see difference (in an almost word-for-word reversal of Hamlet's "Have you eyes" speech to Gertrude, Pandarus displays male sexuality to Cressida at the beginning of the play, I.ii.238-42), but the man himself whose sensuous reason refuses to see "sense." Gertrude destroyed Difference with her incest. Troilus denies No Difference by refusing to recognize Cressida's faithlessness:

> There is a credence in my heart,
> An esperance so obstinately strong,
> That doth invert th' attest of eyes and ears.
>   * * *
> My negation hath no taste of madness.
>   * * *
> Let it not be believed for womanhood!
> Think we had mothers; do not give advantage
> To stubborn critics, apt, without a theme
> For depravation, to square the general sex
> By Cressid's rule . . .
> If beauty have a soul, this is not she;
> If souls guide vows, if vows be sanctimonies,
> If sanctimony be the gods' delight,
> If there be rule in unity itself,
> This was not she. O madness of discourse,
> That cause sets up with and against itself!
> Bi-fold authority, where reason can revolt
> Without perdition, and loss assume all reason
> Without revolt. This is, and is not, Cressid.
> Within my soul there doth conduce a fight
> Of this strange nature that a thing inseparate
> Divides more wider than the sky and earth;
> And yet the spacious breadth of this division
> Admits no orifice for a point as subtle
> As Ariachne's broken woof to enter.

(V.ii.116-48)[24]

We have here come full circle in Shakespeare's meditations on the roots of Difference and No Difference, of the complexities generated by "two distincts, division none." At this point in his career, Shakespeare is seemingly overpowered by the divisive chaos figured in sexual duplicity. The consequent duality seeps through all his images—images of the sacred, of woman, and of the self—as they surrender their integrity to the ambiguity of symmetrical paradox. It is as though in *Twelfth Night* Shakespeare had dramatized the dichotomous erotic possibilities of mediation (Viola as the bifocaled object of two unalterably different desires); as though in *Hamlet* he had in turn dramatized the reflective fusion of those possibilities (Hamlet as a mediator who turns into the ambiguity of his message, his divided revenge being both his suicide and his crime); and, in conclusion, as though in *Troilus and Cressida* Shakespeare had turned against desire itself. Thus *Troilus and Cressida*, the play of violated "degree," is equally the play of perverted mediation (Pandarus) and of definitively untrustworthy woman (Cressida)—and, of course, it is the only Shakespeare play in which, because it is the most vivid narcissistic insult, we have explicit homosexuality presented as the exampling aspect of the theater itself.

Yet Shakespeare is not completely lost in this welter of disgust. If *Troilus and Cressida* is misogynistic, it is so to a creative purpose, one that leads Shakespeare out of the paradoxes of divided identification and toward the imagination of unified masculine desire. In the tragedies that are to follow *Troilus and Cressida*[25] —*King Lear, Macbeth, Coriolanus*—Shakespeare will draw portraits of ever more horrible women, women compared to whom Cressida seems more an unfortunate Ophelia than the world-shattering wanton whom Troilus despises. Lady Macbeth, the insidious maternality of Volumnia, the viperish sexuality of Goneril and Regan—these are a sort of women worthy of Troilus' rhetoric of disgust. Moreover, along with these harridans of the later tragedies, we find in each of these plays male heroes who in the course of the action are correspondingly emasculated, infantilized, almost (and the language of the plays bears this out) feminized by their relationship to the women with whom they are linked. Thus, for example, Lady Macbeth's "unsex me here" is presented as the counterpart both of Macbeth's reluctance to perform the assassination and of his submissiveness to his hectoring wife. This is an inversion of a fixed and dynamic kind, but it is not androgyny, at least not the sort found in the earlier comedies. For the men and women of the tragedies do not exchange roles; they do not become alternatively male and female *manqués*. Rather, the reversal consists of a kind of exaggeration of the qualities Shakespeare associates with mixed gender, so that it is the masculinity of the women that makes them into catastrophic mothers, just as it is the femininity of the men that turns them into terrorized infants.

With this overlay of coupled gender difference, dyadic boundaries become brittle interconnections, tight and fragile—each half linked to the other in the desperation of its desire to be what it is by virtue of what it is to the other. This is a pattern both infantile and adult (or almost adult) at the same time. The plays develop their relationship, reciprocating reference by combining themes of preoedipal dual unit, and of oedipal gender pride into one textured context of desire. This explains why duality and triangularity are for Shakespeare tonic rhythms of each other, so that Lady Macbeth as annihilating Mother—

> I have given suck, and know
> How tender 'tis to love the babe that milks me;
> I would, while it was smiling in my face,
> Have plucked my nipple from his boneless gums,
> And dash'd the brains out—

(I.vii.54–58)

defines for Macbeth the very principle of masculinity:

> Bring forth men-children only!
> For thy undaunted mettle should compose
> Nothing but males.

(I.vii.73–75)

So too in *Coriolanus* it is a continually emphasized dramatic fact that, as Volumnia explains to her son, "Thy valiantness was mine, thou suck'dst it from me." And we have much the same in *King Lear*, when the king, disgusted by his "unnatural hags," prays, "Let not women's weapons, water-drops,/Stain my man's cheeks"; or, the same thing in reverse, when in the pietà scene of IV.vii, a new-born Lear awakens to a nurturing Cordelia and knows himself when he knows her: "For, as I am a man, I think this lady/To be my child Cordelia."

There are, then, two countermovements set up in the tragedies that follow *Troilus and Cressida*. The men are humiliated and undone by women, yet at the same time this is what heroicizes them. Indeed, it is as though the men must discover the justice of their aversion to women in order for their maleness to emerge. Again, this presents a structure of endlessly mirrored opposites; that is, the men become men by being poised against, opposed to, a femininity that is disgusting because it so grotesquely partakes of its opposite. Yet the end result at last breaks the chain of reciprocity, for the men are shown to mature, to throw off their infancy, by the violence of their misogyny. Thus does Shakespeare affirm sex difference with an indictment of female viciousness: the perfidy of women is the condition of male exaltation; Shakespearean men are special because whatever they are, they are not Shakespearean women. In the comedies this was merely a joke, e.g., Touchstone's demonstration that a husband's honor is confirmed by his being cuckolded:

> Horns . . . the noblest deer hath them as huge as
> the rascal. Is the single man therefore blessed?
> No; as a walled town is more worthier than a village,

so is the forehead of a married man more honorable
than the bare brow of a bachelor.

(III.iii.49–54)

Moreover, in the comedies this was a joke that denied itself with its humor, just as comic androgyny disguised itself in the figure of a boy as a woman as a boy. In the tragedies, though, Shakespeare takes the themes of the comedies too seriously to fend them off with humorous negations, and so the joke is transformed into a liberating, if fatal, principle of male maturation. Thus, when Lady Macbeth goes mad, Macbeth is then free to "do all that may become a man," eventually to die at the hands of one "not born of woman." So too, Coriolanus marches on Mother Rome, resolved to act "as if a man were author of himself and knew no other kin," and is promptly doomed when—despite that resolve—he accedes to his mother's entreaties. Yet Coriolanus' concession to his mother is also his farewell to her and the basis of his final boast: "Alone I did it." So too with Lear, who suffers and is ennobled by the vileness of his daughters. In all three plays the heroes experience and then pass beyond female perfidy.

It is no accident, then, that in the tragedies dramatic conflict occurs along an axis of male sexual differentiation developed out of a contempt for maternal femininity. But this, I would like to argue, is not simply an expression of neurotic misogyny (something we can find in abundance in other Elizabethan and Jacobean dramatists), but instead a recapitulation in dramatic terms of the psychological transformations from which masculine gender derives. Indeed, we can explain a good part of the phenomenal success of Shakespeare's plays, especially the tragedies, by pointing to the fidelity with which they reenact common male experience. Here we must remember that Freud picks up his general account of sexual identification at a relatively late stage of psychosexual development. According to Freud, mature sexual identity comes with the resolution of the oedipal dilemma, for which reason gender must be understood as a clarifying vector of triangular conflict. Thus, the boy becomes a man when he resolves his oedipal situation by identifying himself as a desiring subject with his father and, as a result, locates his mother as an object of that directed, subjective desire. Thereafter, of course, different categorically appropriate substitutions can occur. For Freud, then, the consummation of desire constitutes the fulfillment of subjectivity, at least of male subjectivity. On the other hand, by this Freudian reading, girls have a more difficult, complex identification to achieve and therefore a much more problematic—and in this sense more refined—gender subjectivity to accomplish. Freudian girls, in order to become women, must at the oedipal stage first disabuse themselves of their father identification and then reidentify with their mother if they are to coordinate the ι angular system of their discovered desire.

This Freudian theory of sexual development is, of course, highly controversial, primarily because its genetic account of gender begins so late, long after the infantile stages of emerging consciousness otherwise so central to psychoanalytic theory have passed into personal history. Kleinian and more orthodox theoreticians of preoedipal experience have established a greal deal of clinical evidence regarding the infant's first tentative sense of self and its slowly differentiated perception of a maternal environment: long before the infant, boy or girl, is aware of such oedipal categories as mother or father, or of such post-castration-complex distinctions as male and female, the infant has already developed a highly dialectical sense of polarized, categorical experience. At first, the infant is its *umwelt*, but soon enough the infant must negotiate the duality inherent in that unity. Thus, long before there is such a thing as an ego solid enough to accomplish a defense as sophisticated as identification, the infant has already recognized and then reacted against an initial sense of mergedness with female sensibility. Human self-consciousness is therefore predicated upon a proposition that sounds very Shakespearean: the infant must first be and then not be the mother in order to discover its own individuation.

In a way, this obliges us to reverse the poles of Freud's triangulating theory of gender generation.[26] For if the male's first sense of self is implicated in femininity, his masculinity is then conditional upon establishing a self distanced from its first sense of self. Women, on the other hand, because their gender is founded on a bedrock identification with maternality, have a kind of immediate gender reference to which they can refer their sense of self. In contrast to Freud, then, alienation from the object of desire is the preliminary condition both for male self-consciousness and for masculine desire. Perhaps women have an even more complicated sexual identity to discover. But for the male, at least—and this is the problem that Shakespeare repeatedly represents in his plays—there is a psychological need to build a distance between himself and his desire, lest he lapse into the psychotic discovery of No Difference between self and object, between his self-regard and his imagination of his mother, between his identity and the context of his identity.

Here is where the fratricide dialectic of Difference and No Difference becomes more than a taxonomy of social and mythic categories. Shakespeare's horrible, catastrophic women are such because their very negativity generates the distance across which male desire can imagine its satisfaction. His plays create, endeavor to realize in descriptive representation, the distance between men and their mothers, the gap between the masculine ego and its female objects, an opening "for a point as subtle / As Ariachne's broken woof to enter." Men must not become what they fear they are. But the negativity of Shakespeare's feminine characterizations allows them to desire what they would not be.[27] Lady Macbeth is awful so that Macbeth can command her to bear male children. Or, alternatively, Shakespearean man can have a "good" mother like Lady Macduff providing he, or Macbeth as his surrogate, kills her children.

Here too we locate the genetic or topographical function that fratricidal violence plays in Shakespeare's imagination. The structure of doubles is what remains of the original relationship of duality upon whose resolution later oedipal triangularity depends. This is why violence in Shakespeare precedes or conditions sexuality. In *Macbeth*, the conflict between Macbeth and Lady Macbeth is settled on transposed male terms in the battle between the rivals Macbeth and Macduff. In *Coriolanus*, the hero's suicidal concession to maternality becomes self-confirming, maturational, in Coriolanus' final battle with Aufidius. In *King Lear*, the oedipal conflict is resolved by pure fraternal violence, Edgar and Edmund's tournament.

In his early plays, Shakespeare's women are brotherly sisters to his boyish men. In the middle plays, the women are disgusting mothers or faithless whores, or both. In the late plays, the women have turned into incestuously desirable daughters (something that starts to happen in *King Lear*, where daughters are imagined as mothers).[28] The only constant from the twins of *The Comedy of Errors* to Leontes and Polixenes, from *The Two Gentlemen of Verona* to Prospero and Antonio, is the violent relationship of male equals, the enmity of enemy twins.[29] The duality of brothers that generates singularity, along with the mirroring complexities of dual reflexiveness and defused images of the discrete self, is the masculine rephrasing of the original relationship of son and mother, of son and his discovery of an outside world from which he is separated and to which he is attached. The violence between brothers is for Shakespeare the projection into dramatic terms of the infantile experience of cleavage. For, as Shakespeare understands it, fratricide is the road to and away from the mother: a violence *of* desire that confirms the experience of the self; a violence that separates equals and joins, like the "imperial jointress," opposites who have no difference between them. In Lichtensteinian terms, Shakespeare must develop an identity theme with a built-in dissonance, he must clarify a disturbance in identity around which a representative solidity can coalesce. Hence in Shakespeare the homosexuality that founders on its own narcissism. Hence Shakespearean androgyny, fractured in its wholeness. Hence the marriage of Shakespearean opposites, sealed by cuckoldry. Hence Shakespeare's horrible women. Out of this defensive strategy, characteristic of the Shakespearean imagination, come the comedies and the sexuality they release, and out of it, too, come the tragedies and the violence they control. Yet, we should add, out of the dissonance of identity and the acceptance thereof comes also the charity and love of the late romances, which tell another and, I think, an entirely different story.

Notes

1. All Shakespeare quotations are from *The Pelican Shakespeare*, ed. Alfred Harbage (Harmondsworth, Eng.: Penguin, 1967).

2. "The Phoenix and the Turtle," l. 27. The poem, usually dated to 1601, is written about the same time as the plays we discuss here.

3. David Bevington, *From Mankind to Marlowe: Growth of Structure in the Popular Drama of Tudor England* (Cambridge, Mass: Harvard Univ. Press, 1962), especially chapters 5 and 6.

4. Bevington, chapter 5.

5. As developed, for example, in Melanie Klein's theories about the paranoid-schizoid and depressive positions, or Winnicott's conceptualization of the "transitional object." Another way to develop this would be through a discussion of Jacques Lacan's "*objet a.*"

6. This is the title of the seventeenth-century German manuscript that most scholars believe reflects the so-called *Ur-Hamlet.*

7. Shakespeare's name play is consistent: the bad male who balances Olivia-Viola is Malvolio.

8. Malvolio too is exiled to a fool's hermitage, confined to a lunatic's sacred cellar where he receives the ministrations of a fake and comic priest.

9. Compare Francis Bacon on "emulation" and familial relations: "Men have a foolish manner (both parents and schoolmasters) in creating and breeding an emulation between brothers during childhood, which many times sorteth to discord when they are men, and disturbeth families. The Italians make little difference between children and nephews or near kinsfolks; but so they be of the lump, they care not though they pass not through their own body. And to say truth, in nature it is much a like matter; insomuch that we see a nephew sometimes resembleth an uncle or kinsman more than his own parent; as the blood happens." See "Of Parents and Children," in *The Works of Francis Bacon*, ed. J. Spedding, R. L. Ellis, D. D. Heath (New York: Longman, 1864), p. 100.

10. Some modern editors retain the folio's "bonds" over Theobald's traditional emendation. Both readings are equally plausible. We can understand the textual dispute as the elaboration of an ambiguity built into the play—the typographer and the editors each responding to different, though linked, image systems. In *Troilus and Cressida*, the overdetermined fusion of "contract" with sexuality becomes explicit.

11. The unconscious link between comic disguise and cuckoldry comes across in the rush of associations with which Feste hails Olivia early in the play: "As there is

no true cuckold but calamity, so beauty's a flower" (I.v.46–47), followed a few lines later with a common fool's defense of foolery: *"cucullus non facit monachum"* (I.v.51–52). Shakespeare's puns are always pointed. The cowl doesn't make the monk, but neither does the cuckold make a whore. The fool concludes this subliminal syllogism by beginning another that is the consequence of what has just been demonstrated: "Good Madonna, give me leave to prove you a fool" (I.v.52–53). This is the comic opposite of Hamlet's ambiguous "get thee to a nunnery," since Feste is here telling Olivia to forget her dead brother and to forswear her virginal cloister.

12. C. L. Barber, *Shakespeare's Festive Comedy* (Princeton, N.J.: Princeton Univ. Press, 1968), p. 245.

13. This essay is very much indebted to Girard's presentations at the Colloquia of the English Department of The State University of New York at Buffalo, 1969, especially "Myth and Identity Crisis in *A Midsummer-Night's Dream*." See also René Girard, "Lévi-Strauss, Frye, Derrida and Shakespearean Criticism," *Diacritics*, 3 (1973), 34–38, and "Symétrie et dissymétrie dans le mythe d'Oedipe," *Critique*, Feb. 1968, pp. 99–135.

14. Cf. the Jewish prayer of Havdalah, i.e., of Difference, or the many rituals of differentiation described by Mircea Eliade in *Rites and Symbols of Initiation* (New York: Harper and Row, 1958); in *The Myth of the Eternal Return* (Princeton: Princeton Univ. Press, 1971); in *The Sacred and the Profane* (New York: Harcourt Brace Jovanovich, 1959); and in *The Two and the One* (New York: Harper and Row, 1965).

15. "Secret" is important to *Hamlet* because it is the unspeakable message of the father. The Ghost tells Hamlet:

> But that I am forbid
> To tell the secrets of my prison house,
> I could a tale unfold whose lightest word
> Would harrow up thy soul, freeze thy young blood,
> Make thy two eyes like stars start from their spheres,
> Thy knotted and combined locks to part,
> And each particular hair to stand an end
> Like quills upon the fretful porpentine.
>
> (I.v.13–20)

Later, in the closet scene, when the Ghost reappears, Gertrude says:

> Alas, how is't with you,
> That you do bend your eye on vacancy,
> And with th' incorporal air do hold discourse?
> Forth at your eyes your spirits wildly peep,
> And as the sleeping soldiers in th' alarm
> Your bedded hairs like life in excrements
> Start up and stand an end.
>
> (III.iv.118–23)

Placed between maternal presence and paternal absence, Hamlet learns, and becomes, the "secret" of the primal scene.

16. "You go not till I set you up a glass/Where you may see the inmost part of you" (III.iv.20–21). "The precursor of the mirror is the mother's face," says D. W. Winnicott. See "Mirror-Role of Mother and Family in Child Development," in *The Predicament of the Family*, ed. P. Lomas (London: Hogarth Press, 1967). The

infant discovers reality in the face of the mother; what he sees there is what he can allow himself to be. Cf. Paula Elkisch: "It has been my impression in the three cases cited that these patients tried to retrieve, as it were, in their mirrored images what they felt they had lost, their ego, their self, their boundaries." See "The Psychological Significance of the Mirror," *Journal of the American Psychoanalytic Association*, 5 (1965), 235-44. All this is, of course, related to the psychology of twins, about which there is a huge amount of literature. See, for example, Dorothy Burlingham, *Twins: A Study of Three Pairs of Identical Twins* (New York: International Univ. Press, 1952); B. Karpman, "A Psychoanalytic Study of a Fraternal Twin," *American Journal of Orthopsychiatry*, 21 (1955), 735-66; Jacob Arlow, "Fantasy Systems in Twins," *Psychoanalytic Quarterly*, 29 (1960), 175-99.

Lacan would see the ego precipitated in such "mirror" experiences as primarily an imaginary structure; see "Le Stade du miroir" in *Ecrits* (Paris: Editions du Seuil, 1966), 1, pp. 93-100. Eventually, this imaginary, "visual" ego would be resituated in relation to a represented subject of discourse. In my forthcoming book on the development of Shakespeare's canon, I take up Shakespeare's doubling patterns from the point of view of Lacanian psychoanalysis.

17. The unfaithful, promiscuous woman is a secular version of religious apostasy, a development of the moralities' "Infidel." Cf., for example, John Bale's *A Comedy Concerning Three Laws of Nature* or, more interesting in this context, Lewis Wager's *The Life and Repentance of Mary Magdalene*. These earlier plays had a great effect on the organization of later, more sophisticated Elizabethan drama. Thus, for example, notwithstanding his Christian service, Othello as a Moor remains a heathen, an infidel, whose lack of true faith balances Desdemona's supposed infidelity.

18. The compulsion to repeat is more than a function of defense mechanisms. See Sigmund Freud, *Beyond the Pleasure Principle*, in *The Standard Edition of the Complete Psychological Works of Sigmund Freud*, ed. and trans. James Strachey et al., 24 vols. (London: Hogarth Press, 1953-74), 18, p. 63.

19. Niobe is her own opposite, a mother whose narcissistic pride leads to the destruction of her children. See Philip E. Slater, *The Glory of Hera* (Boston: Beacon Press, 1968).

20. Marion Milner, *The Hands of the Living God* (New York: International Univ. Press, 1969). See also D. W. Winnicott, "Transitional Objects and Transitional Phenomena," in his *Collected Papers: Through Paediatrics to Psycho-Analysis* (London: Tavistock Press, 1969).

21. "Emulation" defines a desire divided against itself, a kind of sympathetic rancor best illuminated by Freud's ambiguous account of an ego whose identifications are simultaneously subjective and objective, narcissistic and anaclitic.

22. I cut the speech for the sake of space, but its development of oceanic, musical, and oral imagery corresponds point for point to all the themes we have been dealing with in *Twelfth Night, Hamlet,* and *As You Like It.*

23. Note that as soon as the idea of equality comes up, it immediately suggests cuckoldry. Rosalind continues:

> I would we could do so, for her benefits are
> mightily misplaced, and the bountiful blind woman
> doth most mistake in her gifts to women.

(I.ii.32-34)

To which Celia replies:

'Tis true, for those she makes fair she scarce
makes honest, and those that she makes honest she
makes very ill-favoredly.

(I.ii.35–37)

Cf. also Hamlet's "the power of beauty will sooner transform honesty from what it is to a bawd than the force of honesty can translate beauty into his likeness." (III.i. 111–13).

24. In a recent essay focusing on this speech, J. Hillis Miller makes Troilus' response to Cressida's faithlessness a general hermeneutic model, "Ariachne's Broken Woof," *The Georgia Review*, 31 (1977), 44–60. He argues that the jointure of both the Ariadne and Arachne myths in the idiosyncratic conflation "Ariachne" exemplifies the interweaving of dialogical and logocentric metaphysics in the tangled warp and woof of western culture. Every text is Cressida-like, duplicitous, and every critic, responding thereto, is therefore a Troilus, a "Bi-fold authority." Such an anacoluthic reading leaves one question unanswered: Does this kind of deconstruction undo or merely complete a misogynistic philosophical formula? Perhaps the dialogical critic is not only Troilus-like but Leontes-like as well, in that he invites his betrayal, demands it, for the pleasure of inverting "th' attest of eyes and ears." Leontes boasts that he has "drunk, and seen the spider" (*The Winter's Tale*, II.i.45), but his wife is more than faithful. It is as though the shame of cuckoldry, physical or metaphysical, covered up a deeper shame, as in the well known formula of displaced homosexuality: "I do not love him. She does."

Freud accorded women only one art, weaving, which they invented to cover up the embarrassment of their castration. See *New Introductory Lectures, Standard Edition*, 18, p. 132. This is similar to what we find in Shakespeare, where, as Murray Schwartz points out, the spider often "represents the sexually threatening mother, contact with whom signifies incest. On a deeper level, it signifies the horror of maternal engulfment, frequently confused with the child's own oral-aggressive impulses." See "Leontes' Jealousy in *The Winter's Tale*," *American Imago*, 30 (1973), 270. What is not often noticed is that there is a recuperative value to all of this. In Freud, in Shakespeare, and perhaps in dialogism too, "the spider often emerges as a symbol when an intensely ambivalent person needs to ward off a complete break with reality" (ibid.).

At any rate, my minimal claim is that for Shakespeare there is an important formal difference between the tragedy of a man unable to believe in what he believes is true (Othello, or, for that matter, Lear), and the man who insists upon believing in what he knows is false (Troilus). The former bespeaks disavowal and is as common as fetishism (Othello's handkerchief). The latter, to use Lacan's terms, forecloses castration and the name of the father altogether. Clinically, this last alternative may define psychosis, but in literature it leads to sentimentality, like that of Troilus, precisely because in literature there is always eventually a sense to "the madness of discourse."

25. There is no time to consider the intervening problem comedies, but their place in this development can be readily inferred.

26. Much of this argument depends upon evidence and theory presented by Robert J. Stoller, "Facts and Fancies: An Examination of Freud's Concept of Bisexuality," in *Women and Analysis*, ed. Jean Strouse (New York: Grossman Press, 1974). See also Joel Fineman, "Psychoanalysis, Bisexuality, and the Difference *Before* the Sexes," in *Psychosexual Imperatives: Their Role in Identity Formation*, ed. M. Nelson (New York: Human Sciences Press, 1979).

27. Freud would relate this to his three categories of identification, which, in the manner of Renaissance rhetoricians, he describes in terms of intention: a first type, in which identification leads to an imitation of the object (rhetoric calls this "aemulatio"); a second in which the identification turns into a desire for the object ("convenience" or "copula"); and a third, in which the subject entirely ignores the object and merely copies what it perceives to be the situation of the other ("sympathy," "similitudo," "analogia"). Freud distinguishes the first two cases with an oedipal example: "In the first case one's father is what one would like to *be*, and in the second he is what one would like to *have*." Freud's instance of the third case is an epidemic of contagious hysteria at a girls' school, the disease spread by sympathy. See Freud, *Group Psychology and the Analysis of the Ego, Standard Edition*, 18, pp. 106–07. Clearly, there is a need to relate these kinds of identification to stages of development. The point is, and there is clinical evidence to prove it, that sexual identity precedes oedipality and is conditioned by identificatory styles, rhetorical figures as it were, developed in infancy.

28. I owe this important declension of Shakespearean femininity to Prof. Murray M. Schwartz.

29. The spectrum ends, of course, with *Two Noble Kinsmen*, Shakespeare's retelling of the same enemy-twin story with which Chaucer begins *The Canterbury Tales*. To follow out the theme from Knight's Tale to *Two Noble Kinsmen* would be to show how the Renaissance problematized the more stable, hierarchically organized differences of the medieval tradition—though such destabilization, we can note, had already begun with Chaucerian irony. What distinguishes *Two Noble Kinsmen*, however, and what marks it as an emblematic limit point, is precisely the fact that it is written in collaboration, so that the Shakespearean story of divided unity actually concludes with Shakespeare as "bi-fold author."

6 ✿ The Woman in Hamlet: An Interpersonal View

David Leverenz

> John, I guess there are some people around here who
> think you have some little old lady in you.
>
> —John Dean, *Blind Ambition*

"Who's there?" Bernardo's anxious shout, which begins Shakespeare's most problematic play, raises the fundamental question of Hamlet's identity. Various male authority figures advance simple answers. For the Ghost, Hamlet is a dutiful son who should sweep to his father's revenge and forget about his mother. For Claudius, Hamlet is a possible rebel who should be either made tractable or banished and killed. For Polonius, Hamlet is the heir gone mad through frustrated love for Ophelia, whom Polonius has denied him partly for reasons of state. But for Hamlet, the roles of dutiful son, ambitious rebel, or mad, lovesick heir are just that: roles, to be played for others but not felt for himself. The "who" remains unsettled within and without, "the heart of my mystery" (III.ii.351).[1]

The mixed and contradictory expectations of these father figures— the Ghost, Claudius, Polonius—reflect their own divided image of dutiful reason and bestial lust. At times their power seems to be defined by their ability to order women and children around. Hamlet sees Gertrude give way to Claudius, Ophelia give way to Polonius, and himself at last yield to the Ghost. But Hamlet also sees duplicity and falseness in all the fathers, except perhaps his own, and even there his famous delay may well indicate unconscious perception, rather than the unconscious guilt ascribed to him by a strict Freudian interpretation. Hamlet resists

This chapter first appeared in *Signs: Journal of Women in Culture and Society*, 4 (Winter 1978). Copyright © 1978 by The University of Chicago. Reprinted by permission of the University of Chicago Press.

his father's commands to obey. Despite his illusory idealization of the senior Hamlet as pure and angelic, he senses the Ghost's complicity in the paternal doublespeak that bends Gertrude and Ophelia, indeed bends feelings and the body itself, to self-falsifying reason and filial loyalty. Hamlet is part hysteric, as Freud said, and part Puritan in his disgust at contamination and his idealization of his absent father. But he is also, as Goethe was the first to say, part woman. And Goethe was wrong, as Freud was wrong, to assume that "woman" means weakness. To equate women with weak and tainted bodies, words, and feelings while men possess noble reason and ambitious purpose is to participate in Denmark's disease that divides mind from body, act from feeling, man from woman.

Hamlet's tragedy is the forced triumph of filial duty over sensitivity to his own heart. To fulfill various fathers' commands, he has to deny his self-awareness, just as Gertrude and Ophelia have done. That denial is equivalent to suicide, as the language of the last act shows. His puritanical cries about whoredom in himself and others, his hysterical outbursts to Ophelia about nunneries and painted women, are the outer shell of a horror at what the nurtured, loving, and well-loved soul has been corrupted to. From a more modern perspective than the play allows, we can sense that the destruction of good mothering is the real issue, at least from Hamlet's point of view.

Freudians, too many of whom have their own paternal answers to "Who's there?" see Hamlet as an unconscious Claudius-Oedipus, or as a man baffled by pre-Oedipal ambivalences about his weak-willed, passionate, fickle mother.[2] While acknowledging Hamlet's parricidal and matricidal impulses, we should see these inchoate feelings as responses, not innate drives. Interpersonal expectations, more than self-contained desires, are what divide Hamlet from himself and conscript him to false social purposes. In this perspective, taken from Harry Stack Sullivan, R. D. Laing, and D. W. Winnicott, Hamlet's supposed delay is a natural reaction to overwhelming interpersonal confusion.[3] His self-preoccupation is paradoxically grounded not so much in himself as in the extraordinary and unremitting array of "mixed signals" that separate role from self, reason from feeling, duty from love.

Hamlet has no way of unambiguously understanding what anyone says to him. The girl who supposedly loves him inexplicably refuses his attentions. His grieving mother suddenly marries. His dead father, suddenly alive, twice tells him to deny his anger at his mother's shocking change of heart. Two of his best friends "make love to this employment" of snooping against him (V.ii.57). Polonius, Claudius, and the Ghost all manifest themselves as loving fathers, yet expect the worst and even spy on their children, either directly or through messengers.

Who is this "uncle-father and aunt-mother" (II.ii.366), or this courtier-father? They preach the unity of being true to oneself and others yet are false to everyone; each can "smile, and smile, and be a villain" (I.v. 108). Gertrude's inconstancy not only brings on disgust and incestuous feelings, it is also the sign of diseased doubleness in everyone who has accommodated to his or her social role. The usurping Claudius is the symbol of all those "pretenders," who are now trying to bring Hamlet into line. No wonder Hamlet weeps at the sight of a genuine actor—the irony reveals the problem—playing Hecuba's grief. The male expressing a woman's constancy once again mirrors Hamlet's need. And the role, though feigned, at least is openly played. The actor's tears are the play's one unambiguous reflection of the grief Hamlet thought his mother shared with him before the onset of so many multitudinous double-dealings.

The question of whether to kill or not to kill cannot be entertained when one is not even sure of existing with any integrity. Being, not desiring or revenging, is the question. Freudians assume that everyone has strong desires blocked by stronger repressions, but contemporary work with schizophrenics reveals the tragic variety of people whose voices are only amalgams of other people's voices, with caustic self-observation or a still more terrifying vacuum as their incessant inward reality. This is Hamlet to a degree, as it is Ophelia completely. As Laing says of her in *The Divided Self*: "In her madness, there is no one there. She is not a person. There is no integral selfhood expressed through her actions or utterances. Incomprehensible statements are said by nothing. She has already died. There is now only a vacuum where there was once a person."[4] Laing misrepresents her state only because there are many voices in Ophelia's madness speaking through her, all making sense, and none of them her own. She becomes the mirror for a madness-inducing world. Hamlet resists these pressures at the cost of a terrifying isolation. Once he thinks his mother has abandoned him, there is nothing and no one to "mirror" his feelings, as Winnicott puts it.[5] Hamlet is utterly alone, beyond the loving semiunderstanding of reasonable Horatio or obedient Ophelia.

A world of fathers and sons, ambition and lust, considers grief "unmanly," as Claudius preaches (I.ii.94). Hamlet seems to agree, at least to himself, citing his "whorish" doubts as the cause of his inability to take manly filial action. This female imagery, which reflects the play's male-centered world view, represents a covert homosexual fantasy, according to Freudian interpretation.[6] Certainly Hamlet's idealizations of his father and of Horatio's friendship show a hunger for male close-ness. Poisoning in the ear may unconsciously evoke anal intercourse. And the climactic swordplay with Laertes does lead to a brotherly understanding. But these instances of covert homosexual desire are responses to a lack. Poisoning in the ear evokes conscious and unconscious perversity to intimate the perversion of communication, especially between men. The woman in Hamlet is the source of his most acute perceptions about the diseased, disordered patriarchal society that tries to "play upon this pipe" of Hamlet's soul (III.ii.336), even as a ghost returning from the dead.

The separation of role from self is clear in the opening scene. Anxiety precipitates a genuine question: "Who's there?" It is answered not with "Francisco," the natural rejoinder, but with "Nay, answer me. Stand and unfold yourself" (I.i.2). Francisco restores public ritual by the prescribed challenge of a guard, not the response of a friend. To private uneasiness he responds with public norms. Bernardo's answer to the command to "unfold yourself" is equally self-avoiding. "Long live the King!" he cries (I.i.3). His identity, in the prescribed convention, is equivalent to respect for the King. Yet the not-so-long-lived King has just died, and the new one, who was to have been Hamlet the younger, has been displaced by the old one's brother. Who *is* the rightful King? Who is there? The question returns, under the formulaic phrase that denies any problems of loyalty or succession.

Francisco departs with an odd and disconcerting addition to a conventional farewell: "For this relief much thanks. 'Tis bitter cold,/And I am sick at heart" (I.i.8–9). Tensions between the head and the heart, noble reason and diseased emotion, center the play. Yet this first expression of heartsick feelings has no explanation. The watch has been "quiet"–"Not a mouse stirring," Francisco gratuitously adds (I.i.10). By Act III, Hamlet will be devising a play he calls "The Mousetrap," which would make the new King a mouse and suggest that royal stability is corroded at its base. But for now these jagged interchanges, like the half-lines staggered on the page and the roles confused by the guards, seem simply "out of joint," with no clear perspective on who has been guarding what, why Bernardo seems scared, and why Francisco feels sick at heart. The darker questions recede into the comfortable self-definitions of Horatio and Marcellus, who respond to the next "Who is there?" with "Friends to this ground" (Horatio), "And liegemen to the Dane" (Marcellus, I.i.15). Horatio, whose first word is "friends," is the only one of this group to define himself both within and beyond conventional public deference. As yet we cannot sense the incompatibility between being friends and being liegemen. By Act V the gap is so wide that Horatio declares himself "more an antique Roman than a Dane" (V.ii.330) and tries to drink from the poisoned cup to follow his friend both from and to a poisoned state. All we know

now, though, is that more seems afoot than simply the changing of a guard.[7]

Identity, in the first scene, is defined as role, specifically as loyalty among functionaries of a state. But feelings have been partly voiced that are curiously disconnected from roles. There is no coherent voice for more private feelings—in this case, fear; rote is the norm. The polarity between mind and passions reflects larger polarities in the social order, or rather in a society pretending to be ordered along the father's lines. These polarities become more apparent in the contrast between Claudius's opening speech and Hamlet's first soliloquy. Claudius speaks in the language of public command, with phrases tailored and balanced, the royal "we" firmly affixed to his crown. Oxymorons prescribe a unity of opposites, and his balanced phrasing is only twice disrupted with the reality of seized power: "Taken to wife," and "So much for him" (I.ii.14, 25). For Claudius, reason, nature, and submission are joined in a facile unity.

> Fie, 'tis a fault to heaven,
> A fault against the dead, a fault to nature,
> To reason most absurd, whose common theme
> Is death of fathers, and who still hath cried,
> From the first corse till he that died to-day,
> "This must be so."

> (I.ii.101–06)

To personify an abstraction, reason, is characteristic of Claudius' perspective, in which abstract states are more real than persons. Unfortunately, reality intrudes; in the rush of his logic he misrepresents "the first corse," who was obviously Abel, not a father but a brother killed by a brother, as in Claudius's crime. The heart will intrude its guilt, no matter how speech tries to deny fact and feeling. The rhetoric of formal obedience avoids, while suggesting, the simple stark reality of a father's murder, a son's grief, and a murderer's guilt.

Claudius' speech reveals a second assumption already sensed in the personification of reason. When he speaks of "our whole kingdom . . . contracted in one brow of woe" (I.ii.3–4), he presents his kingdom as a single person. He further connects the language of personal love with the language of public war, since making war among states has the same unity of opposites that he wants to prescribe for individuals, even for his wife. Gertrude, whom he defines only in her disjointed roles as "our sometime sister, now our queen," is thus "Th' imperial jointress to this warlike state" (I.ii.8–9). Marriage is simply the prelude to aggression. The only arena for "joining" is the ordering of the state for war, not the expressing of desire in the marriage bed. Polonius continues the inversion of love and war more explicitly in his advice to Ophelia: "Set your entreatments at a higher rate/Than a command to parley" (I.iii. 122-23). Laertes also echoes the language of war in speaking of love to her: "Keep you in the rear of your affection,/Out of the shot and danger of desire" (I.iii.34-35). In this collusion of ambitious functionaries, the state is the only real person, whose war with other person-states can be told as love, while human loves and fears can be expressed only as warlike obedience to the purposes of states.[8]

Hamlet's first private discourse opposes, point for point, the dehumanizing unities of the King's public preaching. Where Claudius assumes the oneness of reason and nature in filial subjection, Hamlet piles contrary on rebellious contrary, especially that of mind and body. Indeed, Hamlet's soliloquy is obsessed with language of the body—sullied (or solid) flesh, appetite, feeding, father's dead body, tears, incestuous sheets, "gallèd eyes" (I.ii.155), and finally the heart and tongue: "But break my heart, for I must hold my tongue" (I.ii.159), an intuition that precisely describes his fate. Parts of the body, rank, gross, and unweeded, overwhelm any pretense at understanding.

Elsewhere Hamlet attempts to recast the language of public ritual as personal feeling. When his friends say farewell with the conventional "Our duty to your honor," Hamlet responds with a half-ironic inversion: "Your loves, as mine to you" (I.ii.253-54). Duty and love still have something in common, he hopes. But his language in the first act more broadly participates in the most pervasive assumption of Claudius, that reason is what makes a man. Hamlet is disgusted at the thought of "some complexion . . . breaking down the pales and forts of reason" (I. iv.27-28). Those "pales and forts" echo Claudius' equation between war and love. Here is the inward castle of the mind on which, metaphorically, Bernardo and Francisco stand guard, though against what is still uncertain. "Nobility" connotes the mind's royalty, as befits a prince's role. "Nature," on the other hand, is associated with the rabble, reveling in the bestial dregs of "swinish phrase" and scandal, "some vicious mole of nature in them" (I.iv.19, 24) that cannot help but get out. Just as Claudius falsely conjoins nature and obedience into the smooth illusory primacy of reason, so Hamlet, searching for truth at the other extreme, lumps nature, feeling, beasts, and body together, all as negatives.

Hamlet is "unsocialized," a psychiatrist might say, hearing reports of his hostile puns, asides, and soliloquies. Unfortunately, he is far more socialized than he can perceive. He still takes refuge in the shared assumptions of those around him, who locate the self in the mind's obedience to patriarchal order, the body's obedience to abstractions. Whether speaking as Polonius, who can talk so glibly of "wit" as having "soul" and "limbs" (II.ii.90-91) and swear that "I hold my duty as I hold my soul" (II.ii.44), or as Rosencrantz, who expounds so eloquently on how the "single and peculiar life" is only part of the "massy wheel" of majesty (III.iii.11–23), or as Laertes, who takes such pains to instruct Ophelia that Hamlet is "circumscribed/Unto the voice and yielding of that body/Whereof he is the head" (I.iii.22–24), this common public voice denies private feeling and private identity, while asserting the false union of all the parts of the social body in subjection to majesty. As Rosencrantz declares (III.iii.12–13), this power is "much more" than "the strength and armor of the mind" itself. Again the warlike image is symptomatic.

The Ghost seems to be the one father who speaks straight, and Hamlet's encounter with him precipitates clarity about what has happened and what he must do. But while confirming Hamlet's perception of external wickedness, the Ghost invalidates Hamlet's feelings. He speaks to the mind's suspicions of Claudius while denying Hamlet's more profound heartsickness over Gertrude. Claudius' villainy is clear and clearly stated. But many other aspects of the Ghost's account are mixed signals denying simple feeling. After hearing of the "sulph'rous and tormenting flames" awaiting his father, Hamlet cries "Alas, poor ghost!"—a Gertrude-like response (I.v.4). "Pity me not," the Ghost rejoins, rejecting the empathy he has just solicited. He wants only "serious hearing" and revenge. Yet the Ghost then gratuitously describes "my prison house" and forces its horrors on Hamlet by suggesting that knowledge of the truth would shatter his son's body. This is already a Laingian "knot,"[9] designed to exaggerate the father's strength and the son's weakness. Feelings are frivolous; manly endurance is true fortitude. As he will do with Gertrude, the Ghost implies that his son is too frail to hear; so is anyone with "ears of flesh and blood" (I.v.22). Don't pity me, runs the message—but boy, what you *would* feel. . . .Yet why is father in Purgatory? Not because of his heroic or virtuous strength but because of "the foul crimes done in my days of nature" (I.v.12). So in these first few lines the father has: (1) told his son not to pity, yet encouraged him to pity, (2) accentuated his son's earthly weakness and his own immortal strength, yet told Hamlet of "foul crimes," and (3) equated pity with frivolity and dutiful hearing with seriousness, while picturing Hamlet's feelings in language that dismembers the body in its exaggerated seriousness.

The mixed signals persist. We never learn what the "foul crimes" consist of, though they are apparently extensive enough to have the Ghost cry out "O, horrible! O, horrible! most horrible!" at the thought of his "account" for "my imperfections" (I.v.78–80). Yet the major burden of his discourse is to contrast his "dignity" and "virtue" with Claudius' crimes. We have already heard from others, notably Horatio, about

King Hamlet's warlike "frown" and armor (I.i.60–62). There is very little in the Ghost's own speech, however, to support a sense of virtuous integrity. His surprisingly weak affirmation of his love's "dignity" states only that "it went hand in hand even with the vow/I made to her in marriage," presumably to remain faithful (I.v.48–50). Even his love can be fully summarized not by feeling but by "vow" or public ritual. And as King, his peacetime behavior seems to have been primarily sleeping on the job. Otherwise he would not have been killed as he was "Sleeping within my orchard,/My custom always of the afternoon" (I.v.59–60). He is also viciously uncharitable to the Queen, while at the same time forbidding his son from having that same feeling.[10] Throughout his speech, the Ghost is preoccupied with the body, and, as with Hamlet, Gertrude is the focus for that concern. Her change from "seeming-virtuous" behavior to "lust" puts the Ghost into a paroxysm of disgust, not so much at the vile seducer as at the woman who could move from "a radiant angel" to a beast who preys "on garbage" (I.v.46, 55–57). The king of "foul crimes" presents himself as an angel now.

Hamlet's idealization of his father and disgust with Claudius reveals, as Freudians have rightly argued, a splitting of the son's ambivalence toward the father. But the various mixed signals in the Ghost's speech show how the father's communication, not the son's intrapsychic repressions, fosters ambivalence. Father is, in fact, more like Claudius than the Ghost can dare admit. They both speak with the arrogant abstractedness of majesty—"So the whole ear of Denmark/Is . . ./Rankly abused" (I.v.36–38)—yet they both show their particular bodies, in word or deed, subverting the false nobility of royal role. And the Ghost is particularly ambivalent about "nature" itself. Though he invokes his own "foul crimes done in my days of nature" (I.v.12), he concludes: "If thou hast nature in thee, bear it not" (I.v.81). From "Pity me not" to "Bear it not," the Ghost's commands falsify both the father's reality and the son's "nature." They exaggerate father's virtues, demean Hamlet's responses, and establish a confusing set of connections between nature, lust, feeling, and Gertrude, all of which must be resolutely disowned to follow the father's directives toward filial revenge, a "natural feeling" unnatural to Hamlet.[11] Even the minor father figures, like old Priam and Yorick, are vivid in their infirm bodies, not in their dignified precepts. Yet precepts are the "me" that Hamlet has to remember.

Through her impossible attempt to obey contradictory voices, Ophelia mirrors in her madness the tensions that Hamlet perceives. As in Laing's *Sanity, Madness, and the Family*, Ophelia's "madness" is a natural response to the unacknowledged interpersonal falsities of the group.[12] Her history is another instance of how someone can be driven mad by having her inner feelings misrepresented, not responded to, or acknowledged only through chastisement and repression. From her entrance on, Ophelia must continually respond to commands that imply distrust even as they compel obedience. "Do you doubt that?" she opens, after Laertes has told her: "Do not sleep,/But let me hear from you" (I.iii.3-4). The body's natural desire to sleep must yield to the role of always-attentive sister. Without responding, perhaps not even hearing her rejoinder to his demand, Laertes immediately tries to plunge her into a more severe doubt of Hamlet's affection, and therefore of her own. It is simply toying with lust, he says, "a fashion and a toy in blood" (I.iii.6). Reflecting the division between mind and body forced on children by fathers themselves divided, Laertes speaks magisterially of how "nature crescent" in Hamlet must be "circumscribed" to the larger "body" of the state "Whereof he is the head" (I.iii.11, 22-24). Hamlet's voice can go "no further/Than the main voice of Denmark goes withal" (I.iii.27-28). A prince can express no feeling except as it furthers his social role; the rest is transient sensuality, "The perfume and suppliance of a minute,/No more." "No more but so?" Ophelia responds, questioning but trusting, and Laertes rejoins ambiguously: "Think it no more" (I.iii.9-10). So the Ghost speaks to Hamlet and of Gertrude, emphasizing their weakness and strength.

Ophelia accepts Laertes's commands as a "lesson" to "keep/As watchman to my heart . . . " (I.iii.45-46). Yet her advice to him shows her awareness of his possible double self, the pastor and the libertine, the very division he used in describing Hamlet. Punning on "recks" and "reckless," she displays an independent wit, much like Hamlet's more constricted opening puns. But her sense of the necessity for a "watchman" over probable evils of the heart is as unquestioned as her acceptance of the military terminology. The fortress of the female heart needs its Bernardos. She *will* doubt her feelings henceforth. When Polonius reinterprets what she calls Hamlet's "tenders/Of his affection to me" (I.iii.99-100) as monetary transactions leading only to her father's exposure as "a fool," Ophelia hesitantly asserts the "honorable fashion" of Hamlet's loving speech to her (I.iii.111). Yet she mutely accepts her father's assumption that to "tender yourself more dearly" is essential to protect father's self-image (I.iii.107). Polonius is deliberately unconcerned with what his daughter feels. His command to refuse Hamlet any "words or talk" flies in the face of everything Ophelia has said (I.iii. 134). Yet she has no choice but to say, "I shall obey, my lord" (I.iii. 136).

For his part, Polonius is preoccupied only with how he looks. Always the fawning courtier, the man who can say "I hold my duty as I hold my soul" in return for being called "the father of good news" by the new King (II.ii.42-44), his response to Claudius' questions about Ophelia flagrantly reveals his unconcern for anything but his own position. "But how hath she/Received his love?" Claudius inquires. "What do you think of me?" is Polonius' answer; "What might you think?" he anxiously repeats (II.ii.128-29, 139). For Polonius, his daughter is an animal whom he can "loose" (II.ii.162) to catch Hamlet's motive. He cares for Claudius, for his role as "assistant for a state" (II.ii.166), not for his daughter's feelings. The subplot makes clear what the main plot obfuscates: Fathers perceive children as they do their wives and bodies, as beasts to be controlled for the magnification of their self-images, or rather, for the expression of their divided selves, their reason and their lust. These divisions grow from their complicity in playing a leading role in a corrupt state. Polonius, putting the issue squarely, says to Ophelia: "You do not understand yourself so clearly/As it behooves my daughter and your honor" (I.iii.96-97). Ophelia must accept the role of honorable possession and deny her love for Hamlet. This is not a question of repressed sexual desire, though certainly her anxieties, like Hamlet's, have to do with feelings denied. It is a question of what it means to understand oneself when the price is falseness to others.

Hamlet himself fosters Ophelia's crisis, to be sure. He sends her an ambiguous poem that can be read as "Never doubt that I love" or "Never suspect that I love" (II.ii.119). He tells her he loved her; then, "I loved you not" (III.i.119). He seems to confirm Laertes' suspicions by warning her of his lust and ordering her to a nunnery, which of course—another mixed signal—could also be a whorehouse. His crude jokes about "country matters" (III.ii.111) as he lies in her lap, at the play, toy with her role as honorable daughter, confirm his lust, yet contradict the piteous picture he makes of himself in her room, wordless, his clothes in disarray. His oscillating acts of need and aggression are Hamlet's nasty mirroring of what he perceives to be her mixed signals to him: her loving talks, then her inexplicable denial and silence. First he mirrors her silence, then he mirrors the self that Polonius and Laertes have warned her against. More profoundly, her behavior to him—since he has no knowledge of her obedience to Polonius' command—so evokes Gertrude's inconstancy that Hamlet's double messages to Ophelia take on a frenzied condemnation of all women. His soliloquies extend that condemnation to the woman in himself. This Laingian knot of miscommunications compounded, of false selves intensified, leads finally to self-mistrust, even to madness.

Not allowed to love and unable to be false, Ophelia breaks. She goes mad rather than gets mad. Even in her madness she has no voice of her own, only a discord of other voices and expectations, customs gone awry. Most obviously, she does what Hamlet preaches, or at least what he feigns, in going mad. Thinking she is not loved by him, she becomes him, or at least what she conceives to be his "noble mind . . . o'er-thrown" (III.i.150). Just as his absence in Act IV is reflected in the absence of her reason, so her suicide embodies what Hamlet ponders in his soliloquies. After all, Polonius has instructed her that love denied leads to madness (II.i.110), and Ophelia is forever faithful to her contradictory directives. She herself is a play within a play, or a player trying to respond to several imperious directors at once. Everyone has used her: Polonius, to gain favor; Laertes, to belittle Hamlet; Claudius, to spy on Hamlet; Hamlet, to express rage at Gertrude; and Hamlet again, to express his feigned madness with her as a decoy. She is only valued for the roles that further other people's plots. Treated as a helpless child, she finally becomes one, veiling her perceptions of falsehood and manipulation in her seemingly innocent ballads.

Ophelia's songs give back the contradictory voices lodged within her and expose the contradictions. "Where is the beauteous majesty of Denmark?" she asks of Gertrude as she enters (IV.v.21)—a question Hamlet has often asked of the state, as well as of his mother. She then shifts to her first interchange with Polonius, expressed as his question and her answer:

> How should I your true-love know
> From another one?
> By his cockle hat and staff
> And his sandal shoon.
>
> (IV.v.23–26)

Polonius has told her that men are all alike, and Ophelia replies that Hamlet has the constancy of a pilgrim. The first verse also expresses Hamlet's query to Gertrude about her switch in lovers, while the second says goodbye to all faithful true loves, whether brothers, lovers, or fathers. "He is dead and gone, lady" could refer to Polonius, Prince Hamlet, Laertes, Hamlet the King, or the mythical pilgrim. Her next songs replace this faithful male with lusting lovers who deflower young maids, then depart without fulfilling their vows of marriage. "Young men will do't if they come to't. By Cock, they are to blame" (IV.v.60–61). Most readings take this song for Ophelia's own sensual desires under her dutiful exterior—"For bonny sweet Robin is all my joy" (IV.v.185), where Robin is a colloquial Elizabethan term for penis.[13] But "all" implies it is the only joy allowed her. The speaker is Gertrude's helpless, manipulated lust, veering suddenly to Polonius and Laertes telling her about the dangers of male desire, and back again to Hamlet's sense of loss. The songs mirror every level of the play, even Polonius's "flowery" speech; yet they do not express what Ophelia feels, except as sadness. Laertes is right to say, "Thought and affliction, passion, hell itself,/She turns to favor and to prettiness" (IV.v.186–87). Merging with everyone, she speaks in a collage of voices about present sensuality and absent faithfulness, yet dies, as Gertrude says so empathetically, "incapable of her own distress" (IV.vii.177).

Ophelia's suicide becomes a little microcosm of the male world's banishment of the female, because "woman" represents everything denied by reasonable men. In responding to Ophelia's death, Laertes, patently the norm for filial behavior, is embarrassed by his womanly tears. He forbids himself to cry, "but yet/It is our trick; nature her custom holds,/Let shame say what it will." To be manly is to be ashamed of emotion and nature. Saying farewell to her, he says farewell to that part of himself: "When these [tears] are gone,/The woman will be out" (IV. vii.185-88). His genuine feeling cannot be told except as a wish to get rid of the feeling. Even Hamlet, so much more sensitive than others to "nature" and "heart," equates woman with "frailty" (I.ii.146) or worse. "Whore" is his word for changeable feelings, whether those of Gertrude, of "strumpet" Fortune (II.ii.233), or even of himself. Hamlet echoes his stepfather's association of painted woman and painted word (III.i.51-53) as he rails against himself for not being the dutiful son:

> Why, what an ass am I! This is most brave,
> That I, the son of a dear father murthered,
> Prompted to my revenge by heaven and hell,
> Must like a whore unpack my heart with words
> And fall a-cursing like a very drab,
> A stallion!

> (II.ii.568-73)

That women, grief, words, and the heart should be confused with nature, guilt, whoredom, and the body, while filial obedience is equated with noble reason in opposition, is what is rotten in Denmark. Linguistic disorders express social disorders. Ophelia's drowning signifies the necessity of drowning both words and feelings if Hamlet is to act the role prescribed for him, and that is the real tragedy in the play.

Hamlet's focus on ears that are abused stands as a metaphor for the violation of female receptivity. By that token, Hamlet in the end becomes his own violator. Far from being a catharsis or a resolute confrontation, or an integration of the underlying issues, the play's end is a study in frustration and failure.[14] Hamlet retreats to filial duty, allowing the "machine" of his body (II.ii.124) to accomplish the acts required of him. Coming back to a world of fathers and usurpers, where ambition and lust have been defined as the only valid motives, he can speak that language without a qualm. "It is as easy as lying," he has told Rosencrantz and Guildenstern before (III.ii.343). Surrounded by "Examples gross as earth," of sons "with divine ambition puffed," like

Fortinbras, who can breezily risk everything "Even for an eggshell" (IV.iv.46, 49, 53), Hamlet at last resolves himself into a Do by obeying the dictates of his father and of "providence," another abstracted father. "I shall win at the odds," he tells Horatio (V.ii.200). It is a world where winning is the only thing; all else is "foolery" for women. "But thou wouldst not think how ill all's here about my heart," he tells uncomprehending Horatio. "But it is no matter. . . . It is but foolery, but it is such a kind of gaingiving as would perhaps trouble a woman" (V.ii.201–05). To Hamlet's four-times-repeated "but," Horatio ignores the "woman," and responds only: "If your mind dislike anything, obey it." Concerns for mind and obedience are part of the male world, to which Hamlet's stifled heart now responds not with whorish "unpacking" but with silence.

Silence is really the theme of the last act, not the almost farcical excess of deeds and rhetoric. The graveyard scene shows the last perversion of reason, as clowns chop logic over the dead. These mini-Claudiuses at least have the merit of not pretending grief, and their wit calls a spade a spade by asserting the absoluteness of law and power, and of class distinctions even in death. Their jokes have to do with the strong and the weak—the gallowsmaker or the gravemaker "builds stronger" (V.i.40, 55)—because their social roles abet the permanence of death. "Has this fellow no feeling of his business, that 'a sings at grave-making?" Hamlet inquires (V.i.62–63). "Custom hath made it in him a property of easiness," Horatio replies. Feeling and custom, as ever opposed but now with greater clarity, cannot be reconciled. Those who are most at home with "wit" are also most at ease with custom, reasoning, and playing their roles. Words come as glibly to them as to Osric, in proportion as feelings are denied.

It is clear to Hamlet now that words are of no use. "Nay, an thou'lt mouth,/I'll rant as well as thou," he throws back at Laertes (V.i.270–71). This is the posturing of animals, nothing more:

> Let Hercules himself do what he may,
> The cat will mew, and dog will have his day.

(V.i.278–79)

Like Ophelia, Hamlet can mirror how others talk, though with a savage irony that emphasizes the distance between his inward feelings and outward rhetoric. He mocks the foppish Osric, who "did comply, sir, with his dug before 'a sucked it" (V.ii.179). He seems calm, controlled, at arm's length from what he says. Only Gertrude senses the truth:

> This is mere madness;
> And thus a while the fit will work on him.
> Anon, as patient as the female dove

When that her golden couplets are disclosed,
His silence will sit drooping.

                                                              (V.i.271-75)

What seems like a manic-depressive "fit" to Gertrude (a better diagnosis than Freud's "hysteria") is actually Hamlet's response to "the
fit" of a senseless society. He mouths its language and assumes its
stance of male combat, while the "female dove" in him prepares for a
final silence. Earlier he had berated himself for his dove-like gentle-
ness: "But I am pigeon-livered and lack gall/To make oppression bitter" (II.ii.562-63). Now, while he puts on the necessary gall, the unspoken woman in him outwardly obeys paternal commands ("my
purposes . . . follow the king's pleasure" [V.ii.190-91]), whether of
Claudius, the Ghost, or Providence. Inwardly he has already left the
world of fathers, roles, and mixed messages to rejoin Ophelia and Gertrude in death's constancy. Not until Gertrude dies does Hamlet,
dying, fulfill the Ghost's instructions. To kill Claudius as an after-
thought to the Queen's death is his last little "dig" at the "old mole"
(I.v.162).

   So much for Hamlet's "golden couplets," the fledgling poetry of
the self he has tried to "disclose." Ending his drama as he begins it,
with a play on words, he expires with "the rest is silence" (V.ii.347).
That gnomic phrase could mean that there is no afterlife, despite
Hamlet's earlier scruples; that "rest" is equivalent to silence; that
my rest is silence; or that the rest of my story is untold. All of these
ambiguities are true, or at least more true in their ambiguity than the
interpretations that so quickly falsify Hamlet's story. Horatio immediately invalidates the connection between rest and silence by in-
voking singing angels: "And flights of angels sing thee to thy rest!"
The noise of war, the "warlike volley" of drums and guns (V.ii.344),
drives out the silence utterly. We are back in the male world of ambitious sons advancing to their fathers' footsteps.

   The play ends in a mindless sequence of ritual male duties, roles
without meaning. The ambassador informs the court that the King's
"commandment is fulfilled/That Rosencrantz and Guildenstern are
dead." Staring at the dead bodies of the King, Queen, Hamlet, and
Laertes, he can think only of saying, "Where should we have our
thanks?" (V.ii.359-61). Horatio responds not with the story of Hamlet's struggle to keep the integrity of his "noble heart" (V.ii.348) but
with the narrative of Claudius' villainy, and perhaps of Hamlet's as
well:

                         So shall you hear
             Of carnal, bloody, and unnatural acts,

> Of accidental judgments, casual slaughters,
> Of deaths put on by cunning and forced cause,
> And, in this upshot, purposes mistook
> Fall'n on th'inventors' heads. All this can I
> Truly deliver.
>
> (V.ii.369-75)

This is the public story of an unnatural world, not the private record of a heart unspoken. It is a tale of deeds, not feelings. Yet it may be the story Hamlet knows will be told. After all, Horatio himself, "As th'art a man" (V.ii.331), is manfully following his duty to Hamlet's command, sacrificing his wish for suicide. A story born of duty must be a man's story.

All the women are dead, and there are no more womanly tears. Young "Strong-in-arm," who inherits an irrevocably corrupted world, is the arrogant, stupid, blundering finale to the theme of filial duty, to which both the Ghost and Claudius had demanded Hamlet's conformity. His tribute to Hamlet is cast in the rhetoric of a military command: "Let four captains/ Bear Hamlet like a soldier to the stage" (V.ii.384-85). Here Hamlet is finally "fit" to the alien mold of soldier in the stage world of the "captains." At the play's close, Fortinbras ludicrously undercuts Hamlet's final words:

> For he was likely, had he been put on,
> To have proved most royal; and for his passage
> The soldiers' music and the rites of war
> Speak loudly for him.
>
> (V.ii.386-89)

How right for this man without a touch of the female in him to have such confidence in "the rites of war" as confirmation of Hamlet's identity! We are back in the world of the first act, with a more ironic consciousness of what it means for Fortinbras to say, "had he been put on." A body politic cannot take off its clothes and venture, like Hamlet, "naked" and "alone" (IV.vii.50-51); it can only "put on" more roles. From the first anxious question of the guards to the last pointless order to "Go, bid the soldiers shoot," the military atmosphere pervades the language of the play.

Having learned how cruel one must be to be "kind" (I.ii.65), Hamlet puts on a "most royal" corruptedness (V.ii.387). He acts as the world does, speaks as the world speaks. Yet what a mockery it is, a self-mockery, to say of Fortinbras, "He has my dying voice" (V.ii.345). The illegitimate succession instituted by Claudius concludes with the triumph of the son against whom these fathers were at war. It is final proof of the interchangeability, in language and body, of all those in authority, whether enemy or friend. It is also the concluding irony of Hamlet's struggle for speech. His last soliloquy is a voice dying into accord with the senseless ambition and mindless "honor" of Fortinbras: "O, from this time forth,/My thoughts be bloody, or be nothing worth!" (IV. iv.65–66). But now that the guns "Speak loudly for him" (V.ii.389), Fortinbras pompously distinguishes between carnage in field and in court, as if Hamlet's death in battle would have been eminently acceptable: "Such a sight as this/Becomes the field, but here shows much amiss" (V.ii.390–91). Hamlet is right; Fortinbras does inherit his "dying voice," while the rest *is* silence. Just as the hawkish voices of blood, honor, and ambition inherit the world of the fathers, with its false roles and false proprieties, so Hamlet the dove joins Gertrude and Ophelia as a much-too-ravished bride of quietness.

Hamlet is not so much a full-throated tragedy as an ironic stifling of a hero's identity by structures of rule that no longer have legitimacy. It is the most frustrating of Shakespeare's plays precisely because it is the one most specifically about frustration. Shakespeare uses the opposition between male and female to denote the impossibility of speaking truly in a public role without violating or being violated. Too aware of paternal duplicity, Hamlet remains wordlessly modern in his excess of words, unable to center himself in a society whose "offence is rank" (III.iii.36) in every sense, and where the quest for self-knowledge is womanishly at odds with the manly roles he must put on. Even Ophelia only loved his mind. Hamlet's final assumption of a swordsman's identity is not a healthy solution to Oedipal conflicts but a mute submission to his father's command to "whet thy almost blunted purpose" (III. iv.112). The manly identity is imposed, not grown into. Hamlet delays revenging his father's death because his real struggle is to restore his mother's validation of his feelings, though "whore" is the only word available to him for his heartsick disgust. For Freudians to call Hamlet a mini-Claudius, to accept his male world's perspective of ambition and lust as sufficient motives, is to do what all the fathers want to do: explain Hamlet by their own divided selves. Perhaps even incest fantasies, as Laing tells us, may be defenses against the dread of being alone.[15]

What T. S. Eliot took for *Hamlet*'s failure, Shakespeare took for theme, as I have tried to show.[16] It *is* a play "dealing with the effects of a mother's guilt upon her son," not as sexuality but as identity itself. Hamlet's self-doubt is joined to Gertrude's insufficiency. Her "negative and insignificant" character "arouses in Hamlet the feeling which she is incapable of representing," Eliot rightly says, while the demand of his father for revenge calls Hamlet to a clear, though false, role.[17] But these are not flaws in the drama. They are flaws in the patriarchal order, which has cracked all the mirrors for self-confirmation. *Hamlet* succeeds so well, and has lasted so long, because it speaks so keenly to the dissociation of sensibility Eliot elsewhere describes.[18] Whether we call it role and self, reason and nature, mind and body, manly and womanly, or the language of power and the language of feeling, we recognize these dichotomies in our world and in ourselves. How poisonous rule o'ercrows every person's spirit (V.ii.342) is indeed the fundamental answer to "Who's there," as Eliot's critique implies. To pursue the question, Hamlet learns much too well, is not only to fail, but to participate in the collusion.

Notes

1. I am using the Pelican edition of *Hamlet*, ed. Willard Farnham (New York: Pelican Books, 1957). The 1605 edition's title is *The Tragicall Historie of Hamlet, Prince of Denmarke*. The epigraph is taken from John Dean, *Blind Ambition: The White House Years* (New York: Simon and Schuster, 1976), p. 47. I thank Domna Stanton, of *Signs: Journal of Women in Culture and Society*, where this essay first appeared (vol. 4, Winter 1978, pp. 291-308) for her thoughtful and attentive editorial work.

2. See Norman N. Holland, *Psychoanalysis and Shakespeare*, rev. ed. (1964; rpt. New York: Octagon Books, 1976), pp. 163-206, for various parricidal and matricidal interpretations. Erik Erikson discusses Hamlet's identity as delayed adolescent in "Youth: Fidelity and Diversity," *Daedalus*, 91 (1962), 5-27. Neil Friedman and Richard M. Jones develop further psychosocial perspectives, to which my essay is indebted, in "On the Mutuality of the Oedipus Complex: Notes on the Hamlet Case," *American Imago*, 20 (1963), 107-31. More recent psychoanalytic studies include Theodore Lidz, *Hamlet's Enemy: Madness and Myth in "Hamlet"* (New York: Basic Books, 1975), and Norman N. Holland, *"Hamlet*—My Greatest Creation," *Journal of the American Academy of Psychoanalysis*, 3 (1975), 419-27. Avi Erlich's *Hamlet's Absent Father* (Princeton, N.J.: Princeton Univ. Press, 1977) came to my attention after this essay was first drafted. It argues that Hamlet unconsciously fears his mother and needs his father, a conclusion directly opposed to mine. Though Erlich's book has many useful insights, psychoanalytic theory leads him to mistake a wishful male fantasy for interpersonal reality.

3. See Harry Stack Sullivan, *The Interpersonal Theory of Psychiatry* (New York: W. W. Norton, 1953); R. D. Laing, *The Divided Self: An Existential Study in Sanity and Madness* (London: Tavistock Press, 1960); D. W. Winnicott, "Mirror-Role of Mother and Family in Child Development," in *The Predicament of the Family*, ed. P. Lomas (London: Hogarth Press, 1967), pp. 26-33; and D. W. Winnicott, *The Maturational Processes and the Facilitating Environment* (New York: International Univ. Press, 1965). I recognize that the interpersonal approach is in some ways tangential to the major post-Freudian development in psychoanalysis, the British object-relations school. Nevertheless, I believe it is more useful for literary criticism. A quasi-Laingian study of Shakespeare is Terence Eagleton's *Shakespeare and Society: Critical Essays on Shakespearean Drama* (New York: Schocken Books, 1971).

4. Laing, *Divided Self*, p. 95. Laing's dismissal of Ophelia's statements as "incomprehensible" is odd, given his extraordinary sensitivity to the meanings in schizophrenic voices.

5. See Winnicott, "Mirror-Role," pp. 26-33.

6. Ernest Jones, *Hamlet and Oedipus* (London: Victor Gollancz Press, 1949), pp. 86-87, sees "repulsion against woman" as coming from repressed sexual feelings and a "splitting of the mother image"; he connects Hamlet's diatribes against women to unconscious fear of incest wishes. Avi Erlich, in *Hamlet's Absent Father*, explores pre-oedipal dynamics more thoroughly.

7. See Roy Walker, "*Hamlet*: The Opening Scene," in *The Time is Out of Joint* (Folcroft, Pa.: Folcroft Library Editions, 1948), reprinted in *Shakespeare: Modern Essays in Criticism*, ed. Leonard F. Dean (New York: Peter Smith, 1961), pp. 216-21. For broader commentaries on the play's "interrogative mood," see also Maynard Mack, "The World of Hamlet," *The Yale Review*, 41 (1952), 502-23, widely reprinted; Harry Levin, *The Question of Hamlet* (New York: Oxford Univ. Press, 1959); and Bernard McElroy, *Shakespeare's Mature Tragedies* (Princeton, N.J.: Princeton Univ. Press, 1973), pp. 29-88.

8. Laing defines "collusion" as a process by which members of an intimate group, such as the family, conspire knowingly or unknowingly to validate one member's "false self," that self which conforms to other people's expectations. Eagleton's *Shakespeare and Society* analyzes how various false unities in *Hamlet* force the hero's subjectivity into being manipulated as an object.

9. See R. D. Laing, *Knots* (London: Tavistock Press, 1970). This is an extension of Gregory Bateson's "double bind" theory; see G. Bateson et al., "Toward a Theory of Schizophrenia," *Behavioural Science*, 1 (1956), 251-64.

10. Harold C. Goddard, in *The Meaning of Shakespeare* (Chicago: Univ. of Chicago Press, 1951), vol. 1, develops an interpretation along parallel lines, with the Ghost as devil imposing a "divided mind" on Hamlet. Goddard's reading is finally a Christian one, arguing that Art, or the play within the play, could have converted Claudius to repentance if Hamlet's uncontrollable vengefulness had not intervened. Another Christian reader sensitive to the Ghost's duplicity is Eleanor Prosser, in *Hamlet and Revenge* (Stanford, Calif.: Stanford Univ. Press, 1967). Christian readings, like too many Freudian readings, tend to substitute the false answer of duty for the real question of identity.

11. The Ghost has occasioned immense controversy. Of those who see the Ghost as other than benign, see above, and also Richard Flatter, *Hamlet's Father* (New Haven, Conn.: Yale Univ. Press, 1949); G. Wilson Knight, *The Wheel of Fire*, 2nd ed. (London: Methuen, 1965); and J. Dover Wilson, *What Happens in Hamlet* (Cambridge: At the Univ. Press, 1967). Most critics see the Ghost as the good father to whom Hamlet should submit. In *Fools of Time: Studies in Shakespearean Tragedy* (Toronto: Univ. of Toronto Press, 1967), p. 80, Northrop Frye concludes that "God's main interest, in Elizabethan tragedy, is in promoting the revenge, and in making it as bloody as possible." For a Jungian view, which superficially resembles my own in its prescription for men to encounter the woman in themselves, see Alex Aronson, *Psyche and Symbol in Shakespeare* (Bloomington, Ind.: Indiana Univ. Press, 1972). In Aronson's view, the Ghost is Hamlet's dramatized unconsciousness, as Hamlet tries to free himself from "his entanglement with a Hecate-like Magna Mater" (p. 235).

12. R. D. Laing and Aaron Esterson, *Sanity, Madness, and the Family* (London: Tavistock Press, 1964). Esterson expanded one chapter into *The Leaves of Spring: A Study in the Dialectics of Madness* (London: Tavistock Press, 1970).

13. See Harry Morris, "Ophelia's 'Bonny Sweet Robin,'"*PMLA*, 73 (1958), 601–03; also see Carroll Camden, "On Ophelia's Madness," *Shakespeare Quarterly*, 15 (1964), 247-55; and Maurice Charney, *Style in Hamlet* (Princeton N.J.: Princeton Univ. Press, 1969), pp. 107-12.

14. There is near-unanimous critical agreement, except for Goddard, that the last act promotes integration. See Mack, pp. 518-23; McElroy, pp. 85–86; Harold Fisch, *Hamlet and the Word: The Covenant Pattern in Shakespeare* (New York: Ungar, 1971), pp. 85-86; Irving Ribner, *Patterns in Shakespearian Tragedy* (London: Methuen, 1960); Wilson, p. 272; and Michael Goldman, *Shakespeare and the Energies of Drama* (Princeton, N.J.: Princeton Univ. Press, 1972). Goldman goes so far as to say, "The play ends with a final unambiguous discharge of energy," and the gunshots prove that "the air has been cleared" (p. 90). Reuben Brower's more sensitive reading, in *Hero and Saint: Shakespeare and the Graeco-Roman Heroic Tradition* (New York: Oxford Univ. Press, 1971), finds the tension between soldier hero and moral hero reduced to soldier in the end. For a stronger dissent from the consensus, see L. C. Knights, *Some Shakespearean Themes and an Approach to "Hamlet"* (Stanford, Calif.: Stanford Univ. Press, 1966), who finds Hamlet engulfed by evil and the cause of further evil. T. McAlindon, in *Shakespeare and Decorum* (New York: Barnes and Noble, 1973), p. 67, notes that Fortinbras is just "a crude strong-arm," and Frye (pp. 29-30) sees Hamlet as selfish to the end. Lidz's *Hamlet's Enemy* (see n. 2 above) reflects the characteristic adaptive bias of lesser Freudians by discussing the play as a ritual reestablishing appropriate social defenses; he sees Fortinbras as a "direct and uncomplicated hero" who "brings hope for the rebirth of the nation" (p. 112).

15. Laing, *Divided Self*, p. 57. Laing's system suffers from its romanticization of "true self" as aloneness rather than the positive interdependence taught by Winnicott. For a psychoanalytic critique of Laing, see David Holbrook, "R. D. Laing and the Death Circuit," *Encounter*, 31 (1968), 35-45. In *Shakespeare and Society*, Eagleton offers a similar critique of Hamlet himself: "Hamlet's insistence on not being a puppet leads, finally, to a delight in resisting any kind of definition; it becomes, in fact, socially irresponsible, a merely negative response" (p. 61). My own sense is that Hamlet looks to women rather than to men for self-definition and that structures of male rule induce his negation.

16. T. S. Eliot, "Hamlet" (1919), reprinted in *Selected Essays*, 3rd ed. (London: Faber and Faber, 1951), pp. 141-46. In *The Tiger's Heart: Eight Essays on Shakespeare* (New York: Oxford Univ. Press, 1970), p. 76, Herbert Howarth finds Eliot mistaken because the play is about "the helplessness of what is gentle before the onrush of what is rank," a nice formulation. Richard A. Lanham's *The Motives of Eloquence: Literary Rhetoric in the Renaissance* (New Haven, Conn.: Yale Univ. Press, 1976), pp. 129-43, concludes that *Hamlet* is two plays with "two kinds of self," revenger and self-conscious actor looking for the "big scene." Charney's *Style in Hamlet* says Hamlet responds to his world with four styles: self-consciously parodic, witty, passionate, and simple. In my interpretation, the clash Lanham sees between the role-playing "rhetoric" self and the "serious" revenger self mirrors Hamlet's role-inducing world, with no mirror for the real self. In some respects Eliot is right to question Gertrude as an "objective correlative"; she is so much more constant in Hamlet's hopes than in her weak, sensual actuality that she raises the question of whether the woman in *Hamlet* is only in Hamlet.

17. Eliot, "Hamlet," p. 146.

18. Eliot, "The Metaphysical Poets" (1921), reprinted in *Selected Essays*, pp. 281-91.

7 ☼ "Anger's My Meat": Feeding, Dependency, and Aggression in *Coriolanus*

Janet Adelman

Coriolanus was written during a period of rising corn prices and the accompanying fear of famine; rising prices reached a climax in 1608. In May 1607, "a great number of common persons"—up to five thousand, Stow tells us in his *Annales*—assembled in various Midlands counties, including Shakespeare's own county of Warwickshire, to protest the acceleration of enclosures and the resulting food shortages.[1] It must have been disturbing to property owners to hear that the rioters were well-received by local inhabitants, who brought them food and shovels[2] — doubly disturbing if they were aware that this was one of England's first purely popular riots, unlike the riots of the preceding century in that the anger of the common people was not being manipulated by rebellious aristocrats or religious factions.[3] The poor rioters were quickly dispersed, but—if *Coriolanus* is any indication—the fears that they aroused were not. In fact, Shakespeare shapes his material from the start in order to exacerbate these fears in his audience. In Plutarch the people riot because the Senate refuses to control usury; in Shakespeare they riot because they are hungry. Furthermore, the relentlessly vertical imagery of the play reflects the specific threat posed by this contemporary uprising: in a society so hierarchical—that is, so vertical—as theirs, the rioters' threat to level enclosures implied more than the casting down of particular hedges; it seemed to promise a flattening of the whole society.[4] Nor is Shakespeare's exacerbation of these fears merely a dramatist's trick to catch the attention of his audience from the start, or a seventeenth-century nod toward political relevance. For the dominant issues of the uprising—the threat of starvation and the

This chapter first appeared in *Shakespeare: Pattern of Excelling Nature*, ed. David Bevington and Jay L. Halio (Cranbury, N.J.: Associated Univ. Presses, 1978). Reprinted by permission.

consequent attempt to level enclosures—are reflected in not only the political but also the intrapsychic world of *Coriolanus*; taken together, they suggest the concerns that shape the play and particularly the progress of its hero.

The uprising of the people at the start of the play points us toward an underlying fantasy in which political and psychological fears come together in a way that makes each more intense and hence more threatening. For the political leveling promised by the contemporary uprising takes on overtones of sexual threat early in Shakespeare's play:[5] the rising of the people becomes suggestively phallic; and the fear of leveling becomes ultimately a fear of losing one's potency in all spheres. In Menenius' belly fable, the people are "th'discontented members, the mutinous parts," and "the mutinous members" (I.i.110, 148).[6] An audience for which the mutiny of the specifically sexual member was traditionally one of the signs of the Fall, and for which the crowd was traditionally associated with dangerous passion, would be prone to hear in Menenius' characterization a reference to a part other than the great toe (I.i.154). In this initial fantasy, the hitherto docile sons suddenly threaten to rise up against their fathers, the Senators (I.i.76); and it is characteristic of *Coriolanus* that the contested issue in this oedipal rebellion is food.[7] The uprising of the crowd is in fact presented in terms that suggest the transformation of hunger into phallic aggression, a transformation that is, as I shall later argue, central to the character of Coriolanus himself: when the first citizen tells Menenius, "They say poor suitors have strong breaths: they shall know we have strong arms too" (I.i.58-60), his image of importunate mouths suddenly armed in rebellion suggests the source of Coriolanus' rebellion no less than his own.

If the specter of a multitude of hungry mouths, ready to rise and demand their own, is the exciting cause of *Coriolanus*, the image of the mother who has not fed her children enough is at its center. One does not need the help of a psychoanalytic approach to notice that Volumnia is not a nourishing mother. Her attitude toward food is nicely summed up when she rejects Menenius' invitation to a consolatory dinner after Coriolanus' banishment: "Anger's my meat: I sup upon myself/ And so shall starve with feeding" (IV.ii.50-51). We might suspect her of having been as niggardly in providing food for her son as she is for herself, or rather suspect her of insisting that he too be self-sufficient, that he feed only on his own anger; and indeed, he is apparently fed only valiantness by her ("Thy valiantness was mine, thou suck'st it from me" [III.ii.129]). He certainly has not been fed the milk of human kindness: when Menenius later tells us that "there is no more mercy in him than there is milk in a male tiger" (V.iv.28-29), he seems to associate Coriolanus' lack of humanity not only with the absence of any nurturing female element in him but also with the absence of mother's milk itself.[8] Volumnia takes some pride in the creation of her son, and when we first meet her, she tells us exactly how she's done it: by sending him to a cruel war at an age when a mother should not be willing to allow a son out of the protective maternal circle for an hour (I.iii.5–15). She elaborates her creation as she imagines herself mother to twelve sons and then kills all but one of them off: "I had rather had eleven die nobly for their country, than one voluptuously surfeit out of action" (I.iii.24–25). To be noble is to die; to live is to be ignoble and to eat too much.[9] If you are Volumnia's son, the choice is clear.

But the most telling—certainly the most disturbing—revelation of Volumnia's attitude toward feeding comes some twenty lines later, when she is encouraging Virgilia to share her own glee in the thought of Coriolanus' wounds: "The breasts of Hecuba/When she did suckle Hector, look'd not lovelier/Than Hector's forehead when it spit forth blood/At Grecian sword contemning" (I.iii.40–43). Blood is more beautiful than milk, the wound than the breast, warfare than peaceful feeding. But this image is more disturbing than these easy comparatives suggest. It does not bode well for Coriolanus that the heroic Hector doesn't stand a chance in Volumnia's imagination: he is transformed immediately from infantile feeding mouth to bleeding wound. For the unspoken mediator between breast and wound is the infant's mouth: in this imagistic transformation, to feed is to be wounded; the mouth becomes the wound, the breast the sword. The metaphoric process suggests the psychological fact that is, I think, at the center of the play: the taking in of food is the primary acknowledgment of one's dependence on the world, and as such, it is the primary token of one's vulnerability. But at the same time as Volumnia's image suggests the vulnerability inherent in feeding, it also suggests a way to fend off that vulnerability. In her image, feeding, incorporating, is transformed into spitting out, an aggressive expelling; the wound once again becomes the mouth that spits "forth blood/At Grecian sword contemning." The wound spitting blood thus becomes not a sign of vulnerability but an instrument of attack.

Volumnia's attitudes toward feeding and dependence are echoed perfectly in her son. Coriolanus persistently regards food as poisonous (I.i.177–78, III.i.155–56); the only thing he can imagine nourishing is rebellion (III.i.68–69, 116). Among the patricians, only Menenius is associated with the ordinary consumption of food and wine without an allaying drop of Tiber in it, and his distance from Coriolanus can be measured partly by his pathetic conviction that Coriolanus will be malleable—that he will have a "suppler" soul (V.i.55)—after he has had a full meal. But for Coriolanus, as for his mother, nobility consists precisely in *not* eating: he twice imagines starving himself honorably to death before asking for food, or anything else, from the plebians (II.iii. 112-13; III.iii.89-91).[10]

Coriolanus incorporates not only his mother's attitude toward food but also the transformations in mode implicit in her image of Hector. These transformations—from feeding to warfare, from vulnerability to aggressive attack, from incorporation to spitting out—are at the center of Coriolanus' character and of our responses to him: for the whole of his masculine identity depends on his transformation of his vulnerability into an instrument of attack, as Menenius suggests when he tells us that each of Coriolanus' wounds "was an enemy's grave" (II.i.154-55). Cominius reports that Coriolanus entered his first battle a sexually indefinite thing, a boy or Amazon (II.ii.91), and found his manhood there: "When he might act the woman in the scene,/He prov'd best man i'th'field" (II.ii.96-97). The rigid masculinity that Coriolanus finds in war becomes a defense against acknowledgment of his neediness; he nearly succeeds in transforming himself from a vulnerable human creature into a grotesquely invulnerable and isolated thing. His body becomes his armor (I.iii.35, I.iv.24); he himself becomes a weapon "who sensibly outdares his senseless sword,/And when it bows, stand'st up (I.iv.53-54), or he becomes the sword itself: "O me alone! Make you a sword of me!" (I.vi.76). His whole life becomes a kind of phallic exhibitionism, devoted to disproving the possibility that he is vulnerable.[11] In the transformation from oral neediness to phallic aggression, anger becomes his meat as well as his mother's; Volumnia's phrase suggests not only his mode of defending himself against vulnerability but also the source of his anger in the deprivation imposed by his mother. We see the quality of his hunger and its transformation into aggression when, after his expulsion from Rome, he tells Aufidius, "I have . . ./Drawn tuns of blood out of thy country's breast" (IV.v.99-100). Fighting here, as elsewhere in the play, is a poorly concealed substitute for feeding (see, for example, I.ix.10-11; IV.v.191-94, 222-24); and the unsatisfied ravenous attack of the infant on the breast provides the motive force for warfare. The image allows us to understand the ease with which Coriolanus turns his rage toward his own feeding mother, Rome.[12]

Thrust prematurely from dependence on his mother, forced to feed himself on his own anger, Coriolanus refuses to acknowledge any neediness or dependency: for his entire sense of himself depends on his being able to see himself as a self-sufficient creature. The desperation behind his claim to self-sufficiency is revealed by his horror of praise, even the praise of his general.[13] The dependence of his masculinity on warfare in fact makes praise (or flattery, as he must call it) particularly threatening to him on the battlefield: flattery there, where his independence has apparently been triumphant, would imply that he has acted partly to win praise, that he is not self-sufficient after all; it would ultimately imply the undoing of his triumphant masculinity, and the soldier's steel would grow "soft as the parasite's silk" (I.ix.45). The juxtaposition of soldier's steel and parasite's soft silk suggests both Coriolanus' dilemma and his solution to it: in order to avoid being the soft, dependent, feeding parasite, he has to maintain his rigidity as soldier's steel; that rigidity would be threatened were he to be "dieted/In praises sauc'd with lies" (I.ix.51–52). (The same fears that underlie Coriolanus' use of this image here are brought home to him by Aufidius' charges at the end of the play: that he broke "his oath and resolution, like/A twist of rotten silk" [V.vi.95–96]; that he "whin'd and roar'd away" the victory [V.vi. 98]; that he is a "boy of tears" [V.vi.101].)

The complex of ideas that determines Coriolanus' response to praise also determines the rigidity that makes him so disastrous as a political figure. As he contemptuously asks the people for their voices and later gives up his attempt to pacify them, the language in which he imagines his alternatives reveals the extent to which his unwillingness to ask for the people's approval, like his abhorrence of praise, depends on his attitude toward food: "Better it is to die, better to starve,/Than crave the hire which first we do deserve" (II.iii.112–13); "Pent to linger/But with a grain a day, I would not buy/Their mercy at the price of one fair word" (III.iii.89–91). Asking, craving, flattering with fair words are here not only preconditions but also equivalents of eating: to refuse to ask is to starve; but starvation is preferable to asking because asking, like eating, is an acknowledgment of one's weakness, one's dependence on the outside world. "The price is, to ask it kindly" (II.iii.75), but that is the one price Coriolanus cannot pay. When he must face the prospect of revealing his dependence on the populace by asking for their favor, his whole delicately constructed masculine identity threatens to crumble. In order to ask, a harlot's spirit must possess him; his voice must become as small as that of a eunuch or a virgin minding babies; a beggar's tongue must make motion through his lips (III.ii.111–18). Asking, then, like susceptibility to praise, would undo the process by which he was transformed on the battlefield from boy or woman to man. That he imagines this undoing as a kind of reverse voice change suggests the extent to which his phallic aggressive pose is a defense against collapse into the dependent oral mode of the small boy. And in fact, Coriolanus' own use of language constantly reiterates this defense. Instead of using those linguistic modes that acknowledge dependence, Coriolanus spits out words, using them as weapons. His invective is in the mode of Hector's wound, aggressively spitting forth blood: it is an attempt to deny vulnerability by making the very area of vulnerability into the means of attack.[14]

Coriolanus' abhorrence of praise and flattery, his horror lest the people think that he got his wounds to please them (II.ii.147–50), his insistence that he be given the consulship as a sign of what he is, not as a reward (I.ix.26), his refusal to ask—all are attempts to claim that he is *sui generis*. This attitude finds its logical conclusion in his desperate cry as he sees his mother approaching him at the end:

> I'll never
> Be such a gosling to obey instinct, but stand
> As if a man were author of himself
> And knew no other kin.
>
> (V.iii.34–37)

The gosling obeys instinct and acknowledges his kinship with mankind; but Coriolanus will attempt to stand alone. (Since his manhood depends exactly on this phallic standing alone, he is particularly susceptible to Aufidius' taunt of "boy" after he has been such a gosling as to obey instinct.) The relationship between Coriolanus' aggressive pose and his attempts to claim that he is *sui generis* is most dramatically realized in the conquest of Corioli; it is here that Coriolanus most nearly realizes his fantasy of standing as if a man were author of himself. For the scene at Corioli represents a glorious transformation of the nightmare of oral vulnerability ("to th'pot" [I.iv.47], one of his soldiers says as he is swallowed up by the gates) into a phallic adventure that both assures and demonstrates his independence. Coriolanus' battlecry as he storms the gates sexualizes the scene: "Come on;/If you'll stand fast, we'll beat them to their wives" (I.iv.40–41). But the dramatic action itself presents the conquest of Corioli as an image not of rape but of triumphant rebirth: after Coriolanus enters the gates of the city, he is proclaimed dead; one of his comrades delivers a eulogy firmly in the past tense ("Thou wast a soldier/Even to Cato's wish" [I.iv.55–56]); then Coriolanus miraculously reemerges, covered with blood (I.v.22), and is given a new name. For the assault on Corioli is both a rape and a rebirth: the underlying fantasy is that intercourse is a literal return to the womb, from which one is reborn, one's own author.[15] The fantasy of self-authorship is complete when Coriolanus is given his new name, earned by his own actions.[16]

But despite the boast implicit in his conquest of Corioli, Coriolanus has not in fact succeeded in separating himself from his mother;[17] even the very role through which he claims independence was designed by her—as she never tires of pointing out ("My praises made thee first a soldier" [III.ii.108]; "Thou art my warrior:/I holp to frame thee" [V.III.62–63].) In fact, Shakespeare underlines Volumnia's point by the placement of two central scenes. In I.iii, before we have seen Coriolanus himself as a soldier, we see Volumnia first describe her image of her son on the battlefield and then enact his role: "Methinks I see him stamp thus, and call thus:/'Come on you cowards, you were got in fear/Though you were born in Rome'" (I.iii.32–34). This marvelous moment suggests not only the ways in which Volumnia herself lives through her son, but also the extent to which his role is her creation. For when we see him in the next scene, acting exactly as his mother had predicted, we are left with the impression that he is merely enacting her enactment of the role that she has imagined for him.

That Coriolanus is acting under Volumnia's direction even in the role that seems to ensure his independence of her helps to explain both his bafflement when she suddenly starts to disapprove of the role she has created ("I muse my mother/Does not approve me further" [III.ii.7–8]) and his eventual capitulation to her demand that he shift roles, here and at the end of the play. For his manhood is secure only when he can play the role that she has designed, and play it with her approval.[18] He asks her, "Why did you wish me milder? Would you have me/False to my nature? Rather say I play/The man I am" (III.ii.14–16). But "I play the man I am" cuts both ways: in his bafflement, Coriolanus would like to suggest that there is no distance between role and self, but he in fact suggests that he plays at being himself, that his manhood is merely a role. Given that Volumnia has created this dilemma, her answer is unnecessarily cruel, but telling: "You might have been enough the man you are,/With striving less to be so" (III.ii.19–20). Volumnia is right: it is the intensity and rigidity of Coriolanus' commitment to his masculine role that makes us suspect the intensity of the fears that this role is designed to hide, especially from himself. For the rigidity of the role and the tenuousness of the self that it protects combine to make acknowledged play acting of any kind terrifying for Coriolanus, as though he can maintain the identity of self and role, and hence his integrity, only by denying that he is able to assume a role. Because he cannot acknowledge the possibility of role playing, Coriolanus must respond to his mother's request that he act a new role as a request that he be someone other than Coriolanus. When he finally agrees to take on the role of humble supplicant, he is sure that he will act badly (III.ii.105–06) and that he will lose his manhood in the process (III.ii.111–23).

The fragility of the entire structure by which Coriolanus maintains his claim to self-sufficient manhood helps to account for the violence of his hatred of the plebians. For Coriolanus uses the crowd to bolster his own identity: he accuses them of being exactly what he wishes not to be.[19] He does his best to distinguish himself from them by emphasizing his aloneness and their status as multitude as the very grounds of their being.[20] Throughout, he associates his manhood with his isolation, so that "Alone I did it" becomes a sufficient answer to Aufidius' charge that he is a boy. Hence the very status of the plebians as crowd reassures him that they are not men but dependent and unmanly things, merely children—a point of view that Menenius seems to confirm when he tells the tribunes: "Your abilities are too infant-like for doing much alone" (II.i.36-37). His most potent image of the crowd is as an appropriately infantile common mouth (III.i.22, 155) disgustingly willing to exhibit its neediness. Coriolanus enters the play identified by the plebians as the person who is keeping them from eating (I.i.9-10); indeed, one of his main complaints about the plebians is that they say they are hungry (I.i.204-07).[21] Coriolanus himself has been deprived of food, and he seems to find it outrageous that others should not be. His position here is like that of the older brother who has fought his way into manhood and who is now confronted by an apparently endless group of siblings—"my sworn brother the people" (II.iii.95), he calls them—who still insist on being fed by mother Rome,[22] and whose insistence on their dependency threatens the pose of self-sufficiency by which his equilibrium is perilously maintained. To disclaim his own hunger, Coriolanus must therefore disclaim his kinship with the crowd: "I would they were barbarians—as they are,/. . . not Romans—as they are not" (III.i.236-37). But the formulation of the disclaimer itself reveals the very tensions that it is designed to assuage. Insofar as he wishes the people non-Roman, he acknowledges their Romanness; but this acknowledgment of kinship must immediately be denied by the assertion that they are in fact not Roman. The very insistence on difference reveals the fear of likeness.

But the multitudinous mouth of the crowd is horrifying to Coriolanus, not only insofar as it threatens to reveal his own oral neediness to him, but also insofar as it makes the nature of his vulnerability uncomfortably precise. In this hungry world, everyone seems in danger of being eaten. The crowd suspects the senators of cannibalistic intentions: "If the wars eat us not up, they will; and there's all the love they bear us" (I.i.84-85). Since Coriolanus twice dismisses them as ignoble food ("quarry" [I.i.197]; "fragments" [I.i.221]), their fears seem not entirely without basis. But Coriolanus thinks that, without the awe of the Senate, the crowd would "feed on one another" (I.i.187). Given their choice, the tribunes would naturally enough prefer that the "present wars devour" Coriolanus (I.i.257) instead of the populace. The people's belief that the death of Coriolanus would allow them to have corn at their own price (I.i.9) is eventually sustained by the plot, insofar as Coriolanus opposes the giving of corn gratis (III.i.113-17). But at the start of the play, we are not in a position to understand the logic behind their association between killing Coriolanus and an unlimited food supply; and in the context of all the cannibalistic images, the mysterious association seems to point toward a fantasy in which the people, rather than the wars, will devour Coriolanus.[23] Menenius explicates this fantasy:

> *Men.* Pray you, who does the wolf love?
> *Sic.* The lamb.
> *Men.* Ay, to devour him, as the hungry plebeians
>   would the noble Martius.
>
> (II.i.6–9)

And in the third act, as the people begin to find their teeth and rise against Coriolanus, his images of them as mouths begin to reveal not only his contempt for their hunger but also his fear of his own oral vulnerability, fear of being bitten, digested, pecked at: "You being their mouths, why rule you not their teeth?" (III.i.35); "How shall this bosom multiplied digest/The senate's courtesy?" (III.i.130–31); "Thus we debase/The nature of our seats, . . ./. . . and bring in/The crows to peck the eagles" (III.i.134–38). The fear of being eaten that lies just below the surface in these images is made explicit when Coriolanus tells Aufidius that the people have "devour'd" all of him but his name (IV.v.77).

The crowd, then, is both dependent, unmanly, contemptible—and terrifyingly ready to rise up and devour Coriolanus. Through his portrayal of the crowd, Coriolanus can manage to dismiss the specter of his own hunger and insist on his identity as an isolated and inviolable thing ("a thing/Made by some other deity than nature" [IV.vi.91–92], as Cominius says). But he cannot dismiss the danger that exposure to their hunger would bring. His absolute horror at the prospect of showing his wounds to win the consulship depends partly, I think, on the complex of ideas that stands behind his characterization of the crowd. In Plutarch, Coriolanus shows his wounds; in Shakespeare, the thought is intolerable to him and, despite many promises that he will, he never does. For the display of his wounds would reveal his kinship with the plebeians in several ways: by revealing that he has worked for hire (II.ii.149) as they have (that is, that he and his deeds are not *sui generis* after all); by revealing that he is vulnerable, as they are; and by revealing, through the persistent identification of wound and mouth,[24] that he too has a mouth, that he is a dependent creature. Moreover, the exhibition of his wounds to the crowd is impossible for Coriolanus partly because his identity is sustained by exhibitionism of another sort. Coriolanus is right in believing that he must not "stand naked" (II.ii.137) before the crowd, asking for their approval; for this standing naked would reverse the sustaining fantasy by which he hoped to "stand/As if a man were author of himself" (V.iii.35–36). For the phallic exhibitionism of Coriolanus' life as a soldier has been designed to deny the possibility of kinship with the crowd; it has served to reassure him of his potency and his aggressive independence, and therefore to sustain him against fears of collapse into the dependent mode of infancy. To exhibit the fruits of his soldiership as the emblems not of his self-sufficiency but of his vulnerability and dependence, and to exhibit them precisely to those whose kinship he would most like to deny, would transform his chief means of defense into a proclamation of his weakness: it would threaten to undo the very structure by which he lives. And finally, insofar as he would expose himself as vulnerable and dependent by displaying his wounds, he would invite the oral rage of the crowd to satisfy itself on him. "If he show us his wounds and tell us his deeds, we are to put our tongues into those wounds and speak for them" (II.iii.5–8), the Third Citizen says; his grotesque image suggests that the sweet licked by the multitudinous tongue (III.i.155–56) would be "sweet" Coriolanus himself (III.ii.107).[25]

During the first part of the play, Coriolanus uses his opposition to the crowd to define himself and to fend off his vulnerability. But after the exile from Rome, this source of definition fails, and Coriolanus turns toward his old enemy Aufidius to confirm himself. For if Coriolanus has throughout defined himself by opposition, he has defined himself by likeness as well: from the beginning, we have watched him create a mirror image of himself in Aufidius. As soon as he hears that the Volsces are in arms, Coriolanus announces the terms of his relationship with Aufidius: "I sin in envying his nobility;/And were I anything but what I am,/I would wish me only he" (I.i.229–31). But the noble Aufidius is Coriolanus' own invention, a reflection of his own doubts about what he is, an expression of what he would wish himself to be. Shakespeare takes pains to emphasize the distance between the Aufidius we see and the Aufidius of Coriolanus' imagination. The Aufidius invented by Coriolanus seems designed to reassure Coriolanus of the reality of his own male grandeur by giving him the image of himself; his need to create a man who is his equal is in fact one of the most poignant elements in the play and helps to account for his tragic blindness to his rival's true nature as opportunist and schemer. Immediately after Coriolanus has imagined himself Aufidius, he allows us to see the extent to which he is dependent on Aufidius for his self-definition in a nearly prophetic confession: "Were half to half the world by th' ears, and he/Upon my party, I'd revolt to make/Only my wars with him" (I.i.232–34). Later, the Coriolanus who shrinks violently from the praise of others eagerly solicits news of Aufidius' opinion of him; and his oddly touching "Spoke he of me?" (III.i.12) reveals the extent to

which he needs to see himself in Aufidius' eyes.[26] As he approaches
Antium after the exile, he pauses to reflect on the strangeness of his
actions but succeeds only in suggesting that the issue driving him from
Rome and toward Aufidius is a "trick not worth an egg" (IV.iv.21), as
though for the moment the fact of his union with Aufidius is more
important than the circumstances that drove him to it. His attempt to
explain his actions begins and ends with the image of friends "who
twin, as 'twere, in love/Unseparable" (IV.iv.15-16), who "interjoin
their issues" (IV.iv.22). The movement of this soliloquy reveals the
fantasy of twinship underlying his relationship with Aufidius both as
foe and as friend.

The union with Aufidius is for Coriolanus a union with an alter ego;
it represents a flight from the world of Rome and his mother toward a
safe male world. Devoured in all but name by Rome (IV.v.77), Coriolanus enters Antium afraid of being eaten: he fears that the Volscian
wives will slay him with spits (IV.iv.5) and tells the Third Servingman
that he has dwelt "i'th'city of kites and crows" (IV.v.43), a city of
scavengers. (That this city is both the wilderness and Rome itself is
suggested by Coriolanus's echo of his earlier peril, the crows who will
peck the eagles [III.i.138].) Here, far from Rome, Coriolanus at last
allows his hunger and his vulnerability to be felt, and he is given food.
He presents himself to Aufidius during a great feast, from which he is
initially excluded: "The feast smells well, but I/Appear not like a
guest" (IV.v.5-6). But here in Antium, the play moves toward a fantasy
in which nourishment may be safely taken because it is given by a male,
by a father-brother-twin rather than a mother. Coriolanus is finally
taken into the feast. In the safe haven provided by his mirror image, he
will not be devoured; instead, he will eat. Aufidius' servants give us the
final development of this fantasy:

> *First Servant.* . . . Before Corioles he scotched him
>   and notched him like a carbonado.
> *Second Servant.* And had he been cannibally given,
>   he might have broiled and eaten him too.

(IV.v.191-94)

The scene moves, then, from hunger and the fear of being eaten to an
image of Coriolanus triumphantly eating Aufidius. Since his mother will
not feed him, Coriolanus will find in Aufidius the only nourishment
that can sustain him; and insofar as Aufidius is his alter ego, he, like his
mother, will sup on himself.

When Coriolanus is banished from Rome, he responds with an infantile fantasy of omnipotent control: "I banish you!" (III.iii.123). He
then attempts to ensure the reality of his omnipotence by wishing on
his enemies exactly what he already knows to be true of them: "Let

every feeble rumour shake your hearts!/. . . Have the power still/To banish your defenders" (III.iii.125-28). Few curses have ever been so sure of instantaneous fulfillment. Having thus exercised his rage and assured himself of the magical power of his invective, Coriolanus finally makes his claim to true independence: "There is a world elsewhere!" (III.iii.135). His encounter with Aufidius is an attempt to create this world, one in his own image; but even the union with Aufidius leads ultimately back to Rome and his mother. For Coriolanus' rage, like his hunger, is properly directed toward his mother; though it is deflected from her and toward the plebeians and Volscians for much of the play, it finally returns to its source. For Rome and his mother are finally one.[27] In exiling Coriolanus, Rome reenacts the role of the mother who cast him out. Although in his loving farewell, his family and friends are wholly distinguished from the beast with many heads, by the time he has returned to Rome they are no more than a poor grain or two that must be consumed in the general fire (V.i.27). (Even in his loving farewell we hear a note of resentment when he consoles his mother by telling her: "My hazards still have been your solace" [IV.i.28].) As he approaches Rome, the devouring populace becomes indistinguishable from his loving mother. But Menenius has already pointed toward the fantasy that identifies them:

> Now the good gods forbid
> That our renowned Rome, whose gratitude
> Towards her deserved children is enroll'd
> In Jove's own book, like an unnatural dam
> Should now eat up her own!

(III.i.287-91)

The cannibalistic mother who denies food and yet feeds on the victories of her sweet son stands at the darkest center of the play, where Coriolanus' oral vulnerability is fully defined. Here, talion law reigns: the feeding infant himself will be devoured; the loving mother becomes the devourer. In this dark world, love itself is primitive and dangerous: both the First Citizen and Menenius suggest that here to be loved is to be eaten (I.i.84-85; II.i.6-9).

Coriolanus' return to Rome is not ultimately a return to his mother; it is rather a last attempt to escape her love and its consequences. If Coriolanus can make himself a new name, forged in the fires of burning Rome (V.i.14-15), he can construct a new identity independent of his mother: an identity that will demonstrate his indifference to her, his separation from her. For he can stand as author of himself only by destroying his mother. The return to Rome is an act of retaliation against the mother on whom he has been dependent, the mother who has cast him out. But it is at the same time an acting out of the child's fantasy of reversing the roles of parent and child, so that the life of the parent is in the hands of the omnipotent child. The child becomes a god, dispensing life and death (V.iv.24-25): becomes in effect the author of his mother, so that he can finally stand alone.

But Coriolanus can sustain neither his fantasy of self-authorship nor his attempt to realize a godlike omnipotent power. And the failure of both leaves him so unprotected, so utterly devoid of a sense of self that, for the first time in the play, he feels himself surrounded by dangers.[28] The capitulation of his independent selfhood before his mother's onslaught seems to him to require his death, and he embraces that death with a passivity thoroughly uncharacteristic of him:

> O my mother, mother! O!
> You have won a happy victory to Rome;
> But for your son, believe it, O, believe it,
> Most dangerously you have with him prevail'd,
> If not most mortal to him. But let it come.
>
> (V.iii.185-89)

Volumnia achieves this happy victory partly because she makes the dangers inherent in his defensive system as terrifying as those it is designed to keep at bay. Her last confrontation with her son is so appallingly effective because she invalidates his defenses by threatening to enact his most central defensive fantasies, thereby making their consequences inescapable to him.

The very appearance of his mother, coming to beg him for the life of her city and hence for her own life, is an enactment of his attempt to become the author of his mother, his desire to have power over her. He has before found her begging intolerable (III.ii.124-34); when she kneels to him here, making the role reversal of mother and child explicit (V.iii.56), he reacts with a hysteria which suggests that the acting out of this forbidden wish threatens to dissolve the very structures by which he orders his life:

> What's this?
> Your knees to me? to your corrected son?
> Then let the pebbles on the hungry beach
> Fillip the stars. Then let the mutinous winds
> Strike the proud cedars 'gainst the fiery sun,
> Murd'ring impossibility, to make
> What cannot be, slight work!
>
> (V.iii.56-62)

At first sight, this speech seems simply to register Coriolanus' horror at the threat to hierarchy implied by the kneeling of parent to child. But if Coriolanus were responding only—or even mainly—to this threat, we would expect the threatened chaos to be imaged as high bowing to low; this is in fact the image we are given when Volumnia first bows to her son as if—as Coriolanus says—"Olympus to a molehill should/In supplication nod" (V.iii.30-31). But Coriolanus does not respond to his mother's kneeling with an image of high bowing to low; instead, he responds with two images of low mutinously striking at high. The chaos imaged here is not so much a derivative of his mother's kneeling as of the potential mutiny that her kneeling seems to imply: for her kneeling releases the possibility of his mutiny against her, a mutiny that he has been suppressing all along by his exaggerated deference to her. His response here reveals again the defensive function of his hatred of the mutinous and leveling populace: the violence of his images suggests that his mother's kneeling has forced him to acknowledge his return to Rome as a rising up of the hungry and mutinous forces within himself. With her usual acumen, Volumnia recognizes the horror of potential mutiny in Coriolanus' response and chooses exactly this moment to assert, once again, his dependence on her: "Thou art my warrior" (V.iii.62).

Coriolanus' forbidden wish to have power over his mother was safe as long as it seemed impossible. But now that protective impossibility itself seems murdered, and he is forced to confront the fact that his wish has become a reality. Nor are the hungry and mutinous forces within him content to murder only an abstract "impossibility": the murderousness of the image is directed ultimately at his mother. And once again, Volumnia makes Coriolanus uncomfortably clear to himself: after she has enacted his terrifying fantasy by kneeling, she makes it impossible for him to believe that her death would be merely an incidental consequence of his plan to burn Rome.[29] For she reveals exactly the extent to which his assault is on both. Her long speech builds to its revelation with magnificent force and logic. She first forces him to see his attack on his country as an attack on a living body by accusing him of coming to tear "his country's bowels out" (V.iii.103). Next, she identifies that body as their common source of nurture: "the country, our dear nurse" (V.iii.110). Finally, as she announces her intention to commit suicide, she makes absolute the identification of the country with herself. After she has imagined him treading on his country's ruin (V.iii.116), she warns him:

> Thou shalt no sooner
> March to assault thy country than to tread—
> Trust to't, thou shalt not—on thy mother's womb
> That brought thee to this world.
>
> (V.iii.122-25)

The ruin on which Coriolanus will tread will be his mother's womb—

a warning accompanied by yet another assertion of his dependence on her as she recalls to him the image of himself as a fetus within that womb.

If Coriolanus' mutinous fantasies are no longer impossible, if his mother will indeed die as a result of his actions, then he will have realized his fantasy of living omnipotently without kin, without dependency. In fact this fantasy, his defense throughout, is articulated only here, as he catches sight of his mother (V.iii.34–37), and its expression is the last stand of his claim to independence. Throughout this scene, Volumnia has simultaneously asserted his dependence on her and made the dangers inherent in his defense against that dependence horrifyingly clear; and in the end, it is the combination of her insistence on his dependency and her threat to disown him, to literalize his fantasy of standing alone, that causes him to capitulate. Finally, he cannot "stand / As if a man were author of himself / And knew no other kin"; he must become a child again, a gosling, and admit his neediness. The presence of his own child, holding Volumnia's hand, strengthens her power over him. For Coriolanus seems to think of his child less as his son than as the embodiment of his own childhood and the child that remains within him; even when we are first told about the son, he seems more a comment on Coriolanus' childhood than on his fatherhood. The identification of father and child is suggested by Coriolanus' response as he sees wife, mother, and child approaching: "My wife comes foremost; then the honour'd mould / Wherein this trunk was fram'd, and in her hand / The grandchild to her blood" (V.iii.22–24). Here Coriolanus does not acknowledge the child as his and his wife's: he first imagines himself in his mother's womb and then imagines his child as an extension of his mother. Even Coriolanus' language to Menenius as he earlier denies his family reveals the same fusion of father and son: "Wife, mother, child, I know not" (V.ii.80), he says, in a phrase that suggestively identifies his own mother as the mother of the child and the child he attempts to deny as himself. Volumnia had once before brought Coriolanus to submission by reminding him of himself as a suckling child (III.ii.129); now virtually her last words enforce his identification with the child that she holds by the hand: "This fellow had a Volscian to his mother; / His wife is in Corioles, and his child / Like him by chance" (V.iii.178–80). But at the same time as she reminds him of his dependency, she disowns him by disclaiming her parenthood; she exacerbates his sense of himself as a child, and then threatens to leave him—as he thought he wished—alone. And as his fantasy of self-sufficiency threatens to become a reality, it becomes too frightening to sustain. Just as his child entered the scene holding Volumnia's hand, so Coriolanus again becomes a child, holding his mother's hand.

The ending of this play leaves us with a sense of pain and anxiety; we are not even allowed the feelings of unremitting grief and satiation that console us in most of the other tragedies. The very nature of its hero insists that we keep our distance. Coriolanus is as isolated from us as he is from everyone else; we almost never know what he is thinking, and—even more intolerably—he does not seem to care what we are thinking. Unlike an Othello or an Antony, whose last moments are spent endearingly trying to ensure our good opinion, Coriolanus makes virtually no attempt to affect our judgment of him: he dies as he has tried to live, heroically mantled in his self-sufficiency, alone. Nor is it only our democratic sympathies that put us uncomfortably in the position of the common people throughout much of the play: Coriolanus seems to find our love as irrelevant, as positively demeaning, as theirs; in refusing to show the people his wounds, he is at the same time refusing to show them to us. In refusing to show himself to us, in considering us a many-headed multitude to whose applause he is wholly indifferent, Coriolanus denies us our proper role as spectators to his tragedy. The only spectators Coriolanus allows himself to notice are the gods who look down on this unnatural scene and laugh, who are so far removed from men that they find this human tragedy a comedy. And as spectators, we are in danger of becoming as distant from human concerns as the gods: for Coriolanus' isolation infects the whole play and ultimately infects us as well. There are very few moments of relaxation; there is no one here to love. We are made as rigid and cold as the hero by the lack of anything that absolutely commands our human sympathies, that makes us feel our own status as dependent creatures, part of a community. Even the language does not open out toward us, nor does it create the sense of the merging of meanings, the melting together, that gives us a measure of release in *King Lear* or *Antony and Cleopatra*, where a world of linguistic fusion suggests the dependence of all parts. Instead, the language works to define and separate, to limit possibilities, almost as rigidly as Coriolanus himself does.[30]

Finally, the nature of our involvement in the fantasies embodied in this distant and rigid hero does not permit any resolution: it also separates and limits. For Coriolanus has throughout given free expression to *our* desire to be independent, and we delight in his claim. But when he turns on his mother in Rome, the consequences of his claim to self-sufficiency suddenly become intolerably threatening to us. We want him to acknowledge dependence, to become one of us; but at the same time we do not want to see him give in, because to do so is to force us to give up our own fantasy of omnipotence and independence. Hence at the final confrontation we are divided against ourselves, and no solution is tolerable: neither the burning of Rome nor the capitulation and death of our claims to independence. Nor is the vision of human dependency that the play allows any compensation for the brutal failure of our desire to be self-sustaining. In *Lear* and *Antony and Cleopatra*, dependency is finally shown to be what makes us fully human: however much the characters have tried to deny it, it finally becomes their salvation, and ours, as we reach out to them. But dependency here brings no rewards, no love, no sharing with the audience; it brings only the total collapse of the self, the awful triumph of Volumnia, and Coriolanus' terribly painful cry: "O mother, mother / What have you done?"

Notes

1. John Stow, *Annales* (London, 1631), p. 890. See Sidney Shanker, "Some Clues for *Coriolanus*," *Shakespeare Association Bulletin*, 24 (1949), 209-13; E. C. Pettet, "*Coriolanus* and the Midlands Insurrection of 1607," *Shakespeare Survey*, 3 (1950), 34-42; and Brents Stirling, *The Populace in Shakespeare* (New York: Columbia Univ. Press, 1949), pp. 126-28, for discussions of the uprising and its political consequences in the play.

2. Stow, p. 890.

3. See Edwin F. Gay, "The Midland Revolt and the Inquisitions of Depopulation of 1607," *Transactions of the Royal Historical Society*, N.S.18 (1904), 195–244, for valuable contemporary commentary on the uprising and an analysis of it in comparison with earlier riots of the sixteenth century. See also Pettet, p. 35.

4. The participants in the uprising were commonly called "levelers" and their activity "leveling," in startling anticipation of the 1640s. The common use of this term suggests the extent to which their fight against enclosures seemed to threaten hierarchy itself. (See, for example, Stow, p. 890, and Gay, p. 213, n. 2; p. 214, n. 1; p. 216, n. 3; and p. 242). The vertical imagery is so prominent in the play that it scarcely needs to be pointed out; at its center is Cominius' warning that the tribunes' stirring up of the people is "the way to lay the city flat, / To bring the roof to the foundation, / And bury all which yet distinctly ranges / In heaps and piles of ruin" (III.i.201-05). The threat of the people to rise and cast Coriolanus down from the Tarpeian rock, Coriolanus' horror of kneeling to the people or of his mother's kneeling to him, and ultimately the image of the prone Coriolanus with Aufidius standing on him—all take their force partly from the repetition and intensity of the vertical imagery throughout.

5. Shakespeare had in fact just used the word *level* to suggest a sexual leveling at the end of *Antony and Cleopatra*, when Cleopatra laments: "The soldier's pole is fall'n: young boys and girls / Are level now with men" (IV.xv.65-66).

6. All references to *Coriolanus* are to the new Arden edition, ed. Philip Brockbent (London: Methuen, 1976).

7. Coriolanus himself occupies an odd position in the psychological myth at the start of the play: though he is a father, we almost always think of him as a son; though the populace considers him prime among the forbidding fathers, he himself seems to regard the patricians as his fathers. His position midway between father and sons suggests the position of an older sibling who has made a protective alliance

with the fathers and now fears the unruliness of his younger brothers. Instead of fighting to take possession of the undernourishing mother, he will deny that he has any need for food.

8. Menenius' words point to the rigid and ferocious maleness so prized by Rome. Phyllis Rackin, in an unpublished paper entitled "*Coriolanus*: Shakespeare's Anatomy of *Virtus*" and delivered to the special session on feminist criticism of Shakespeare at the 1976 meeting of the Modern Language Association, discusses the denial of female values in the play as a consequence of the Roman overvaluation of valor as the chiefest virtue. Rackin's analysis of the ways in which the traditionally female images of food, harvesting, and love are turned to destructive purposes throughout the play is particularly revealing.

The ideal Roman woman is in fact one who denies her womanhood, as we see not only in Volumnia but in Coriolanus' chilling and beautiful description of Valeria (V.iii.65-67). (Indeed, Valeria seems to have little place in the intimate family gathering of V.iii; she seems to exist there largely to give Coriolanus an excuse to speak these lines.) The extent to which womanhood is shrunken in Roman values is apparent in the relative unimportance of Coriolanus' wife Virgilia; in her, the female values of kindly nurturing have become little more than a penchant for staying at home, keeping silent, and weeping. (Given the extreme restrictions of Virgilia's role, one may begin to understand some of the pressures that force a woman to become a Volumnia and live through the creation of her exaggeratedly masculine son. In "Authoritarian Patterns in Shakespeare's *Coriolanus*," *Literature and Psychology* 9 [1959], 49, Gordon Ross Smith comments perceptively that, in an authoritarian society, women will either be passive and subservient or will attempt to live out their thwarted ambition via their men.)

At the end of the play, Rome sees the consequences of its denial of female values as Coriolanus prepares to deny nature in himself and destroy his homeland. When Volumnia triumphs over his rigid maleness, there is a hint of restitution in the Roman celebration of her as "our patroness, the life of Rome" (V.v.1). But like nearly everything else at the end of this play, the promise of restitution is deeply ironic: for Volumnia herself has shown no touch of nature as she willingly sacrifices her son; and the cries of "welcome, ladies, welcome!" (V.v.6) suggest an acknowledgment of female values at the moment when the appearance of these values not in Volumnia but in her son must mean his death.

9. The association of nobility with abstinence from food—and of the ignoble lower classes with excessive appetite for food, in connection with their traditional role as the embodiment of appetite—was first demonstrated to me by Maurice Charney's impressive catalog of the food images in the play. See "The Imagery of Food and Eating in *Coriolanus*," in *Essays in Literary History*, ed. Rudolf Kirk and C. F. Main (New Brunswick, N.J.: Rutgers Univ. Press, 1960), pp. 37-54.

10. In fact, Coriolanus frequently imagines his death with a kind of glee, as the badge of his noble self-sufficiency. See, for example, III.ii.1-5, 103-04; V.vi. 111-12.

11. The extent to which Coriolanus becomes identified with his phallus is suggested by the language in which both Menenius and Aufidius portray his death. For both, it represents a kind of castration: "He's a limb that has but a disease:/Mortal, to cut it off; to cure it, easy" (III.i.293-94); "You'll rejoice/That he is thus cut off" (V.vi.137-38). For discussions of Coriolanus' phallic identification and its consequences, see Robert J. Stoller, "Shakespearean Tragedy: *Coriolanus*," *Psychoanalytic Quarterly*, 35 (1966), 263-74, and Emmett Wilson, Jr., "Coriolanus: The Anxious Bridegroom," *American Imago*, 25 (1968), 224-41. In "An Interpretation

of Shakespeare's *Coriolanus*," *American Imago*, 14 (1957), 407–35, Charles K. Hofling sees Coriolanus as a virtual embodiment of Reich's phallic-narcissistic character. Each of these analysts finds Coriolanus' phallic stance to some extent a defense against passivity (Stoller, pp. 267, 269–70; Wilson, passim; Hofling, pp. 421, 424).

12. David B. Barron sees Coriolanus' oral frustration and his consequent rage as central to his character. See "*Coriolanus*: Portrait of the Artist As Infant," *American Imago*, 19 (1962), 171–93. This essay anticipates mine in some of its conclusions and many of its details of interpretation.

13. Most critics find Coriolanus' abhorrence of praise a symptom of his pride and of his desire to consider himself as self-defined and self-sufficient, hence free from the definitions that society would confer on him. See, for example, A. C. Bradley, "Coriolanus," reprinted in *Studies in Shakespeare*, ed. Peter Alexander (London: Oxford Univ. Press, 1964), p. 229; G. Wilson Knight, *The Imperial Theme* (London: Methuen, 1965), p. 169; Irving Ribner, *Patterns in Shakespearean Tragedy* (London: Methuen, 1960), p. 190; Norman Rabkin, *Shakespeare and the Common Understanding* (New York: Free Press, 1967), p. 131; and James L. Calderwood, "*Coriolanus*: Wordless Meanings and Meaningless Words," *Studies in English Literature 1500–1900*, 6 (1966), 218–19.

14. In his discussion of Coriolanus' cathartic vituperation, Kenneth Burke suggests that invective is rooted in the helpless rage of the infant. See "*Coriolanus*—and the Delights of Faction," *Hudson Review* 19 (1966), 200.

15. To see Corioli as the mother's womb here may seem grotesque; the idea becomes less grotesque if we remember Volumnia's own identification of country with mother's womb just as Coriolanus is about to attack another city (see discussion elsewhere in this chapter). Wilson suggests (pp. 228–29) that the attack on Corioli represents defloration—specifically, that it expresses the equation of coitus with damaging assault and the resultant dread of a retaliatory castration.

16. The force of this new name is partly corroborated by Volumnia, who delights in reminding her son of his dependence on her: she has trouble learning his new name from the start (II.i.173) and eventually associates it with the pride that keeps him from pity for his family (V.iii.170–71). But several critics have argued convincingly that the self-sufficiency implicit in Coriolanus' acquisition of his new name is ironically undercut from the beginning by the fact that naming of any kind is a social act, so that Coriolanus' acceptance of the name conferred on him by Cominius reveals his dependence on external definition just at the moment that he seems most independent. See, for example, Rabkin, pp. 130–32; Lawrence Danson, *Tragic Alphabet: Shakespeare's Drama of Language* (New Haven, Conn.: Yale Univ. Press, 1974), pp. 150–51; and Calderwood, pp. 219–23.

17. The father's role in the process of individuation and the consequent significance of Coriolanus' fatherlessness have been pointed out to me by Dr. Malcolm Pines: the father must exist from the start in the potential space between child and mother in order for separation from the mother, and hence individuation, to take place; the absence of Coriolanus' father thus becomes an essential factor in his failure to separate from his mother. Coriolanus' father is in fact extraordinarily absent from the play: he is never mentioned. That Menenius repeatedly is identified as Coriolanus' father at the end of the play (V.i.3; V.ii.62, 69; V.iii.10) merely underscores this absence: insofar as this weak old man is associated with nurture, he might serve Coriolanus more adequately as a mother-substitute than as a father-substitute. The absolute absence of the father here points toward a parthenogenesis fantasy in which the son is literally the creation of the mother alone, a reversal of the more typical Shakespearean fantasy of male parthenogenesis (see, for example, *King Lear* or *The Tempest*).

18. Volumnia's place in the creation of her son's role, and the catastrophic results of her disavowal of it here, have been nearly universally recognized. For a particularly perceptive discussion of the consequences for Coriolanus of his mother's shift in attitude, see Derek Traversi, *Shakespeare: The Roman Plays* (Stanford, Calif.: Stanford Univ. Press, 1963), pp. 247–54. In an interesting essay, D. W. Harding suggests Shakespeare's preoccupation during this period with the disastrous effects on men of their living out of women's fantasies of manhood. See "Women's Fantasy of Manhood," *Shakespeare Quarterly*, 20 (1969), 252–53. Psychoanalytically oriented critics see Coriolanus as the embodiment of his mother's masculine strivings, or, more specifically, as her longed-for penis. See, for example, Ralph Berry, "Sexual Imagery in *Coriolanus*," *Studies in English Literature*, 13 (1973), 302; Hofling, pp. 415–16; Stoller, pp. 266–67, 271; and Wilson, p. 239.

Several critics have noticed the importance of acting and the theatrical metaphor in the play. See, for example, William Rosen, *Shakespeare and the Craft of Tragedy* (Cambridge: Harvard Univ. Press, 1960), pp. 171–73, and Kenneth Muir, *Shakespeare's Tragic Sequence* (London: Hutchinson, 1972), pp. 184–85. Harold C. Goddard in *The Meaning of Shakespeare* (Chicago: Univ. of Chicago Press, 1951), pp. 216–17, discusses acting specifically in relation to the role that Volumnia has cast for her son. Berry points to the acting metaphors as a measure of Coriolanus' inner uncertainty and his fear of losing his manhood if he shifts roles (pp. 303–06).

19. Goddard (p. 238), Hofling (p. 420), and Smith (p. 46), among others, discuss Coriolanus' characterization of the crowd as a projection of elements in himself that he wishes to deny, though they do not agree on the precise nature of these elements.

20. And so does Shakespeare. In Plutarch, Coriolanus is accompanied by a few men both when he enters the gates of Corioli and when he is exiled from Rome. Shakespeare emphasizes his isolation by giving him no companions on either occasion. Eugene Waith, in *The Herculean Hero* (New York: Columbia Univ. Press, 1962), p. 124, and Danson (p. 146) emphasize Coriolanus' position as a whole man among fragments.

21. Barron associates Coriolanus' hatred of the people's undisciplined hunger with his need to subdue his own impulses; here, as elsewhere, his argument is very close to my own (pp. 174, 180).

22. See note 7 above. The likeness of the plebeians to younger siblings who threaten Coriolanus' food supply was first suggested to me by David Sundelson in conversation.

23. See Leonard Tennenhouse, "*Coriolanus*: History and the Crisis of Semantic Order," *Comparative Drama*, 10 (1976), 332. In the course of his suggestive essay on the semantic, historical, and psychological issues informing the significance of the people's voices in *Coriolanus*, Tennenhouse comes very close to the center of my argument when he says: "Coriolanus, the child denied love in the service of patrician ideals, is perceived by the mob as the one who denies. The mysterious source of the cannibalistic rage directed against him is the recognition by the plebeians that he would withhold from them what the patrician mother would withhold from her son—nurturance and thus life itself" (p. 335). Although his essay came to my attention after most of the present essay was written, this statement and the suggestions of Zan Marquis initiated my understanding of cannibalism in the play.

24. See, for example, I.iii.40–43 (discussed early in this chapter) and II.iii.5–8. Exposed, Coriolanus' wounds would become begging mouths, as Julius Caesar's do (*Julius Caesar*, III.ii.225–26).

25. The Third Citizen's image points also toward the possibility that Coriolanus

would be inviting homosexual rape by standing naked before the crowd. Dr. Anne Hayman has suggested to me that Coriolanus' fear of his unconscious homosexual desires, especially of a passive feminine kind, is central to his character; she sees his fear of the wish for passive femininity as part of his identification with his mother, who shares the same fear. I am indebted to Dr. Hayman for her careful reading of this paper and her many helpful comments. (The relationship with Aufidius, though presented in decidedly homosexual terms [see, for example, IV.iv.12-16, 22; IV.v. 110-19, 123-24], seems to me more significant as an expression of Coriolanus' need for a mirror image of himself than as the expression of his homosexual desires, as I argue later in this chapter.)

26. That Coriolanus' identity is at issue in the turning toward Aufidius is made uncomfortably clear by the scene in which he comes to Antium. Despite the servingmen's comic and belated assertions that they had nearly pierced Coriolanus' disguise (IV.v.150-64), they clearly had no inkling of his stature before he revealed himself. Furthermore, Coriolanus' gradual unmasking before Aufidius suggests that he wants to be known as himself before he names himself (IV.v.55-66). The scene is in part a test of the power of Coriolanus' identity to make itself known without external definition; the results are at best ambiguous.

27. Donald A. Stauffer, in *Shakespeare's World of Images* (New York: W. W. Norton, 1949), p. 252, points out that Rome is less *patria* than *matria* in this play; he discusses Volumnia as a projection of Rome, particularly in V.iii. Virtually all psychoanalytic critics comment on the identification of Volumnia with Rome; Barron comments specifically that Coriolanus turns the rage of his frustration in nursing toward his own country at the end of the play (p. 175).

28. It is a mark of the extent to which external dangers are for Coriolanus merely a reflection of internal ones that he feels himself in no danger until the collapse of his defensive system. Unlike Coriolanus, we know that he is in danger before its collapse: Aufidius plans to kill him no matter what he does (IV.vii.24-26, 56-57).

29. Rufus Putney, in "Coriolanus and His Mother," *Psychoanalytic Quarterly*, 21 (1962), pp. 368-69, 372, finds Coriolanus' inability to deal with his matricidal impulses central to his character; whenever Volumnia threatens him with her death, he capitulates at once.

30. G. Wilson Knight discusses the hard metallic quality of the language at length; he associates it with the self-containment of the hostile walled cities and distinguishes it from the fusions characteristic of *Antony and Cleopatra* (p. 156). In a particularly interesting discussion, Danson associates the rigidity and distinctness of the language with the play's characteristic use of metonymy and synecdoche, which serve to limit and define, in place of metaphor, which serves to fuse diverse worlds (pp. 155-59).

8 ❀ "Since first we were dissevered": Trust and Autonomy in Shake- spearean Tragedy and Romance

Richard P. Wheeler

In the earlier phases of his career, Shakespeare writes interchangeably —perhaps often simultaneously—comedies, history plays, three widely divergent tragedies, and narrative and lyric poetry.[1] But in the later phases, the last two of Dowden's four periods, Shakespeare tends to write within the inclusive framework of a single, exceptionally flexible genre: tragedy from *Hamlet* to *Coriolanus*, and then, with some overlap, the late romances.[2] In this paper I will try to identify polarized trends in Shakespeare's development, separated by generic distinctions in the earlier work, which confront each other in the drama of the tragic period, and which help to shape Shakespeare's artistry in the tragedies and the romances. Although I will suggest some of the ways these trends are manifested in various plays, my main concern is to state as simply and as sharply as I can a complex pattern, itself composed of smaller, interrelated patterns, that emerges from a long view of Shakespeare's development.[3] I hope that the effort to achieve synoptic clarity justifies sacrificing the very detailed reading that would be necessary to situate fully any one play within this developmental outline.

The tragedies and the romances dramatize polarized modes of seeking self-fulfillment in conditions of extreme crisis. This polarity, which persists through an astonishing range of transformations, is itself hardly unique to Shakespeare; Margaret S. Mahler generalizes its essential qualities when she speaks of "man's eternal struggle against fusion on the one hand and isolation on the other."[4] What is characteristic of Shakespeare is a full imaginative investment in mutually necessary

This chapter also appears in Richard Wheeler, *Shakespeare's Development and the Problem Comedies: Turn and Counter-Turn*, forthcoming from the Univ. of California Press. Reprinted by permission.

but mutually incompatible modes of self-experience at either end of this spectrum, and a recurrent pattern of oscillation between them. At one extreme, a deeply feared longing for merger subverts relations of trust; at the other, failed autonomy gives way to helpless isolation.

The destructive potential in conflicting needs for trust and autonomy, averted in the festive comedies and displaced away from Hal's quest for power in the *Henriad*, shapes the drama in a new way in *Hamlet*. A polarity that begins to take form in the movement from *Hamlet* to *Troilus and Cressida* recurs regularly in the drama that follows; it is refined to exceptional purity in *Antony and Cleopatra* and *Coriolanus* at the end of the period of the tragedies, and again in *The Winter's Tale* and *The Tempest*. This polarization is expressed in a pattern of contrast that cuts across other lines of development; with varying degrees of clarity and comprehensiveness, it tends to sort the later drama into two groups of plays. The fear of and longing for merger with another provide the primary driving force in the plays of one of these groups. In the other, a comparably ambivalent relation to the prospect of omnipotent autonomy provides the psychic context in which the protagonists seek self-definition.

I will refer to the two groups as the trust/merger group and the autonomy/isolation group. The terms paired across a slash mark designate the primary positive and negative trends—the need and the characteristic danger that accompanies it—that are held in tension within the plays of each group, and that together distinguish the two groups from each other. It must be stressed, however, that these distinctions indicate emphasis and subordination, not exclusion; they point to shifts in relations among basic needs and psychological hazards, present in all the plays.

The tragedies I include in the trust/merger group are *Hamlet, Othello, King Lear,* and *Antony and Cleopatra.* In these plays, the effort to establish power and autonomy is ultimately subordinated to what proves to be a stronger need for a lost or jeopardized relation of mutuality. A characteristic fear underlying the experience of the protagonists of these plays is loss of autonomy in a union that destroys both self and other. But the longing for merger shapes the action, and is culminated, tragically, in the endings of these plays. Hamlet's final sense of enclosing himself within the sphere of "a divinity that shapes our ends,/Rough-hew them how we will" (V.ii.10–11), completes in a dramatically ambiguous religious resolution a movement more directly realized in the human context of the other plays of this group. Othello, after he labors desperately to reconstruct an image of his heroic self, joins Desdemona on her death bed, "to die upon a kiss" (V.ii.359). The dying Lear, with dead Cordelia in his arms, tragically consummates the overreaching longing that has driven him throughout the play. Antony dies in the arms of Cleopatra, to be reborn through the fertile womb of her imagination into a transcendent image of manhood he has been unable to achieve in his life.

In each of these instances, an extravagant effort to protect a deeply threatened ideal of manly selfhood gives way to a more powerful longing, completed with tragic irony, for merger with another. In skeletal form, the culminating action of these plays is a movement through loss of identity in isolation toward a tragic realization, in mutual destruction, of the longing for merger.

The tragedies I include in the autonomy/isolation group are *Troilus and Cressida, Macbeth, Timon of Athens,* and *Coriolanus.* In these plays, relations of the self to others that promise fulfillment instead prohibit the achievement of stable autonomy. The protagonists of these plays, unlike those of the trust/merger group, move away from relations of unqualified trust, which ultimately prove to be destructive. Each of these relationships is grounded in a perilous overinvestment of self in others—a mistress, a wife, a whole society, a mother—that negates the autonomy these characters will make desperate efforts to retrieve. Troilus' naive faith in Cressida, Macbeth's desperate reliance on the will of his powerful wife, Timon's bizarre attempt to appropriate for himself the role of nurturant mother to all of Athens, and Coriolanus' bond to his mother—all of these shape dependent, contingent identities that define both the strength and vulnerability of the characters involved.

The psychic separateness that each of these characters initially either denies or surrenders is in each case tragically realized as complete estrangement, isolation, and impotent rage against a world perceived as hostile, intrusive "other." The culminating action of these plays moves through destructive merger toward isolation and emptiness. Rather than die, like the protagonists of the trust/merger group, in a union with a beloved other, Troilus is left in impotent, empty rage; Macbeth and Coriolanus, desperately and defiantly alone, are hacked to death by enemies; Timon dies, in a grave of his own making, after petitioning the "common mother," the "common whore of mankind": "Ensear thy fertile and conceptious womb/Let it no more bring out ingrateful man!" (IV.iii.177; 43; 187-88).

The contrasting movements of the two groups can be summarized by a glance at key developments in the experience of Lear and Macbeth. In the opening scene of *King Lear,* there is a clear incompatibility between Lear's implicit assumption of absolute power and freedom and his actual forfeiture of political power to his daughters. Driving Lear, and underscoring his desire to "shake all cares and business from our age," is his longing for a condition of childlike dependency with his beloved Cordelia: "I loved her most, and thought to set my rest/On her kind nursery . . ." (I.i.39; 123-24). After he banishes Cordelia, and after Regan and Goneril have refused to comply with his demands on them, Lear is unable to articulate the "true need" they have failed to accommodate. But after the shattering experience of the storm, in which his effort to assert hallucinatory omnipotence by commanding the heavens to serve his will gives way to his own collapse, Lear can express that need, and the joy that attends its apparent fulfillment, when he would transform imprisonment into the earthly paradise of a sacred union with Cordelia:

> Come, let's away to prison.
> We two alone will sing like birds i' th' cage.
> When thou dost ask me blessing, I'll kneel down
> And ask of thee forgiveness.
>
> (V.iii.8-11)

Lear's final experience oscillates between the unbearable awareness of Cordelia's death—"Thou'lt come no more,/Never, never, never, never, never . . ." (V.iii.308-09)—and the undeniable longing to retrieve her, to exist in the presence of the radiant, human, feminine face and voice that alone can confer wholeness and meaning: "Look on her! Look her lips,/Look there, look there—, . . ." (V.iii.311-12). The sum of Macbeth's experience, by contrast, is realized as absolute aloneness, bereft even of desire for relations with others. The death of Lady Macbeth offstage releases Macbeth's vision of life as a "walking shadow, a poor player" emptied of any context, within the self or external to it, that could provide meaning: "It is a tale/Told by an idiot, full of sound and fury,/Signifying nothing" (V.v.24; 26-28). There is an enormous gulf between Lear's "never" and Macbeth's "nothing." Lear necessarily fails to achieve the conditions he covets for living through Cordelia's presence. Macbeth annihilates in himself the capacity even to imagine a context that would redeem him from absolute, empty isolation.

Whereas *King Lear* begins with the separation of Lear from his daughters, the quest for royal manhood in *Macbeth* requires that Macbeth's ambition be nurtured into action by others. After the first exchange with the witches, Macbeth is driven to achieve a magically compelling ideal of manhood articulated for him by his wife. Macbeth cannot refuse this ideal, but he cannot pursue it except by making himself a child to the demonic motherhood held out to him by Lady Macbeth. As the merger of these two characters dissolves, Macbeth's sustained violence, always exercised in the context of family relations—a fatherly king, a father and son, and finally a mother and her "babes"—only serves to isolate him further, until even the illusion of omnipotence nurtured by the witches collapses before the force of a man "not born of woman."

As my emphasis on family relations in *King Lear* and *Macbeth* suggests, the psychological polarity I am tracing is grounded in experience in a family, particularly in the crises that accompany the maturational process of forming a separate self out of an originally undifferentiated matrix. Early development involves, according to Margaret Mahler, "a gradual growing away from the normal state of human symbiosis, of 'oneness' with the mother." As the child discovers that he is not identical with the essential source of nurture provided by the mother, and that his world is not magically responsive to urgent demands originating in him, he must struggle to master the first and most profound divisions in the development of the human self. This development proceeds along the lines of what Mahler calls the "gradual process of separation-individuation." The movement through individuation is essential to the establishment of autonomous identity, but it is accompanied by unavoidable and repeated traumas of separation. This leads Mahler, with other analysts, to see the "growing away process" as a "lifelong mourning process."[5] Erik Erikson calls the achievement of the early phases of the separation-individuation process "basic trust," the confidence manifest at the very core of experience that inner urges and external providers are trustworthy enough to allow further development of the self and its relations to others. But as Erikson observes:

> Even under the most favorable circumstances, this stage seems to introduce into psychic life (and become prototypical for) a sense of inner division and universal nostalgia for a paradise forfeited. It is against this powerful combination of a sense of having been deprived, of having been divided, and of having been abandoned—that basic trust must maintain itself throughout life.[6]

The establishment of basic trust, and out of it the first gains toward the achievement of autonomy, underlies all later development, both toward relations with others and toward the consolidation of individual identity. Mahler suggests that "the entire life cycle" pivots on the double "process of distancing from and introjection of the lost symbiotic mother, . . . the 'all-good' mother, who was at one time part of the self in a blissful state of well-being."[7] But as the ego develops along boundaries that distinguish the world from the self, crises in the process of separation can engender the wish to reinhabit the symbiotic unity of infant and mother; crises within the environment provided by the mother, including those that provoke fears of "reengulfment," can lead to the defiant repudiation of essential others and to fantasies of a powerful autonomous self that magically incorporates symbiotic omnipotence. Neither the longing for fusion nor the longing for omnipotent autonomy can be integrated fully into the contingencies of living, and the separation-individuation process to which they are bound is never complete. Arnold H. Modell emphasizes that, in the development of an individual self:

> the acceptance of separateness, as is true for the establishment of one's identity, is never absolute or final. Even if one has established the capacity for mature love, established a sense of identity, and accepted the uniqueness of the beloved—there is a wish to merge, to fuse, to lose one's separateness.[8]

The wish to merge with another, however, if felt to endanger one's need to be separate, may in turn intensify the effort to establish total separation through withdrawal and isolation. Both the movement toward separation and the longing for fusion may jeopardize the equilibrium of the self that emerges from their interaction. The longing for merger threatens to destroy precariously achieved autonomy; the longing for complete autonomy threatens to isolate the self from its base of trust in actual and internalized relations to others.

Shakespearean tragedy dramatizes conditions of extreme crisis that bring these longings directly into the felt experience of the protagonist's vulnerable, heroic identity. As C. L. Barber observes, "the roots in infancy from which identity grows outward in healthy situations become, in tragic situations, the source of impossible, destructive, and self-destructive demands."[9] In much of the earlier drama, however, Shakespeare uses generic boundaries to reinforce selectively barriers that protect "enterprises of great pitch and moment" from the intrusion of deep psychic conflict. The longing for trustworthy feminine control that often lies near the psychological center of the festive comedies asserts itself independently of, or in triumph over, fears of encroachment and sexual degradation that can attend the movement toward intimacy. In the second tetralogy of English history plays, Prince Hal engineers his way toward the assumption of royal authority in an almost entirely masculine world.[10] The *Henriad* works through tensions of father and son conflict uncomplicated by a directly expressed maternal presence; the actions of the festive comedies proceed under the direction of benign feminine control—but again without the explicit presence of mothers. In the *Sonnets*, the loving poet often sacrifices claims for his own autonomy to live through an idealizing identification with the adored friend. Self-denial in the *Sonnets* is transcended by merger with the friend, in which the poet assumes a generous, nurturant role that derives from experiences of maternal cherishing.

Hamlet, because it brings into tragic drama the full range of family-based conflict, forecloses solutions available in earlier works that exclude or minimize potentially disruptive conflict. It seems that the tragedies culminating in relations of destructive merger seek to reinhabit the world of love grounded in trust, often presided over by benign female presences, as dramatized in the festive comedies. The women of these tragedies—Ophelia, Desdemona, Cordelia, Cleopatra—often recall the women who establish the conditions for loving in the comedies, but they cannot accomplish the comedies' goals of stable relations of mutuality. By contrast, the desperate recoil into movements toward travestied autonomy in Troilus, Macbeth, Timon, and Coriolanus recall the simpler world of masculine authority, uncomplicated by the presence of captivating women, that Prince Hal negotiates in the *Henriad*.[10]

The split in the *Sonnets* between the chaste, almost sacred idealization of the friend and the degraded sexuality of the dark lady—a split that originates in conflicted responses to a single maternal figure—is taken up and refocused in the tragedies of the trust/merger group, usually in a single relation to a woman, as when Othello inscribes "whore" upon the brow of "divine Desdemona." A sense of desperate isolation, which emerges in those sonnets that suggest failures in Shakespeare's identification with the friend, anticipates the tragic intensity of helpless separation in the plays of the autonomy/isolation group. In *Timon of Athens*, this helplessness is given dramatic shape by Timon's desperate denial of it when he rails savagely against a society that has failed to reciprocate his nurturant generosity.

In the development of Shakespeare's later drama, the two groups balance and perhaps beget each other in a rhythmic unfolding of plays—or in one instance, pairs of plays—in the same genre. From this vantage point, *Hamlet* in the trust/merger group is closely linked to *Troilus and Cressida* in the autonomy/isolation group, *Othello* and *King Lear* to *Macbeth* and *Timon of Athens, Antony and Cleopatra* to *Coriolanus*, as if the movement through isolation to union and the movement through union to isolation recurrently engender each other.[11] This rhythmic, oscillating pattern can be traced into the reconstructive actions of the late romances, blurred a little in the experimental gestures toward new form in *Pericles* and *Cymbeline*, and worked to great clarity in *The Winter's Tale* and *The Tempest*.

Like Roethke's woman, "lovely in her bones," Shakespeare's art "moved in circles, and those circles moved."[12] The interanimations of turn and counterturn within this psychic dance are virtually infinite and occur at every level. But it is useful to conceive of four separable contexts in which a movement through an enduring polarity—of trust inseparable from the fear of destructive merger and of autonomy entangled with the threat of isolation and emptiness—is realized in these plays: in the interaction of conflicting needs for trust and autonomy in the protagonist of a single play; in the oscillating movement from a play in the trust/merger group to a play in the autonomy/isolation group—from *King Lear* to *Macbeth*, for instance; in a spiraling movement toward increased polarization in the development first of tragic and then of romance form; and in the polarized relation of the two genres to each other, as the central experience of loss in the tragedies gives way to the restoration of lost relations in the reunions of the late romances.

Lying behind these developments, as a half mythic paradigm of stable family harmony, is Hamlet's nostalgic remembrance of his father's kingly authority, complemented by the loving union of royal husband and wife. But at the outset of *Hamlet*, this private paradise of familial order has become an "unweeded garden." The tragedies pursue fragmentary, aberrant, self-destructive gestures toward reestablishing either half of the balance of trust and autonomy Hamlet recalls in his idealization of the past. The late romances move toward reinstatements of the identity anchored in images of manly autonomy and familial unity, which Hamlet has lost through his father's murder and his mother's remarriage. Although in *Hamlet* the need to be an autonomous, active self and the need to find a relation of trust in which to ground that self are closely balanced, Hamlet must locate himself within a relation to transcendent providence before completing his personal mission, and both achievements are dramatically ambiguous. But Hamlet's efforts to incorporate the image of vengeful, heroic manhood stipulated by his father's ghost, and to recover the capacity for trust shattered by Gertrude's incestuous union, identify the psychological directions in which the ensuing drama will move. The tragedies that follow intensify this polarization of mutuality based on merger and an autonomy that requires separation. The polarization reaches extreme form in Antony's death in the arms of Cleopatra, set against Coriolanus' death in an alien city. The late romances, by extension and by contrast, culminate in the mutuality reachieved in *The Winter's Tale* and in Prospero's movement toward benevolent autonomy in *The Tempest*.

Antony's bond to Cleopatra expresses a longing denied by the Roman ideal of manly honor and autonomy. Once he has been ensnared by Cleopatra's "strong toil of grace" (V.ii.346), Antony can neither retrieve full rapport with that ideal nor fully articulate an identity for himself independent of it. When he fails to live up to a Roman ego ideal he cannot abandon or qualify, the essential imagery of self-experience becomes for him as "indistinct as water is in water"

(IV.xiv.10–11).[13] The deep antagonism between Antony's Roman self and the mode of relatedness into which he is drawn by Cleopatra is ironically manifest in Antony's death. He declares himself "a Roman, by a Roman/Valiantly vanquished" (IV.xv.57–58) while lying in the arms of the woman who has led him beyond the experiential limits of Roman manhood.

Shakespeare makes it clear that Antony's failure to integrate the two poles of his experience is a necessary, tragic failure. To be Cleopatra's "man of men" (I.v.72) is to be enmeshed in the contradictory imperatives realized as paradox in Antony's death. In his life, they are realized by a series of circular movements in which the union of Antony and Cleopatra is severed and then renewed with heightened intensity. The longing for this union is the most powerful need driving Antony: it at once allows him to achieve a richer, more inclusive humanity, and estranges him from political resources established by Caesar's deflection of all human impulse into the quest for power.

The longing for identity in mutuality continues to seek elaboration after Antony has been sacrificed to it. It remains for Cleopatra to articulate a dream of an Antony adequate to her own shrewdly exploited dream of herself. From Cleopatra's vantage point, "'Tis paltry to be Caesar" (V.ii.2). In the dream she describes to Dolabella, an extravagant consummation of human longing for transcendent identity finds in her vigorous, earthy imagination the home it cannot maintain in ongoing human experience: "His delights/Were dolphin-like, they showed his back above/The element they lived in" (V.ii.88–90). This dream of her lover's endless "bounty" ("an autumn 'twas/That grew the more by reaping" [V.ii.88–89]), which embraces Antony in Cleopatra's bountiful imagination of him, is the exalted counterpart of Lady Macbeth's effort to live through her husband in the image of a manhood she covets. Underlying this dream is the longing to reinhabit the serenely mysterious realm of complete unity that Lady Macbeth shatters in her violent repudiation of maternal nurture:

> Peace, peace!
> Dost thou not see my baby at my breast,
> That sucks the nurse asleep?
> . . . . .
> As sweet as balm, as soft as air, as gentle—
> O Antony!
>
> (V.ii.307–11)

Cleopatra has offered Antony a mode of relating in which his manhood is completed in his response to the feminine in Cleopatra, and which releases the mutual interchange of masculine and feminine in both lovers.[14] Although this union is tragically incompatible with the structures of sustained life as they are understood in this play, its ideal imaginative completion holds the stage even as Cleopatra's corpse is scrutinized by curious Romans seeking a cause of death in a world that does not crack, even with "the breaking of so great a thing" (V.i.14).

The restless expansiveness that often makes *Antony and Cleopatra* seem as much like comedy or romance as tragedy, the inclusiveness of an action that holds contradictory modes of living and understanding in its wide embrace, and the rich lyrical imperialism that can melt Rome in Tiber to establish new heaven, new earth, make this play a fitting culmination of the tragedies of the trust/merger group. Wide-ranging dramatic movements concerned with establishing a source of irreducible value characterize these plays: Hamlet's imperiled nobility is set off by the rotten world of Denmark; the precious womanhood of Desdemona is dramatized against Othello's "lust-stained" imagination of her; Cordelia's truth survives the sacrifice of Cordelia in Lear's quest to fulfill "true need." More than in any of these plays, in *Antony and Cleopatra* Shakespeare dramatizes value in a dream of fulfillment plainly incompatible with pragmatic reality. Cleopatra's folly, as Janet Adelman observes, "is the folly of vision; and the whole play moves toward the acknowledgement of its truth."[15]

Coriolanus, by contrast, completes a group of tragedies centered from the beginning in movements toward disillusionment and devaluation. Cressida's infidelity and the bankruptcy of heroic ideals define the world of *Troilus and Cressida*; the "imperial theme" is transformed into royal butchery in the action of *Macbeth*; Timon's grand generosity collapses into vindictive misanthropy in *Timon of Athens*. Like *Antony and Cleopatra*, *Coriolanus* exaggerates trends in the group it completes. The strong Egyptian fetters that bind Antony are liberating as well as destructive; Cleopatra's immortal longings are illusions that illuminate a human truth; together the two lovers appropriate the right to define, against Caesar's might, what is noble, what is great. On the other hand, psychological patterns that entrap Coriolanus are explored in ways that severely qualify the glory of Roman manhood to which he aspires. The "lonely dragon" is accorded no visionary power to counterpoise the relentlessly reductive force of the action in the last tragedy of the autonomy/isolation group.

Volumnia creates in Coriolanus a self that expresses "my very wishes / And the buildings of my fancy" (II.i.188–89). As Coriolanus fulfills her wish to be a man, embodying the "valiantness" he has sucked from her, the relation also takes unto itself a deep maternal antagonism toward the son who becomes the man such a mother longs to be herself.[16] Within the context of her exalted identification of herself with her son, the glory Volumnia takes in Coriolanus' wounds expresses a deep resentment toward a manhood she cannot realize in her own person. The inseparability of the nurturant maternal bond and violent attack of the infant who has become manly warrior is established strikingly in Volumnia's own imagery:

> The breasts of Hecuba,
> When she did suckle Hector, looked not lovelier
> Than Hector's forehead when it spit forth blood
> At Grecian sword, contemning.
>
> (I.iii.38–41)

In his brutal successes at war, Coriolanus both localizes his mother's ideal of manhood and absorbs her fierce inner rage. In battle, Coriolanus will display his bloody body to urge on the Roman troops, for the wounds he receives are in balance with the destruction he metes out, in a kind of desperate homeostasis of violence. But in peace, his wounds become a source of vulnerability and shame. Coriolanus' angry refusal to show his wounds to the citizens reflects a fear of exposing himself as incomplete, piecemeal, a collection of fragments held together only by his mother's idea of him.

Coriolanus' fear of gaps in himself—represented by the wounds his mother has enjoined him to suffer, and which she regards as emblems of her own self-fulfillment—betrays his perpetual indebtedness to Volumnia for what provisional psychic wholeness he possesses. Coriolanus is ashamed to show the wounds that reflect his own fear of being female, of being identical with that part of his mother which she repudiates by identifying herself with him. This fear of being female, of being possessed by "some harlot's spirit" (III.ii.112), is linked to a hidden hatred of the bond with his mother, which the play expresses by dwelling on Coriolanus' turning against his motherland and on his role as destroyer of family units in battle. But the action bends this resentful impulse back toward its origins, until Coriolanus' imminent assault on Rome is equated with an assault on "thy mother's womb/That brought thee to this world" (V.iii.124–25). Coriolanus is forced to renounce in direct confrontation a matricidal impulse implicit in his effort to "stand/As if a man were author of himself/And knew no other kin" (V.iii.35–37).

The impotent rage released in Coriolanus when Aufidius calls him "boy" completes an understanding developed throughout the play—that Coriolanus' savage masculinity remains bound to the overpowering mother who invented it and filled it with her son. Coriolanus would rather die than acknowledge this psychic incompleteness:

> Cut me to pieces, Volsces. Men and lads,
> Stain all your edges on me. Boy? False hound!
> If you have writ your annals true, 'tis there
> That, like an eagle in a dovecoat, I

Fluttered your Volscians in Corioles.
Alone I did it. Boy?

(V.vi.110-15)

He is destroyed amidst cries that define him as the arch-enemy of the family and reflect his deep hostility toward the familial constraints that underlie his very being:

ALL PEOPLE Tear him to pieces!—Do it presently!—
He killed my son!—My daughter!—He killed my
cousin Marcus!—He killed my father!

(V.vi.119-21)

Like his own challenge to the Volscians, the cry of the people to tear the hero to pieces clarifies the fragmentation that results from Coriolanus' futile effort to assert a manly autonomy independent of his bond to Volumnia.

The late romances as a group retrieve a place for the basic needs sacrificed in the tragedies to destructive impulses within those needs. A psychological index to the development through the tragedies to the romances can be constructed from D. W. Winnicott's understanding of the role of aggression in the formation of the self. Winnicott specifies conditions that enable the self to "use" objects that exist "out in the world."[17] This "capacity to use objects" includes the capability of relating to others in a manner that acknowledges their full, independent existence. In locating others in a world outside the realm of mere projection and exploitation, Winnicott argues: "It is the destructive drive that creates the quality of externality." The object can be "used" in a world recognized as external to the self only if it is first destroyed in a psychic world not yet differentiated from the world beyond it: "It is the destruction of the object that places the object outside the area of the subject's omnipotent control." Winnicott points to the importance of the mother (and the often analogous role of the analyst) as "the first person to take the baby through this first version of the many that will be encountered, of attack that is survived." Acknowledgment of a separate world, not completely independent of projective fantasy, but which does not exist simply as a creation of projection, can only be achieved when a world beyond omnipotent control reveals itself as such by surviving its destruction within the sphere of omnipotence. The completion of this process is crucial to the establishment of both trust and autonomy; it makes possible relations to others that can unite persons who acknowledge the separateness of one another.[18]

In the crises of Shakespeare's later drama, the boundary that establishes the condition of externality is blurred by protagonists who replace actuality with worlds that reflect inner need and conflict. In movements either toward fusion or radical isolation, encounters with essential others recreate in drama the conditions of infantile destruction Winnicott describes. But in these plays, the implications of this aggression extend far beyond a two-person encounter grounded in one individual's regression to deep conflict; destructiveness based in fantasy leads to actual destruction in the plays' dramatic reality. Often, as in *King Lear*, this destruction becomes the image of permanent, generalized loss:

> *Kent.*   Is this the promised end?
> *Edgar.* Or image of that horror?
> *Albany.*   Fall and cease.

(V.iii.264–65)

But each of these plays, at its psychological core, participates in part or all of the process Winnicott describes, in which an essential other is denied a place in reality, is destroyed in fantasy, survives that destruction, and thus becomes a part of the actual world, separate from the subject, but united with him in a bond of trust. Within the complexities of their whole dramatic movements, the romances dramatize the renewed completion of this process, but the tragedies return it to and abort it at the destructive phase.

In the tragedies, essential others, replaced by projective fantasies, are denied places in the actual world. Tragic protagonists who lose touch with actuality attempt to recapture it within the sphere of omnipotent control: "Now he'll outstare the lightning" (*Ant.* III.xiii.195), Enobarbus observes of an Antony who has forfeited his actual resources of power; "I banish you!" (*Cor.* III.iii.124) cries Coriolanus to the Rome that has banished him. Frustrations that penetrate the assumption of omnipotent control, rather than lead to its dissolution, tend to divert magical, projective thinking toward a negative vision no less grandiosely self-centered. Othello, "the noble Moor whom our full Senate/Call all in all sufficient" (IV.i.257–58), expects the universe to suffer a cosmic repetition of his own unbearable loss after he murders Desdemona:

> I have no wife.
> O, insupportable! O heavy hour!
> Methinks it should be now a huge eclipse
> Of sun and moon, and that th' affrighted globe
> Should yawn at alteration.

(V.ii.98–102)

Timon would annihilate Athens, indeed humanity ("Destruction fang mankind!" [*Tim.* IV.iii.23]), when Athenian ingratitude annihilates in him the illusion of a world defined by the nurturant generosity through which he has lived. But Timon's raging belongs no less to the projective realm of omnipotent control than his earlier generosity, and it is Timon, not mankind, who cannot survive his destructiveness: "'Timon is dead, who hath outstretched his span./Some beast read this; there does not live a man'" (V.iii.3-4).

More than that of any other tragic protagonist, Timon's fate reflects the catastrophe of infantile self-annihilation that Winnicott associates with the failure to be able to create the quality of externality. It is a limitation of *Timon of Athens* that Timon's misanthropic reconstruction of the world is inadequately balanced by a dramatic reality independent of it. The Athenian world Timon rejects is never compellingly established in the first place, and it is scarcely affected by Timon's withdrawal of himself from it into impotent rage. More typically in the tragedies, destructiveness that originates in the sphere of omnipotent control does lead to actual destruction in a fully rendered world that sustains life for the protagonist who has belonged to it. When Lear gives up his kingdom, he relinquishes such a world, one that Cordelia and Kent struggle at the outset to keep intact and struggle throughout to reinstate.

In doing this, Lear trades actual power for illusory omnipotence. When he banishes Cordelia, he does not send her out into the world, but expels her from an imaginary world of omnipotent control defined by magical, automatic responsiveness to the demands of his psyche. When Lear is ready to go with her to prison, he continues to deny her a place in a world beyond that created by his own need. In his longing, Lear destroys Cordelia by creating her presence in the image of his own need and imprisoning her in that image.[19] But the consequences of Lear's actions extend throughout the world of the play. He has tragically altered the conditions of an actual world in which Cordelia must be destroyed, cannot be retrieved, cannot be used. In the play's symbolic action, the malevolence of that outer world mirrors the inner destructiveness of Lear.

The late romances create a comparable intermingling of symbolic and actual destruction. The resolutions of these plays hinge on the restored presence of those who "survive destruction," but often at considerable cost in the actual world. After Leontes retreats into persecutory fantasy in *The Winter's Tale*, he cannot begin to recover a world apart from his omnipotent recreation of it until his "psychic murder of Hermione."[20] The eventual recovery of Hermione, who survives Leontes' hatred, will reinstate the creative rapport between inner need and external reality that Leontes annihilates in jealous delusion. But this process of recovery is decisively complicated when the attack on Hermione destroys in actuality the one figure who provides for Leontes a link between the world of fantasy and the actual world. That link is Mamillius, whom Leontes both loves as a son in the world and endows with projected attributes that reflect his persecutory fantasies: "Though he does bear some signs of me, yet you/Have too much blood in him" (II.i.57–58).

In the infantile struggle that Winnicott interprets, the external world can only be recognized and lived in after it survives destruction, but in the complex dramatic reality of *The Winter's Tale*, Leontes can recognize a world apart from fantasy only when an essential part of it does not survive. Even the oracle of Apollo is powerless to free Leontes from his delusion until news comes of Mamillius' death. Mamillius is a real victim of the assault on Hermione that takes place within the sphere of Leontes' destructive omnipotence; Mamillius dies when he is deprived of the essential maternal presence Leontes destroys in fantasy. The loss of Mamillius in the actual world confirms its independent existence, but cannot enable Leontes fully to assume his own place in it. The completion of Leontes' mourning must reestablish the boundary that both connects and separates the inner and outer world, and must prepare him to acknowledge that outer world as a place to live in. Only then can he and his wife be newly united, in a bond of trust that confirms the autonomy of each, "at the point in time and space of the initiation of their state of separateness."[21]

Each of the romances culminates in the restoration of figures who have survived destruction. The romances also tend to divide into pairs of plays which extend the groups within the drama that precedes them. *Pericles* and *The Winter's Tale* follow in the line of those plays that move toward tragically achieved relations of merger, and I regard them as part of the trust/merger group. *Cymbeline* and *The Tempest* have stronger affinities with the tragedies of the autonomy/isolation group, in which the protagonists move toward isolation and emptiness. The resolution of *Pericles* in the reunion of the protagonist with his daughter and wife is facilitated by the intervention of the goddess Diana. Like that of *Pericles*, the ending of *The Winter's Tale* is centered emotionally in the protagonist's recovery of lost relations of mutuality and trust. Hermione's reappearance in *The Winter's Tale* takes unto itself the quality of sacredness suggested by the appearance of Diana in *Pericles*.

By contrast, Jupiter, god of masculine power and autonomy, must intervene to allow the resolution of the tangled action of *Cymbeline*. Autonomous patriarchal power is restored to the human sphere in *The Tempest* through the actions of Prospero. In the ending of *The Tempest*, and to a lesser extent in *Cymbeline*, feelings of loss and separation qualify the spirit of restoration and renewal. *The Tempest* closes on a Prospero who has given up his beloved daughter, his beloved Ariel, and his beloved magic, and for whom henceforth "every third thought shall be my grave" (V.i.311).

In *The Winter's Tale*, the longing for merger and the violent recoil from it are ultimately subordinated to achieved trust and mutuality.

Perdita, Hermione, and Paulina together enable Leontes to recover a place in the world of relations he has himself destroyed in the delusional rages of the first three acts. In the hallowed presence of Hermione, maternal and wifely, sacred and human, Leontes recovers the base for potent, sustained selfhood lost to Hamlet, Lear, Othello, and Antony. In *The Tempest*, the need for autonomy is purged of the drive toward omnipotence and the collapse into failure. Rendered helpless by his misplaced trust in Antonio, Prospero wrests new power away from the savage legacy of the "foul witch Sycorax," malevolent symbol of feared maternal power. In Prospero, Troilus' "venomed vengeance" yields to the "rarer action" of a mercy that seems to contain, rather than transcend, his vindictive impulses. Macbeth's usurpation by a demonic wife and three cunning witches is superseded by the liberation of those powers imprisoned by Sycorax. Timon's fantastic quest for maternal omnipotence and his collapse into misanthropic rage are transformed into artfully exploited magical power and Prospero's final resignation of himself to his own human limitations. Finally, the mutual banishment of Coriolanus and Rome gives way to the mutual recovery of Prospero and Italy.

In Leontes, Shakespeare allows the richness of relations grounded in mutual trust to flow back into the life of a character who has fearfully transformed those riches into a nightmare of violent jealousy. *The Winter's Tale* moves beyond the poisoned cup that fragments psychic wholeness to the mutuality Leontes finds through a magic "lawful as eating" (V.iii.111). In Prospero, Shakespeare provides a character who subdues the longing for omnipotent control to responsible power, who can release the daughter whose loss leaves an unfillable void in himself and not collapse around his own experience of emptiness. Leontes' recovery of himself in the embrace of Hermione and Prospero's assertion of self-sufficient autonomy through the power of his mind extend, and perhaps embody in its purest form, the division I have tried to trace through the drama leading up to these plays.

The restoration of Leontes in the facilitating presence of Hermione reverberates back through the plays of the trust/merger group to complete an image of manhood complementary to the feminine powers invested in Portia and Rosalind in the festive comedies. Hermione "hangs about his neck," restoring to health not only the mind that has imagined a Polixenes who "wears her like her medal, hanging/About his neck" (V.iii.112; I.ii.306-07), but also Hamlet's anguished memory of Gertrude, who would "hang on [King Hamlet] / As if increase of appetite had grown/By what it fed on" (*Ham.* I.ii.143-45). Essential to the comic achievement that takes *The Winter's Tale* beyond the catastrophic world of tragedy is the movement toward a reciprocal, mutually creative relation between a vigorously rendered manhood and a comparably complete realization of essential womanly power. But the play can only come to this point through Leontes' trusting submission of himself to the active, guiding spirit of Paulina.

The trusting investment of self in others gives way in *The Tempest* to exacting control and shrewd vigilance; the mature womanly powers embodied in Paulina and Hermione drop out altogether. The maternal capacities to give and withhold essential nurture, which inform Timon's initial generosity and his subsequent withdrawal of nurture in the feast of stones and water, are incorporated into Prospero's magic, as in the banquet Ariel first provides and then withdraws from the distraught visitors to the island. In order to dramatize the controlling presence of Prospero, Shakespeare must split his imagination of the feminine into the compliant, innocent daughterhood of Miranda and the evil, maternal power bequeathed to the island by Sycorax. Prospero's autonomy, which completes with new intensity an ideal of manhood anticipated in the *Henriad*, is achieved by the rigorous subordination of trust to power. In the world of *The Tempest*, trust exercised within the sphere of human activity "like a good parent" (I.ii.94) begets a contrary falsehood great as itself.

Taken together, *The Winter's Tale* and *The Tempest* relate to each other across a division in Shakespeare's imagination that is never closed nor completely bridged. This division separates a potential identity sought in a trusting investment of self in another, and which turns on the mutual dependence of male and female, from a potential identity sought in a counterturn toward the assertion of self-willed masculine autonomy over destructive female power or over compliant feminine goodness. But *The Winter's Tale* and *The Tempest* look across this division toward needs that form the separate, incompatible centers of the previous drama.[22] Perhaps, like Leontes and Polixenes, these two plays, written at the end of Shakespeare's career, "shook hands, as over a vast; and embraced, as it were, from the ends of opposed winds" (*WT* I.i.28-29). From the vantage point of this conceit, it is well to recall what happens when that vast is dissolved by intimate contact in *The Winter's Tale*. But nonetheless, Leontes, restored fully to himself in the arms of Hermione, presides over the ending of *The Winter's Tale* with kingly power and autonomy. And Prospero, having willed his own autonomy in triumph over the threatening power invested in Sycorax's heritage, submits himself to the playwright's ultimate "other" for the life-giving applause that only can save him from isolation and despair. Together, these plays culminate a vast dramatic enterprise that encounters with incomparable courage and skill human vulnerabilities that entered into Shakespeare's life, and enter into our own, in that "wide gap of time since first/We were dissevered" (*WT* V.iii.154-55).

Notes

1. In my title I quote from Leontes' closing speech in *The Winter's Tale*; all quotations from Shakespeare are from *William Shakespeare: The Complete Works*, gen. ed. Alfred Harbage (Baltimore: Penguin Books, 1969). Earlier versions of this chapter were presented at the annual meeting of the Shakespeare Association of America, April 1977, and included in a lecture given at the University of California, Berkeley, and the University of California, Santa Cruz, in February 1978. The present form is adapted from the final chapter of my book, *Shakespeare's Development and the Problem Comedies: Turn and Counter-Turn* (Berkeley: Univ. of California Press, 1980).

2. See Edward Dowden, *Shakspere: A Critical Study of his Mind and Art*, 3rd ed. (New York: Harper and Brothers, 1881). His division of the works into periods is entangled with speculations regarding "spiritual tendencies" in Shakespeare's "personality" that occasionally make Dowden's Shakespeare almost unrecognizable to modern readers. But the groups themselves provide a useful way of identifying important shifts in Shakespeare's development of dramatic form, and I think his insistence that the critic must in some way "attempt to pass through the creations of a great dramatic poet to the mind of the creator" (p. xii) is as appropriate to our age, with its speculative tools, as it was to Dowden's.

The chronology Dowden provides has been altered by modern scholarship, which pushes *Julius Caesar* back to 1599 from Dowden's date of 1601–03. I do not include *Julius Caesar* in my discussion of plays from the tragic "period," although it anticipates them more than it recalls either *Titus Andronicus* or *Romeo and Juliet*. *Twelfth Night*, according to modern dating, may have been written after *Hamlet*, and its comic world reflects some of the concerns of the tragedies, but its deepest affinities, in spirit and form, are to the festive comedies that precede it. Two comedies contemporaneous with the tragedies, *All's Well that Ends Well* and *Measure for Measure*, can be assimilated to the pattern I trace through the tragedies and the romances (see n. 22).

3. The idea of "psychological development," as Heinz Lichtenstein has observed, requires the "postulation of an invariant, to which all transformations must be related." See "The Role of Narcissism in the Emergence and Maintenance of a Primary Identity," *The International Journal of Psycho-Analysis*, 45 (1964), 55. In his own work, Lichtenstein postulates "the concept of a primary identity as an invariant, the transformations of which we could call development" (p. 55). My purpose is not to disclose a primary identity for Shakespeare, but to establish the presence of polarized modes of self-experience that are repeatedly transformed in the tragedies and romances without losing their identifying characteristics. Because I see this polarity as both an animating force and a structural principle in Shakespeare's development of the drama, one that persists as an "invariant" against which complex variations can be measured, it serves a purpose in my argument analogous to that served by the concept of primary identity in Lichtenstein's work.

4. Margaret Mahler, "On the First Three Subphases of the Separation-Individuation Process," *Psychoanalysis and Contemporary Science*, 3 (1974), 305.

5. Mahler's theory of "the psychological birth of the individual" specifies a series of subphases, each of which contributes differently to the separation-individuation process, and each of which has its specific forms of psychic hazard (pp. 295–96). But all the subphases are understood within the larger context of opposing gestures toward fusion and separation, a context that she sees as active throughout the life span. It is this larger context that I have found most pertinent in formulating an overview of Shakespeare's development in the tragedies and the romances.

Mahler's full-length studies of early development, which summarize and extend work reported on in many articles, are *On Human Symbiosis and the Vicissitudes of Individuation* (London: Hogarth Press, 1969) and *The Psychological Birth of the Human Infant* (New York: Basic Books, 1975).

6. Erik H. Erikson, *Childhood and Society*, 2nd ed. (New York: W. W. Norton, 1974), p. 250.

7. The "'all-good' mother" is not an actual person but an aspect of the infant's experience of maternal care as a "blissful state of well-being." Mahler links this experience with an "actual or fantasied 'ideal state of self,'" which is a source of longing identical with the longing for fusion ("On the First Three Subphases," p. 305).

8. Arnold H. Modell, *Object Love and Reality* (New York: International Univ. Press, 1968), pp. 61–62.

9. I quote from the opening chapter of C. L. Barber's book (in progress at this writing) on the place of the tragedies in the development of Shakespeare's drama and the drama of the Elizabethan stage. This note gives me an opportunity to acknowledge my large indebtedness to Barber's work generally, and in particular to strategic comments he offered in response to an earlier draft of this paper. Painstaking readings of earlier drafts of this paper by Carol Thomas Neely have also contributed substantially to its present form.

10. Ernst Kris, in his essay on "Prince Hal's Conflict," makes this point in distinguishing Hal's relations to parental conflict from Hamlet's: "In Hamlet, the oedipus [conflict] is fully developed, centering around the queen. In Shakespeare's historical dramas women are absent or insignificant. Prince Hal's struggle against his father appears therefore in isolation, enacted in male society." See *Psychoanalytic Quarterly*, 17 (1948), 502.

11. Although the chronology can never be made totally secure, there is considerable consensus among recent scholars and editors. Harbage provides the following dates for the tragedies, which vary little from those supplied by G. Blakemore Evans in *The Riverside Shakespeare* (Boston: Houghton Mifflin, 1974) and by Sylvan Barnet in *The Signet Classic Shakespeare* (New York: Harcourt Brace Jovanovich, 1963, 1972): *Hamlet*, 1601; *Troilus and Cressida*, 1602; *Othello*, 1604; *King Lear*, 1605; *Macbeth*, 1605; *Timon of Athens*, 1606; *Antony and Cleopatra*, 1607; and *Coriolanus*, 1608. Harbage's dates for the late romances are: *Pericles*, 1607; *Cymbeline*, 1609; *The Winter's Tale*, 1610; and *The Tempest*, 1611.

12. "I Knew a Woman," in Theodore Roethke, *Words for the Wind* (Bloomington, Ind.: Indiana Univ. Press, 1961), p. 151.

13. Janet Adelman perceptively explores the movement in the play by which Antony's Roman identity is dissolved and transcended through its immersion in the fluid, hyperbolical, erotic world of Cleopatra's Egypt in *The Common Liar: An Essay on 'Antony and Cleopatra'* (New Haven, Conn.: Yale Univ. Press, 1973): "The Roman horror of that loss [of oneself in the sexual process] and the ecstatic union which the lovers feel as they die are two elements in the same process: for the dissolution of personal boundaries is both our greatest fear and our highest desire" (p. 149).

14. Murray M. Schwartz emphasizes the "interpenetration of opposites, self and other, male and female," in *Antony and Cleopatra*, as he explores shifts in Shakespeare's use of the "playspace" of drama in the development from the tragedies to the late romances. Schwartz's paper, now Chapter 2 of this book, was delivered at the International Shakespeare Association Congress, Washington, D.C., in April 1976. In the same session, Janet Adelman presented a paper that is now Chapter 7 of this book; it helped focus for me the discussion of *Coriolanus* that follows.

15. Adelman, *The Common Liar*, p. 163.

16. Cf. Philip E. Slater's analysis of the "oral-narcissistic dilemma" in Greek family structure and mythology in *The Glory of Hera* (Boston: Beacon Press, 1968). Slater describes "a deeply narcissistic ambivalence in which the mother does not respond to the child as a separate person, but as both an expression of and a cure for her narcissistic wounds. Her need for self-expansion and vindication requires her both to exalt and to belittle her son, to feed on and to destroy him" (p. 33).

17. D. W. Winnicott, *Playing and Reality* (New York: Basic Books, 1971), p. 91.

18. Winnicott summarizes his argument by providing the following sequence of development: "(1) Subject *relates* to object. (2) Object is in process of being found instead of placed by the subject in the world. (3) Subject *destroys* object. (4) Object survives destruction. (5) Subject can *use* object" (p. 94; see also pp. 90, 92, 93).

19. M. Masud R. Khan provides a clinical instance of this process in a discussion of three patients whose progress in analysis was blocked by their incapacity to relinquish "symbiotic omnipotence": "They needed my *presence*—in the analytic situation so they could disregard and negate me, and in their life so they could be related to themselves." See *The Privacy of the Self* (New York: International Univ. Press, 1974), p. 84.

20. Murray M. Schwartz, "*The Winter's Tale*: Loss and Transformation," *American Imago*, 32 (1975), 156. This illuminating discussion of "how Shakespeare transforms the fears and realities of loss into the theatrical revelation of fulfillment" (p. 146) completes a thorough psychoanalytic interpretation begun in "Leontes' Jealousy in *The Winter's Tale*," *American Imago*, 30 (1973), 250-73. I am also indebted to Stephen Greenblatt for emphasizing the importance of Mamillius' death in the whole design of *The Winter's Tale* (personal communication).

21. Winnicott, p. 97. The quoted words are italicized in the original.

22. *The Winter's Tale* and *The Tempest* also look back to the more problematic resolutions of two comedies from the tragic period, *All's Well That Ends Well* and *Measure for Measure*. The resolution of the plot in *All's Well* through the efforts of Helena suggests the roles of such heroines as Portia and Rosalind in earlier comedies, but Helena's cure of the king's fatal disease and her arrangement for her own miraculous reappearance after rejection and apparent death anticipate the roles divided up among Paulina, Perdita, and Hermione in *The Winter's Tale*. The design of *All's Well* places it among the trust/merger group ("we should submit ourselves to an unknown fear," says Lafew [II.iii.5-6]), although Bertram resists trusting submission up to the very end and does not then embrace it very convincingly.

Measure for Measure, by contrast, comes under the control of a man, Vincentio, who, as many have noted, anticipates the role of Prospero in *The Tempest*. *Measure for Measure* belongs with the autonomy/isolation group; indeed, Vincentio's autonomy is purchased at the expense of isolating him from direct involvement in the range of human conflict that besets lesser mortals in this play. His proposal to Isabella in the comic resolution suggests a denial of that isolation more than a fully successful triumph over it. The book from which this essay is adapted is a study of *All's Well* and *Measure for Measure* and the place they occupy in Shakespeare's development (see n. 1).

9 ❀ "I wooed thee with my sword": Shakespeare's Tragic Paradigms

Madelon Gohlke

> Traditional textual interpretation founds itself on this particular
> understanding of metaphor: a detour to truth. Not only individ-
> ual metaphors or systems of metaphors, but fiction in general is
> seen as a detour to a truth that the critic can deliver through her
> interpretation.
> —Gayatri Chakravorty Spivak, translator's preface to Jacques
> Derrida, *Of Grammatology*

Much of what I am going to say about Shakespeare and about the
possibility of a feminist psychoanalytic interpretation of literature, or,
for that matter, of culture, depends on a reading of metaphor. It is
metaphor that allows us to subread, to read on the margins of discourse,
to analyze what is latent or implicit in the structures of consciousness
or of a text. A serious feminist critic, moreover, cannot proceed very
far without becoming paranoid unless she abandons a strictly intention-
alist position. To argue sexism as a conscious conspiracy becomes both
foolish and absurd. To pursue the implications of metaphor, on the
other hand, in terms of plot, character, and possibly even genre, is to
adopt a psychoanalytic strategy that deepens the context of feminist
interpretation and reveals the possibility at least of a feminist psychohistory.

Metaphor provides a convenient entrance into a text, as it provides a
point of departure for psychoanalytic interpretation because of the way
in which vehicle consistently outdistances tenor. For instance, the following two lines from *A Midsummer Night's Dream*—"Hippolyta, I
wooed thee with my sword,/And won thy love, doing thee injuries"

(I.i.16-17)—convey far more than the simple prose explanation offered in my text: "Theseus had captured Hippolyta when he conquered the Amazons."[1] These lines, in which the sword may be the metaphoric equivalent of the phallus, in which love may be either generated or secured by hostility, and in which the two partners take up sadistic and masochistic postures in relation to each other, are not irrelevant to the concerns of the play. They may be seen to reverberate in the exaggerated submission of Helena to Demetrius, in the humiliation of Titania by Oberon, in the penetration by violence of the language of love. They even bear an oblique relation to the "lamentable comedy" of *Pyramus and Thisbe*, the failed marriage plot contained within the larger structure of successful heterosexual union celebrated at the end of the play.

Metaphor may also elucidate character, as in the case of Claudio in *Much Ado*, whose speech is relatively poor in imagery until it erupts into his condemnation of Hero in the middle of the play. There he claims, among other things: "But you are more intemperate in your blood/ Than Venus, or those pamp'red animals/That rage in savage sensuality" (IV.i.58-60). It is Claudio's suspicious predisposition that composes this violent and disproportioned outburst. It is no accident that the "solution" to this conflict hinges on the fiction that Claudio has killed Hero through his slander. In this sense, the conventional marriage plot of Shakespeare's comedy may also be read metaphorically. The prospect of heterosexual union arouses emotional conflicts that give shape to the plot, unleashing a kind of violence that in the comedies remains symbolic, imagined rather than enacted.

In the following pages, I shall be considering the uses of metaphor in several related ways. In some instances, I will refer to the function of metaphor in individual discourse, assuming that it is this kind of highly charged imagistic expression that offers the most immediate clues to unconscious awareness, that metaphor in some sense structures awareness. I am assuming furthermore that metaphor may be seen to structure action, so that some features of plot may be regarded as expanded metaphors. Moving outward from this premise, I then want to consider the possibility that certain cultural fictions may be read metaphorically, that is, as expressions of unconsciously held cultural beliefs. I am especially interested in Shakespeare's tragedies, in what seem to me to be shared fictions on the part of the heroes about femininity and about their own vulnerability in relation to women—fictions interwoven with violence, which generate a particular kind of heterosexual dilemma.

The primacy of metaphor in the structures of individual consciousness, as in the collective fiction of the plot, appears in an early tragedy, *Romeo and Juliet*, where the failure of the play to achieve the generic status of comedy may be read as the result of the way heterosexual relations are imagined. In the conversation between the servants Sampson and Gregory, sexual intercourse, through a punning reference to the word maidenhead, comes to be described as a kind of murder:[2]

> *Sampson.* 'Tis all one. I will show myself a tyrant. When I have fought
> with the men, I will be civil with the maids—I will cut off
> their heads.
> *Gregory.* The heads of the maids?
> *Sampson.* Ay, the heads of the maids or their maidenheads. Take it in what
> sense thou wilt.
>
> (I.i.23–28)

To participate in the masculine ethic of this play is to participate in the feud, which defines relations among men as intensely competitive, and relations with women as controlling and violent, so that women in Sampson's language "being the weaker vessels, are ever thrust to the wall" (I.i.17–18). That Romeo initially rejects this ethic would seem to redefine the nature and structure of male/female relationships. What is striking about the relationship between Romeo and Juliet, however, is the extent to which it anticipates and ultimately incorporates violence.

Both lovers have a lively imagination of disaster. While Romeo ponders "some vile forfeit of untimely death" (I.iv.111), Juliet speculates "If he is married,/My grave is like to be my wedding bed" (I.v.136–37). Premonition, for both, has the force of self-fulfilling prophecy. While Romeo seeks danger by courting Juliet and death by threatening suicide in the wake of Tybalt's death, Juliet, under pressure, exclaims: "I'll to my wedding bed;/And death, not Romeo, take my maidenhead!" (III. ii.136–37). Read metaphorically, the plot validates the perception expressed variously in the play that love kills.

The paradigm offered by *Romeo and Juliet*, with some modifications, may be read in the major tragedies as well. Here the structures of male dominance, involving various strategies of control expressed in the language of prostitution, rape, and murder, conceal deeper structures of fear, in which women are perceived as powerful and the heterosexual relation is seen as either mutually violent or at least deeply threatening to the man.

Murder in the Bedroom: *Hamlet* and *Othello*

Hamlet's violent behavior in his mother's bedroom expresses some of the violence of his impulses towards her. Obsessed as he is with sexual betrayal, the problem of revenge for him is less a matter of killing Claudius than one of not killing his mother.[3] Hamlet's anger against women, based on his perception of his mother's conduct, finds expression in the language of prostitution in his violent outburst against Ophelia:

> I have heard of your paintings, well enough. God hath given you one face,
> and you make yourselves another. You jig and amble, and you lisp; you
> nickname God's creatures and make your wantonness your ignorance. Go to,
> I'll no more on't; it hath made me mad.
>
> (III.i.143-48)

It is painting that makes women two-faced, which allows them to deceive, to wear the mask of chastity, while lust "Will sate itself in a celestial bed/And prey on garbage" (I.v.56-57). Like whores, they cannot be trusted. The paradox of prostitution in these plays is based on the masculine perception that the prostitute is not so much the victim as the agent of exploitation. If women are classed as prostitutes and treated as sexual objects, it is because they are so deeply feared as sexually untrustworthy, as creatures whose intentions and desires are fundamentally unreadable. Thus, while Helen in *Troilus and Cressida* is verbally degraded (the Trojans discuss her in terms of soiled goods and contaminated meat) she is, through her infidelity to Menelaus, the source of the sexual pride and humiliation that animates the entire conflict between the two warring nations. Honor among men, in this play, though it takes the form of combat, is ultimately a sexual matter, depending largely on the fidelity or infidelity of women. For a man to be betrayed by a woman is to be humiliated or dishonored. To recover his honor he must destroy the man and/or woman who is responsible for his humiliation, for placing him in a position of vulnerability.

In *Hamlet*, it is the player queen who most clearly articulates the significance attributed to feminine betrayal. "A second time I kill my husband dead/When second husband kisses me in bed" (III.ii.188-89). It hardly matters whether Gertrude was implicated in the actual death of Hamlet. Adultery is itself a form of violence and as great a crime. Hamlet, who reacts as an injured husband in seeking revenge against Claudius, also seeks retribution against his mother. Not having any sanction to kill his mother, however, he must remind himself to "speak daggers to her, but use none" (III.ii.404). That his manner suggests physical violence is confirmed by Gertrude's response: "What wilt thou do? Thou wilt not murder me?/Help, ho!" (III.iii.22-23). It is at this point that the violence Hamlet seeks to contain in his attitude towards his mother is deflected onto another object presumed to be appropriate.

This single act of displaced violence, moreover, has further ramifications in terms of Hamlet's relation to Ophelia, whose conflicted responses to the fact that her lover has killed her father increase the burden of double messages she has already received from the men in the play, culminating in her madness and death. It is not his mother whom Hamlet kills (Claudius takes care of that) but Ophelia. Only when she is dead, moreover, is he free to say clearly that he loved her. Similarly

Othello, in whom the pathology of jealousy, the humiliation and rage that plague the man supposedly dishonored by the woman he loves, are more specifically and vividly portrayed, will say of Desdemona late in the play: "I will kill thee,/And love thee after" (V.ii.18-19).

If I seem to be arguing that the tragedies are largely about the degeneration of heterosexual relationships, or marriages that fail, it is because I am reading the development from the comedies through the problem plays and the major tragedies in terms of an explosion of the sexual tensions that threaten without rupturing the surface of the earlier plays. A woman's power throughout is less social or political (though it may have social and political ramifications) than emotional, expressed in her capacity to give or to withhold love. In a figure like Isabella, the capacity to withhold arouses lust and a will to power in someone like Angelo, whose enforcing tactics amount to rape. In Portia, the threat of infidelity, however jokingly presented, is a weapon in her struggle with Antonio for Bassanio's allegiance. Male resistance, comic and exaggerated in Benedick, sullen and resentful in Bertram, stems from fears of occupying a position of weakness, taking in essence a "feminine" posture in relation to a powerful woman.

The feminine posture for a male character is that of the betrayed, and it is the man in this position who portrays women as whores. Since Iago occupies this position in relation to Othello, it makes sense that he seeks to destroy him, in the same way that Othello seeks to destroy the agent of his imagined betrayal, Desdemona. There is no reason to suppose, moreover, that Iago's consistently degraded view of women conceals any less hostile attitude in his actual relations with women. He, after all, like Othello, kills his wife. The difference between the two men lies not in their fear and mistrust of women, but in the degree to which they are able to accept an emotional involvement. It is Othello, not Iago, who wears his heart on his sleeve "for daws to peck at" (I.i. 62). Were it not for Othello's initial vulnerability to Desdemona, he would not be susceptible to Iago's machinations. Having made himself vulnerable, moreover, he attaches an extraordinary significance to the relationship: "And when I love thee not,/Chaos is come again" (III.iii. 91-92); "But there where I have garnered up my heart,/Where either I must live or bear no life,/The fountain from the which my current runs /Or else dries up" (IV.ii.56-59).

Once Othello is convinced of Desdemona's infidelity (much like Claudio, on the flimsiest of evidence), he regards her not as a woman who has committed a single transgression but as a whore, one whose entire behavior may be explained in terms of lust. As such, he may humiliate her in public, offer her services to the Venetian ambassadors, pass judgment on her, and condemn her to death. Murder in this light is a desperate attempt to control. It is Desdemona's power to hurt that Othello seeks to eliminate by ending her life. While legal and social sanctions may be invoked against the prostitute, the seemingly virtuous woman suspected of adultery may be punished by death. In either case, it is the fear or pain of victimization on the part of the man that leads him to victimize women. It is those who perceive themselves to be powerless who may be incited to the acts of greatest violence.

The paradox of violence in *Othello*, not unlike that in *Macbeth*, is that the exercise of power turns against the hero. In this case, the murder of a woman leads to self-murder, and the hero dies attesting to the erotic destructiveness at the heart of his relationship with Desdemona: "I kissed thee ere I killed thee. No way but this,/Killing myself, to die upon a kiss" (V.ii.357–58). If murder may be a loving act, love may be a murdering act, and consummation of such a love is possible only through the death of both parties.

"Of Woman Born": *Lear* and *Macbeth*

The fantasy of feminine betrayal that animates the drama of *Othello* may be seen to conceal or to be coordinate with deep fantasies of maternal betrayal in *Macbeth* and *Lear*.[4] Here the emphasis falls not so much on the adult heterosexual relation (though there are such relations) as on the mother/son or the fantasy of the mother/son relation. In these plays, to be feminine in the masculine consciousness is to be powerless, specifically in relation to a controlling or powerful woman. For Lear, rage as an expression of power acts as a defense against this awareness, while tears threaten not only the dreaded perception of himself as feminine, and hence weak, but also the breakdown of his psychic order:

> Life and death, I am ashamed
> That thou hast power to shake my manhood thus!
> That these hot tears, which break from me perforce,
> Should make thee worth them. Blasts and fogs upon thee! (I.iv.298–301)

> You think I'll weep.
> No, I'll not weep.
> I have full cause of weeping, but this heart
> Shall break into a hundred thousand flaws
> Or ere I'll weep. O Fool, I shall go mad! (II.iv.279–83)

> O, let me not be mad, not mad, sweet heaven!
> Keep me in temper; I would not be mad! (I.v.45–46)

It is not Lear who annihilates his enemies, calling down curses on the organs of generation of Goneril and Regan, but rather he who is being banished by the women on whom he had depended for nurturance. It is they who are the agents of power and destruction, allied with the storm and he, like Edgar, who is "unaccomodated man," a "poor, bare, forked animal," naked and vulnerable. That the condition of powerlessness gives rise to compassion in Lear is part of his dignity as a tragic hero. It does not, however, alter his perceptions of women as either good or bad mothers. Moreover, if the banishment of Cordelia initiates a process by which Lear becomes psychotic, it may be argued that her return is essential to the restoration of his sanity. The presence or absence of Cordelia, like Othello's faith in Desdemona's fidelity, orders the hero's psychic universe. When Cordelia dies, Lear must either believe that she is not dead or die with her, being unable to withstand the condition of radical separation imposed by death.

In *King Lear*, the most powerful image of separation, of the child who is banished by his mother, is that of birth. "We came crying hither: /Thou know'st, the first time that we smell the air/We wawl and cry" (IV.vi.178–80). In this sense, the mother's first act of betrayal may be that of giving birth, the violent expulsion of her infant into a hostile environment. In other passages, a woman's body itself is perceived as a hostile environment:

> But to the girdle do the gods inherit,
> Beneath is all the fiend's.
> There's hell, there's darkness, there is the sulphurous pit. (IV.vi.126–29)

> The dark and vicious place where thee he got
> Cost him his eyes. (V.iii.174–75)

Intercourse imaged as violent intrusion into a woman's body may be designed to minimize the cost.

If it is birth itself—the condition of owing one's life to a woman and the ambivalence attending an awareness of dependence on women in general—that structures much of Lear's relations to his daughters, *Macbeth* may be read in terms of a systematic attempt by the hero to deny such an awareness. The world constructed by Macbeth attempts to deny not only the values of trust and hospitality, perceived as essentially feminine, but to eradicate femininity itself.[5] Macbeth reads power in terms of a masculine mystique that has no room for maternal values, as if the conscious exclusion of these values would eliminate all conditions of dependence, making him in effect invulnerable. To be born of woman, as he reads the witches' prophecy, is to be mortal. Macbeth's program of violence, involving murder and pillage in his kingdom and the repression of anything resembling compassion or remorse within, is designed, like Coriolanus' desperate militarism, to make him author of himself.

The irony of *Macbeth*, of course, is that in his attempt to make himself wholly "masculine" or uncontaminated, so to speak, by the womb, he destroys all source of value: honor, trust, and—to his dismay—fertility itself. It is his deep personal anguish that he is childless. The values associated with women and children, which he considers unmanly, come to be perceived as the source of greatest strength. In this play, it is procreation rather than violence that confers power—"The seeds of Banquo kings!" (III.i.70). To kill a child or to imagine such an act, as Lady Macbeth does in expressing contempt for her husband's vacillations, is to betray not only the bonds of human society but to betray one's deepest self. To reject the conditions of weakness and dependence is to make oneself weak and dependent. Macbeth's relentless pursuit of power masks his insecurities, his anxieties, and ultimately his impotence. *Macbeth, more clearly than any of the other* tragedies (with the possible exception of *Coriolanus*), enacts the paradox of power, in which the hero's equation of masculinity with violence as a denial or defense against femininity leads to his destruction.

Macbeth's attempt to avoid the perception of Lear that "we cry that we are come/To this great stage of fools" (IV.vi.182-83), that the human infant is radically defenseless and dependent on the nurturance of a woman, gradually empties his life of meaning and leads to his perception of it as "a tale/Told by an idiot . . ./Signifying nothing" (V.v. 26-28). Of all the tragic heroes, moreover, he is the most isolated in his death, alienated from himself, his countrymen, his queen. He has become what he most feared, the plaything of powerful feminine forces, betrayed by the "instruments of darkness," the three witches.

"The Heart of Loss": *Antony and Cleopatra*

Interwoven into the patriarchal structure of Shakespeare's tragedies is an equally powerful matriarchal vision. They are even, I would argue, aspects of one another, both proceeding from the masculine consciousness of feminine betrayal. Both inspire a violence of response on the part of the hero against individual women, but more importantly, against the hero's perception of himself as womanish, in which he ultimately hurts himself. The concurrence of these themes is particularly evident in *Antony and Cleopatra*, a play that both recalls the ritual marriage conclusion of the comedies as it deepens the sexual dilemma of the tragic hero.

Antony's relation both to Cleopatra and to Caesar may be read in terms of his anxieties about dominance, his fear of self-loss in any intimate encounter. Early in the play, Cleopatra uses this perception to her advantage by suggesting that for Antony to respond to the Roman messengers is to acknowledge his submission either to Caesar or to Fulvia. Her own tactics, of course, are manipulative and a form of dominance that Antony himself recognizes: "These strong Egyptian fetters I must break/Or lose myself in dotage" (I.ii.117-18). The advice of the soothsayer to Antony concerning his proximity to Caesar is similar in structure if not in content: "Near him thy angel/Becomes afeard, as being o'erpow'red" (II.iii.20-21). When Antony returns to Egypt, he is in effect "o'erpow'red by Cleopatra: "O'er my spirit/Thy full supremacy thou knew'st (III.xi.58-59); "You did know/How much you were my conquerer, and that/My sword, made weak by my affection, would/Obey it on all cause" (III.xi.65-68). Antony, like Romeo earlier, perceives himself as having been feminized by love: "O sweet Juliet,/Thy beauty hath made me effeminate/And in my temper soft'ned valor's steel!" (*Rom.* III.i.115-17). "O, thy vile lady!/She has robbed me of my sword" (*Ant.* IV.xiv.22-23).

If affection makes Antony weak, it also makes him suspicious of Cleopatra's fidelity: "For I am sure/Though you can guess what temperance should be,/You know not what it is" (III.xiii.120-22). He falls easy prey to the conviction that Cleopatra has betrayed him to Caesar, making him the subject of sexual as well as political humiliation. "O, that I were/Upon the hill of Basan to outroar/The horned herd!" (III.xiii.126-28). In this light, Cleopatra becomes a "witch," a "spell," a "triple-turned whore":

> O this false soul of Egypt! This grave charm,
> Whose eye becked forth my wars, and called them home,
> Whose bosom was my crownet, my chief end,
> Like a right gypsy hath at fast and loose
> Beguiled me, to the very heart of loss.
> What, Eros, Eros!
>
> (IV.xii.25-30)

Antony, under the power of erotic attachment, feels himself, like Othello, to have been utterly betrayed. Under the impact of this loss, moreover, his sense of psychic integrity begins to disintegrate: "Here I am Antony,/Yet cannot hold this visible shape, my knave" (IV.xiv.13-14). Chaos is come again.

While the fiction of Cleopatra's death restores Antony's faith in her love, it does not restore his energy for life. Rather, the withdrawal of her presence destroys any vestige of interest he has in the world of the living. "Now all labor/Mars what it does; yea, very force entangles/Itself with strength" (IV.xiv.47-49). It is Cleopatra who not only dominates Antony's emotional life but invests his world with meaning. The fact that she—unlike Juliet, Ophelia, Desdemona, Cordelia, and Lady

Macbeth—dies so long after her lover, not only reveals her as a complex figure in her own right, but also attests to her power to give imaginative shape to the hero's reality.

Cleopatra in many ways is the epitome of what is hated, loved, and feared in a woman by Shakespeare's tragic heroes. She is, on the one hand, the woman who betrays, a Circe, an Acrasia, an Eve, the Venus of *Venus and Adonis*. To submit to her or be seduced by her is to die. She is the player queen, for whom adultery is also murder. She is a Goneril, a Lady Macbeth, a nonnurturing mother. What she takes, on the other hand, she also has the power to give. She is imaginative, fertile, identified with the procreative processes of the Nile. If Antony lives in our imagination, it is because of her "conception" of him. In this sense, she, like Desdemona and Cordelia, is the hero's point of orientation, his source of signification in the world. Union with her is celebrated as a curious comic counterpoint to the tragic structure of double suicide and also portrayed as a literal impossibility. Moreover, for this sexually powerful woman to escape censure, the fate of a Cressida or a Helen, she must negate her own strength; she must die. While Theseus' phallic sword in Antony's hands turns against him, Cleopatra, like Juliet, will accept death "as a lover's pinch,/Which hurts, and is desired" (V.ii. 295-96). Throughout Shakespeare's tragedies, the imagery of heterosexual union involves the threat of mutual or self-inflicted violence.

Looked at from one angle, what Shakespeare's tragedies portray is the anguish and destruction attendant on a fairly conventional and culturally supported set of fictions about heterosexual encounter. The tragedies, as I read them, do not themselves support these fictions, except to the extent that they examine them with such acute attention. The values that emerge from these plays are, if anything, "feminine" values dissociated from the traditional masculine categories of force and politics, focused instead on the significance of personal relationships or the fact of human relatedness: the values of feeling, kinship, loyalty, friendship, and even romantic love. That the recognition of these values entails the destruction of the hero and everyone who matters to him attests perhaps to a kind of cultural determinism, or at least to the very great difficulty of reimagining habitual modes of behavior. It is the basis in cultural fictions of certain kinds of heterosexual attitudes to which I now wish to turn.

On the Margins of Patriarchal Discourse

Shakespeare's tragic paradigms offer the possibility of a deconstructive reading of the rape metaphor that informs Theseus' words to his captured queen.[6] Violence against women as an aspect of the structure of male dominance in Shakespeare's plays may be seen to obscure deeper patterns of conflict in which women as lovers, and perhaps more importantly as mothers, are perceived as radically untrustworthy. In this structure of relation, it is women who are regarded as powerful and men who strive to avoid an awareness of their vulnerability in relation to women, a vulnerability in which they regard themselves as "feminine." It is in this sense that one may speak of a matriarchal substratum or subtext within the patriarchal text. The matriarchal substratum itself, however, is not feminist. What it does is provide a rationale for the structure of male dominance in Shakespeare's tragedies, while it provides an avenue of continuity between these plays and the comedies in which women more obviously wield power.

The preceding analysis may be seen, moreover, to parallel the movement of psychoanalytic theory from an emphasis on oedipal to preoedipal stages of development. Roughly speaking, the shift has occurred in terms of a decrease of concern with father-son relations and a corresponding increase of concern with mother-son relations.[7] Certainly it may be said that the theories of object-relations, narcissism, schizophrenia, and separation-individuation have more to do with the child's early relations with the mother than with the father. Whether or not these theories are read in consonance with Freud's formulation of the Oedipus complex, the shift in focus relocates the discussion of certain issues. This relocation in turn reveals new interpretive possibilities. Specifically, it reopens the question of femininity.

A deconstructive reading of the rape metaphor in Shakespeare's tragedies leads directly or indirectly to a discussion of the masculine perception of femininity as weakness. The "macho" stance thus becomes a form of "masculine protest," or a demonstration of phallic power in the face of a threatened castration. It is for the male hero, however, that femininity signifies weakness, while actual women are perceived by him as enormously powerful, specifically in their maternal functions. It is not the female herself who is perceived as weak, but rather the feminized male. To project this problem back onto women—as Freud does in his discussions of femininity, in which the little girl perceives herself as castrated—is to present it as incapable of resolution.[8] If femininity itself is defined as the condition of lack, of castration, then there is no way around the masculine equation that to be feminine is to be castrated, or as Antony puts it, to be robbed of one's sword.

It is the so-called masculine consciousness, therefore, that defines femininity as weakness and institutes the structures of male dominance designed to defend against such an awareness. Shakespeare's tragedies, as I read them, may be viewed as a vast commentary on the absurdity and destructiveness of this defensive posture. However, while Shakespeare may be said to affirm the values of feeling and vulnerability associated with femininity, he does not in dramatic terms dispel the anxiety surrounding the figure of the feminized male. At this point, I would say that dramatic metaphors intersect with cultural metaphors.[9]

Freud's views of femininity may be useful to the extent that they articulate some deeply held cultural convictions. In one sense, what they do is reveal the basis of some powerful cultural metaphors, so powerful in fact that they continue to find formulation in the midst of our vastly different social and intellectual context. In the midst of profound structural changes in habits of philosophic and scientific thinking, as a culture we cling to the language of presence and absence, language and silence, art and nature, reason and madness, to describe the relations between the terms masculine and feminine. It is as though the breakdown of hierarchical modes of thought, of vertical ways of imagining experience, finds its deepest resistance in our habits of imagining the relations between the sexes. Some, like the Jungian James Hillman, would even argue that in order to effect real changes in our intellectual formulations of reality, we must find ways of reimagining femininity.[10] Sexual politics may lie at the heart of human culture, of our constantly shifting and evolving world views.

The preceding discussion, of course, rests on assumptions to which Freud would not have subscribed, chief among them a hypothesis concerning the relation between cultural metaphors and the concept of a cultural unconscious. What I would like to propose is that the notion of the unconscious may be culture specific—that is, the guiding metaphors of a given society or culture may legitimately be seen to express the structure of its unconscious assumptions, just as the metaphoric structure of individual discourse may be seen to convey some of the unconscious freight of a given life. If Kuhn is correct in assuming that scientific revolutions are the result of paradigm shifts or profound changes in our habits of imagining the world, then it may also be possible to consider the unconscious implications of certain habits of imagining.[11] Literary conventions may then be viewed as aspects of these imaginative habits, as codifications of a certain spectrum of unconscious attitudes, at the same time that they change and evolve, live and die according to their relation to the society out of which they arise and to which they respond. Cultural changes, to pursue the implications of Kuhn's argument, are in effect profound metaphoric changes, which in turn involve changes in the structuring of the unconscious.

In this light, literary history may be read psychologically. The questions one might ask, then, would concern the spectrum of psychic needs served by specific conventions and genres. Tracing the uses of a convention would then also yield a literary version of psychohistory.

To offer an example close to the subject of this essay, I would like to pursue briefly some of the ramifications of the rhetoric of courtly love.

It is interesting to observe the language of Denis de Rougement, who is so careful to situate the courtly love phenomenon in a historical sense, when he refers to the rhetorical trope of love as war: "There is no need, for example, to invoke Freudian theories in order to see that the war instinct and eroticism are fundamentally allied: it is so perfectly obvious from the common figurative use of language."[12] Obvious to whom? Is the war instinct, for instance, perceived as an aspect of the feminine psyche? Here the common (and to many readers unquestioned) assumption that reference to the male of the species includes women may be seen to obscure a process by which a fundamentally "masculine" attitude is proposed as a universal norm. More important, however, is the interpretive process by which de Rougemont reads a metaphor specific to a certain set of conventions, albeit powerful ones, as an unalterable aspect of the unconscious life of the species: "All this confirms the natural—that is to say, the physiological—connexion between the sexual and fighting instincts."[13]

It is this supposedly natural "connexion between the sexual and fighting instincts" that structures the language of the courtly love lyric, as it structures the language of sexual encounter in Shakespeare. To term this rhetoric "conventional" is not to demean it but rather to call attention to its psychological power, to which de Rougemont himself assents, at the same time that one recognizes its mutability, its historicity. Images of sexual intercourse as an act of violence committed against a woman run deep in our culture. The depth and persistence of these images, however, may tell us more about the anxieties of a culture in which femininity is conceived as castration and women are perceived paradoxically as a source of maternal power than it does about the actual or possible relations between the sexes.

Toward a Feminist Discourse

> And, as I have hinted before, deconstruction must also take into account the lack of sovereignty of the critic himself. Perhaps this 'will to ignorance' is simply a matter of attitude, a realization that one's choice of evidence is provisional, a self-distrust, a distrust of one's own power, the control of one's vocabulary, a shift from the phallocentric to the hymeneal.
> —Gayatri Chakravorty Spivak, translator's preface to Jacques Derrida, *Of Grammatology*

Literary history, finally, is an aspect of cultural history. Both attest to changing patterns of awareness, to the constant refiguring of our relation to our specific location in time and space, to our own historicity. If individual history, as Ortega y Gasset writes, may be conceived as a process of casting and living out or living through metaphors of the self, is it not possible to imagine cultural history in similar terms?[14] To interpret these metaphors, to read on the margins of discourse, is not only to engage in a process that is characteristic of psychoanalytic interpretation but also to become engaged in a fundamentally historical process, that of making what is unconscious conscious and thus altering and displacing the location of the unconscious. This process, obviously akin to that of psychotherapy, is not to be perceived statically as an attempt to eliminate the unconscious but rather to dislodge it, to transform its metaphoric base.

Psychoanalytic theory in this sense may also be read in the historical dimension, as a means of reading the unconscious figurings of a given life within a specific cultural moment. As such, it will of course be subject to change and will to some extent serve the interests of the society that supports it. I am not here arguing against psychoanalytic theory in any sense but rather *for* a recognition of its historicity.[15] While Freud's elaboration of the Oedipus complex may have served to assuage the neurotic dilemmas of his society, it does not serve the needs of contemporary feminism. In a society like ours, in which most women can expect to work for a significant part of their lives and to bear fewer than three children, the interpretive myths offered by Freud for women are increasingly pathological. In order to be useful, the theory must bear a demonstrable relation to perceived reality. To argue that the social reality of women should be altered to fit the theory is not only reactionary but naive. It would make more sense to pursue the directions of contemporary psychoanalytic theory toward a redefinition of femininity, assuming, as I do, that implicit within the current focus on the mother/child relation is a reawakening of interest in the question of femininity. There are even some theorists, like Dorothy Dinnerstein, who would argue that such a reformulation is necessary for cultural survival, given the political destructiveness of the masculine ethic.[16]

What then, in psychoanalytic terms, would constitute the beginnings of feminist discourse? How is a woman, according to the painful elaborations of Julia Kristeva and others, to avoid the Scylla of silence or madness and the Charybdis of alienated or masculine discourse?[17] Gayatri Spivak has lately been suggesting that what we need is something like a Copernican revolution: from the phallocentric formulation of femininity as absence to a gynocentric language of presence.[18] If it makes sense that the male child should perceive his own sex as primary and difference as an inferior version of himself, then it makes as much sense that the little girl should also initially perceive her sex as primary. That each sex should take itself as the norm is perhaps part of the Ptolemaic universe of children, which must undergo several stages of decentering before maturity. Not to undergo this process of decentering is to elaborate structures in which dominance becomes the mask of weakness and submission a subversive strategy in the mutual struggle for power. For a woman to read herself obliquely through the patriarchal discourse as "other" is to assent to this structure. For a critic, male or female, to read this discourse as representative of the true nature of masculinity or femininity is to accept this structure. For a feminist critic to deconstruct this discourse is simultaneously to recognize her own historicity and to engage in the process of dislocation of the unconscious by which she begins to affirm her own reality.

Notes

1. *A Midsummer Night's Dream, The Complete Signet Classic Shakespeare,* ed. Sylvan Barnet (New York: Harcourt Brace Jovanovich, 1963, 1972), p. 530. Quotations from Shakespeare in this chapter refer to this edition.

2. Two critics have dealt specifically with the relationship between sex and violence in this play. A. K. Nardo notes that "To the youths who rekindle the feud on a point of honor, sex, aggression, and violence are inextricably united." While Juliet undergoes an extraordinary process of development, Nardo argues, she is ultimately unable to survive in this hostile atmosphere and is finally "thrust to the wall by the phallic sword her society has exalted." See "Romeo and Juliet Up against the Wall," *Paunch,* 48–49 (1977), 126–32. Coppélia Kahn, in a more extensive consideration of this subject, relates the ethic of the feud, in which sex and violence are linked, to the patriarchal structure of the society, commenting on the extent to which the conclusion of the play, associating death with sexual consummation, is also contained within this structure. Fate is thus not only a result of powerful social forces but also of the individual subjective responses to these forces. See "Coming of Age in Verona," *Modern Language Studies,* 8 (1977-78), 5-22.

3. Theodore Lidz represents Hamlet as torn between the impulse to kill his mother for having betrayed his father and the desire to win her to a state of repentance and renewed chastity. My reading of Hamlet is very much indebted to his analysis in *Hamlet's Enemy: Madness and Myth in "Hamlet"* (New York: Basic Books, 1975).

4. Murray M. Schwartz discusses the difficulty of the hero's recognition of his relation to a nurturing woman in Chapter 2 of this book. While Lear's dilemma, according to Schwartz, results from a "refusal to mourn the loss of maternal provision," Macbeth's difficulty may be seen as the result of an attempt to usurp maternal functions and to control the means of nurturance himself.

5. My discussion of the ways in which masculinity and femininity are perceived in this play is indebted to Cleanth Brooks' classic essay on *Macbeth* in *The Well*

Wrought Urn (London: Dobson Books, 1968), pp. 17–39. For Brooks, it is Macbeth's war on children that reveals most clearly his own weakness and desperation. Ultimately the issue of manliness, for Brooks, is related to the theme of humanity or lack of it, but he does not raise questions about masculine and feminine stereotypes.

6. I would assent to the following description by Gayatri Spivak of the task of deconstruction: "To locate the promising marginal text, to disclose the undecidable moment, to pry it loose, with the positive lever of the signifier; to reverse the resident hierarchy, only to displace it; to dismantle in order to reconstitute what is always already inscribed. Deconstruction in a nutshell." See Jacques Derrida, *Of Grammatology*, translator's preface (Baltimore: Johns Hopkins Univ. Press, 1976), p. lxxvii. While Spivak points out that there is no end to this process, in that the work of deconstruction is itself subject to deconstruction, she also notes that "as she deconstructs, all protestations to the contrary, the critic necessarily assumes that she at least, and for the time being, means what she says" (p. lxxvii). While it may not be strictly necessary to borrow this terminology for the reading I am proposing, it may be useful to observe that any large-scale reinterpretation, from a minority position, of a majority view of reality must appear at least in the eyes of some as a "deconstruction."

7. Although the shift from father to mother is clear in the work of such theorists as John Bowlby, Melanie Klein, Margaret Mahler, and D. W. Winnicott, the child or infant, partly for grammatical reasons, tends to be regarded as male. Here, the problem inherent in the use of the masculine pronoun to refer to both sexes emerges. Textually speaking, the construction often obscures a shift of consideration from the development of the infant, male or female, to the exclusive development of the male infant. This convention is related to the cultural assumption by which the male of the species is taken as a norm, of which the female then becomes a variant. To remove this convention would not merely introduce a stylistic awkwardness (for some people at least), but it would also reveal a fundamental awkwardness in the structure of the author's argument. While the use of the male pronoun often *is* used generically to indicate both men and women, it as frequently serves to exclude consideration of the female without calling attention to the process by which she has been removed from the discussion.

8. Although Freud approaches the subject of femininity from different angles in his three major discussions of it, there is no question that he links the process of feminine development indissolubly to the recognition on the part of the little girl that she is castrated. It would seem at least reasonable to argue, however, that the presence or absence of a penis is of far greater significance to the boy or man, who feels himself subject to the threat of its removal, than it could ever be to the girl or woman, for whom such a threat can have little anatomical meaning. I wonder too, why, in Freud's argument, a little girl would be inspired to give up the manifestly satisfying activity of masturbation on the basis of the illusion of a loss—the assumption perhaps that she might have had more pleasure if she had once had a penis, of which she seems mysteriously to have been deprived?

The problem that gives rise to these baroque speculations is of course Freud's assumption that there must be some reason why the little girl would withdraw her love from her mother in order to bestow it upon her father. Freud can imagine no other reason than the little girl's recognition of her own inferiority and thus "penis envy," and her resentment of her mother, equally deprived, for not having provided her with the desired organ. There can be no heterosexual love, in this account, without the theory of feminine castration. One can understand, from this vantage point, why Freud was reluctant to give it up. See "Some Psychical Consequences of the Anatomical Distinction Between the Sexes." "Female Sexuality," and "Femininity," in *The Standard Edition of the Complete Psychological Works of Sigmund Freud*, ed. and trans. James Strachey et al., 24 vols. (London: Hogarth Press, 1953–74), 19, 21, 22, pp. 241–60, 221–46, 112–35. For various critiques of Freud, see also Roy Schafer, "Problems in Freud's Psychology of Women," *Journal of the American Psychoanalytic Association*, 22 (1974), 459–85; Jean Strouse, ed., *Women and Analysis* (New York: Grossman Press, 1974); Jean Baker Miller, ed., *Women and Psychoanalysis* (Baltimore: Penguin, 1973).

9. One might wish to argue that social, psychic, and literary structures are so intimately interwoven that the relation between plot and culture is like that between Hamlet and his fate, between a text that is given and one that is generated, enacted, in part chosen. With this in mind, one might begin to speak of "patriarchal plots," the complex set of figures by which western culture has elaborated its relation to the structures by which it lives. The question then becomes the extent to which a powerful social movement warps, flexes, alters, and reimagines these essential structures and how genres are born and transformed.

10. James Hillman, *The Myth of Analysis: Three Essays in Archetypal Psychology* (Evanston, Ill.: Northwestern Univ. Press, 1972), pp. 215–98.

11. Thomas Kuhn, *The Structure of Scientific Revolutions* (Chicago: Univ. of Chicago Press, 1966).

12. Denis de Rougemont, *Love in the Western World*, trans. Montgomery Belgion (New York: Harcourt Brace, 1956), p. 243. I have chosen the passages from de Rougemont because they are central to the elucidation of the courtly love tradition and because they are so clearly, though unintentionally, biased. A more contemporary (and more complex) example of the same kind of bias might be found in the concluding chapters of Leo Bersani's *A Future for Astyanax: Character and Desire in Literature* (Boston: Little, Brown, 1977).

13. de Rougemont, p. 244.

14. Ortega y Gasset, *History as a System, and Other Essays Toward a Philosophy of History* (New York: W. W. Norton, 1961), pp. 165–233.

15. The following articles make a case for the relevance of Freud's personal history to the structure of his thought: Arthur Efron, "Freud's Self-Analysis and the Nature of Psychoanalytic Criticism," *The International Review of Psychoanalysis*, 4 (1977), 253–80; Jim Swan, "*Mater* and Nannie: Freud's Two Mothers and the Discovery of the Oedipus Complex," *American Imago*, 31 (1974), 1–64; Patrick Mahony, "Friendship and its Discontents," unpublished paper presented to the Canadian Psychoanalytic Society, Montreal, May 19, 1977. Freud's instrument of self-analysis, from the point of view of these critics, becomes a double-edged sword, a manifestation of his genius for the articulation of the structural principles of his own psyche, as well as a measure of the necessary limitation of his method. Murray Schwartz elucidates this point further in Chapter 2 of this book. Juliet Mitchell might be seen to treat this subject on a large scale in *Psychoanalysis and Feminism* (New York: Pantheon Books, 1974), when she argues that the Oedipus complex acts as a structural representation of the psychic organization of patriarchal society.

16. Dorothy Dinnerstein, *The Mermaid and the Minotaur: Sexual Arrangements and Human Malaise* (New York: Harper and Row, 1976).

17. Julia Kristeva, who seems to accept the Lacanian explanation of the process of the child's induction into the symbolic order in western culture, presents the position of women within this construct as one of agonized conflict. See the opening

chapters of *About Chinese Women*, trans. Anita Barrows (New York: Urizen Books, 1977). Shoshana Felman states the problem of defining a feminist discourse within a masculine ethic as follows:

> If, in our culture, the woman is by definition associated with madness, her problem is how to break out of this (cultural) imposition of madness *without* taking up the critical and therapeutic positions of reason: how to avoid speaking both as *mad* and as *not mad*. The challenge facing the woman today is nothing less than to "re-invent" language, to *re-learn how to speak*: to speak not only against, but outside of the specular phallocentric structure, to establish a discourse the status of which would no longer be defined by the phallacy of masculine meaning. An old saying would thereby be given new life: today more than ever, changing our minds—changing the mind—is a woman's prerogative.

See "Women and Madness: The Critical Phallacy," *Diacritics* 4 (1975), 2–10.

18. This statement derives from remarks made by Gayatri Spivak near the end of a session at the 1977 convention of the Midwest Modern Language Association. She spoke of "the womb as a tangible place of production," as the point of departure for a new discourse of femininity. She has suggested, since the work on which this comment is based is not yet in print, that I refer to my memory of her statements. I wish to apologize in advance for any error in understanding her position.

10 ❀ The Family in Shakespeare's Development: Tragedy and Sacredness

C. L. Barber

The loss that we feel in Shakespeare's greatest tragedies is not just the loss of human beings, though that is part of it; nor yet the loss of heroic human beings, though that is a great deal of it. I think our deepest sense in the greatest tragedies is the loss of what one can call the sacred-in-the-human. The qualm of awe we feel comes from the fact that the sacredness the tragedy generates is shown by the logic of the tragic action to be something that human life and society cannot sustain, something indeed that can be destructive, with tragic consequences.

This experience of sacredness does not, in my judgment, involve a religious, supernatural eschatology. On the contrary, it seems to me that Shakespeare's extraordinary relevance to the modern age that began in his period comes partly from his having so consistently done without any religious supernatural. He takes up into his tragedy human needs that might look to religious fulfillment, but the tragic situation he presents is the natural world. He thus presents what one can call the post-Christian situation. One way to put it is that he dramatizes the search for equivalents of the Holy Family of Christianity in the human family.

Shakespeare's art is distinguished by the intensity of its investment in the human family, and especially in the continuity of the family across generations. This investment is extended out into society and up into the royal family. Everything we know about his own family and his relation to it—and we know a great deal, really—is consistent in middle-class terms with what we find in the art, chiefly in aristocratic and royal terms.

This chapter is a revised version of a paper delivered at The English Institute, Cambridge, Mass., in September 1976.

The distinctive facts are that he was the son of a tenant farmer's son who rose to eminence in the thriving town of Stratford while Shakespeare was a child, married the youngest daughter and chief heir of his father's yeoman landlord, and then, when Shakespeare was twelve, fell into debt, withdrew from civic life, and lost the bulk of his wife's inheritance. Shakespeare as eldest son joined in the long, heartbreaking, unsuccessful legal struggle to recover his mother's inheritance; in the late nineties he was still involved in legal action in chancery. But meanwhile he had of course succeeded wonderfully, in middle-class terms, by his own role in a booming joint stock company. He pursued personal and family success, not in London nor in court terms, but in Stratford, by going through with his father's earlier application for a coat of arms to make his father and himself gentry, and by buying the property of New Place.[1]

One cannot, of course, derive Shakespeare's creative achievement from such facts. But one can, I think, see that the shape of his artistic development is consistent with them. A salient fact is that he did not make tragedy his central form of expression until after he had outdone his father in the rising middle class. Only then did he turn to dramatizing all-or-nothing, male-to-male oedipal conflict and the crucial stresses that relationship to the feminine brings into such conflict. The dramatization was in terms of all-or-nothing issues about rule and royalty, as the meaning of kingship had been developed in the history plays. But it was made in the commercial theater, an independent standing place from which Shakespeare could look with his awesome ironic understanding at the great world and its magic.

Another kind of security was also involved. The dramatist could now risk testing the possibility of becoming the ideal, omnipotent father of infancy: he could begin the major tragedies' expression of the longing for that figure of authority, of the parricidal rage, of the immense anxiety, of the feared destruction. The caste difference between middle-class author and royal subjects obviously contributed to the awe with which figures of authority were invested, in accord with the worshipful patterns of the secular hierarchy. His middle-class difference also contributed to the increasing ironic clarity with which the whole struggle was presented in successive tragedies as Shakespeare managed to get it increasingly under the artistic control of tragic form.

The shift into the preoccupations of the major tragedies can be summarized by the change from a special investment of self in Falstaff to such an investment in Hamlet. Falstaff, as William Empson long ago suggested, relates to Prince Hal somewhat as the speaker of the sonnets relates to the high-born young man, but with "a savage and joyous externalization of self-contempt."[2] Hamlet, endowed with wit, imaginative energy, and dramatic resource to the point where, like Falstaff, he tends to come out of the control of the play, is potentially the thing itself, a prince who encounters and must redeem the buried majesty of an ideal royal father, brought back as an immediate presence by the magic of theatrical power.

The matrix of sensibility that Shakespeare brings to his major tragedy can be seen by considering how in the works written before that period—more than half of his production—as well as in the romances after it, Shakespeare characteristically internalized relationships within the family constellation. Marlowe in his middle twenties had already launched heroic drama of titanic oedipal victory, envisaging in Tamburlaine a protagonist taking over a male identity capable of dealing with the stress of suffering beauty by mastering it in mastering the world. "Conceiving and subduing both" was necessary to Marlowe as a defense against surrender to transcendent beauty and power.[3] Shakespeare was clearly far less immediately threatened by giving himself. He was not subject to the compulsive need we see in Marlowe to resort to a defensive cruelty, a need that limits the range of Marlowe's art while at the same time giving it its special intensity. How is it that Shakespeare could suffer so much more beauty? Or not need to suffer in giving himself to it?

Shakespeare's earlier work is shaped by a very strong identification with the cherishing role of the parents of early infancy. This is the role the poet adopts in cherishing the young man addressed in the sonnets. Such relationship is grounded most deeply in very early modes of relation, dyadic rather than triadic. Triangular relationships involve a predominantly negative resolution of the Oedipus complex. This orientation is consistent with the almost complete absence, in the early work, of confrontations between sons and fathers—the very thing that is to become central in the first major tragedies. In the early work, there is a very strong tendency to submerge or transcend conflict by identification, so that the sensibility is profoundly sociable. Concern for kinship and kindness extends benign family relationships out into larger contexts of society and nature and focuses on unkindness in violations of family and extended family. Figures of adult male authority in the older generation are characteristically weak or vulnerable, and they command loyalty or sympathy. Active male-to-male rivalry and violence is typically between brothers, or brotherly friends or enemies within the same generation. The chief source of menace, however, is in women. For behind the identification with maternal, cherishing attitudes, motivating it at deep levels, is the danger of being abandoned or overpowered. So a central preoccupation of the early work is with overpowering women—either being overpowered by them or overpowering them.

All these problematic stresses in the family constellation come into the major tragedies. But what is new is their presenting crises of heritage centered in the effort to achieve or maintain a positive resolution of the Oedipus complex, identification with heroic adult male authority. The first major tragedies, *Julius Caesar* and *Hamlet*, with *Macbeth* a little later, center in man-to-man confrontations, tragic struggles to take over heritage and male identity by destroying paternal figures of authority, attempts to destroy them so as to become them—only to find self-destruction in the process. In *Hamlet* and *Macbeth*, relationship to women that the hero cannot manage contributes decisively to the tragic failure. In the whole sequence, there is a shift from the slight role of women in *Julius Caesar* to a greater and greater emphasis on the protagonist's inability to cope with the demands made by or on women, from *Othello*, through *Lear, Macbeth, Antony and Cleopatra,* and *Coriolanus.* In *Timon of Athens* there is an abortive attempt to dramatize a man who tries to *be* the all-providing, feeding parent.

In the first three late romances, Shakespeare turns to dramatizing the fulfillment of the need men have to be validated by feminine presences, now presented as achieved in visionary reunions—reunions anticipated within tragedy in *Lear* and *Antony and Cleopatra.* A daughter restored leads to the recovery of a lost wife, Thaisa, Hermione. The finale is a tempest distanced and managed. Prospero gives up the daughter with whom he has been isolated in his cell as Lear dreamt of being isolated in a prison cell with Cordelia. By his "art" he masters a usurping younger brother as well as the temptation to talion violence: "The rarer action is/In virtue than in vengeance" (*Tmp.* V.i.27-28).[4] "In my end is my beginning."

One can summarize the development by reference to different ways of coping with the incest taboo, which is necessarily an urgent problem in such family-centered art and the temperament that produced it. The early work is much preoccupied with diversions of sexual energy embedded in family ties—in cruelty on the one side and tenderness on the other. The Pandora's box of horrors opened in *Titus* centers on family relations, in blood ties and blood feud. The revenge play structure is used to enact a fantasy that separates overt sexuality, linked with violence, from the family and extreme family loyalty. The menace of maternal sexuality is dealt with by making Tamora, that "unhallowed dam,/Like to the earth, swallow her own increase" (V.ii.190-91)—which is brute sexuality embodied in her rapist sons "baked in this pie" (V.iii.60). The strongest feeling is directed by Titus to a daughter disfigured in a way that is at once sexually disabling and suggestive. Strangely, Titus the official martial hero becomes an embodiment of a maternally cherishing father; the sentimental farewells, after his death, center on his grandson: "Many a time he danced thee on his knee,/Sung thee asleep" (*Tit.* V.iii.162–63).

Much of the strangeness in the attitudes we find expressed in the sonnets toward the young man becomes comprehensible when one recognizes relationships to parental attitudes, and more deeply still, to childlike feelings of total dependence—in summary, to vertical relationships that originate in the transmission of heritage and identity, as they are now shaping relationships within a single generation or half-generation. The poems to him start out, after all, precisely with this subject. In urging the young man to have a child, the first seventeen poems encourage him to make for himself a renewing mirror image such as the poet soon makes for *himself* of the young man:

> Look in thy glass and tell the face thou viewest
> Now is the time that face should form another . . .
>
> (Sonnet 3)

The lines describe almost exactly what Shakespeare himself does in later poems with the young man as mirror:

> My glass shall not persuade me I am old,
> So long as youth and thou are of one date . . .
>
> (Sonnet 22)

The poet's renewal by identification is compared to that of a parent with a child. In one sonnet it is a father:

> As a decrepit father takes delight
> To see his active child do deeds of youth,
> So I, made lame by Fortune's dearest spite,
> Take all my comfort of thy worth and truth.
>
> (Sonnet 37)

Or it is the youth's own mother:

> Thou art thy mother's glass, and she in thee
> Calls back the lovely April of her prime;
> So thou through windows of thine age shalt see,
> Despite of wrinkles, this thy golden time.
>
> (Sonnet 3)

Relationship by identification is less familiar from our conscious social experience than relationship to people as objects, because it is less accessible to observation. We observe our objects, but people whom we take into ourselves by identification are matter less for our observation than for our conservation. In fact, as Freud's later writings and more recent studies repeatedly insist, identification is particularly important not only in relationship to parents but generally as a means of dealing with the loss of objects by estrangement or death. And a person lost who has been internalized and so preserved, as well as grieved for, can often be found again in a new object. One of the most extraordinary sonnets makes explicit the beloved's function as heir to earlier attachments:

> Thy bosom is endearèd with all hearts
> Which I by lacking have supposèd dead;
> And there reigns love and all love's loving parts,
> And all those friends which I thought burièd.

(Sonnet 31)

The third quatrain specifies that those lost become "parts of" the poet now projected in the friend:

> Thou art the grave where buried love doth live,
> Hung with the trophies of my lovers gone,
> Who all their parts of me to thee did give;
> That due of many now is thine alone.
>   Their images I loved I view in thee,
>   And thou, all they, hast all the all of me.

(Sonnet 31)

There is no reference here to parental figures; the earlier figures are "lovers" in the broad Elizabethan sense, but the kind of feeling for them, "dear religious love" calling forth "many a holy and obsequious tear" (ll.6 and 5), is consistent with original familial love.

The poet's identification of himself with the young man, and the passive dedication of himself to dependence on his love, is far more visible than the poet's identification with the cherishing parent, because for the most part the latter is expressed or embodied in the process of creating the sonnet. What is crucial for the whole view of Shakespeare's development in its early stages is that adopting the cherishing role permits a reception of heritage and the maintenance of a self grounded in it, without confronting centrally the problem of manliness. The poet in effect becomes the nurturing parent(s) in his/her/their earliest desirable function, the function that creates and validates life.

This way of maintaining heritage does not involve confronting the self-asserting male egotism of the father. I do not mean to suggest that such a "normal" development was outside Shakespeare's range of feeling and attitude. Freud and others stress that two-sided residues of the oedipal history are normally present in everybody, identifications with the father and with the mother in both *their* bisexual aspects.

In the comic mode, Shakespeare's strong family orientation comes out early in *The Comedy of Errors.* He transforms Plautus' libertine male comedy into a thoroughly domestic affair, ending with a moving family reunion presided over by a holy abbess who proves to be the mother. We have also the taming of a shrew, with the abbess' assistance —and soon Petruchio turns Katherina into a good household Kate.

As the festive form of comedy comes into its own, what is dramatized is release from family ties on a tide of communal, seasonal, holiday feeling presided over by benignly masterful young women. The younger generation leaves the family to go out into what Northrop Frye has called "the green world," to go through something like a saturnalian revel, and in the process to experience a release from family sexual taboos. Release brings clarification about the claims of nature within the natural and generational cycle. *Romeo and Juliet* is a tragedy that begins like a festive comedy and dramatizes the failure of the young lovers to escape from destructive family ties after their marvelous moment of release in a liminal world where they leave family names and ties behind.

In the histories of this very productive period, we have men largely without women; in *Richard II* the feminine presence is "the lap of this green land" on which men struggle. In life, we often first encounter an insuperable problem in thinking that we have solved it. In *Henry IV* and *Henry V*, Shakespeare dramatizes the successful positive resolution of the latent conflict of Hal with his usurper father, with all the resources of social control brought into play, as well as the ritual process of the sacrifice of "that father ruffian," Falsaff (*1H4*.II.iv.45). Hal internalizes his father to become, officially, all king and a guiltless man, "the offending Adam" whipped out of him by "Consideration" (*H5*.I.i.28–29). But as Peter Erickson is showing, in work in progress at this writing, his unresolved passional needs keep coming out in ways that make the underside of him surprisingly like Hamlet. Another young critic, Richard P. Wheeler, who is exploring Shakespeare's development with the problematic comedies as a fulcrum, points out that the separation of genres in this period between male-dominated history and festive comedy with its delightful, enthralling heroines keeps separate areas that come together in the next period of more drastic, deeper conflicts.[5]

The problematic comedies have lost the confident reliance on a community feeling for sexuality as benign and sanctioned by natural rhythms. Sexuality instead is either disassociated from family ties and social sanctions and so a pernicious degradation, as in *Measure for Measure*, or else it is too closely bound up with having grown up together and remaining under the aegis of the older generation, as with Helena and Bertram in *All's Well that Ends Well*. Meanwhile, the major tragedies show violence erupting from the pull of family ties that are too close, "more than kin" (*Ham*.I.ii.65). The whole heroic identity is invested in "holy cords" (*Lr*. II.ii.76) that have an incestuous content, direct or displaced. The investment is at once ennobling and ironically destructive.

In the late romances, we have symbolic action that, instead of freeing sexuality from the ties of family, works to restore family ties by disassociating them from the threat of degradation by physical incest. The romance mode of presentation insists that the action is *symbolic*, even though the ecstatic reunions are also actual happenings within a playspace that has been enfranchised by a new understanding of the way magic *can* work. Murray M. Schwartz has developed the view that the tragedies use up the playspace in which the psyche makes the transition from the world as mother to the larger social world.[6] Presences without which "the wine of life is drawn" (*Mac*.II.iii.95) are destroyed by the demand to become or possess them totally. The romances, in Schwartz's splendid formulation, restore the playspace. In the reunions of *Pericles* and *The Winter's Tale*, Shakespeare finds his way to his composite version of Dante's "Virgine madre, filia del tuo filio."

II

If I were writing this essay in 1876 instead of 1976, it would be called "Shakespeare: Poet of the Family." I want to sketch now very briefly how, as I see it, he dramatizes the investment of feeling and need in the human family, by relation to the way that investment is made in the religious worship of God and the Holy Family.

The creation of a new art form puts men in a new relation to their experience. The new repertory theater provided a new location for language and gesture. Human possibilities could be envisaged with the freedom of a special place apart, alternative to the church and to courtly situations. The new vantage point of the audience watching action on a stage made the drama a new organ of culture, a *novum organum*. It was an agent in the historical shift of the Renaissance and Reformation from a ritual and ceremonial view of life, with absolutist assumptions about meaning and reality, towards a psychological and historical view. The historical understanding Shakespeare develops sees absolutist assumptions motivating relative, dramatic events.

The new theater came into its own a generation after most of the symbolic actions of the Old Religion had been forbidden in England by the Protestant reformers around Elizabeth. Most of its visible embodiments, Christ on the Rood, the saints and the Virgin Mary in statues, paintings and stained glass, had been swept from the churches on orders from the Privy Council in the years immediately preceding Marlowe and Shakespeare's birth in 1564. One of the official homilies, in rebuking the people for not faithfully attending the new service, speaks of their "gross carnal imaginations" missing "the gay gazing sights" of the old worship. One homily denounced "our churches . . . full of great puppets, wondrously decked and adorned . . . you would believe our men saints were some princes of Persia with their proud apparel, and the idols of our women saints were nice and well-trimmed harlots."[7] Soon there were "gay gazing sights" in the theater, with living puppets and Marlowe's Tamburlaine, self-made prince of Persia, and his captured princess bedecked "with precious jewels of mine own,/More rich and valurous than Zenocrate's" (*1 Tamb.*,I.ii.292–93). But the trend was not simply secular. If the Old Religion's holy images had been partly secularized, the new theater's secular personages could be invested with meanings cognate to those that had entered into worship: "Now walk the angels on the walls of heaven/. . . To entertain divine Zenocrate" (*2 Tamb.*, II.iii.2983, 85).[8]

I can imagine no way to prove it, but it seems to me that the very central and problematical role of women in Shakespeare—and in the Elizabethan drama generally—reflects the fact that Protestantism did away with the cult of the Virgin Mary. It meant the loss of ritual resource for dealing with the internal residues in all of us of the once all-powerful and all-inclusive mother. The threatening mother survived as an immediate, physical supernatural presence in Protestant countries after the benign Holy Mother had been drastically reduced in scope and presence—for the terrible mother was still conjured up and pursued with terrible persecution in the witch manias well into the seventeenth century. Keith Thomas, in his fine study *Religion and the Decline of Magic*, notes that the belief in witches survived in England after many Catholic resources of exorcism had been dispensed with.[9]

Witches proper are of course among Shakespeare's repertory of overpowering women: Joan La Pucelle in a history at the outset, the Weird Sisters in the most intense of all the tragedies. *Macbeth*, in its complex way, is an exorcism, for it presents the witches as the outstretched shadows of Lady Macbeth and understands their power as depending on masculine insecurity. But they are also objectively supernatural beings. After the Reformation, the benign supernatural figure of the Holy Mother could not be present in a comparable way. Not only was her image gone, but prayers like *Sancta Maria Virgo* were not taken over from the *Lay Folks Prayer Book* to the *Book of Common Prayer*: "Saint Mary, maid of maidens, mother and daughter of the king of kings . . . holy gate of heaven, set us all in peace, changing the name of Eve . . . show that thou art our mother."[10] Hermione is a statue in a chapel before she comes back down into life.

I do not agree with critics who see intimations of a Christian resolution in Shakespeare's tragedy. As I see it, he presents versions of the Oedipus complex tragically unresolved. His tragedies present the post-Christian situation where, with some of the expectations and values of Christianity, we do not have God and the Holy Family, only the human family. In this situation he makes us feel that human life is supremely valuable as well as terrible. The fact that Shakespeare could do this must be one main reason for the rise of bardolatry since the mid-eighteenth century.

The rites of passage of traditional Christianity, Catholic or Anglican, are regularly structured to take people through threshold moments of losing or changing family ties by turning their need for total relationship to Christ and God. This is very clear in the services of baptism, confirmation, marriage, and burial. Shakespeare's mature plays show people in passage from one stage of life to another, succeeding in comedies, failing in tragedies. Some tragedies start with the failure of ritual. In *Hamlet* it is burial. The service begins with "I am the resurrection and the life (saith the Lord)" to lead the bereft past loss with recognition that we are dust that returns to dust. Hamlet looks for his buried father in the dust; then the father returns from death to ask for a total, uncritical commitment. As in all the tragedies, there is a swerve back to the deepest family ties. And since on its positive side the tie to the father is the core of human and social values, Hamlet's Galilean turbulence is potentially creative as well as terribly destructive.

Lear begins with a failure of the passage that might be handled by the marriage service, as it is structured to persuade the father to give up his daughter. Regan and Goneril, though married, pretend to meet Lear's demand on them in all-but-incestuous terms. Cordelia defends herself by reference to the service:

> Haply, when I shall wed,
> That lord whose hand must take my plight shall carry
> Half my love with him, half my care and duty.
> Sure I shall never marry like my sisters,
> To love my father all.

(I.i.100–04)

Shakespeare presents social arrangements in the Christian terms of his society, and with a critical perspective that implies *part* of the Christian norm. But only part. The full Christian norm would deal with the need for a complete union in love, the need Lear looked for from Cordelia in his hope "to set my rest/On her kind nursery" (I.i.123–24), by redirecting it to divine objects, with the discipline of humility before God as the condition of being "one with Christ and Christ with us." What a father would give up in the marriage service would ideally be given compensation in the communion service that immediately followed.

In Catholic worship, there would have been compensation also for him by relationship with the Blessed Virgin, Holy Mother, Queen of Heaven. The relationships toward which the incestuous love tends, to make the daughter a mother, whether by impregnating her or depending totally on her, are shown fulfilled in the traditional Christian scenes of the Annunciation and the Madonna with Child—fulfilled in a sacred way that expresses the latent wishes and protects against acting them out, against pursuing in human objects the total fulfillment reserved for the divine persons. So a Christian Lear might be provided with the Presence whose lack drives him to madness; his daughters might be spared the demand that they be that presence, that all their tenderness be arrogated to a father who asks them to make him, in effect, their god. In the two older daughters, resistance to the demand, in the situation of sibling rivalry, has atrophied their tenderness, making them sexually avid and demonically vengeful, eager to destroy the impossible old man who has destroyed their full humanity.

Obviously Lear's world is not Christian in this full sense. On the contrary, in the opening acts Shakespeare emphasizes pagan, pre-Christian references: "by the sacred radiance of the sun,/The mysteries of Hecate . . ." (I.i.109–10); "Hear, Nature, hear; dear Goddess, hear . . ." (I.iv. 277). But as we go through Lear's suffering with him, and the sufferings of Gloucester and Edgar, Christian *expectations* come increasingly into play. By the time Cordelia returns, significantly without her husband, we share with at least part of our sensibility the need she comes to meet. As regularly happens in Shakespeare's mature work, religious language comes into play to express the investment in the family bond:

> There she shook
> The holy water from her heavenly eyes,
> And clamor moistened. . . .
>
> (IV.iii.31–33)

What the play presents, however, is not a Christian resolution, but the tragic consequences of this investment. In the scene of Lear's reunion with Cordelia—for me as for many the most moving moment in Shakespeare—Lear's summary image on coming back into sanity is shaped by Christian conceptions: "Thou art a soul in bliss; but I am bound/Upon a wheel of fire" (IV.vii.45–48). And in Cordelia's "No cause, no cause," we get a full expression of Christian love without a Christian supernatural.

How fully Shakespeare understood the destructive side of human bonds, the value of which he so movingly expresses, is manifest in his having changed the happy ending of all his sources. The English win, and among the English Edmund. Lear's great speech in response to that situation is often quoted by those who, caught up in the Christian feeling, want to see the play's ending as wholly redemptive, with intimations of a reunion of father and daughter in a hereafter:

Come, let's away to prison: . . .
When thou dost ask me blessing, I'll kneel down
And ask of thee forgiveness: so we'll live,
And pray, and sing, and tell old tales, . . .
And take upon's the mystery of things,
As if we were God's spies . . .

(V.iii.8-21)

Lear has undergone a discipline of humility and achieved something like Christian disillusion with worldly things, together with a sense of the wrong he did Cordelia. He has seen through royal vanity. But he still wants his daughter "to love [her] father all." A chasm of irony opens as we realize that he is leading her off to death. His vision of prison amounts, almost literally, to a conception of heaven on earth—*his* heaven, the "kind nursery" after all.

To talk about what Shakespeare is appealing to (and controlling) in such a moment, one needs to understand the religious traditions or situation he is drawing on, but also the roots of potential religious feeling in the family. For he is presenting the modern situation where religious need, or need cognate to what has been dealt with by worship of the Holy Family, has no resource except the human family and its extensions in society, including the problematic ideal of kingship. William Elton's *King Lear and the Gods*[11] shows how highly relevant religious thought of the period is to the play—notably the idea of a *Deus Absconditus*. The play's adumbration of religious ritual is exhibited in Herbert Coursen's fine new study of *Christian Ritual and the World of Shakespeare's Tragedies*.[12]

For my purposes, psychoanalysis is a useful supplement because it amounts, in some aspects, to a sociology of love and worship within the family, or as derived from the family, especially as experienced in infancy. The experiences of infancy were not, as such, a focus of much analytical attention in Shakespeare's period; our acute consciousness of them goes back to romanticism and develops along with the decreasing hold of religion. Infantile experience as such is also not a major concern of Shakespeare's art, since his culture little regarded it. Yet his plays find equivalents and shape action in ways that, with their central familial preoccupations, can be understood by reference to infantile residues. Thus it is useful, I think, to understand Lear's vision of prison as a regressive wish demanding that Cordelia join in it. In the large design of the play, this tendency of course connects with the childishness and playfulness, often charming and liberating in the midst of anguish, that floods through the Fool's part and flashes in moments of Edgar's impersonation of Mad Tom, as in Lear's own sprightliness in madness. The tendency also relates to Lear's confident assumption at the outset of relationship to a benign Nature, even as he asks the "dear Goddess" to

convey sterility into the womb of Goneril—with all the developing ambiguities: Edmund's "lusty stealth of nature" (I.ii.11), Lear's incredu-
lous "Is there any cause in Nature that make these hard hearts?" (III.vi.
76-77).

It is surely because the plays are centered so much in family that
they can make comprehensible to the widest variety of auditors their
enormous range of thought, lore, myth, and literary commonplace (as
well as uncommon place). Such matters as the ambiguous status of Nature in the thought of the period, or again the fear that God has withdrawn from the world, need not be understood in systematic terms as
we watch the play, fruitful as such understanding is in extending its significance. We understand distinctions that are potentially systematic by
reference to the concrete social world and the family center of it: "Why
brand they us/With base? With baseness? Bastardy? Base? Base?/Who
in the lusty stealth of nature . . ." (I.ii.9-11). So too with *Deus Absconditus*. One way the theological anxiety is brought home is that God's
representative on earth, the king, begins the play by in effect abscond-
ing. And he is first and foremost a father. The first, most important
order of understanding is "close to home."

Shakespeare dramatizes the implication of fixation as Cordelia's
death—also the result, of course, of a whole complex social process that
has been set in motion by Lear's abdicating and dividing authority, by
Gloucester's sensuality and credulity, by the brute fact of chance in
war. Those who insist on seeing the play as Christian rather than post-
Christian have to ignore or "transcend" the fact that the heavens do not
respond to the repeated appeals made to them, as by Albany:

> If that the heavens do not their visible spirits
> Send quickly down to tame these vile offenses,
> It will come,
> Humanity must perforce prey on itself,
> Like monsters of the deep.

> (IV.ii.47-51)

Heaven's vault merely reverberates Lear's "Howl, howl, howl, howl!"
as he enters with the dead Cordelia in his arms. And yet humanity does
not simply prey on itself like monsters. Without attempting here to describe the play's extraordinary final effect of affirmation along with
tragic loss, the argument I have been indexing needs to be completed by
noting that Lear and Cordelia, while they are represented with marvelous understanding as human individuals, also become in effect icons.
Lear with Cordelia in his arms is a *pietà* with the roles reversed, not
Holy Mother with her dead Son, but father with his dead daughter. In
the new situation, where it was necessary to do without the supernatural
figures and refind them in secular manifestations, Shakespeare's art

finds new intensity of grace possible in human life, and new intensity of tragic loss. As the plays become part of the ongoing culture, particular figures within particular family constellations become themselves icons important for us, "Presences/That passion, piety or affection knows":

> All perform their tragic play,
> There struts Hamlet, there is Lear,
> That's Ophelia, that Cordelia. . . .

In using the term "icon" about Lear and Cordelia, there is the difficulty that the Christian associations imply an image that stands for something holy which it only represents—for something beyond, transcendent. True, in a holy place an icon can come to be itself holy, something set apart—as with saints' relics, or the icons of the Eastern Orthodox tradition. But it does so in a context of worship and belief. In talking or writing about Shakespeare's use or adumbration of religious language and action, it is easy to slip into implying such a context. And so it is crucial to check the powerful tendency of the Christian vocabulary to imply the whole Christian situation—crucial because his art does so.

Lear and Cordelia do not stand for transcendent persons beyond them—for God and the Virgin. They are themselves finite persons in a finite world. The play generates sacredness about them by the same development that makes their tragic destiny. The sacredness in Shakespeare's tragedy goes with recognition of the human impossibility of being divine, realized by the dread attempt, which brings destruction. The attempt is to have a total relationship, satisfying the assumption of omnipotence of mind—or better, in Lear's case, omnipotence of heart.

To attempt this is to make no difference, to use René Girard's terms, no difference between a daughter and the all-providing mother. Othello makes no difference between the mother and the wife; he makes Desdemona sacred in this way and then destroys her, with Iago's diabolical prompting, on the assumption that if she is a secular woman she will make no difference between him and Cassio (the mother's handkerchief in Cassio's hand is confirmation). His expectations and demands are absolutes: "My soul hath her content so absolute/That not another comfort like to this/Succeeds in unknown fate" (*Oth*.II.i.189–91). Here again what is lost is the sacred-in-the-human as humanity creates and destroys it.

Notes

1. Samuel Schoenbaum's *William Shakespeare: A Documentary Life* (Oxford:

Clarendon Press, 1975) makes the significance of the evidence clearer than ever before.

2. William Empson, *Some Versions of Pastoral* (London: Chatto and Windus, 1935), p. 104.

3. C. L. Barber, "The Death of Zenocrate: 'Conceiving and subduing both' in Marlowe's *Tamburlaine*," *Literature and Psychology*, 16 (1966), 15-24.

4. Citations are to *The Complete Signet Classic Shakespeare*, ed. Sylvan Barnet (New York: Harcourt Brace Jovanovich, 1963, 1972).

5. Richard P. Wheeler, *Shakespeare's Development and the Problem Comedies: Turn and Counter-Turn* (forthcoming from the Univ. of California Press in 1980. See chapter 4.)

6. Schwartz outlines his view of the development from the major tragedies through the late romances in Chapter 2 of this book.

7. *Sermons or Homilies Appointed to be Read in Churches in the Time of Queen Elizabeth* (Oxford: Clarendon Press, 1816), 2, pp. 8, 219-20. The first passage is cited by Philip Hughes, *The Reformation in England*, 5th ed. (rev.) (London: Burns and Oates, 1963), 3, p. 104.

8. Citations are to *The Works of Christopher Marlowe*, ed. C. F. Tucker Brooke (Oxford: Clarendon Press, 1946).

9. Keith Thomas, *Religion and the Decline of Magic* (London: Weidenfeld and Nicolson, 1971), pp. 493-501.

10. I have taken phrases from several prayers to the Virgin Mary in *The Prymer or Lay Folks Prayer Book*, ed. Henry Littlehales (London: 1895), EETS original series, p. 105.

11. William Elton, *King Lear and the Gods* (San Marino, Calif.: Huntington Library, 1966).

12. Herbert Coursen, *Christian Ritual and the World of Shakespeare's Tragedies* (Lewisburg, Pa.: Bucknell Univ. Press, 1976).

11 ❂ Interpreting Posthumus' Dream from Above and Below: Families, Psychoanalysts, and Literary Critics

Meredith Skura

Shakespeare's *Cymbeline* is an extraordinarily complicated play, even for a romance. Set in prehistoric Britain, it combines elements of history play and Roman play, but it still ranges over an Elizabethan Italy and a timeless pastoral world in Wales. By allusion, it also ranges widely over Shakespeare's own earlier plays. Its wicked Queen evokes Lady Macbeth; Iachimo evokes Iago; and the hero Posthumus recalls Othello, although Shakespeare seems to be making mere cartoon versions of those earlier complex characters.

If the external allusions are complicated, the on-stage action is even more so. There are more than twenty separate strands of action, and although sorting them out into three major plot lines helps some, the action is still confusing, even in the way that it is primarily about Posthumus' marriage to Imogen, rather than about Imogen's father Cymbeline, who gives the play its name. And finally, the play is written in a very mannered, elliptical, and self-conscious style. While most modern audiences can respond immediately to Othello, Posthumus' adventures in *Cymbeline* present many difficulties and call for an acquired taste.

These difficulties are precisely what interest me, however. This essay will be an experiment to see how a psychoanalytic bias can be of use in coming to terms with difficult works, like *Cymbeline*, which do not readily fit into expected patterns. I am not interested in trying to psychoanalyze either Shakespeare or the reader, nor in discovering all an analyst might say about the "unconscious meaning" of the play, but only in trying to use some psychoanalytic categories to explain its puzzling details. I hope to *avoid* the familiar dichotomy between analyst's and critic's explanations—or between "unconscious" and "conscious" meaning. "Meaning is an affair of consciousness," says critic E. D.

Hirsch, while the analyst Ferenczi claims that the conscious meaning cannot be understood until the unconscious "depths are plumbed."[1] I think, though, that what happens as we look at *Cymbeline*, even more clearly than with the other plays, is that we can see the terms conscious and unconscious as a misleading polarity. What we really experience instead of either of these extremes is a range of different ways of being aware.

There is no such thing as a neatly separable conscious meaning, nor a meaning of which we are totally unconscious, but only a range of different ways of being aware of and representing things—different "modes of consciousness," as one analyst has called them.[2] Locating their effect is not simply a matter of finding an unconscious meaning behind the action, but rather of finding a play between two ways of seeing the details already visible in the action. The effect, as two French analysts have described it in their revisionary essay on "The Unconscious,"[3] is like a newspaper puzzle-game in which Napolean's hat is hidden—though perfectly "visible"—in the leaves of a tree. This ambiguous interplay affects all levels of *Cymbeline*, from moral interpretation to plot to language, and it recreates for us the shifting ambiguities of experience in our own lives that we normally do not notice.

I want to begin not with psychoanalysis but rather with the simple fact that Shakespeare's plays are about families. It is remarkable how many of the plays develop out of specific moments in what we might call the cycle of generations that makes up a family. Both comedies and tragedies begin in those moments of crisis or transition that open new worlds, the *rites de passage* through Jaques' seven ages of man—or, rather, in Shakespeare, the ages of the family. Characters grow up in and then out of families; they start their own families and struggle to keep them together; they watch their children leave to set up new families; and, finally, they fall back to become their children's children.

The early plays, for example, are often organized around the transition from childhood to adult passion and its responsibilities. *A Midsummer Night's Dream*, its action poised on the threshold of a royal marriage, reveals the passage from a sexless spring when Hermia and Helena sat sewing together as calm as two cherries on a branch (while Leontes and Polixenes, in *The Winter's Tale*, frisked together like twinned lambs in their boyhood days), to the midsummer heat that sends the girls to the forest scrabbling at each other like animals. We watch Romeo's passage from a sexless puppy love for Rosaline—which his family could approve—to the dog days of passion that nearly tear Verona apart.

The plays written near the turn of the century often show another kind of transition, when the young heroes emerge from their boyish isolation and irresponsibility to take over leadership, whether from a literal or a symbolic father. Prince Hal leaves his prodigal days behind to become a sober king when his father dies; Hamlet moves from his student days to an even more sobering burden of leadership when his father dies, because for him it soon requires that he really must steal the crown. Brutus—historically Caesar's stepson—moves from a quiet filial devotion to a sense of authority that leaves no more room for Caesar as soon as Brutus thinks of himself as head of Rome. And even Angelo in *Measure for Measure* crosses the threshold, leaving the cloistered virtues and an "unsounded self" to confront adult responsibilities and temptations. Elsewhere we can see a movement in the other direction, when a Titus or a Lear thinks he can retire to his children's nursery.

Cymbeline and the other romances differ from the earlier plays in their scope; they present the whole cycle, often ranging over several crises in different generations. The histories present such cycles too, of course, but what distinguishes the romances is the way they focus on one particular aspect of family experience that I want to examine here. The romances make explicit a paradox about families that Shakespeare put at the center of his plays long before the anthropologists began to study kinship relations: the family is so important that characters cannot even imagine themselves without one, yet every family must bring on its own destruction. Its very success in raising children ensures that they will want to leave—or to take over in the wrong way. As the crisis recurs in each generation, both parents and children have to find the right balance between holding on and letting go; they must avoid both the threat of an ingrown family collapsing in on itself and the threat of an explosion that will tear the family apart.

The romances stage several of these crises, and in them the two threats take many forms. The threat of holding on too tightly is seen most strikingly in the threat of incest in these plays.[4] *Pericles* opens with a story about incest; incestuous longing is just hinted in *The Winter's Tale*, when Leontes sees his daughter for the first time in sixteen years; and there may be a more obscurely implied incestuous attraction making Prospero jealous of his potential son-in-law. Shakespeare also suggests an incestuous ambition on the part of characters like Cloten and Caliban, who want to marry their lovely step-sisters, usurping their proper role within their foster families and refusing to leave.

But incest is only one form of a more general danger that family bonds will become too strong. Parents in particular threaten to swallow up their children. Mothers are quite literally ready to eat their "little darlings" during the famine in *Pericles* (reversing the threat from Lear's "pelican" daughters). More often the parents simply do not want their children to leave or to shake off parental power. Antiochus in *Pericles* delays his daughter's wedding because he wants her for his own use, but even the less perverse parents like Simonides in *Pericles*, or Cymbeline or Prospero, delay weddings. And Alonso—who lets his daughter go—is sorry: she is in another country; it's as if the wench were dead.

The opposite threat of families exploding outwards comes sometimes from parents who throw their children out, as Dionyza does in *Pericles*, or as Leontes does. Cymbeline merely loses track of his sons, but the effect is the same. More often, however, it comes from the children who try to break out of the family too soon. So Florizel refuses to ask his father's blessing on a dubious marriage, and Perdita herself denies her shepherd "father" in running off with Florizel, just as Cymbeline's sons defy their shepherd "father."

These family dramas are interesting in themselves, but they are also the outward accompaniment of an equally important inner drama that I want to look at more closely. It is a drama that each new generation feels: the conflict between family inheritance and personal individuality, between old memories and new perceptions, between being part of the family unit and being the head of a new family. This is the universal drama that Freud saw in the very specific fate of Oedipus. What psychoanalysis adds to the traditional western understanding that the past shapes us is the idea that the past works on us unconsciously and in even stranger, less direct ways than it did for Oedipus, permeating our present lives without being literally true as it was for him.

Too much emphasis on the past, of course, is reductive, and we have all read psychoanalytic criticism that reduces an ongoing drama to a perpetual repetition of the same old family drama. So the analyst finds that Prince Hal and Hamlet commit oedipal crimes—as do Brutus, Macbeth, Angelo, and Florizel. Shakespeare's plays resist such reductions— but they do so partly by taking them into account.

The plays present a uniquely balanced vision. Without ever reducing present experience to mere repetition of the past, they never leave out the shadowy resonances that the analyst finds in present experience. Indeed, Shakespeare finds a way of representing the ambiguity of *current* experience that re-creates "out there" some of the complexity of what it is like inside our own overlaid minds. We are each tied to a family with bonds stronger than any an overbearing father can impose because those bonds are part of our sense of ourselves, taking the form of memories or attitudes of mind and perception. The child can leave his family behind, but he cannot escape its influence, and in some sense he cannot know who he is until he knows where he has come from—until he knows his roots.

One way Shakespeare portrays all this, of course, is to put the literal parents onstage. Thus Hamlet really is struggling with his parents, and so is Coriolanus. No wonder the analyst takes to these plays, as Norman Holland says, like a kitten to a ball of wool. But another way Shakespeare portrays the family influence is by symbolic reenactments of the original family situations, so that a character leaves home and comes to a new world, seemingly to a new family, but we can see that he is also simultaneously working out his relationships to his old family as he tries out the new one. We can neither reduce his current to his past experience, nor can we ignore his past. The family references flicker on the surface. They are neither a psychoanalytic skeleton behind the surface, nor are they quite part of the literal meaning. And this is precisely the role they have in life. The family's role comes out most strikingly in the case of Posthumus in *Cymbeline*, and it is to his adventures that I want now to turn, to see how the cycle of family crises reverberates as part of his own separate experience as an individual, and particularly how all this emerges in the strange climactic dream he has at the turning point of the play.

Of course, to the casual audience, Posthumus in this play is primarily a husband, but we shall see that there is no way for him to find himself as husband until he finds himself as son, as part of the family he was torn from long ago. The story of Posthumus learning to be a proper son is not literally part of the main plot, and in fact it is hardly noticeable and seldom noted in discussions of the play. But it is nonetheless a shaping influence on the story of his learning how to be a husband.

No one would claim that *Cymbeline* is solely about families. It is, in fact, about several different relationships that hold men together. Its three main plots examine political, generational or familial, and marital ties, so that the story of Posthumus' marriage takes place only in this larger context. All three plots are about human bonds gone wrong—exploded or imploded—and then being righted by a new faith or mutuality of trust.

The first, or political, plot is the story of King Cymbeline of Britain, who refuses to pay tribute money to Rome and is getting ready to go to war about it. In the second or dynastic plot, we learn that Cymbeline's two sons disappeared long ago, and his good wife has died. He is now remarried to a wicked Queen with an unsavory son whose name Cloten, rhymes with "rotten." Cymbeline is foolish enough to insist that his daughter Imogen marry Cloten instead of letting her marry the orphan Posthumus, whom Cymbeline has been bringing up as his own son.

In the third plot (really the main one), Imogen and Posthumus do get married secretly anyway, but with almost disastrous results. Posthumus is banished, and while he is away he succumbs to an Iago-like villain, Iachimo, and makes a bet with him on his wife's chastity. Iachimo promptly worms his way into Imogen's bedroom by hiding himself inside a trunk so that he can come out in the night to inspect her room and see the telltale mole on her left breast—and to take the bracelet Posthumus gave her. All this ocular proof convinces Posthumus that Imogen has betrayed him, and, rashly, he orders her killed. Of course he soon repents—too late, as he thinks, to save her, so instead he vows to serve her father, Cymbeline, by fighting in the British army against Rome. (We begin to see how the plots mesh.) He makes a heroic stand with three other rustic soldiers, and these happy few save the King and win the war. Posthumus, however, gets himself arrested as an enemy to Britain, still trying to repent and now willing to die.

Although, as I said, these plots are not literally about families, all three have family resonances behind them. Even in the first plot, Cymbeline's politics are a magnification of family rebellion. He was brought up at the court of Rome where he learned a Roman honor that now teaches him to rebel against Rome itself. The second plot is literally about family conflicts, and it presents the crisis I have described. Cymbeline is Imogen's possessive father; he wants to "pen her up," as he says, and make his Queen her jailer. Such restraint takes an alternate form in Cymbeline's pastoral alter-ego, Belarius, who has stolen the King's two sons and keeps them penned up in a cave. The two fathers have opposite motives—Cymbeline wants to prevent Imogen from marrying outside the courtly circles appropriate to his dynastic expectations, and Belarius wants to keep his stolen "sons" from entering into the same courtly world. But in both cases the children are being kept at home and treated as things, not people ("Foolish thing!" Cymbeline calls Imogen, "Disloyal thing!"). Cymbeline further tightens the family circle by insisting that Imogen marry "his wive's sole son."

It is in the Posthumus plot, as I have suggested, that the family resonances are most striking, however. Posthumus' trouble at the beginning of the play is that he does not know who he is—and this is partly because he does not know who his family is. Literally, of course, everyone does know his family, but he is introduced as an orphan—his very name, Posthumus, proclaims his status as one born out of his parents' death, just as he was "ript" from his dying mother's womb. The first thing we hear about him is that he cannot be "delved to the root"—a dubious note in a play about family trees, in which every man who founds one is associated with a tree. And, just listening to Posthumus, we hear an immature young man—good, but not yet able to distinguish independence from rash rebellion. Posthumus is cut off from his elders; he himself tells us that the weakness which led him to wager on Imogen's chastity in the first place was his swaggering refusal to "be guided by others' experience." If Cymbeline imposes his own experience in too stifling a way, Posthumus tries too soon to break free from the experienced elders—as perhaps he broke free too soon from his mother's womb when he was "ript" from it.

Though his real family is dead, Posthumus' story is a sequence of substitute-family adventures. It is not at all obvious, but we can see that he associates himself with two new families and works out his relation each time to a new father and two older brothers, all as part of his other adventures. His first foster family is Cymbeline's, and here he makes a mistake and usurps his proper place when he elopes with Imogen. We may certainly sympathize with his desire to marry Imogen, but it is at best precipitous and at worst tainted with the disrespect and incest that show most clearly in the stepson Cloten. For, in a sense, Cymbeline's degenerate stepfamily is a symbolic reflection of Posthumus' actions, and Cloten is a parody of Posthumus himself.[5] Cloten is of course Posthumus' opposite in so many ways: mean, proud, and cowardly—and he smells. Yet there are similarities, and these lie in more than their common passion for wagers and gambling. Imogen mistakes Cloten's *body* for Posthumus', and as for the spirit, Cloten's potential for selfish possessiveness is the very thing Posthumus must come to terms with. In fact, it is a Clotenish trait that nearly kills Posthumus' marriage, when he makes that bet and gives in to a boorish rage.

So Posthumus' mistakes with his first family coincide with his mistakes in his marriage. But he goes on to a second foster family, and this one leads to the healing of his marriage. Having killed Imogen (or so he thinks), Posthumus repents by joining Imogen's father's army, as we saw, and he promptly winds up fighting beside an unidentified father and two sons. (We of course know that these are really Cymbeline's own sons and their kidnapper, in disguise, and we can appreciate the ironic play among various levels of "real" and only apparent family ties.) This time Posthumus takes his proper place: brave, but not overbearing; accepting his position as nameless third son; subduing his own ends to those of the little family. He stands with Belarius in the "narrow lane," but instead of killing "the old man" in a repetition of an oedipal crime at the crossroads,[6] he defends him selflessly, and the group single-handedly saves Britain. It is only when he has become a proper son that he becomes a man and takes his father's place, for Posthumus' father was known and named for his brave defense of Britain. Significantly, it is only when Posthumus goes into battle that he invokes his family's protection and takes on its name.

It is only when Posthumus moves from the older, suffocating family bonds, in which members are imprisoned and imprisoning, to this more generous conception of what it means to be part of a family, that he can establish a new and more mature relationship with his wife. At first he himself had been like a possessive parent, jealously guarding Imogen;

when exiled, he left her with a "manacle of love," the bracelet he comes to believe in more than he believes in Imogen herself. Finally he winds up in his own prison, manacled and doomed. But once the characters find the right way of giving themselves to each other, the manacles of love become living, strengthening bonds. And when Imogen and Posthumus finally find each other at the end of the play, whether we hear "rock" or "lock" in the disputed word of Imogen's greeting, her words transform all the rocky prisons, bonds, bolts, and locks we have heard about earlier. Posthumus, not recognizing her, had pushed her away, but she embraces him, saying:

> Think that you are upon a [l] ock, and now
> Throw me again.

(V.v.262–63)

All the strongholds in the play are similarly transformed: the British island, "paled in with rocks unscalable," or the "temple" Imogen, whose "lock" Iachimo did not pick after all.

Posthumus' prison is itself transformed by the dream he has there, in which his family forms a strong, unbroken circle around him and we see the bondage of the prison walls replaced by family bonds. (The stage directions are perfectly clear: beginning with a call for *solemn music*, they specify each family member and then order them all to "circle Posthumus round as he lies sleeping" [V.iv.28].) For Posthumus' achievement as a husband and a son is crowned by this vision of his family. Dead though they are, they appear physically on stage, breaking into the current action and revealing their implicit presence all along. They appear just when Posthumus finds himself, and the dream is a perfect climax to his story.

The dream is a climax for the whole play as well, and I want to turn finally to it now to see more clearly the general role of the family in the play. The dream comes at the moment when the action has gotten more tangled than we ever see it elsewhere in Shakespeare, and when the levels of duplicity and sheer misunderstanding have multiplied so that even the audience, which sees everything, has some trouble sorting them out. The dream reassures both the characters and the audience that the complexities will be made simple and the separations will become reunions, and that the "extraordinary blindness"[7] of the characters has been countered all along by the insight of an all-seeing god.

What sort of dream can achieve all this? The critics have come to call it the vision of Jupiter, and so it is. I have left out the best part of the dream, actually, in my first description. The great god comes down from the sky in a marvelous flourish: "Jupiter descends in thunder and lightning, sitting upon an eagle. He throws a thunderbolt. The Ghosts fall on their knees" (V.iv.). And when he leaves, "The marble pavement closes; he is entered/His radiant roof" (V.iv.90–91). But the more homely aspect of the dream, which is a vision of Posthumus' family, is just as important, if not more so. The family frames Jupiter's appearance and is responsible for it. They are the ones who summon him and ask him to account for himself. (Why has he been treating their son this way?!) And they remain behind to have the last word after he leaves.

The dream can be interpreted either as a revelation of the divine forces in human affairs, or as a revelation of the familial matrix that underlies all human experience. We can name the force that guides the action in Cymbeline's world, either by interpreting "from above" and calling it Jupiter, or by interpreting "from below" and calling it the effect of family.

The two phrases "from above" and "from below" allude purposely to Freud's account of the interpretation of dreams, in which he distinguishes on the one hand between traditional dream interpretation, which looks to the bizarre images in dreams for prophecies and god's word, and Freud's own more mundane interpretation, which looks for derivatives of early infantile complexes.[8] Freud would not be surprised to discover that a dream about God was "really" about the dreamer's father. Of course, Freud's answers to questions about how gods and fathers were related were often reductive answers: the "illusions" of art and religion derive from the forgotten mundane truths about the family. But the play insists on both interpretations. What is revealed in the dream is a guiding force that comes out of the family and is associated with it but is as "rare," to use a recurring word from the play, as a divine power would be.

My point is that while Shakespeare avoids the Freudian reduction of the divine vision, he still "psychologizes" or internalizes it. Shakespeare's originality lies not only in joining gods and fathers, combining two different aspects of experience, but in joining and transforming two familiar literary traditions so that each takes on new meaning. The first of these is the divine epiphany, the entrance of a *deux ex machina*, who was expected in the narrative romances on which Shakespeare drew and who literally appeared in machines of various subtlety on the sixteenth-century stage, including Shakespeare's own plays: Hymen in *As You Like It* and Diana in *Pericles*. What is extraordinary about Posthumus' epiphany, however, is that while Jupiter does indeed descend, he neither does nor says anything of substance—no rescues, no revelations, and only the flimsiest, most circumstantially creaky, of oracles. Essentially all he does is say "I am here."

The same is true of Shakespeare's transformation of the second tradition that he drew upon for the dream—the family recognition scene. For just as Shakespeare gives us an intervening god who does nothing, he gives us a recognition scene in which nothing is recognized. Posthumus is not literally reunited with his family, the way children in romances always are, and he does not learn anything literally new about his identity. He is not a prince and was not meant to be; he is merely his father's son. After the dream, nothing has changed except his state of mind; Posthumus has simply recognized his past and therefore recognized himself. Here, as with the divine epiphany, what is usually staged as an outward movement of the plot—and what appears as such in Shakespeare's other romances—has become instead an inward movement of the mind. Other young heroes (or more often heroines) in the romances must also find their parents in order to find themselves. What is different here is that Posthumus cannot find his parents in the flesh; he must find the idea of his parents. "Sleep, thou hast been a grandsire and begot/A father to me," says Posthumus when he wakes: he is the child of his own vision (V.iv.93-94). Shakespeare is not Sophocles, and he has not written another *Oedipus*. What he has done in this play is just what Freud did in his theory *about* Oedipus: he has rationalized a myth by making it into a psychological truth.

I want now to suggest that this semi-psychoanalytic insight about the family's presence can help us to understand and cope with the difficulties, obscurities, and ambiguities in *Cymbeline*—because the family's ambiguous presence in the characters' lives is closely related to the remarkable degree of confusion unique to this play, and to the pervasive uncertainty about just what is going on. Of course, no one finally trusts appearances in any Shakespearean world—at least we do not usually trust those characters who trust appearances and demand ocular proof. But in this Shakespearean world, appearances are almost never right or even determinable; the characters are literally nearsighted and otherwise inclined to misinterpret or overinterpret. But even more unsettling, not only do we mistrust external appearances here but also internal ones. We mistrust even those overwhelming inner passions that seem to be the rock-bottom reality of life.

This is the kind of distrust more familiar to the psychoanalysts, and *Cymbeline*, more than any other Shakespearean play, comes closest to the strange unsettling revelation of depths below depths unearthed in psychoanalysis. It presents a world where identities shift—and so do loyalties (Posthumus dresses like a Briton to defend Britain and then puts on Roman clothes and is arrested); where past suddenly overtakes present; where one emotion turns into its opposite. *Cymbeline* shows us what it is like to be a creature of the past, a creature with a latency period and latent meanings in everything we do. The play shows what it is to be an individual whose identity paradoxically depends on being part of a family in which that identity is threatened; an individual whose conscious experience is colored by *un*conscious, and whose current life is always shaped by a quiet, or not so quiet, symbolic force from the past.

Cymbeline has been called a history play, but it is a history play of the individual too, and it shows that what we are now comes out of what we *were*. Like Oedipus, its characters keep meeting their past and must give it a place,[9] just as Cymbeline must finally "pay tribute" to the Rome that generated him and his ideals, even though he has outwardly defeated the Roman army. The play presents a world in which a "posthumus" child finds life only be recreating his dead parents, and where people who had seemed dead come alive in strange ways. Interestingly enough, the play also ensures that we in the audience also keep meeting figures like Iachimo/Iago from our past lives with Shakespeare, and it forces us to find a way of incorporating that past without letting it take over.

There are many scenes in *Cymbeline* where Shakespeare demonstrates the family resonances enriching—and confusing—the characters' experience, but I will mention only one here. The scene comes just past the middle of the action, when everyone is moving to Wales. In the political plot, the Roman forces are gathering there; in the second, or dynastic plot, Cymbeline's kidnapped sons are living there; and in the marriage plot, Imogen is heading there (in disguise, of course) to find her husband. In addition, when Imogen arrives in Wales (disguised as the boy Fidele), she accidentally wanders into the cave where her kidnapped brothers have been living for the last twenty years with their kindly kidnapper, though neither they nor she realizes anyone else's true identity. The scene I am talking about comes after Imogen, alias "Fidele," has been living with the brothers for a while and is suddenly discovered "dead" by one of them, though *we* know she isn't really dead but only drugged.

The scene begins when the young man, whose real name is Arviragus but who is known as Cadwal, comes onstage carrying the dead body of what he thinks is the boy Fidele. This death makes the young man remember the death of their mother (rather, of the woman they have taken all along to be their mother, but whom we know was merely the kidnapper's wife). But this is not all the death evokes. For us in the audience, the scene evokes Lear's entrance with the dead Cordelia in his arms, and, if we are loose enough, it evokes the *pietà* behind Lear's posture. Behind the *pietà*, it evokes an original image of the mother with a living child in her arms. In addition, when we hear Fidele called a "lily" in this scene, we may remember an earlier scene in the play—a time when Imogen was not dead but asleep and Iachimo spied on her in order to get information to mislead Posthumus. Then too she was called a "lily" as she lay senseless.

Now Fidele is not Fidele, of course—"he" is Imogen; nor is he dead. He has merely taken a potion that the wicked Queen gave to his friend thinking it was poison, but which we know is a harmless sleeping medicine. For that matter, not only isn't this Fidele dead, but Arviragus' mother, whom he mourned before, was not his mother either. Nonetheless, all these confusions do not invalidate Arviragus' emotion—any more than they invalidate the audience's esthetic and even playful appreciation of the scene. We take it for granted that we who are watching can bring something to our experience of this scene: other scenes in the play, scenes in other Shakespearean plays, a whole cultural matrix, and all our common human experience as well. What Shakespeare shows, in addition, is that even the characters most directly and least esthetically involved in the experience also bring things to it, making it richer and more complicated that it "really" is.

But experience is always richer than it "really" is, so long as there are people to observe it. The exaggerated complications in *Cymbeline* make us realize with even more force than usual that "reality" finally lies in the enrichment, and the truth lies in the excess. Arviragus' "excessive" or mistaken emotion, we finally realize, is appropriate after all: Fidele really is his sister. Arviragus is responding to a larger truth than the literal—just like Freud's patients, whose literally false *déjà vu* experiences are yet true representatives of their "psychological constellation" of the moment.[10]

Partly because the play's twists and self-consciousness encourage our detachment, they also encourage us to consider curiously those things we usually take for granted, and to ask not only "Who is that?" but "How do I know?"—to wonder about the nature of identity. The action suggests and discards several answers to that question and leaves us, I think, with a more amorphous and unsettling one—one more like the psychoanalyst's. We already knew that identity is more than a surface phenomenon. Only in the case of a sham like Cloten do clothes make the man and give him a lineage (his "tailor" was his "grandfather" [IV. ii.81–82]). And only a promiscuous Italian "jay" (whore) finds her beauty's "mother" in her painting, as Imogen says (III.iv.50–51). But identity is more than skin deep too, in this play. A mole identifies Guiderius at the end, but it was just such a mole that misled Posthumus about Imogen's true nature earlier. And not only moles but whole trunks can mislead; the trunk in which Iachimo hides to observe the mole is only a prelude to the more spectacular confusion of identities when Imogen mistakes Cloten's headless trunk for Posthumus'.

To discover his identity, Posthumus must look not only at the present trunk but at the roots. He must look to his family—but he must look in the very special, imaginative way we have seen. Instead of literally discovering his family, he must simply reimagine them; he must make what he can of the past, recreate his family in his dreams. And if the puns on which I have partly based this argument seem tenuous already, I will add one that is even more far-fetched and seemingly peripheral. There are some literal or vegetable "roots" that appear in the play during Imogen's pastoral interlude as Fidele. For she takes on the job of cooking for her hosts and makes them dishes, as they say, fit for the gods, when she "cut[s] our roots in characters" to make her brothers' broth (IV.ii.49). I am not suggesting that Shakespeare here is giving away *his* recipe for making characters out of their roots (for one thing, "character" did not yet mean quite what it means for us). But I am suggesting that the farcical misunderstandings in this play are matched by its seemingly trivial puns. And that it is in just such flickering, uncertain, off-center signs that the unconscious meaning of our love manifests itself, and the unconscious depths of character, which are always *felt*, make themselves *known*.

Notes

1. E. D. Hirsch, Jr., *Validity in Interpretation* (New Haven, Conn.: Yale Univ. Press, 1967), p. 4.

2. George S. Klein, *Perception, Motives and Personality* (New York: Knopf, 1970), p. 303.

3. Serge Leclaire and Jean Laplanche, "The Unconscious, a Psychoanalytic Study," in *French Freud: Structural Studies in Psychoanalysis*, Yale French Studies, 48 (1972), 118–75.

4. For suggestive treatment of this and related points, see C. L. Barber, "'Thou that beget'st him that did thee beget': Transformation in *Pericles* and *The Winter's Tale*," *Shakespeare Survey*, 22 (1969): 59–67; Leslie Fiedler, *The Stranger in Shakespeare* (New York: Stein and Day, 1972); and A. D. Nuttall, "Two Unassimilable Men," in *Shakespearean Comedy*, gen. ed. Malcolm Bradbury and David Palmer, Stratford-on-Avon Studies 14 (New York: St. Martin's Press, 1972).

5. See Murray M. Schwartz's "Between Fantasy and Imagination: A Psychological Exploration of *Cymbeline*," in *Psychoanalysis and Literary Process*, ed. Frederick Crews (Cambridge, Mass.: Winthrop Publishers, 1970).

6. Suggestions of unwitting oedipal confrontation emerge more directly in Shakespeare's source. The Posthumus figure in Holinshed, Brute, fled from his family because he found that he had killed his father instead of a deer; the hero of *The Rare Triumphs of Love and Fortune* flees, like Posthumus, because of a taboo attachment, and then meets his father disguised as a hermit. (Note: *Rare Triumphs*, an anonymous dramatic romance acted in 1582, was edited by W. W. Greg in the Malone Society Reprints, 1931.)

7. Northrop Frye, *A Natural Perspective: The Development of Shakespearean Comedy and Romance* (New York: Columbia Univ. Press, 1965).

8. Along with the model of layered analogies described by Freud and others (e.g., Ernst Kris and Erik Erikson), see the model of mutually interacting analogies described by Paul Ricoeur in the first chapter of *Freud and Philosophy: An Essay on Interpretation*, trans. Denis Savage (New Haven, Conn.: Yale Univ. Press, 1970). Elsewhere, of course, Freud was more interested in completely *nonanalogous* relationships between manifest and latent meanings, such as the ones produced by the distortions of dream work.

9. See n. 6.

10. See Sigmund Freud, *The Psychopathology of Everyday Life*, in *The Standard Edition of the Complete Psychological Works of Sigmund Freud*, ed. and trans. James Strachey et al., 24 vols. (London: Hogarth Press, 1953–74), 6, pp. 265–68.

12 ❂ The Providential Tempest and the Shakespearean Family

Coppélia Kahn

I

Shakespeare rarely portrays masculine selfhood without suggesting a filial context for it. Of all his heroes, only Timon has neither kith nor kin—but through his obsessive giving he tries vainly to make all Athens his family, dependent on him for nurturance. Even the most pathologically solitary hero, Richard III, defines himself by systematically exterminating his family and violating its bonds in novel ways. It goes without saying that Shakespeare depicts all his women characters as sisters, daughters, wives, or mothers. Cleopatra is only superficially an exception, for her milieu of Egyptian fecundity binds her profoundly to the human family through sexuality and procreation. Yet, at the same time, an intense ambivalence toward the family runs through Shakespeare's works, taking the familiar shape of conflicts between inheritance and individuality and between autonomy and relatedness. As Meredith Skura observes: "The family is so important that characters cannot even imagine themselves without one, yet every family must bring on its own destruction."[1] That is, characters must break out of their families in order to grow up, and when they have founded families of their own, they must learn both to accept and then to let go of their children.

In this essay, I will set the Shakespearean quest for masculine selfhood in the context of the family and the life cycle. From the beginning of his career to the end, Shakespeare sought a dramatic and psychological strategy for dealing not only with our common ambivalence toward our families but specifically with the male passage from being a son to being a father. He found it through the romance, in one of its

This chapter also appears in Coppélia Kahn, *Man's Estate: Masculine Identity in Shakespeare*, forthcoming from the Univ. of California Press. Reprinted by permission.

typical patterns of action that I shall call "the providential tempest."[2] The five plays following this pattern are *The Comedy of Errors, Twelfth Night, Pericles, The Winter's Tale,* and *The Tempest,* all directly or indirectly based on narrative romance. They depict the separation of family members in a literal or metaphorical tempest; the resulting sorrow and confusion; and the ultimate reunion of the family, with a renewed sense of identity or rebirth for its members. This pattern is that of a journey, and it suggests a passage through time as well as through space—the individual's passage from emotional residence within the family to independence and adulthood. As depicted in the plays, the tempest and shipwreck initiating the main action represent the violence, confusion, and even terror of passing from one stage of life to the next, the feeling of being estranged from a familiar world and sense of self without another to hang onto.[3]

The only female protagonists in these tempest plays are Viola and Olivia in *Twelfth Night,* and Viola plays a man's part in most of the action. Marina, Perdita, and Miranda of the romances are accessory to their fathers' development as characters, rather than characters developed for their own sakes, and their spheres of action are severely restricted. While Hermione is strongly defined, it is Leontes' identity crisis that the play stresses. Clearly, with the exception of *Twelfth Night,* the pattern I am describing—of separation from and reunion with the family— reflects a male passage, and the point of view within the five plays shifts significantly from that of son to that of father.

Reading these five plays as a group, we watch a process of identity formation highlighted in two significantly interrelated crises: that of the youth emerging from the family, more than a child but still not quite a man, and that of the father who has not yet fully accepted his father-hood. Erik Erikson's division of the lifelong process of identity formation into stages can help us to grasp the tempest action as a symbol for the way family relationships shape the growing self.[4] The great normative crisis of identity occurs in adolescence; it is then that instinctual and social imperatives for intimacy with the opposite sex and pressures toward a settled choice of work and way of life create a crisis, defined by Erikson as "a necessary turning point, when develop-ment must move one way or another."[5] These imperatives and pressures create a recoil, a "regressive pull" back into the family, into the identifications of the early, preoedipal stage of ego building. In effect, the adolescent reexperiences separation and individuation, but not solely through his mother.

Peter Blos characterizes adolescence as dominated by two broad affective states: mourning and being in love.[6] Confronted with the great imperative of finding someone to love, the adolescent must give up the strongest love he has known thus far, his love for his parents. To give it up, he must mourn them, and in mourning them, he has recourse to the usual mechanism of mourning: he identifies with them, or one of them. But he does this indirectly, by merging narcissistically with persons who can mirror him as that parent once did. In effect, he recapitulates the symbiotic merger with the mother preceding separation and individuation.[7] This recapitulation occurs in what Blos calls the transitory narcissistic stage of adolescence, which normally precedes the definitive stage, the search for a heterosexual object. It is characterized by an overwhelming hunger for a love object of the same sex, in which the real identity of the object, the parent of the same sex, is denied. Whether it is positive or negative, identification with this same-sex object is necessary, as part of the mourning process, before heterosexual love can exist.[8] It is this process of mourning the loss of the parent by identification, and finding a new object of love after working through identification, that *The Comedy of Errors* and *Twelfth Night* depict.

The next three plays take up the process of maturing at a later turning point in which identity is again a generational issue. Though the father-protagonists of the three romances have broken away and formed families of their own, they return to fighting old battles with their internalized original families in the attempt to redefine themselves as fathers instead of sons. They struggle to accept their difference from and dependence on women and to take parenthood as the measure of their mortality. Shakespeare resolves this crisis through the father-daughter relationship, using the daughter's chaste sexuality and capacity to produce heirs as a bridge to the hero's new identity as father. In the history plays, it was the son on whom the father relied for a reaffirmation of his identity through the male line of succession. In these tempest plays, the patriarchal stress on lineage is softened, but not really changed; the daughter instead of the son carries on the father's line. But whereas the history plays bypassed the role of women in the definition of male identity, these plays recast it. The daughters don't inherit a patrimony in the same sense as the sons did; rather, they *are* the inheritance of purified female sexuality that the father-heroes pass on to their sons-in-law.

In the first group of plays, the fear animating the identity crisis is the fear of losing hold of the self—in psychoanalytic terms, the fear of losing ego identity. Often it is expressed as the fear of being engulfed, extinguished, or devoured in the sea or in some oceanic entity. The adolescent in the throes of establishing that continuity of self-image, that basic inner stability on which identity is based, fears losing his still-emergent self in another through erotic fusion, which at the same time he ardently desires. What Erikson separates into two stages, adolescence and youth, Shakespeare treats as one in these comedies through courtship, the traditional comic action.[9] Courtship is a time of self-exploration through amorous adventure and testing, which leads to the final choice of a mate, signifying the transition from youth to maturity.

The second group of plays, the romances, are more oedipally oriented than the first. In them, incestuous threat or wish motivates action, rather than the fear of losing ego identity, or identity confusion more closely related to preoedipal formation. C. L. Barber characterizes the difference between the comedies and the romances thus:

> The festive comedies move out to the creation of new families; *Pericles* and *The Winter's Tale* move through experiences of loss to the recovery of family relations in and through the next generation. . . . where regular comedy deals with freeing sexuality from the ties of family, these late romances deal with freeing family ties from the threat of sexual degradation.[10]

That threat comes, in various ways, from the psychic remnants of old filial relationship, persisting into maturity and preventing fathers from fully accepting the sexual powers of women and their own implication in the cycle from birth to death. *Pericles, The Winter's Tale*, and *The Tempest* all mirror anxiety about—and even disgust at—desire, female sexuality, and procreation.

Shakespeare also brings out the emotional structure underlying these crises of filial identity through a striking device of repetition or doubling.[11] He first uses the twin as a double for the self in relation to the mother; then the daughter, repetition through generation, is a double for the self in relation to the father. Finally, in *The Tempest* he uses revenge—repeating what was done to you but reversing it onto the other—and the renunciation of revenge as a way of ending the contest of the self against time and against its own children.

Any psychoanalytic discussion of doubling is of course indebted to Rank and Freud, who first described it in literature as a neurotic manifestation of the Oedipus complex.[12] Freud discusses the double as an example of "the uncanny," a mental representation of something familiar and homelike but at the same time secret, strange, and sinful—a representation, in short, of our earliest sexual feelings and wishes with regard to our parents, which we later perceive as guilty, repress, and hide. The double expresses the idea that these filial ties are inescapable and will cling forever, no matter how hard we try to shake them off. The double's typical activity in the literary sources cited by Rank and Freud is to pursue and unnerve the hero with his persistent, baffling presence, which specifically prevents the hero from loving a woman. Intervening at crucial moments to poison the hero's attempts at intimacy, the double thus prevents him from becoming independent from his family.

Freud and Rank also stress the double's power to bind the hero to his oedipal past in another way. The double, they maintain, is a potential death bringer, a projection of the castrating oedipal father, while at the same time it represents the hero's beloved, narcissistically overestimated self. The double makes the hero's life a torment, but the hero's life also depends on the double's existence. If the hero tries to kill his double, he too will die; they are symbiotically bound to each other.

By expressing his protagonists' struggles toward identity through doubles, Shakespeare brings out the fear of ego loss and the regressive narcissistic pull of the family that Freud and Rank stress. But he also uses the double as a means of negotiating the difficult passage from filial rootedness to independence, to suggest a normal resolution of identity crises. Defining himself in and then against his double, the Shakespearean protagonist discovers and affirms his sexual identity and loosens confining family ties, so that "twinship and kinship are replaced by selfhood."[13]

II

Now the twin-sibling plays, *Errors* and *Twelfth Night*. In each, the protagonist feels an intense affection for his twin that inspires his crucial actions, and the confusion caused by being mistaken for his twin leads ultimately not only to the desired reunion with the twin but to a previously unsought union with a marriage partner. The double of these plays, the beloved twin, brings with him not just the morbid anxieties Freud and Rank find but also an ultimately benign confusion that acts as a catalyst for reunion, rebirth, and fulfillment. The twin is a compromise figure, a projection of contending desires; it is through the twin that the protagonist retains ties with the filial past but also through the twin that he finds a mate and breaks with that past to create his own future. Searching for his twin and mistaken for him, Antipholus of Syracuse (Antipholus S.) meets Luciana and falls in love; grieving for her twin and disguised as him, Viola meets Orsino and falls in love.

But in their searching and grieving, Antipholus S. and Viola are both regressing to the earliest stage of identity formation: identification with one perceived as being the same as oneself, which is distinct from object choice, love for someone distinct from and outside the self, predicated on an already formed ego. Identification is first experienced at the mother's breast, when the infant fuses with one who is not yet perceived as "not me." It is also in infancy that the mother's face mirrors the child to himself, confirming his existence through her response to him before he has an inner sense of his separateness and permanence.[14] Thus the twin, as narcissistic mirror, represents the mother as the earliest, most rudimentary confirmation of the self.

In *Errors*, the twins' very names stress the idea behind the whole action, that identity is formed in relationship to "significant others." Shakespeare changed the names from Menaechmus (in his source, Plautus' *Menaechmi*) to Antipholus, from the Greek *anti* + *philos*: love against or opposed to.[15] The entire family, we realize as the play proceeds, has landed in Ephesus as either the direct or indirect result of storm, shipwreck, and separation. As each character is introduced, we see that he feels uprooted and alienated from himself because he has lost that "other" closest to him. The dominant metaphor for this collective psychic state is being lost in or on the sea—precisely the event that caused the state. Shakespeare thus internalizes the external and conventional events of the romance plot.

The focus of psychological interest rests on Antipholus of Syracuse, the melancholy, questing brother who comes to Ephesus in search of a self as well as a family. His first soliloquy crystallizes the interior action of the family romance:

> He that commends me to mine own content
> Commends me to the thing I cannot get.
> I to the world am like a drop of water
> That in the ocean seeks another drop,
> Who, falling there to find his fellow forth,
> (Unseen, inquisitive) confounds himself.
> So I, to find a mother and a brother,
> In quest of them, unhappy, lose myself.[16]
>
> (*Err.* I.ii.33–40)

One might argue that Antipholus seeks to repeat an oedipal triangle, with his brother taking his father's place. But as the action focuses exclusively on his relationship to his brother, it seems, rather, that he wants to make a mirroring mother of his brother. He envisions extinction—total merger with an undifferentiated mass—as the result of his search. The image of a drop of water seeking another drop stresses his need for his identical twin but also suggests the futility of this means of self-definition. As half of a single drop of water, will Antipholus be more "content" or have more of a self? And the image of that one drop falling into a whole ocean conveys the terror of failing to find identity: irretrievable ego loss.

I hesitate to place much weight on Antipholus S. himself as a character with a complex inner world. Rather, his speech adds a powerful psychological dimension to the farcical action as a whole: it encourages us to see the incipient confusion and the ensuing descent into madness as fantasies of identity confusion and ego loss in adolescence, attendant on the break away from filial identifications and into adult identity. Erikson notes that when "identity hunger" is extreme, young people:

> . . . are apt to attach themselves to one brother or sister in a way resembling that of twins. . . . They seem apt to surrender to a total identification with at least one sibling . . . in the hope of regaining a bigger and better [identity] by some act of merging. For periods they succeed, but the letdown which must follow the artificial twinship is only the more traumatic. Rage and paralysis follow the sudden insight—also possible in one of a pair of twins—that there is enough identity only for one, and that the other seems to have made off with it. [17]

The irony for Erikson's adolescent and for Shakespeare's character is that seeking identification by narcissistic mirroring leads only to the obliteration, not the discovery, of the self.

That obliteration takes the form of the "errors," the comic confusions of identity, which provide the mirth of the play. The metaphorical and dramatic forms the errors take, however—metamorphosis, engulfment, and enchantment—allow for a psychological reading along with a farcical one and continue the theme of identity confusion and loss of ego identity. Shakespeare shifts the scene of Plautus' comedy from Epidamnum to Ephesus in order to call on all the associations of that city with magic and witchcraft (well-known to his audiences through St. Paul's visit to Ephesus), and he gains a language in which he can express that theme.

Metamorphosis is first hinted at when Antipholus S., quite naturally fearing he has been robbed, voices deeper anxieties about the robbery of his very identity, by "Dark-working sorcerers that change the mind,/ Soul-killing witches that deform the body" (*Err.* I.ii.99–100). When at first he accedes, dazed and passive, to the new identity rather harshly attributed to him by his brother's wife, his response is parodied by that of his servant, who feels that he is being "transformed . . . both in mind and in my shape" to be an ape; to one who only plays a part, who isn't really who he seems to be (*Err.* I.ii.195–99). Then, falling in love with Luciana when she tenderly persuades him that he is someone else, Antipholus S. envisions her as a god, who would "create" him anew.

Calling her a mermaid and a siren, he picks up the oceanic imagery of his earlier soliloquy, and at this point the idea of metamorphosis shades into that of engulfment. Her sister would drown him, but she will rescue him. Metaphorically, she will save him from that obliteration of self, that inauthentic metamorphosis into another person, which her sister promised:

O, train me not, sweet mermaid, with thy note
To drown me in thy sister's flood of tears;
Sing, siren, for thyself, and I will dote;
Spread o'er the waves thy golden hairs,
And as a bed I'll take thee, and there lie, . . .

(*Err.* III.ii.45–49)

In raptures he continues, while she protests that he, as her sister's hus-band, ought to be saying such things to her sister, Adriana. Identifying himself ever more closely with Luciana as "mine own self's better part,/ Mine eye's clear eye, my dear heart's dearer heart"—even saying "I am thee," he asks her to marry him (*Err.* III.ii.61–66). But again parody questions this instant surrender of self to another, when Dromio of Syracuse wails: "I am an ass, I am a woman's man, and besides myself" (*Err.* III.ii.76–77). He equates metamorphosis with possession by a woman and possession by a woman with loss of self in the form of engulfment. In a hilariously disgusting blazon of the fat cook Luce, he identifies parts of her body with countries and continents: "spherical, like a globe," she gushes grease, sweat, and rheum, and "lays claim" to Dromio, believing he is his twin. Woman becomes identified with those engulfing waters in which Antipholus S. feared to "confound" himself in Act I. Dromio's fears of being lost in Luce prove contagious; by the end of Act III, Antipholus S. regards Luciana as a mermaid luring him to death by drowning, and he hastens to leave on the next ship.

The play now takes up a third metaphor for loss of ego identity: possession by spirits. The mistaken arrest of Antipholus of Ephesus (Antipholus E.) for debt is described as seizure by "a devil," "a fiend, a fury," and the courtesan in the play is called "the devil's dam" who appears, like Satan, as "an angel of light" to gain men's souls. Metaphor becomes dramatic reality when the conjurer Dr. Pinch arrives to exorcise Antipholus E. But his efforts, of course, are vain. The real deliverance from the bonds of error is by angelic power. Pauline word play runs through the scenes focusing on Antipholus E.'s arrest; mistakenly and to no avail, he seeks deliverance from the sergeant's bonds with the coins—angels—which will pay his debt.[18] These echoes of Paul's miraculous deliverance from prison prepare us for the denouement at the abbey, wherein the evil powers of Lapland sorcerers and Circe's cup show themselves to be providence in disguise.

Counterpointing this series of metaphorical and dramatic projections of what it is like to lose or "confound" one's identity, one's relationship to others, and one's grasp of reality in general, are two other senses of reality. Both involve a sense of time. As an aspect of its concern with the development of identity as process rather than a fixed state, *Errors* fittingly stresses the importance of time in two ways. First, from the beginning of the play, time is the means by which the network of obligations and relations in ordinary life is maintained, allowing people to experience and reaffirm their identities constantly. When the twins are mistaken for each other, appointments are broken, people are late, and the network breaks down. Much of the comic action depends on this precise and mundane sense of time. Contrasted with it is the idea that time is an organic process analogous to conception, birth, and growth. It proceeds at a proper pace toward a destined goal, can neither be hurried nor stopped, and is controlled by God, like the tempest itself. Emilia's final lines firmly link this sense of time with a sense of identity as growth in time—the serious and realistic theme underlying the farce:

> Thirty-three years have I but gone in travail
> Of you, my sons, and till this present hour
> My heavy burden ne'er delivered.

(Err. V.i.400–402)

Identity grows through time and through loss, confusion, and challenge. Errors are part of a process whereby youth grows into and out of the family to find itself.

In *Errors*, the twin provides an affective bridge from filial to individual identity; seeking the twin, the hero finds his mate, but only when he is able to distinguish himself firmly from his twin. In *Twelfth Night*, we move a step further from the family, and the twin and other doubles function at first as projections of emotional obstacles to identity and then, in Viola and Sebastian, as the fulfillment of a wish for a way around the obstacles. The play abounds in images of engulfment and devouring connected with the sea and love; often it is suggested that love, like the sea, is boundless and voracious, swallowing up the lover. As John Hollander points out, the play is saturated in watery media, just as two of the main characters (and several of the minor ones) are suffused by their desires.[19] Images of the sea (reinforced by allusions to ships, sailing, and sea trading), of tears, rain, liquor, urine, and the humors surge forth. The images are first stated in Orsino's famous opening speech:

> O spirit of love, how quick and fresh art thou,
> That notwithstanding thy capacity
> Receiveth as the sea, nought enters there,
> Of what validity and pitch soe'er,
> But falls into abatement and low price,
> Even in a minute!

(TN I.i.9–14)

The idea of the sea is reiterated in the succeeding image of Orsino—like Actaeon, being torn apart by his desires. Orsino reverses the image in comparing his love to a woman's, saying:

> Alas, their love may be call'd appetite,
> No motion of the liver, but the palate,
> That suffers surfeit, cloyment, and revolt;
> But mine is all as hungry as the sea,
> And can digest as much.
>
> (*TN* II.iv.98–102)

Still, everything about Orsino proclaims that it is he who is consumed by desire and not the opposite. Skittish, giddy, "a very opal" of erotic whim, he himself is like the mutable sea. Similarly, when love comes stealing upon Olivia like the plague, her self-mortifying dedication to a dead brother vanishes instantly, and she becomes a bold wooer. When Orsino and Olivia love, they lose themselves in desire.

Interacting with this tendency to lose the self in surrender to Eros, however, is the attempt to retain identity, through a narcissistic mirroring similar to what Antipholus S. sought in *Errors*, and through distancing oneself from the object of desire. Viola copes with the supposed loss of her twin brother by in effect becoming him; when she disguises herself as a man, she is another Sebastian, her twin's twin. Viola is parallelled and contrasted with Olivia, another grieving sister; "to season a brother's dead love" she vows to water her chamber once a day with tears. Sequestered with the memory of her brother, she rejects Orsino's constant suits and punishes the world by withdrawing her beauty from it. When Viola falls in love with Orsino, she devotes herself to a martyrdom similar to Olivia's. As long as her disguise proves convincing, she can never confess or consummate her love, and, as Orsino's page, can only express it by furthering his suit to Olivia, her rival. Viola's disguise, it must be said, is to some extent necessitated by her circumstances, and unlike Olivia's attachment to her brother, it is a conscious assumption of a different identity that she maintains in tandem with her real one. Both move, however, from loving dead brothers to loving unattainable male figures, maintaining love with a distance that does not threaten their persistent ties to the family through their brothers.

Orsino's love parallels theirs in the sense that his object is hopelessly unattainable, and in the exacerbated self-consciousness and distancing it involves. His desire for Olivia can never be satisfied. Even though Orsino, like Olivia when she falls in love with Cesario, gives himself over to passion, the fact that he chooses an unyielding object with whom real intimacy is impossible argues his fear of losing himself in passion.

Thus, while all three characters fall madly in love, they all, in different ways, defend against Eros as a threat to the integrity and stability of the self. It is the narcissistic mirroring in which Viola and Olivia engage, however, that is most relevant to the Shakespearean family romance. The twin and the sibling, for Viola and for Olivia, are versions of a need for primary ontological reassurance. Like the mother, they are not fully differentiated from the self (they look the same, or similar, and are of the same blood), and thus they reaffirm the self at the most basic level but keep it from developing further.

However, the fact that mirroring is sought from a double of the opposite sex focuses the issue specifically on sexual identity rather than on identity per se, as in *Errors*. The errors of *Twelfth Night* are not merely those of mistaken identity, as in the earlier play, but errors that create an aura of doubt about the characters' sexual identity—for *us* rather than for them. *Twelfth Night* is frequently read as a play about masking, about the conscious and unconscious assumption of false identities and about levels of self-knowledge and self-deception;[20] this theme is played out prominently through Viola's transsexual disguise.

For the greater part of the play, until Act V, scene 2, each of the three major characters is wholly certain of who it is that he or she loves: Orsino, unaware of his growing attachment to Cesario, ardently pursues Olivia; Olivia gives herself passionately to a man she knows as Cesario; and Viola is constant to Orsino. Viola's transsexual disguise, until she and Sebastian are mistaken for each other in the duel with Sir Andrew, works on us more deeply and disturbingly than it does on the characters it fools, precisely because it fools them and doesn't fool us. As we watch Viola mediating between Olivia and Orsino, inhabiting one sex with them and another with us, we are forced to conceive of several novel and conflicting ways in which sexual identity might be detached from personal identity; we are cut loose from our habitual assumption that the two are inextricable, that the person is defined by his or her sex. In effect, we experience that state of radical identity confusion typical of adolescence, when the differences between the sexes are as fluid as their desires for each other, when a boy might feel more like a girl than a boy, or a girl might love another girl rather than a boy.[21]

Consider these several possibilities. Olivia believes Cesario to be a man, but we know he isn't, and are titillated by the suggestion that Olivia, loving a woman instead of a man, isn't the woman she should be. Similar doubts arise with Orsino, who has unclasped his bosom so readily to a charming boy. At the same time, Shakespeare lets us see that both Olivia and Orsino are drawn to Viola because they find in her those characteristics of the opposite sex to which they are attracted. Orsino says:

> For they shall yet belie thy happy years,
> That say thou art a man. Diana's lip
> Is not more smooth and rubious; thy small pipe
> Is as the maiden's organ, shrill and sound,
> And all is semblative a woman's part.
> I know thy constellation is right apt for this affair.
>
> (*TN* I.iv.30–35)

Olivia, musing on Cesario's statement that he is "a gentleman," declares:

> I'll be sworn thou art;
> Thy tongue, thy face, thy limbs, actions, and spirit
> Do give thee five-fold blazon. Not so fast: soft! soft!
> Unless the master were the man.
>
> (*TN* I.v.295–98)

At some level, Cesario is a homosexual object choice for each of them, and at another, a heterosexual one. Yet "she" or "he" is the same person, one person. Creatures whose sexual identity is not simply and clearly male or female—hermaphrodites or eunuchs—threaten the binary opposition on which sexual identity, and much else in culture, is based. Without the strict differentiation of male from female, psychic integrity disappears and chaos impends. When Viola refers to herself as a "poor monster," she but touches on the fearsome aspects of her disguise that have been evident to us as she moves ambiguously from Orsino to Olivia.

Yet, in the delicate comic irony of the scenes between Viola and each of the other two, Shakespeare reminds us through Viola's poignant double entendres of what Viola herself never forgets: that no matter how the duke and countess see her, she is not androgynous but irreducibly a woman. The fluid sexual proclivities of youth promise to clash with the reality principle, for that "little thing" she thinks she lacks of being a man is crucial.

The early introduction of Sebastian into the play, however, assures us that all will end properly with a mate of the opposite sex for both Orsino and Olivia. When Sebastian and Viola recognize each other as brother and sister in the last scene, and Olivia is reprieved from the shadow of our doubt that she might have been in love with a woman, Sebastian says: "So comes it, lady, you have been mistook. / But nature to her bias drew in that" (*TN* V.i.257–58). Nature's bias is usually regarded as a heterosexual one, but the line is actually ambiguous.[22] "Nature's bias" can mean that Olivia followed nature in loving a woman for a short and perhaps necessary period, before actually marrying a man.[23] Similarly, Orsino perhaps needed to see Viola as a girlish boy before he could accept her as a real and ardent woman. The dramatic device of identical, opposite-sex twins allows Orsino and Olivia to navigate the crucial passage from identification to object choice, from adolescent sexual experimentation to adult intimacy, from filial ties to adult independence, without even changing the objects of their desires.

Feste's song, "When that I was and a little tiny boy," which concludes the play, states in its offhand, colloquial, cryptic way the conception of a man's life cycle in terms of psychosexual stages that underlies the action of *Twelfth Night*. Several interpreters have suggested that the "foolish thing" of the first stanza is the *membrum virile*. [24] Before the speaker comes to "man's estate," sexuality can be like a toy, playful and open to experimentation, fluid, spontaneous, and uncommitted. But man's estate in the second stanza implies status, responsibility, wealth, and property, which "knaves and thieves" may cheat him out of. He must leave sexual play behind and, in the third stanza, take himself a wife. Now the issue is "swaggering," the pretense and display of courtship, as we have seen it in the play through Orsino's elegant embassies of love and Sir Andrew's pathetic attempts at valor, neither of which "thrive."

The song skips over marriage and parenthood, coming to rest in the puzzling fourth stanza at the last stage of life, a decline into drunkenness and sleep,[25] before ending with a sigh at the perpetual recurrence of the cycle: "A great while ago the world began . . ./ But that's all one, our play is done." *Twelfth Night* traces the evolution of sexuality as related to identity, from the playful and unconscious toyings of youthful courtship, through a period of sexual confusion, to a final thriving in which swaggering is left behind and men and women truly know themselves through choosing and loving the right mate.

III

With *Pericles*, written six or seven years after *Twelfth Night* and toward the end of Shakespeare's career, the family romance moves to its second stage: the protagonist as father, and his daughter as a different kind of double than the twin, one who repeats but reverses his experience and lifts him decisively out of the oedipal family of his past. Through her he becomes a father anew, accepting his fatherhood as his identity, and stops trying vainly to deny his mortality.

Pericles begins by plunging boldly into a representation of the oedipal family. The hero, seeking the hand of a princess, must win her by answering the riddle her father Antiochus has devised, or lose his head. The riddle simultaneously proclaims and hides the incest between father and daughter:

> I am no viper, yet I feed
> On mother's flesh, which did me breed.
> I sought a husband, in which labour
> I found that kindness in a father.
> He's father, son, and husband mild;
> I mother, wife, and yet his child:
> How they may be, and yet in two,
> As you will live, resolve it you.

(*Per.* I.i.65–72)

Riddles occur at points of life crisis in folklore and literature because the riddle structure offers an expressive model for the reconciliation of essential dualities. It creates confusion and then establishes clarity, reaffirming the rules and essential distinctions on which social life depends.[26] Underlying the riddle in *Pericles* is the ancient image of the *uroboros,* the mythical snake swallowing its own tail, nourishing itself from its own substance. In a Jungian sense, the *uroboros* is:

> an expression of the archetypal domination of nature and the unconscious over life. . . . In this phase the Archetypal Feminine not only bears and directs life as a whole, and the ego in particular, but also takes everything that is born of it back into its womb of origination and death.[27]

It signifies the mystical and perhaps sinister unity of life and death in woman, a mortal creature who gives birth to another creature who will also die. In the specific context of incest that the riddle traces, however, this mystical continuity of life and death is perverted. The union between the princess and her father denies the ongoing process of producing life from one generation to the next; her womb, receiving the seed from which she herself was generated, is a haven of sterility and death instead of the source of life. The *uroboros* suggests the incestuous oedipal family doubling back upon itself, consuming generational differences instead of sending forth new generations. The riddle and the Antioch experience as a whole are thus a negative analogue for "the family romance in *Pericles* [which] brings together a separated father, mother, and daughter only to divide the generations again for reproduction and rule."[28] In particular, the riddle stresses the destructive confluence of father and daughter, which will be canceled out by the role Marina is to play as one who figuratively and positively "gives birth" to her own father.

Clearly the father-daughter incest of the riddle is a projection of the son's desire to possess the mother and is associated with Pericles as a son. Whether he answers the riddle or feigns ignorance, he is helpless in Antiochus' hands, and through the rest of the play, he is dogged with miseries—though he does nothing to deserve them. Not his character, but the action of the providential tempest demands that he suffer punishment for a guilty desire not dramatized as his. Antiochus' riddle-scheme impressively depicts the castration threat (the stage is decked with the heads of failed suitors), while Pericles' meek, passive response to it represents the son's desire to renounce his phallic challenge to the father and regain his love, in effect taking the mother's place.

Pericles' episodic voyages from place to place, and his successive experiences of loss, are symbolic confrontations with oedipal desire and oedipal fear. The recurrent father figures he encounters represent his continuing difficulty in resolving his image of the father and his position in relation to him. Simonides, on whose shores Pericles is washed up half-dead after the first tempest, is a jolly, generous, nurturant figure who at first delights in playing the possessive father as a joke, then gives his daughter Thaisa to Pericles with his blessing. Cleon, the governor of a kingdom decimated by famine, is aided by the hero with gifts of food; out of gratitude, Cleon takes in Pericles' daughter Marina after the second tempest, when her mother (Thaisa) supposedly dies. But Cleon proves spineless before his envious, scheming wife, who arranges for the girl's death; thus he betrays Pericles' trust. Cerimon, a holy, wise, and kindly magus, restores Thaisa to life by his art. Lysimachus, the governor of Mytilene whom Marina redeems from carnal vice, charitably reunites her with her father and becomes his son-in-law.

Collectively, these figures bear an array of ambivalent traits: generous and impoverished, powerful and powerless, ascetic and fleshly. Throughout his encounters with them, Pericles can only bow his head, suffer, and endure. Only once does he show initiative and act a hero's part—whereupon the second tempest hits him. He is pointedly enjoined to learn patience, the virtue analogous to renunciation of the oedipal project. Unable to do so, he withdraws from the world in a deathlike trance, from which only his daughter can save him.

The shift from twin to daughter as the figure through whom the hero gains his final identity is crucial. What it means is that he breaks out of time conceived as a repetition of oedipal patterns and breaks into the future through his daughter and his own new family. The twin is the hero's physical and temporal double; born at the same time and looking just like him, he represents the hero's ties to the preoedipal past. But the daughter, of the opposite sex, born from but after the hero, the product of his union with a woman, is not his mirror image but his successor and opposite. Her fruitful chastity is the opposite of his mother's problematical oedipal sexuality, and (in *Pericles* and *The Winter's Tale*) reunion with her precedes reunion with his wife. Thus she validates his separateness from his own father, his fatherhood, his uniqueness.

Pericles falls conspicuously into two halves, the first tracing the hero's adventures, the second beginning some years later when his daughter approaches maturity and centering on her. Her life recapitulates his in that she too suffers several "tempests". She is threatened with death by her foster mother, captured by pirates, and finally delivered to a brothel to become a whore. Her name and her character make her a walking symbol of the tempest action:

> Ay me! poor maid,
> Born in a tempest, when my mother died,
> This world to me is as a lasting storm,
> Whirring me from my friends.
>
> (*Per.* IV.i.18–20)

In addition, her oblique, cryptic, enigmatic mode of speech links her to the riddling, incestuous princess of Antioch. Plainly enough, her relationship with Pericles in the reunion scene is the reverse of the father-daughter incest of the play's beginning, her redemptive chastity paradoxically more truly fruitful than the princess' lust. Pericles calls her "Thou that beget'st him that did thee beget" (*Per.* V.i.195). Her purity banishes the shadow of oedipal sexuality and brings the hero back to his wife and to the world.

IV

In an illuminating essay, C. L. Barber says that "the primary motive which is transformed in *The Winter's Tale* . . . is the affection of Leontes for Polixenes, whatever name one gives it."[29] Though Leontes is a mature man—king, husband, father—the nine-months' visit of his boyhood friend reveals that he is still split between two identities, the boy of the past and the father of the present. Following J.I.M. Stewart (who follows Freud) in interpreting Leontes' jealousy, I would argue that the hero's belief that his wife loves his best friend is his defense against the horrified realization that he too still loves that friend, his way of saying: "Indeed, I do not love him, she loves him!"[30] Recall the appealing imagery used to describe the affection that "rooted" between Leontes and Polixenes in their boyhoods. It portrays a paradise of sameness and oneness, the complete untroubled identity of each with the other:

> We were as twinn'd lambs that did frisk i' th' sun,
> And bleat the one at th'other: what we chang'd
> Was innocence for innocence: we knew not
> The doctrine of ill-doing, nor dream'd that any did.
>
> (*WT* I.ii.67–71)

Clearly, Polixenes is Leontes' double, one of the same sex and age who only mirrors him; loving Polixenes is depicted as guiltless, Edenic, and asexual, as opposed to loving a woman. It is also a love that denies time; Leontes and his friend were "Two lads that thought there was no more behind/But such a day to-morrow as to-day, and to be boy eternal" (*WT*, I.ii.63–65).

The homosexual implications of this nostalgic fantasy are less important than what it suggests about Leontes' attitude toward his mature sexuality, his manliness. He would like to escape and repudiate it, because being a husband and father means entrusting one's sexual dignity to a daughter of Eve, ceding the future to one's children, and facing death. Being "boy eternal," on the other hand, means being free of sexual desire, with its risks, its complications, and its implication in the procreative cycle, and being, though only in fantasy, immortal. In Polixenes' idyllic picture of boyhood, childish innocence is contrasted with adult sinfulness, and that sinfulness is then specifically associated with the women he and Leontes married, the "temptations" later "born" to them. The association of sin with the carnal pleasure legitimized by marriage betokens a guilt-ridden reluctance to accept, let alone appreciate, the natural desire of men for women—a reluctance soon rationalized in the violent misogyny through which Leontes voices his jealousy, the conviction that women are false through and through.

Having lost the mirror of his masculine identity in Polixenes, Leontes then seeks it in Mamillius, as he normally would in the patriarchal Shakespearean world. But his jealousy provokes him, ironically, to misinterpret the strong physical resemblance between himself and Mamillius. While Shakespeare makes it clear that this resemblance is the legitimate confirmation of Leontes' sexual union with Hermione, and the proof of her fidelity, Leontes finds Hermione's assertion of it another indication of female treachery:

> . . . they say we are
> Almost as like as eggs; women say so,
> (That will say anything) . . .

(WT I.ii.129–31)

In several significant ways, Shakespeare makes Mamillius a symbol of the union of male and female. His name associates him with the maternal function of nursing, and he is shown in the female company of his mother and her attendants. But he is also "a gentleman of the greatest promise" and universally acknowledged as the future ruler of Sicily, Leontes' heir. The news of his death arrives immediately upon Leontes' denial of the oracle, an act that spells Hermione's doom. That is, Mamillius dies when Leontes denies most absolutely his natural and legitimate sexual union with the feminine, with Hermione, of which Mamillius is the sign and seal. And he is driven to deny it because he cannot sustain it. Despite his age, his kingship, and his fatherhood, emotionally Leontes is stuck at the developmental stage preceding the formation of identity, the stage of undifferentiated oneness with the mother, on which his oneness with Polixenes was modeled.[31] He cannot sustain a relationship with a woman based on the union of his and her separate identities, in which trust and reciprocity mediate that separateness.

Fittingly, in robbing Leontes of an heir, Mamillius' death deprives him of a supremely important aspect of his male identity. Just as Macbeth cannot rest content with kingship so long as he lacks heirs to pass it on to, so Leontes is incomplete without an heir, and his lack of one is the direct result of his inability to accept his dependence on feminine power and to sustain a trusting union with Hermione. With the deaths of Mamillius and (seemingly) Hermione, Leontes' delusion lifts, and he enters into a period of realization and repentance. At this point Shakespeare makes explicit, through the figure of Father Time, connections that have been implicit in the first half of the play: those between the human experience of time in the life cycle, women, and the formation of masculine identity.

Inga-Stina Ewbank shows how Leontes, crazy in his jealousy, acts with feverish haste, "goes against time and is therefore blind to truth." In the tradition of Renaissance iconography appropriated by Shakespeare in this play, time is a father, an old man, just what Leontes does not want to be. Ironically, in defying Father Time, he denies his own fatherhood and deprives himself of a son and a future. He is plunged into seemingly endless mourning for his past actions. As Ewbank says, now Leontes "has to become aware of truth in a wider sense . . . through subjection to Time the Revealer."[32] It is in this second half of the play that women, Paulina and Perdita, gain effective dramatic power to nurture men; concurrently, time becomes the revealer, whose daughter is truth, rather than the destroyer, *tempus edax*, who seized Mamillius and Hermione. The play moves to "a world ransomed" (Bohemia), and through a number of parallels in dramatic structure and action, Shakespeare keeps alive his "primary motive," Leontes' feeling for Polixenes, now changed into the wide gap of enmity dividing the once "twinn'd" brothers. But this time the younger generation, the sons and daughters, are to redeem (or in Shakespeare's metaphor "beget") their fathers, restoring them to new identities as fathers.

Camillo's plot to present Florizel as his father's ambassador to Leontes provides the middle term by which the breaches between father and son, and brother and brother (Leontes and Polixenes), can both be healed at once. As Murray Schwartz argues: "By impersonating his father, Florizel can replace him without really replacing him."[33] But more important for the play's main action, the transformation of Leontes' affection for Polixenes, Florizel in the latter's place bridges the gap between the two men and makes them friends again, not as "twinn'd lambs" but as men who have erred, suffered, and lost. The king's greeting to his future son-in-law makes this change clear:

> Your mother was most true to wedlock, prince;
> For she did print your royal father off,
> Conceiving you . . . .
> . . . . Most dearly welcome!
> And your fair princess—goddess! O! alas,
> I lost a couple that 'twixt heaven and earth
> Might thus have stood, begetting wonder, as
> You, gracious couple, do; and then I lost
> (All mine own folly) the society,
> Amity too, of your brave father, whom
> (Though bearing misery) I desire my life
> Once more to look on him.
>
> (*WT* V.i.123-25, 129-37)

Florizel and Perdita represent complementary modes of mediating separation and difference from significant others, a crucial task in identity formation. He fights his father, then reconciles with him. Perdita, on the other hand, does not fight but subsumes opposites into a transcendent reality. On the sexual level, she reconciles virginity and erotic appeal, modesty and abandonment; mythically, through the imagery and ambiance of Bohemia, she is associated with "things dying" and "things newborn," with mother earth, the womb and tomb of all. She combines the qualities of the chaste preoedipal mother and the sexually desirable oedipal mother, symbolically uniting Leontes' divided attitudes toward women.

Significantly, though, Leontes' recognition of Florizel precedes his recognition of Perdita; he regains a son before he regains a daughter, thus recasting his relationship with his "brother," Polixenes, before he goes on to recognize and recast his relationship with the feminine in Perdita and then Hermione. This sequence of reunions recapitulates the sequence of identity development for which I am arguing. The total identity of like with like which Leontes found with Polixenes was an effort to repeat the mother-child symbiotic unity and to avoid male identity. When Leontes "takes" Florizel "for" Polixenes as well as "for" Mamillius, he is accepting paternity, his and Polixenes', as the crucial component of his male identity—and paternity is equally based upon his separateness from the feminine and his union with it. To acknowledge Perdita as his daughter is to accept the sexuality he had wanted to repudiate; to acknowledge her as his heir is to accept the mortality he had wanted to escape. It is fitting that Leontes, as he clasps Hermione's hand (that crucial gesture again), characterizes his reunion with her in terms of the most primitive, elemental human activity, begun at the mother's breast:

> O, she's warm!
> If this be magic, let it be an art
> Lawful as eating.
>
> (*WT* V.iii.109–11)

V

The island setting of *The Tempest* and the centrality of Prospero as demiurge make it a fantasy of omnipotence. Prospero not only controls; he creates. He devises scenarios of his deepest wishes and causes them to be enacted, redesigning his world so as to rectify or compensate for his past. The play's several interwoven actions—the courtship of Ferdinand and Miranda, the ordeal and illumination of the court party, the usurpations attempted by Antonio and Sebastian, and by Caliban, Stephano, and Trinculo—are all foreseen or overseen by Prospero. They are his attempts to work through his oedipal past, to complete himself. As such, they are only partly successful. He redefines himself as man rather than magician, and regains his dukedom. But while he gives up his omnipotence in the end, he never recognizes and accepts his sexuality and his relationship to women as Leontes does. Unlike *Pericles* and *The Winter's Tale, The Tempest* does not depict the rebirth of a family as well as of a man, and thus Prospero's final identity lacks the fullness of that achieved by the other heroes. [34]

Unlike them, Prospero has no wife; strangely, he doesn't even allude to his duchess' fate in the otherwise detailed account of his past that he gives Miranda. Moreover, his only mention of his wife is highly ambivalent, at once commending and questioning her chastity: "Thy mother was a piece of virtue, and / She said thou wast my daughter" (*Tmp.* I.ii.56–57). In addition to Miranda, the only other woman in the play is Sycorax, the "foul witch" and bad mother who penned Ariel in a cloven pine and gave birth to Caliban the freckled whelp. Marina and Perdita as doubles of their fathers grow up independently from them, their qualities and powers developing spontaneously and freely. They then function as mothers to their fathers by "delivering" them to new identities as fathers. They also serve as doubles of their mothers, uniting chastity with fertility and countering their mothers' oedipally tinged sexuality. Miranda, on the other hand, has never left her father. She is his creation, exclusively nurtured, tutored, and controlled by him on the island. Her sexuality, like that of the other daughter-doubles, is firmly allied with the divine order behind nature. But it is Prospero who defines and guards that sexuality, subsuming it into his larger project for the settling of old scores and the resumption of his role in Milan.

On a larger scale, Prospero's subjugation of sexuality in Miranda is figured in the antithesis between Ariel and Caliban. Spirit and flesh, air and earth, god and beast: these facets of human existence, it is implied, are decisively sundered in Prospero as in his underlings, whom he keeps separate by anxious, vigilant control. Ironically, neither character is actually as distinct from the other or as one-dimensional as Prospero thinks he is; each has potential that the magus is too busy with his task of defensive control to notice. Though Ariel is not human and cannot feel, he knows what sympathy and love are and moreover, values them as a human being would:

> Ariel.   The King,
> His brother, and yours, abide all three distracted,
> And the remainder mourning over them,
> Brimful of sorrow and dismay . . . .
> . . . . Your charm so strongly works 'em,
> That if you now beheld them, your affections
> Would become tender.
> Prosp.   Dost thou think so, spirit?
> Ariel. Mine would, sir, were I human.
> Prosp.   And mine shall.
> Hast thou, which art but air, a touch, a feeling
> Of their afflictions, and shall not myself,
> One of their kind, that relish all as sharply,
> Passion as they, be kindlier mov'd than thou art?
>   (Tmp. V.i.11–14, 16–24)

Prospero, who is human, has to be reminded that he has a heart by one who lacks it. The terms of endearment with which he plies Ariel and no one else are wasted on the spirit, who nonetheless has a touch of humanity. On the other hand, the savage and deformed slave on whose nature, Prospero claims, nurture will never stick, reveals a touching sensitivity to beauty and a capacity for wonder to which his master is oblivious. Caliban gives his heart, however foolishly, to Stephano and Trinculo, but at least he has affections. All that matters to Prospero, though, is that Caliban tried to rape his daughter; it was then that the magician abandoned the task of educating his creature and removed him from the cell to imprisonment in a rock (Tmp. I.ii.346–64). In the last scene, Prospero hardly gives Caliban's moral enlightenment its due, though he hints he'll pardon him and directs him back to the cell instead of the rock. Ariel finally gains his freedom, as Prospero gains his, in renouncing revenge, but Caliban is likely to remain confined on the island, as Prospero's sexuality remains confined in himself and in Miranda's chaste marriage.

Essentially, in coming from Milan to the island, Prospero went from childlike, self-absorbed dependency to paternal omnipotence, skipping the steps of maturation in between. Whether he surrendered the cares of state to Antonio or whether Antonio stole the state for himself (Prospero's self-contradictory account suggests both; see *Tmp.* I.ii.66–132), Antonio in effect served as his brother's parental provider before casting him out.[35] Then, assuming dominion over the island, Prospero became free to pursue his studies in a boundlessly nurturant environment, without significant rivalry. The island was his virgin space: he was the first man on it. Having previously withdrawn from all competition in the world of men, under these special conditions he was given a second chance to eradicate his father's preeminence and priority in time, and become his father's equal, through preeminence and priority on the island. As Harry Berger argues, the island is like a child's microsphere, where he makes a model of his painful experiences so as "to play at doing something that was in reality done to him," and thus "redeems his failures and strengthens his hopes."[36] This "playing" is a magical, wish-fulfillment form of delayed growing up for Prospero.

Specifically, he plays out rivalries which he never fully confronted before, using his brother as a stand-in for his father. He does so through a brilliant compromise between revenge and charity, which allows him to have his cake and eat it too. When Providence brings his treacherous brother and his brother's confederate Alonso to the island in a tempest, he re-creates for them his own near-fatal voyage "in a rotten carcass of a butt" years before. He subjects Alonso to the threat of usurpation and the seeming loss of his son, again versions of their actions against him. These trials would add up to a tidy revenge were they not sheer illusion, the product of Prospero's strenuous art, and were they not perpetrated for the sake of arousing "heart-sorrow and a clear life ensuing." They are and are not revenge. For Prospero to take revenge in reality would be to repeat what was done to him and become mired in the family past, in a cycle of successive revenges. But not to take revenge would be passivity and impotence. By recognizing his own anger in the realization that "the rarer action lies in virtue than in vengeance," and by stopping short of revenge, he breaks out of repetition, out of the revenge cycle, and out of his oedipal past. But he fails to re-create in any sexual relationship the life-giving love experience first known with the mother.[37]

Delineating the centrality of the rival sibling motif to the Shakespearean conception of masculinity, Joel Fineman argues that "branching pairs of siblings, real or virtual, male and female, rooted together in synonymous rivalry" are crucial to male identity. For since the male's first sense of self is implicated with the mother, in order to define himself he must separate decisively from her; he must establish a crucial difference. Fineman sees fratricidal rivalry as the adult rephrasing of this early, essential differentiation, and he regards it as essential to the next step in masculine identity formation, the oedipal conflict and its resolution.[38] Among Shakespearean rivals, Prospero neither fights his brother to the death, as Claudius does King Hamlet, or Hal Hotspur, nor reconciles with him as does Oliver with Orlando, or Proteus with Valentine. Rather, he effects the unique compromise I have described. But that compromise brings him no closer to acknowledging his sexuality or to uniting with the feminine, because he has still not fully worked through his oedipal past, or perhaps because he has sublimated it too well in his art.

Presumably, Prospero's years on the island were devoted to two ends: perfecting his art and perfecting Miranda. Her chastity, like Marina's and Perdita's, functions as a denial of her father's past desires. By giving her to Ferdinand, the son of his brother's partner in crime, and ensuring legitimate heirs to his regained dukedom, he symbolically resolves his old rivalries and validates his new identity as duke. The summit of Pericles' and Leontes' lives is reunion with their daughters and then with their wives: recovery of what they denied and lost before. In contrast, the triple crown of Prospero's life is to give up revenge, then to give his daughter away, and finally to give up his art.

A final question suggests itself. All through the play, Shakespeare stresses in Prospero a superb combination of power and control. There are signs of strain in his tetchiness with Ariel, his disgust with Caliban, his obsession with Miranda's virtue, his hatred of Antonio. But on the whole, he commands his art in the service of giving vent to but transcending his violent feelings. Why must he renounce his art? Why can't he keep it and hold his dukedom too, since it has served his worldly and his personal aims so well? He gives it up because he doesn't need it any more, because with its aid he has accomplished the project of emerging from the family and becoming his own man, the Duke of Milan. The cost of this achievement, however, is sexual and social isolation.

A romance is a fiction of wish fulfillment. The plays I have discussed are all romances by virtue of their sources, or their nature as dramas, or both. They articulate the ambivalent wish to get free of the family and find a self outside it, while at the same time to stay within it, nurtured by its loves. All these plays seek a compromise between the two conflicting urges, and the compromise turns on the finding of a mate. From the male protagonist's point of view, this means that it turns on his ability to accept woman and sustain intimacy with her. She is at once the seal of his male identity and the obstacle to it; he fears her and he needs her. Without her, he can neither leave his family of origin and find himself, nor father his own family and play his part in the patriarchal world. At the cost of great suffering, Leontes wins the fullest acceptance of woman, and *The Winter's Tale* presents the richest vision of male identity defined within the family. Leontes is both, and equally, husband and father. Significantly, though, the family romance concludes with *The Tempest*, in which woman is most strongly repressed. Prospero's identity is based entirely on his role as father, and his family is never united or complete. The Shakespearean family romance, then, remains closer to the imperfect realities we live with than to the wishes we cherish.

Notes

1. Meredith Skura, "Interpreting Posthumus' Dream from Above and Below: Families, Psychoanalysts, and Literary Critics" (Chapter 11 in this book).

2. See Frank Kermode's Introduction to the new Arden edition of *The Tempest* (London: Methuen, 1954) for a useful discussion of this motif in relation to its literary and historical sources and its intellectual background.

3. Several Shakespearean critics have written perceptively on the tempest motif. First and notable is G. Wilson Knight, *Myth and Miracle* (London: Chatto and Windus, 1929) and *The Shakespearian Tempest* (London: Chatto and Windus, 1932), who finds the storm "percurrent in Shakespeare as a symbol of tragedy" and sees the opposition of storm and music as central to the canon. Others are Northrop Frye, *A Natural Perspective: The Development of Shakespearean Comedy and Romance* (New York: Columbia Univ. Press, 1965) and Douglas Peterson, *Time, Tide, and Tempest: A Study of Shakespeare's Romances* (San Marino, Calif.: Huntington Library, 1973). So far as I know, no one has pursued the psychological interpretation of the tempest that I will present here.

4. For Erikson's concept of identity, see his *Identity: Youth and Crisis* (New York: W. W. Norton, 1964), 22-23, 50, 159-60 and passim; for the eight stages of psychosexual development, see his *Childhood and Society*, 2nd ed. (New York: W. W. Norton, 1974), 247-75. I will be concerned here with three of the four stages succeeding latency: adolescence, characterized by a conflict between identity and role confusion; youth, by a conflict between intimacy and isolation; and maturity, by a conflict between generativity and stagnation.

5. Erikson, *Identity: Youth and Crisis*, p. 16.

6. Peter Blos, *On Adolescence: A Psychoanalytic Interpretation* (New York: Free Press, 1962), 100, but see 87-128 and passim.

7. Symbiotic merger and the separation-individuation process are described and analyzed in Margaret S. Mahler, Fred Pine, and Anni Bergman, *The Psychological Birth of the Human Infant: Symbiosis and Individuation* (New York: Basic Books, 1975).

8. Blos, pp. 90-91.

9. For a brief description of these stages, see Erikson, *Childhood and Society*, pp. 261–66; for a more extensive discussion, see Erikson, *Identity: Youth and Crisis*, pp. 142–207.

10. C. L. Barber, "'Thou that beget'st him that did thee beget': Transformation in *Pericles* and *The Winter's Tale*," *Shakespeare Survey*, 22 (1969), 59–67.

11. I am greatly indebted to John T. Irwin, *Doubling and Incest/Repetition and Revenge: A Speculative Reading of Faulkner* (Baltimore: Johns Hopkins Univ. Press, 1975), for the ideas of the sibling as a double, of incest and revenge as forms of repetition, and the relation of doubling, incest, and revenge to the sequence of generations within the family.

12. Otto Rank, *The Double: A Psychoanalytic Study*, ed. and trans. Harry Tucker, Jr. (Chapel Hill, N.C.: Univ. of North Carolina Press, 1971), first published in 1914, expanded 1925. See also Sigmund Freud, "The 'Uncanny'" in *The Standard Edition of the Complete Psychological Works of Sigmund Freud*, ed. and trans. James Strachey et al., 24 vols. (London: Hogarth Press, 1953–74), 17, pp. 217–52.

13. Marjorie Garber, "Coming of Age in Shakespeare," *The Yale Review*, 66 (1977), 517–33. Her understanding of sexual maturation in Shakespeare parallels mine at several salient points.

14. See D. W. Winnicott's description of this process in *Playing and Reality* (New York: Basic Books, 1971), pp. 111–18. Paula Elkisch, "The Psychological Significance of the Mirror," *Journal of the American Psychoanalytic Association*, 5 (1965), 235–44, relates the need to see oneself in a mirror to narcissistic crises of identity; one who fears ego loss turns to the mirror for protection against it, trying to retrieve in the mirrored image his self, his boundaries. Morris W. Brody, "The Symbolic Significance of Twins in Dreams," *Psychoanalytic Quarterly*, 21 (1952), 172–80, claims that twins in dream and folklore, whether of the same or opposite sexes, represent the dreamer and his or her mother in the fusion of the womb or of nursing; they symbolize the ambivalent wish to maintain union with the mother but at the same time not to be swallowed up in her, maintaining separation through duplication of the self.

15. See R. A. Foakes, new Arden edition of *The Comedy of Errors* (London: Methuen, 1962), p. 2.

16. This and subsequent quotations from the plays discussed here are taken from the new Arden edition (London: Methuen): *The Comedy of Errors*, ed. R. A. Foakes, 1962; *Twelfth Night*, ed. J. M. Lothian and T. W. Craik, 1975; *Pericles*, ed. F. D. Hoeniger, 1963; *The Winter's Tale*, ed. J.H.P. Pafford, 1963; *The Tempest*, ed. Frank Kermode, 1954.

17. Erikson, *Identity: Youth and Crisis*, 178.

18. Antipholus E.'s hoped-for redemption from arrest by money in the form of angels parodies the liberation of Peter from prison in *Acts* 12:1–11, and it adds a spiritual dimension to the subsequent liberation of Antipholus from the errors of mistaken identity and domestic dissension plaguing him.

19. John Hollander, "*Twelfth Night* and the Morality of Indulgence," *Sewanee Review*, 67 (1959), 222–35.

20. See L. G. Salingar, "The Design of *Twelfth Night*," *Shakespeare Quarterly*, 9 (1958), 118–35, and Joseph H. Summers, "The Masks of *Twelfth Night*," in *Shakespeare: Modern Essays in Criticism*, ed. Leonard F. Dean (New York: Oxford Univ. Press, 1961), 128–37.

21. Blos explains that in adolescence the withdrawal of love from the parents, or

from their object representations in the ego, deflects love onto the self; the adolescent thus enters into the "transitory narcissistic stage" described in n. 6, which precedes attachment to a heterosexual object. In the boy, this narcissism may lead to a same-sex object choice based on an ego ideal. Blos cites Tonio Kröger's crush on Hans Hansen as an example; Mann says that Tonio "loved him in the first place because he was handsome; but in the next because he was in every respect his own opposite and foil" (quoted in Blos, p. 80). Helene Deutsch describes "a strongly bisexual tendency" in girls in early adolescence, which leads them to stress masculine traits, to suffer the same kind of homosexual crushes as boys do, or to have bisexual fantasies about a brother (often a twin) endowed with all the qualities the girl herself would like to have, or blamed for the impulses she represses and rejects. See *The Psychology of Women: A Psychoanalytic Interpretation* (New York: Grune and Stratton, 1944; rpt. New York: Bantam Books, 1967), 1, pp. 88-89).

22. The editors of the new Arden edition of *Twelfth Night*, J. M. Lothian and T. W. Craik, comment that "Nature followed its inborn tendency, to mate female with male and so undo the effects of Viola's misleading disguise."

23. C. L. Barber, *Shakespeare's Festive Comedy* (Princeton, N.J.: Princeton Univ. Press, 1959), makes this suggestion.

24. Hollander, p. 236; Leslie Hotson, *The First Night of Twelfth Night* (New York: Macmillan, 1954), 173.

25. Furness and Halliwell in the *Variorum* edition, and Craik and Lothian in the new Arden edition, cite Sir Thomas Overbury's *Characters* for "beds" as denoting old age.

26. Phyllis Gorfain, "Riddles and Tragic Structure in Shakespeare," *Mississippi Folklore Register, Special Issue: Shakespeare and Folklore,* ed. Philip C. Kolin, 10 (1976), 187-209.

27. Erich Neumann, *The Great Mother: An Analysis of the Archetype* (Princeton, N.J.: Princeton Univ. Press, 1972), 30.

28. Phyllis Gorfain, "Puzzle and Artifice: The Riddle as Metapoetry in *Pericles,*" *Shakespeare Survey*, 29 (1976), 11-20.

29. Barber, "'Thou that beget'st him,'" 65.

30. J.I.M. Stewart, *Character and Motive in Shakespeare* (London: Longmans, Green, 1949), p. 34. See also Sigmund Freud, "Some Neurotic Mechanisms in Jealousy, Paranoia, and Homosexuality," *Standard Edition*, 18, pp. 221-33.

31. See Sigmund Freud, "Leonardo da Vinci and a Memory of His Childhood," *Standard Edition*, 11; "On Narcissism: An Introduction," *Standard Edition*, 14; and Murray M. Schwartz, "Leontes' Jealousy in *The Winter's Tale,*" *American Imago*, 30, (1973), 250-73, and "*The Winter's Tale*: Loss and Transformation," *American Imago*, 32, (1975), 145-99. Arguing that Leontes is motivated by a "fear of separation from idealized others" and that he attempts "to reunite himself with a fantasized ideal maternal figure," Schwartz analyzes the paranoia of the hero's jealousy as a radical denial of separation. He sees the second half of the play as a successful reconstitution of continuity and union rooted ontogenetically in the mother-son symbiosis. His interpretation of the play's psychology is rigorous, comprehensive, and brilliant; I am greatly indebted to it.

32. Inga-Stina Ewbank, "The Triumph of Time in *The Winter's Tale,*" in *Shakespeare's Later Comedies*, ed. D. J. Gordon (Harmondsworth, England: Penguin, 1971).

33. Schwartz, "Loss and Transformation," p. 178.

34. Carol Thomas Neely, in "Women and Issue in *The Winter's Tale*," a paper delivered at the Central Renaissance Conference in April 1975, firmly distinguishes Shakespeare's treatment of sexuality in *The Winter's Tale* from that in the other romances, which "hover uneasily between the extreme idealization of sex and its extreme degradation," while in *The Winter's Tale*, "fully developed women characters play central roles" to free men from distorted sexual attitudes. I came upon her paper after writing this essay to discover that its view coheres with my own at many points.

35. Karl M. Abenheimer, "Shakespeare's *Tempest*: A Psychological Analysis," *Psychoanalytic Review*, 33 (1946), 399–415, suggests this interpretation.

36. Harry Berger, Jr., "Miraculous Harp: A Reading of Shakespeare's *Tempest*," *Shakespeare Studies*, 5 (1970), 253–83, makes this point.

37. Hans W. Loewald, *Psychoanalysis and the History of the Individual* (New Haven, Conn.: Yale Univ. Press, 1978), remarks that "ego development does not proceed in a straight line, does not consist in a movement further and further away from id. . . . One might come close to human time by saying that it consists in an interpretation and reciprocal relatedness of past, present, and future. . . . an ascending spiral in which the same basic themes are re-experienced and enacted on different levels of mentation and action" (p. 23).

38. Joel Fineman, "Fratricide and Cuckoldry: Shakespeare's Doubles" (Chapter 5 in this book).

13 ❀ Shakespeare's Nothing

David Willbern

> *Hamlet.* Do you see nothing there?
> *Gertrude.* Nothing at all; yet all that is I see.
> *Hamlet.* Nor did you nothing hear?
> *Gertrude.* No, nothing but ourselves.
>
> (III.iv.131–33)

"The quality of nothing," according to Gloucester, "hath not such need to hide itself. Let's see," he commands Edmund, who is displaying his forged letter by obviously concealing it. "Come, if it be nothing, I shall not need spectacles" (*King Lear*, I.ii.32–35).[1] Gloucester looks at the letter, but does not see that it is nothing, a hoax. Only when he is blind, cruelly enlightened, does he finally see nothing. Paradoxically, for us to see Shakespeare's Nothing we do need spectacles, or rather a spectacle: the play of nothing in Shakespeare's theater. His tragedies enact somber scenes in such a spectacle. They are Renaissance No-drama.

To see Shakespeare's Nothing we must open our eyes. A familiar geometrical figure offers an opening glimpse of its form. We can start with the circle: sign of nothing and all, cosmos and zero. Then we can divide it into two equal parts (zero divided is still zero), marking the division not with a line but with a curve (*curve* derives from *circle*):

not ◗ but ◐ —to suggest mutuality and not bifurcation of the halves. "Two distincts, division none." We can even give each "half-zero" a mathematical sign: positive and negative, or negative and positive. They are reciprocal yet equal.

This fanciful mathematics and geometry inscribe a structure for my essay—a circle that is also a point of departure. Since our usual order puts absence before presence, zero before one, I'll begin with the negative sign of nothing: the notion of absence, negation, denial, or lack. The most dramatic appearance of this sign in Shakespeare occurs in Cordelia's fateful silence and voiced "Nothing": her refusal to give Lear what he asks for; to pretend, as her father and sisters do, that words are like things, given and received—a reified rhetoric that wins property. Cordelia's answer doesn't add up. It is not proportional to the third part of the kingdom Lear has reserved to reward the part she was to play. It does not fit the ratio of his irrationality.[2]

Yet Cordelia's answer signifies more than these arithmetical or geometrical metaphors can directly suggest. Shakespeare's overdetermined language typically includes bawdy meanings, and there is a specific, though latent, bodily sense of Cordelia's "nothing"—as *no thing*—the sense which Hamlet intends in his notorious joking with Ophelia just before the play-within-the-play (his byplay is verbal foreplay):

> Lady, shall I lie in your lap?
> No, my lord.
> I mean, my head upon your lap?
> Ay, my lord.
> Do you think I meant country matters?
> I think nothing, my lord.
> That's a fair thought to lie between maids' legs.
> What is, my lord?
> Nothing.

(III.ii.112-21)[3]

This genital sense of "thing" functions in *Lear* most evidently in the Fool's traditional phallic jokes ("She that's a maid now, and laughs at my departure,/Shall not be a maid long, unless things be cut shorter" [I.v.51-52].)[4] It relates to ubiquitous anxieties in the play concerning bodily injury or loss, such as Gloucester's eyes, Lear's "cut off" train of soldiers, naked unaccommodated man as a "poor, bare, fork'd animal," Lear himself as nothing ("an O without a figure"). Moreover, Cordelia's defense of her spoken "Nothing" alludes to the latent notion of no thing as some thing missing. "I yet beseech your Majesty," she says to the father who has just banished her,

> If for I want that glib and oily art
> To speak and purpose not, since what I well intend,
> I'll do't before I speak—that you make known
> It is no vicious blot, murther, or foulness,
> No unchaste action, or dishonored step,
> That hath depriv'd me of your grace and favor,
> But even for want of that for which I am richer—
> A still-soliciting eye, and such a tongue
> That I am glad I have not, though not to have it
> Hath lost me in your liking.

(I.i.223-33)

One deprivation (her banishment) follows others (her "Nothing," her lack of eye and tongue). Shakespeare's imagery is significantly organic and sexually suggestive as well. Not having, or having nothing, is Cordelia's loss, and ultimately Lear's. Through its imagery of licentiousness denied and organs deprived, the language of Cordelia's defense alludes to the hidden genital significance of her "Nothing." Against this bodily background, France's previous words to Lear also disclose hidden senses. "This is most strange," he notes, that Cordelia

> should in this trice of time
> Commit a thing so monstrous, to dismantle
> So many folds of favor. Sure her offense
> Must be of such unnatural degree
> That monsters it. . . .

(I.i.213-20)

Shakespeare's imagery evokes a vision of Cordelia stripped ("dismantled") of her father's love ("folds of favor"),[5] and a hint of some secret sin ("a thing so monstrous . . . , of such unnatural degree"), which Cordelia then denies ("It is no vicious blot . . ."). Hidden in the folds of Shakespeare's imagery is a vision of a woman disrobed and the sight of something monstrous and unnatural: an early glimpse, through metaphor, of the later image of woman and female genitals that incites Lear's rage and terror in ensuing acts. "Thorough tatter'd clothes small [great] [6] vices do appear;/Robes and furr'd gowns hide all," he exclaims in Act IV (IV.vi.164-65), but nothing is hidden to his maddened sight, which uncovers *no thing*:

> Down from the waist they are Centaurs,
> Though women all above;
> But to the girdle do the gods inherit,
> Beneath is all the fiends': there's hell, there's darkness,
> There is the sulphurous pit, burning, scalding,
> Stench, consumption. Fie, fie, fie! pah, pah!

(IV.vi.124-29)

Lear's response to this malignant and demonic image of no-thingness is first rage, then insanity, and then a kind of infancy (*infans*, speechless). Confronted with his own grotesque fantasies of destructive female "organs of increase," facing the face he cannot banish from his unsweetened imagination ("whose face between her forks presages snow"—presages "no" [IV.vi.119]), he lapses into inarticulation, trying, as I hear him, literally to spit out what disgusts him: "*F*ie, *f*ie, *f*ie! *p*ah, *p*ah!" Another moment of nonverbal *infans*-y occurs in the next scene (IV.vii), when Lear, clothed and carried by others, is brought silent to his reunion with Cordelia. A similar event is enacted at their final meeting, in Lear's last vision of Cordelia's face and lips, which leads him back (a regression) into fantasy and final delusion: seeing what is not there, as he exclaims, "Look on her! Look her lips,/Look there, look there!"; and hearing what is not there, as he reaches through the ultimate silence for her voice, "ever soft,/Gentle, and low, an excellent thing in woman" (V.iii.273-74).

From her voiced "Nothing" to her mute voice as "an excellent thing," Cordelia's discourse traces a circle of absent presence. She is the queen of silence, reciprocating Lear's tragic stature as the king—"every inch"—of nothing (Hamlet: "The King is a thing ... of nothing" [IV.ii.27-30]). *Rex* becomes *res* becomes *rien*. Or in the uncanny wisdom of Lear's Fool, "uncle" is "nuncle" ("none"-cle): "Can you make no use of nothing, nuncle?" (I.iv.130). Cordelia's nothing, at beginning and end, circumscribes or pinpoints the elemental absence at the center of Lear's world. She is, to use Kent's phrase, "the true blank of thine [Lear's] eye" (I.i.159). Her silence and absence describe the center of the target of his sight, and the "blank" (target center) is blank (vacant, nothing). Lear's banishment of Cordelia shuts out a symbolic vision he cannot bear to see. "We/Have no such daughter," he says to France, "nor shall ever see/That face of hers again" (I.i.262-64). Its features remind him of nothing (the "face between her forks"). Eventually he will meet its most traumatic mask, represented by Gloucester's bloody eyeless face, into whose vacancy he stares as he delivers his "Down from the waist" diatribe.

Yet this design of denial and negation traces only half of our original circle. Its reciprocal, the positive half, represents fullness rather than emptiness, presence rather than absence, whole rather than hole. It rests on or borders its negative twin in a relationship of primary creativity. Nothing, in other words, is the very ground of being, just as silence is the ground of speech. Speech happens in silence, silence happens in speech (without intervals of silence, speech is gibberish). Silence, too, can speak: it is, as we say, pregnant. And when silences are broken, they are also filled. They are spaces or times for talk, occasions for creation. [7]

I want now to consider the potential positive generativity of Shakespeare's Nothing—although what is generated is not always benign. For instance, in *Romeo and Juliet*, after that fairy fantasy turned nightmare of the "Queen Mab" speech, Romeo interrupts Mercutio's barely controlled words by insisting, "Peace, peace, Mercutio, peace!/Thou talk'st of nothing." Mercutio replies:

> True, I talk of dreams,
> Which are the children of an idle brain,
> Begot of nothing but vain fantasy. . . .

> (I.iv.95-98)

Nothing, begot of itself. As Lear warns Cordelia, "nothing will come of nothing." Yet even Lear's words imply a generativity of nothing: his verb is future imperative. This ability of nothing to generate other versions of itself attains its most potent moment in *The Winter's Tale*, as the product of Leontes' barely coherent jealous obsessions:

> Affection! thy intention stabs the centre.
> Thou dost make possible things not so held,
> Communicat'st with dreams (how can this be?),
> With what's unreal thou co-active art,
> And fellow'st nothing. Then 'tis very credent
> Thou mayst co-join with something, and thou dost
> (And that beyond commission), and I find it
> (And that to the infection of my brains
> And hard'ning of my brows).
>
> (I.ii.138–46)

Moments later, after watching Hermione and Polixenes converse, he demands of Camillo, "Is whispering nothing?/Is leaning cheek to cheek? is meeting noses?"

> . . . Is this nothing?
> Why then all the world and all that's in't is nothing,
> The covering sky is nothing, Bohemia nothing,
> My wife is nothing, nor nothing have these nothings,
> If this be nothing.
>
> (I.ii.284–96)

"Nothing" gets obsessively repeated into thing-ness: an abstraction made concrete, which subsumes everything else. It becomes a self-reflexive, self-generating agent of its own creation, produced out of the mysterious, violent, sexual "co-action," or coitus, of "dreams," the "unreal," "something," and "nothing."[8] Like Othello's "cause," which grounds itself on a nonreferential pronoun, "it," Leontes' obsessions and fantasies have a literal and reified "nothing" at their origin. Still, this nothing accompanies something, or it hints of "possible things." These hints reside in covert connotations of the "innocent" language of the play, just as Leontes perceives hidden meanings in the "innocent" behavior of his wife and friend. For instance, when Polixenes enters the world of *The Winter's Tale*, he immediately emphasizes "nine changes of the wat'ry star" (the human gestation period), refers to "burthens" and to being "fill'd up," and concludes:

> And therefore, like a cipher
> (Yet standing in rich place), I multiply
> With one "we thank you" many thousands moe
> That go before it.
>
> (I.ii.1–9)

Shakespeare's language is literally pregnant with connotation. The verb "multiply" carries sexual as well as arithmetical sense, and the simile of "standing in rich place" symbolically imitates Leontes' own carnal fantasies of Polixenes' secret relationship with Hermione. In a real sense, the origins of Leontes' jealousy lie in the vocabulary of the scene. Leontes' "nothings" complement the potent nothing of Polixenes' "cipher": they both multiply meanings.

Leontes has created something out of nothing; or, he has deciphered a hidden meaning in Polixenes' simile of the cipher. His creation, like Othello's green-eyed monster, is a destructive progeny, yet the fact of its existence represents a version, however malignant, of the generativity that linguistic or dramatic production *ex nihilo* involves.[9] "Nothing" signifies the opportunity, indeed the imperative, to create "something"— some meaning or sense: a name for absence. This play of occasion and necessity characterizes various aspects of Shakespeare's art. While Leontes' creation is dangerous and potentially tragic, others seem initially heroic, like Coriolanus' self-nomination: "He was a kind of nothing," says Cominius: "titleless,/Till he had forg'd himself a name" (V.i.13–14). (Of course, Coriolanus' "forg'd" name is also a forgery, since it denies his family origin.) This naming of nothing manifests itself in happier terms in *A Midsummer Night's Dream*, in the assertions of Duke Theseus. His characterizations (but not use) of imagination and poetic creativity make him a benevolent version of Leontes:

> And as imagination bodies forth
> The form of things unknown, the poet's pen
> Turns them to shapes, and gives to aery nothing
> A local habitation and a name.

(V.i.14–17)

(Again there are metaphors of physical procreation: birth and baptism.)

The idea of naming nothing is coincidentally built into the very word, through its probable pronunciation in Shakespeare's time. That is, "nothing" would have sounded like "noting" (hard "t"). So that *noting* (knowing, naming, or designating) coexists with and represents the awareness of *nothing*.[10] Moreover, the sound of "noting" includes the aural aspect of the shape of nothing. That is, Shakespeare's Nothing looks like "O" (zero) and sounds like "O" (oh), the basic ejaculation that predicts speech, the infant's Word. Its functions range from trivial to extreme, from the common, "Oh, I see," to Albany's "O, see, see!," or to Lear's final howling "O" (V.iii.258, 305). It is an infinitely mean-ingful phoneme, in which are rooted our most basic words about speech. The Latin *os* (mouth) and *orare* (to speak) are sources for many of our words about speech and the mouth ("orator," "orality").

"Orifice" means literally to make a mouth. To say "O" we make the shape with our own mouths. "O"—the sign of nothing, the sound of nothing—underlies speech itself. Its design underlies writing as well. "The circle is found at the origin of almost all the alphabets or ideograms."[11] *Ab ovo*, zero.

Psychoanalytic theories of the origins and acquisition of language, of perception, of reality testing, of the capacity to symbolize or to interact creatively with an environment, all start from the primary fact of absence, separation, loss. The loss of an immediate, felt relationship to an object or person stimulates a need to restore the relationship: to bring things symbolically to mind when they are not really present, or to make them present through some communicative act (like a cry). Awareness of absence thus results in imagined or reenacted presence: a re-collection or re-membering of what was lost.[12] Contemporary French psychoanalysis emphasizes this primary myth of loss in specifically linguistic terms. Describing Lacan's "diacritical theory of meaning," whereby words rest finally not on anything real (that is, not on any thing) but only on the circularity of mutual interdefinition, Anthony Wilden explains that "it is this implied circularity and autonomy of language that leads Lacan into postulating a sort of fault in the system, a hole, a fundamental lack into which, one might say, meaning is *poured*." This is Lacan's "primordial *manque*." It corresponds to Derrida's idea that "the signature is a *wound*—and there is none other at the origin of the work of art." These metaphors of an original lack, hole, defect, or wound signify that anatomical manifestation of presence and absence which demonstrates the fact of genital difference (*la différence* in the Derridean "*différance*"). The sexual, bodily senses of Shakespeare's Nothing and O thus connect to various myths of symbolic origins.[13]

Psychoanalytic theorists frequently refer, in their discussions of the development of symbolic representation, to what is becoming a kind of Freudian exemplum: the little game (which Freud's grandson invented at age one-and-a-half) of discarding and then retrieving a wooden reel with string attached: the so-called "*Fort! Da!*" game.[14] Freud interpreted the child's activity as a representation of his mother's disappearance and reappearance, events originally only suffered but now under the child's symbolic control. When he threw the reel away, or dropped it beneath his crib, it was *fort* (gone); when he pulled it back to his hands, it was *da* (there). Actually, the little boy seems not to have uttered these words. Instead, he made the sounds "o" and "ah," which Freud and the boy's mother heard as childish efforts at the adult terms *fort* and *da*. This is a good, reasonable interpretation (by two good analysts), yet it distances us from the verbal (or preverbal) reality of the event. What the child actually did, according to Freud, was to "give vent to a loud, long-drawn-out 'o-o-o-o.'" Our first language, as Lear reminds us, is a cry: "We came crying hither . . . " (IV.vi.178–80).

This primal dialectic between absence and presence, loss and re-creation, sounds its opening note in a pun I hear (thanks to Peter Brook's recent film) at the very beginning of *King Lear*. Brook's Bergmanesque, black-and-white, Scandanavian production opens in stark, wintry silence, as the camera slowly pans past Lear's waiting subjects and into the throne room. It gradually focuses on a slowly closing door at one end of the room. When the door swings shut, the heavy repercussion of its closing is the initial sound in the film. Paul Scofield, as Lear, then speaks a single word: "Know." He waits several seconds before continuing the line: "that we have divided in three . . ." (I.i.37). The cinematic sequence sounds like this: *slam* / "Know" / *silence*. For a moment, Lear's word "Know" is separate from the rest of his sentence. What I hear first, before the ensuing words resolve the ambiguity, is the single word, "No," accented by a closing door. In that brief moment, "No" and "Know" coalesce in the same audible syllable, harmonizing the dialectical theme of knowledge and negation which *King Lear* proceeds tragically to play out, and which Shakespeare's Nothing subsumes as part of its whole.

Of course, not all hearers and few productions of *King Lear* will automatically construe this "Know" / "No" pun. Yet that brief auditory event can be considered paradigmatic of an audience's responses, moment by moment, to a play. That is, knowing or noting fills up the space of nothing in at least three ways: through the genius of the poet (Theseus' argument), through the events of the production and the theatrical locus within which it happens, and ultimately through the imaginations of the audience that sees and hears (and reads) the play. A better model of such an audience, filling silence and nothing with meanings (notings), is available in *Hamlet*, in the Gentleman's report of Ophelia's mad discourse. "Her speech," he says, "is nothing":

> Yet the unshaped use of it doth move
> The hearers to collection; they yawn [aim]¹⁵ at it,
> And botch the words up fit to their own thoughts,
> Which as her winks and nods and gestures yield them,
> Indeed would make one think there might be thought,
> Though nothing sure, yet much unhappily.
>
> (IV.v.7–13)

The ways in which we give meaning to nothing, botching up words to fit our own thoughts, are essential processes of seeing, hearing, or reading plays. We also give airy nothing a habitation and a name; we make "nothing sure" by interpreting it, just as Freud interpreted the sounds and senses of his grandson's game. The passage from *Hamlet* provides its own demonstration of its point. For instance, does "which," or "them," in line eleven ("Which as her winks and nods and gestures yield them") refer to *her* words or *their* (the hearers') thoughts? Syntax and sense are obscure here. The best and fullest reading, I would claim, rejects exclusivity and accepts all the possible senses, in an effort to appreciate how speaker and hearer get con-fused in the act of communicating and interpreting symbolic discourse.

To interpret Shakespeare's Nothing is a much larger task. One way to begin is to collect several senses of "O" as sign and sound and symbol—various significations that circumscribe and circulate through Shakespeare's Nothing, especially in *King Lear*. These various meanings coexist and interpenetrate throughout Shakespeare's text; their confusions are elaborate. In an effort to sustain the complexity while undoing the confusion, I have isolated separate sets of meanings and briefly characterized them. The ensuing fragmentation in my own text is a result of the necessarily artificial disintegration of Shakespeare's inimitable linguistic integrity.

Nothing / Zero / Cipher

These mathematical terms include various synonyms of "nothing," such as "nil," "null," "none," "naught" ("nought"), and "aught" ("ought"). "Zero" and "cipher" share the same Arabic root: *sifr*, meaning "empty." The two meanings of "cipher" convey the primary dialectic of presence and absence. As a synonym for zero it means "empty," "nothing"; it also means "secret letter" or "code" (it signifies the absence of a specific and salient presence). Nothing by itself, in context its meanings are multiple, like Polixenes' "cipher . . . standing in rich place."

Void / Vacancy / Absence / Lack

These terms occupy the primary ground of nothing, which can be perceived as a threat ("negative nothing") or as a potential for re-creation ("positive nothing")—from Lear to Lacan. In psychoanalytic terms, it represents an occasion for castration anxiety or primitive fears of dissolution, and/or the potential reconnections of symbolic relationships.

Hole / Whole

A primary pun, catching in a single sound the dialectic of nothing and all. Shakespeare's language is insistently homophonic.

Circle / Cycle / Orb / Ring / Wheel

These words describe both objects and motions. Circles and circlings are crucial throughout *King Lear*, especially. For instance, "the orbs / From whom we do exist and cease to be" (I.i.111-12) symbolize a whole matrix of elements, such as stars, planets, orbits, celestial (Ptolemaic) spheres—as well as womb, testicles, semen, eggs, or eyes. Other circles include Lear's crown, the sun (nothing, like the sun), and the Wheel of Fortune that becomes the wheel of fire (IV.vii.46) as it and the play come full circle.

Womb / Genitals / Mouth / Eyes / Egg

These are the organic embodiments of the dialectic. In *Lear*, they underlie Cordelia's spoken "Nothing" and her final silence ("Look there! . . . her lips"), and Gloucester's "bleeding rings, / Their precious stones new lost" (V.iii.190-91)—an image that reemphasizes the symbolic connection between eyes and genitals. A reciprocal image— the symbolic castrating threat—underlies Edgar's words to Edmund about their father: "The dark and vicious place where thee he got / Cost him his eyes" (V.iii.173-74). Less darkly, the womb is traditionally the circle incarnate: see religious representations of the Virgin's womb or the medieval *topos* of the enclosed circular garden.[16] Our word "egg" is *ovum* in Latin, *ōion* in Greek. Zeros are commonly known as "goose eggs," suggesting their imagined procreative powers.

Tomb / Pit / Hell

The tomb is the womb's reciprocal, as *Romeo and Juliet* and hundreds of medieval and Renaissance poems proclaim. Shakespeare often connects the theological hell with the genital one, as places where men are consumed by fire (venereal burning): see Sonnet 144. In *Titus Andronicus* the symbolic identity of the "detested, dark, blood-drinking pit" (II.iii.224), destructive female genitals, and the devouring maternal mouth (Tamora) is explicit.[17] Lear's tirade against women repeats these connections. Recall that Shakespeare's stage had a trapdoor hellmouth at its center. (Dante's Inferno is built of descending concentric circles, an abyss that leads to Satan's mouth.)

God / Heavenly Spheres

"God is a circle (or a sphere) whose center is everywhere and whose circumference is nowhere."[18] An inversion of the geometry of Hell, Dante's Mount Purgatory consists of ascending concentric circles, which lead to Beatrice's smile and the gates of Paradise. Paradise itself is a perfect Ptolemaic cosmos of concentric spheres.

Necromantic Circle

This is the magic circle that summons up spirits and protects the summoner from them. It represents a parody, or blasphemy, of God's creative power and is one of the basic geometric and symbolic figures that structures the theatrical stage itself. Speech (dialogue) gives life to (inspires) spirits (actors). Prospero is magician, stage director, actor, and audience.

Speech / Glottis / Globe / Theater

The sound of O and its shape coalesce in these two primary potencies—of the spoken word and dramatic representation on a stage: Shakespeare's "wooden O," his global theater.

Here is much ado about nothing—indeed, almost too much. As Laertes remarks of his sister's mad, bawdy songs, "This nothing's more than matter" (IV.v.174). Like the widening circles that emanate from a single disturbance in the surface of a pond, or like some protean Joycean process of "the abnihilisation of the etym," my divisions of O multiply into an almost "infinite deal of nothing."[19] I researched O and discovered that research itself is circular. The universe of knowledge is not linear but curved.[20] It all becomes an unending *histoire d'O*, of which I can trace only a part. Where I have carefully to sort out various meanings of "nothing" and "O," Shakespeare's incredibly inclusive language reintegrates this variety into a unified word or metaphor. For instance, as Romeo lies prostrate in Friar Laurence's cell, the Nurse urges him to "stand up, stand up, stand, and you be a man. / For Juliet's sake, for her sake, rise and stand;/Why should you fall into so deep an O?" (III.iii.88-90). Shakespeare plays here with several senses of O as sound and shape and symbol—the naughty meanings. Romeo's "O" is his hyperbolic moaning and groaning; the Nurse's meanings include that female (genital) "O" for which rising and falling defines virility, and that grave "O" into which Romeo ultimately will fall (Act V is a set of variations on the theme of womb and tomb). Mercutio earlier teases Romeo in similar bawdy terms. "This cannot anger him," he says:

> 'twould anger him
> To raise a spirit in his mistress' circle,
> Of some strange nature, letting it there stand
> Till she had laid it and conjur'd it down.
>
> (II.i.23-26)

Mercutio's bawdiness, like the Nurse's, plays with sexual senses of "stand" and further imagines copulation as conjuration. Exactly this latter image, of conjuring up and raising spirits within a female circle, is elaborated in Burgundy's remarks to Henry in *Henry V*. When Henry laments that he "cannot so conjure up the spirit of love" in Katherine, so "that he will appear in his true likeness," Burgundy replies:

> If you would conjure in her, you must make a circle;
> if conjure up Love in her in his true likeness, he must
> appear naked and blind. Can you blame her then, being a maid
> yet ros'd over with the virgin crimson of modesty, if she deny
> the appearance of a naked blind boy in her naked seeing self?
> It were, my lord, a hard condition for a maid to consign to.
>
> (V.ii.288-99)

The genital meanings are straightforward ("naked seeing self" combines eye and vagina, through their physical similarities).[21]

With this naughtiness in mind, and an ear to further bawdy punning, we can now attend to Shakespeare's famous Prologue to *Henry V*, often considered his most glorious evocation of the magical relationship between actor, stage, and audience. It begins with an "O":

> O for a muse of fire, that would ascend
> The brightest heaven of invention!
> A kingdom for a stage, princes to act,
> And monarchs to behold the swelling scene!
> . . . . But pardon, gentles all,
> The flat unraised spirits that hath dar'd
> On this unworthy scaffold to bring forth
> So great an object. Can this cockpit hold
> The vasty fields of France? O. may we cram
> Within this wooden O the very casques
> That did affright the air at Agincourt?
> O, pardon! since a crooked figure may

Attest in little place a million,
And let us, ciphers to this great accompt,
On your imaginary forces work.
Suppose within the girdle of these walls
Are now confin'd two mighty monarchies,
Whose high, upreared, and abutting fronts
The perilous narrow ocean parts asunder.
Piece out our imperfections with your thoughts;
Into a thousand parts divide one man,
And make imaginary puissance;
Think, when we talk of horses, that you see them
Printing their proud hoofs i' th' receiving earth. . . .

The speech opens with a dramatic wish for fiery ascent and a "swelling scene"—a wish initially frustrated by "flat, unraised spirits" who lack the phallic potency to "bring forth" their object. The actual "cockpit" (a genital juncture in pun) is too small: the "wooden O" of the Globe Theater cannot physically contain the objects it wishes to represent. Yet through a metaphoric shift from geometry (the architectural "O") to mathematics ("O" as number, zero)—bridged by the shared image of shape ("a crooked figure")—Shakespeare transmutes impotence into omnipotence. The actors who are nothing in themselves become representative "ciphers to this great accompt," and now they count for something. They symbolically multiply, through the reciprocal paradox of being divided: one man becomes a thousand. That multiplication involves sexual as well as mathematical senses (like Polixenes' cipher). The wooden O then re-presents itself as "the girdle of these walls," which now confine high, upreared, mighty monarchies: an image of potency (male within female) that mirrors and is made possible by the "imaginary puissance" of the audience. That imaginative potency is very fertile, as Shakespeare's image suggests. We translate a mere word, "horses," into a symbolic vision of fecundation that condenses the procreative relationship between word, drama, actor, and audience into a poetic image—one that also alludes to the written text: "*printing* their proud hoofs i' th' receiving earth."[22]

Just as "O" as exclamation represents a primitive word at the threshold of speech, and "O" as mark designates the origins of writing, so the various symbolisms of "O" as creative no-thing, or circle, mouth, or womb, underlie primitive conceptions of the theatrical stage itself—connecting human procreation and reproduction with stage production. "O" is the germinal image of Shakespeare's stage (hence the other meaning of my title: "Shakespeare is Nothing"): "this wooden O," the oral stage, and the womb from which that primary relationship develops. Shakespeare's O, his Nothing, thus becomes a dialectic, circumscribing the fruitful interplay between the theatrical mode (what is actually onstage) and the imaginative mode (what is represented to and in the minds of an audience). His O describes a *relationship*; its original models are infantile and maternal, involving the "primal cavities" of womb and mouth.[23] The image of the stage as pregnant enclosure— "*cette enceinte de bois*," in J. P. Petit's felicitous phrase,[24] lies at the basis of Shakespeare's conception of theatrical space as generative— and destructive—female interiority. For him, the metaphor of dramatic and poetic creation as procreation was more than merely metaphor; it was the ground, the primary embodiment, of his art.[25]

Images of feminine enclosures appear throughout Shakespeare's works. At the negative extreme are such catastrophic enactments as the witches' cauldron in *Macbeth*, or the devouring and dismembering pit in *Titus Andronicus*—images that return in their bodily loci in Lear's maddened vision of female genitals, just as Gloucester's ravaged and bleeding face mirrors Lavinia's. The tragedies sternly unfold in terms of this negative or destructive conception of nothing. *Hamlet, Macbeth,* and *King Lear* occupy a stage that seems to offer only danger, confinement, loss, and ultimate death. Yet even the tragedies do not wholly surrender to nihilism. The sheer fact of their existence as dramatic works that re-present negation is an assertion of potency (compare Shakespeare's boasts of poetic immortality in the *Sonnets*). The image-making power of poetry and drama provides a positive balance to the images of negation they construct.[26] Even that most desperate and apparently nihilistic statement of the nothingness of theatrical significance, which Macbeth utters at the end of his play, sounds some positive notes of affirmation: that it is the player, the stage, and the tale that *signify*, award significance to, exist within and create images for, nothing. Macbeth's famous moment of despair is the reciprocal negative version of Theseus' positive characterization of drama as that which gives airy nothing a habitation and a name:

> Out, out, brief candle!
> Life's but a walking shadow, a poor player,
> That struts and frets his hour upon the stage,
> And then is heard no more. It is a tale
> Told by an idiot, full of sound and fury,
> Signifying nothing.

(V.v.23–28)

All comes to nothing, as nothing comes to all. Yet this is not solely the darker or tragic vision. The implicit sense of creative power that tragedies like *Macbeth* or *King Lear* ambiguously suggest becomes explicit in a play like *The Tempest*, where "the great Globe itself" contains and becomes a world, an every-thing, while in itself it is a no-thing, airy nothing, "melted into air, into thin air": an all-inclusive sphere where fragility encloses emptiness, like those emblematic bubbles and dewdrops of Metaphysical and Baroque poetry.[27] Dissolved, insubstantial, the stuff of dreams, both the stage and our lives are finally "rounded"—like a circle or a cipher—"with a sleep" (*The Tempest*, (IV.i.148-58). Joyce's pun is perfect: "Shapesphere" (*Finnegans Wake*, 295.4).

Prospero's final dissolution of his own theatrical magic, though hardly an unambiguous evocation of the positive values of dramatic generativity, does offer an alternative, reciprocal view to the darkly tragic perspective of *King Lear*. Both Lear and Prospero, as old men approaching death (and with daughters to give away, reluctantly), confront the fact of inevitable nothing—but in different ways. Lear tries heroically to stand up to the threat and assert his power in the face of its decline: to say "I" in the midst of nothing ("They told me I was everything"), to be the integer "one" alongside the zero. Yet he becomes, in the Fool's words, "an O without a figure; . . . nothing." ("Power," notes Sigurd Burckhardt, "was the integer before the zero.")[28] Hamlet makes an epigram of the tragedy of heroic assertion in the midst of nothing when he claims that "a man's life's no more than to say 'one'" (V.ii.74).[29] The fearful idea of being *no one* (none, noun)[30] motivates tragedies of identity like *King Lear* and the rest of Shakespeare's tragedies. *Coriolanus* is an extreme example of the denial of circularity (family relationship, origins) in favor of hyperbolically heroic "one-ness" (self-authorship). Heroic assertion in such a world culminates in tragedy; it adds up finally to nothing. In the shorthand of psychoanalytic terminology, oral disintegration encompasses phallic affirmation.

Shakespeare's romances entertain another alternative. Prospero's willing surrender of his "most potent art," his admission of loss and awareness of ultimate nothingness ("Every third thought shall be my grave"), represent a will, not to power, but to surrender power: to give up, to lose, to be lost. Prospero gives up his daughter, while Lear holds on to his to the end, and beyond. Lear refuses to surrender, to mourn, to learn to die. Prospero's exit—and his *return* as Epilogue—enact the enduring value of philosophical acceptance instead of heroic denial in the face of nothing.[31]

Ultimately, the spherical world of Shakespeare reintegrates all the circles and semicircles of my fragmented vision. I must finally abandon the fanciful mathematics of plus and minus zero, since what Shakespeare actually attempts is to incorporate the malignant images of "negative nothing" into the "positive nothing" of the global theater he creates. He erects a sphere (thus being symbolically both father and mother) that contains and momentarily controls those catastrophic fantasies of death and dismemberment that underlie his tragedies (and other plays as well). Nothing, ultimately, is what the plays are *about*, in a spatial as well as thematic sense.

Yet Shakespeare's theatrical playspace, with all its positive procreativity, is also simultaneously the most encompassing representation of that "unmanly," "female" Nothing that arouses tragic anxiety. In other words, Shakespeare cannot escape the primary ambivalence of his global image. All he can do—and he can do almost all—is to work within the voluminous confines of that figure's largest spaces (the theater, the world), constructing in imagination and dramaturgy smaller versions of its powers and paradoxes. Shakespeare's imaginatively vast theatrical space can symbolize a female interior heroically occupied by male "spirits" (actors, phalli), a maternal womb inhabited by playful children (such as the Forest of Arden), or a malignant mouth consuming its victims. It can represent the interior of a confined male psyche—as in *Hamlet*, where the actual Globe Theatre becomes a mirror of the hero's mind, and vice-versa: "Remember thee!/Ay, thou poor ghost, whiles memory holds a seat/In this distracted globe" (I.v.95–97). It also mirrors the "mind's eye" of the audience enclosed within the theater and imaginatively re-creating the play. The particular predominance from play to play of any one symbolic significance does not dissipate the resonant energies of others. All these symbols of Shakespeare's Nothing coexist in his idea of the theater. His movement from tragedy to romance may demonstrate a shift from a dark, malevolent perspective on this idea to a brighter, more benign one—or from tragic denial to philosophical acceptance of the inexorability of being "rounded with a sleep," surrounded and finished by the inevitable nothing of death. But the primary ambivalence never disappears.

Yet how can I sum up? An infinity of nothings is nothing, and infinity. The totality of Shakespeare's Nothing cannot be circumscribed by any figure of speech or design, unless it be his own wooden O. Shakespeare's Nothing is a paradox: a living world that willingly announces itself as a mere bubble, words that disappear into a void. Shakespeare's theater is finally only a momentary enactment of sight and sound and symbol, surrounded by silence and a bare stage, at the last returning to where it began, in emptiness and absence. Yet while it is there, in the playspace of creative nothingness, it is wondrous: beautiful and dreadful, ruinous and renascent, and uniquely worth noting.

Notes

1. Citations are to *The Riverside Shakespeare*, ed. G. Blakemore Evans et al. (Boston: Houghton Mifflin, 1974).

2. Employing the terms of Eric Berne's Transactional Analysis, a recent critic suggests that Cordelia tries to bring Lear—who acts as "Parent" but really is 'Child"—to "Adult" level by short-circuiting his role-playing ritual, thus making him laugh. Her "Nothing" is a jest, and its strategy fails. See Duncan Fraser, "Cordelia's 'Nothing,' " *The Cambridge Quarterly*, 8 (1978), 1-10.

3. Shakespeare's bawdy usage of "nothing" in *Hamlet* has been noted by most commentators. See Thomas Pyles, "Ophelia's 'Nothing,' " *Modern Language Notes*, 64 (1949): 322-23; and of course Eric Partridge, *Shakespeare's Bawdy: A Literary and Psychological Essay and a Comprehensive Glossary*, rev. ed. (London: Routledge and Kegan Paul, 1968). Its use in *King Lear* is noted by Samuel Abrams and Leonard Shengold, "The Meaning of 'Nothing': (I) A Note on 'Nothing', (II) More about the Meaning of 'Nothing,' " *Psychoanalytic Quarterly*, 43 (1974), 115-19. Pyles, who assumed that this sort of naughtiness would have produced "guffaws" and "leers" from Shakespeare's audience, considered it "safe to assume that Shakespeare was perfectly well aware of the 'loose' meaning of *nothing* and *naught(y)* in the venereal vocabulary of his day."

4. The word "thing" is unique. Practically meaningless in itself, it can fill in any blank, replacing any other noun. It has a kind of semantic omnipotence by displacement. For the possible etymological origins of the phallic sense of "thing," see Theodore Thass-Theinemann, *The Interpretation of Language*, 2 vols. New York: Jason Aronson, 1973), II.61-63. On "nothing," see II.69-70.

5. The British psychoanalyst, Ella Freeman Sharpe, reads "folds of favor" as a reference to the maternal breast, which "child Lear" has been denied. See her essay, "From *King Lear* to *The Tempest*," in her *Collected Papers on Psycho-Analysis* (London: Hogarth Press, 1968), pp. 229-30.

6. The first and second Quarto editions have "small"; the first Folio has "great." Either reading is defensible. (Lear, I imagine, would prefer the Folio text.) Partridge glosses the bawdy meaning of "vice" as "pudend" (see *Shakespeare's Bawdy*).

7. See Norman O. Brown, *Love's Body* (New York: Vintage, 1966), pp. 256-66 and Susan Sontag, *Styles of Radical Will* (New York: Dell, 1969), pp. 3-34. On silences in *King Lear*, see Jill Levenson, "What the Silence Said: Still Points in *King Lear*," in *Shakespeare 1971: Proceedings of the World Shakespeare Congress*, ed. Clifford Leech and J.M.R. Margeson (Toronto: Univ. of Toronto Press, 1972), pp. 215-29; Emily Leider, "Plainness of Style in *King Lear*," *Shakespeare Quarterly*, 21 (1970), 45-53; and Richard D. Fly, "Revelations of Darkness: The Language of Silence in *King Lear*," *Bucknell Review*, 20 (1972), 73-92.

8. See Murray M. Schwartz, "Leontes' Jealousy in *The Winter's Tale*," *American Imago*, 30 (1973), 250-73. Schwartz describes the "Affection!" passage as "an abstract version of the primal scene, the intercourse of something and nothing" (pp. 264-65).

9. For commentary on traditional theological and philosophical notions of creation *ex nihilo* in the Renaissance, see William R. Elton, *"King Lear" and the Gods* (San Marino, Calif.: Huntington Library, 1966), especially pp. 179-90; Paul A. Jorgensen, "Much Ado about *Nothing*," *Shakespeare Quarterly*, 5 (1954), 287-95; and Rosalie Colie, *Paradoxica Epidemica* (Princeton, N.J.: Princeton Univ. Press, 1966), pp. 220-51.

10. See Helge Kökeritz, *Shakespeare's Pronunciation* (New Haven: Yale Univ. Press, 1953). The Latin *nota*, meaning mark of designation, is related to *nosco* ("I begin to know") and thus to our word "know."

Several of Shakespeare's senses and uses of the word "nothing," as well as the auditory pun on "noting," are cited in Jorgensen, pp. 287-95. See also Robert F. Fleissner, "The 'Nothing' Element in *King Lear*," *Shakespeare Quarterly*, 13 (1962), 62-71.

11. Bruno Munari, *The Discovery of the Circle*, trans. Marcello and Edna Maestro (New York: George Wittenborn, 1966), p. 65. Consider the "Om" of Eastern mythology, or the "Mu" of Zen. (On the latter, see Tetsumaro Hayashi, "The Concept of Nothingness in *King Lear*—A Buddhist Interpretation." *Persica* (Eng. Lit. Soc. of Okayama), 6 [1978], 77-82.)

12. This is a central and continuing theme in Freudian theory. Freud's 1925 essay on "Negation" offers a brief statement; see *The Standard Edition of the Complete Psychological Works of Sigmund Freud*, ed. and trans. James Strachey et al., 24 vols. (London: Hogarth Press 1953-74), 19, pp. 235-41. See also David Bleich, "New Considerations of the Infantile Acquisition of Language and Symbolic Thought," *Psychoanalytic Review*, 63 (1976), 49-72.

Yet, as Jacques Lacan points out in "The Agency of the Letter in The Unconscious," *Ecrits: A Selection* (New York: W. W. Norton, 1978), p. 150, the remembered object remains only a symbolic substitute. Language reconstitutes loss but does not undo it:

> If we try to grasp in language the constitution of the object, we cannot fail to notice that this constitution is to be found only at the level of concept, a very different thing from a simple nominative, and that the *thing*, when reduced to the noun, breaks up into the double, divergent beam of the "cause" (*causa*) in which it has taken shelter in the French word *chose*, and the nothing (*rien*) to which it has abandoned its Latin dress (*rem*).

Michel Leiris substantiates and personalizes this abstract idea when he writes, in *Manhood* (New York: Grossman Press, 1963):

> I am imbued with the notion that a Muse is necessarily a dead woman, inaccessible or absent; that the poetic structure—like the cannon, which is only a hole surrounded by steel—can be based only on what one does not have; and that ultimately one can write only to fill a void or at the least to situate, in relation to the most lucid part of ourselves, the place where this incommensurable abyss yawns within us. (Quoted by John Hawkes, preface to *Travesty* [New York: New Directions, 1976])

13. See Jacques Lacan, *The Language of the Self: The Function of Language in Psychoanalysis*, trans. with notes and commentary by Anthony Wilden (Baltimore, Johns Hopkins Press, 1968), p. 217, and Jacques Derrida, *Glas* (Paris: Editions Galilée, 1974). For a recent semiotic essay on the dialectic of writing and nothingness, see Jean-Louis Schefer, "La mort, le corps, rien," *Sub-stance*, 14 (1976), 117-25. Besides Lacan, these Gallic myths of primordial absence and "zero degree" writing are most eloquently related by Derrida and Roland Barthes. See Derrida, "Genesis and Structure of [Rousseau's] *Essay on the Origin of Language*," in Derrida, *Of Grammatology*, trans. Gayatri Spivak (Baltimore, Johns Hopkins Univ. Press, 1977), pp. 165-268, and Barthes, *Writing Degree Zero*, trans. A. Lavers and C. Smith (New York: Hill and Wang, 1968).

These myths of nothing at the nodal point recur throughout human thought. All of our counting numbers literally start from, and derive from, zero. Proof of their mathematical generation (by Gottlob Frege, Bertrand Russell, and other theorists) is elaborate: see Martin Gardner's "Mathematical Games" section of *Scientific American*, Feb. 1975, pp. 98–101. Recent astrophysical speculation about "black holes" posits an all-engulfing emptiness which is often imaged as a mouth, or "the navel of the universe," and which has at its core something termed a "naked singularity"—an entity which one excitable science writer considers a "gorgonlike horror": see Dietrick E. Thomson, "The Blob That Ate Physics," *Science News* 12 July 1975, pp. 28-29. Martin Gardner has recently reviewed the growing literature on this mysterious phenomenon, in "The Holes in Black Holes," *New York Review of Books*, 29 Sept. 1977, pp. 22-24.

Among narrative myths of origin, there seem to be two primary versions. In Judaeo-Christian mythology, the Beginning is characterized by a *void* (Old Testament), and by a *word* (New Testament). The two myths together create the primary dialectic of void and word, nothing and noting, which Joyce captures in his most "original" pun: "In the buginning is the woid, in the muddle in the sound-dance" (*Finnegans Wake*, [New York: Viking, 1959] 378.29). For a whimsically philosophical negative narrative, see Donald Barthelme's brief "Nothing: A Preliminary Account," *Guilty Pleasures* (New York: Farrar, Straus, and Giroux, 1974), pp. 161–65. Amidst his tangle of nots, Barthelme remarks, "For an ampler account, see Shakespeare."

14. See Freud, *Beyond the Pleasure Principle* (in *Standard Edition*, 18, pp. 3–65. The incident is central to Lacanian theory: see *The Language of the Self.*

15. The quartos have "yawne," the folios "ayme."

16. See Georges Poulet, *The Metamorphoses of the Circle*, trans. Carley Dawson and Elliott Coleman (Baltimore: Johns Hopkins Press, 1966), especially pp. xxii-iv.

17. See my essay, "Rape and Revenge in *Titus Andronicus*," *English Literary Renaissance*, 8 (1978), 159–82.

18. See Poulet, pp. 1-14.

19. *Finnegans Wake* 353.22. Anthony Burgess glosses this phrase as, "optimistically, the re-creation of meaning out of nothing." See his *Re Joyce* (New York: Ballantine, 1965), p. 239. "An infinite deal of nothing" is Bassanio's opinion of Gratiano's loquacity in *The Merchant of Venice*, I.i.114.

20. "Search" derives from Middle English *serchen* or *cerchen*, out of Old and Middle French *cercher* or *chercher*, from the Latin *circum* and *circare* ("to go around or about"). "Know" derives from Greek *gnotus* and Latin *nosco* (root: *NO*), related to *notus, nota.* See Eric Partridge, *Origins: A Short Etymological Dictionary of Modern English*, 3rd ed. (New York: Macmillan, 1963), s.v. "circulate," "search."

21. See Partridge, *Shakespeare's Bawdy*, p. 152.

22. The term *"fécondation"* is J. B. Petit's: see " 'This wooden O': Théâtre et signe dans les choeurs de *Henry V*," *Etudes Anglaises*, 21 (1968), 286–92. For an excellent brief evocation of the imaginative range of Shakespeare's stage, see A. B. Kernan, "This Goodly Frame, the Stage: The Interior Theater of Imagination in English Renaissance Drama," *Shakespeare Quarterly*, 25 (1974), 1-5. On the pregnancy of words and the potency of images, see Inga-Stina Ewbank, " 'More pregnantly than words': Some Uses and Limitations of Visual Symbols," *Shakespeare Survey*, 24 (1971), 13-18.

23. See René Spitz, "The Primal Cavity: A Contribution to the Genesis of Perception and Its Role for Psychoanalytic Theory," in Spitz, *No and Yes: On the Genesis of Human Communication* (New York: International Univ. Press, 1957); and Spitz,

The First Year of Life (New York: International Univ. Press, 1965). Excellent use of Spitz's theories has been made by Donald Kaplan, in "Theatre Architecture: A Derivation of the Primal Cavity," *The Drama Review*, 12 (1968), 105–16. Using Spitz's notion of "primal dialogues"—nonverbal communications between infant and mother—Kaplan argues that "a theatre . . . structures an opportunity for a primal dialogue between the audience and the actors" (p. 109). No dramatist was more aware of this opportunity, and its primitive origins, than Shakespeare.

24. Petit, p. 291.

25. After quoting the famous line from Theseus' speech about the imagination, and citing the gentleman's remark about the effect of Ophelia's mad discourse on her audience, Paul Jorgensen writes: "One must not, of course, try to build Shakespeare's concept of imaginative creation upon the fanciful, and at best figurative, references to Nothing in these passages. At the same time, analogy with the doctrine of divine creation, which was neither fanciful nor figurative, helps explain the remarkable persistence with which the concept of nothingness, and usually the word itself, appears in his statements on poetry and dreams" (p. 284). I am arguing that the primary analogy is not with "divine creation" (a doctrine that was and is both fanciful and figurative, even though believed), but with natural human procreation. Moreover, I am willing to build an idea of Shakespearean imaginative productivity on these various figures and fantasies of Nothing.

26. See K.T.S. Campbell, "'The Phoenix and the Turtle' as a Signpost of Shakespeare's Development," *British Journal of Aesthetics*, 10 (1970), 169–79.

27. See Poulet, pp. 15–31.

28. "*King Lear*: The Quality of Nothing," in Howard S. Babb, ed., *Essays in Stylistic Analysis* (New York: Harcourt, Brace, Jovanovich, 1972), p. 242.

29. See Ralph Berry, "'To Say One'": An Essay on *Hamlet*," *Shakespeare Survey*, 28 (1975), 107–15.

30. The "noun" pun comes from Brown, p. 262: "I'm no one. I'm a noun."

31. Murray M. Schwartz concludes his study of *The Winter's Tale* by writing: "Finally Shakespeare . . . looks toward reality and fantasy simultaneously, toward loss, the beginning of death, and toward re-creation, its negation. He gives us nothing and all." "*The Winter's Tale*: Loss and Transformation," *American Imago*, 32 (1975), 198.

A Bibliography of Psychoanalytic and Psychological Writings on Shakespeare: 1964-1978

David Willbern

> *Ophelia.* Will he tell us what this show meant?
> *Hamlet.* Ay, or any show that you will show him.
>   Be not you ashamed to show, he'll not shame to
>   tell you what it means.

As psychoanalytic criticism has gradually assumed a prominent place in the Shakespeare industry, many literary critics have begun to use or to acknowledge the theories and techniques of psychological interpretation in writing about Shakespeare. Because it is sometimes difficult to draw clear lines between interpretive perspectives in criticism, the boundaries of this bibliography are elastic enough to hold onto—or permeable enough to let in—a wide range of studies that answer in various ways to my own sense of the intentionally "psychological." I have spread my nets wide enough to include those studies of Shakespeare and his art that focus on such issues as identity, family, sexuality, irrationality, creativity, aggression, narcissism, role playing, dreams, play, ambivalence, or anxiety, and that employ the terms and techniques of psychological theory or use interpretive strategies that rely on an awareness of such theory. Contemporary critics are accommodating psychoanalysis to their views of Shakespeare in innovative and productive ways, a development exemplified by the continuing—nay, relentless—emergence of new critical studies. The field is thriving.

I have taken 1964 as my starting point because Norman Holland's *Psychoanalysis and Shakespeare* (item 184 below), a book that thoroughly and superbly reviews previous psychological writings on Shakespeare, beginning with Freud, is complete up to that year. Any reader interested in checking pre-1964 studies can do so easily with Holland's book. (Readers can also see the bibliography compiled by Bette Green-

An earlier version of this bibliography appeared in *The International Review of Psycho-Analysis*, vol. 5 (1978). Reprinted by permission.

berg and Albert Rothenberg [item 152 below], which confines itself to "medico-psychological" studies and cites writings before Freud.) The bibliography does not include references to dissertations, abstracts of papers, or book reviews. Beyond these conscious exclusions, there will be some essays, particularly recent ones, that have escaped my grasp. I regret in advance any such omission.

The listing here is alphabetical by author, followed by an index that allows its user to find those items pertaining to specific works of Shakespeare. For those wishing to pursue the literature after 1978, various sources are available. The annual bibliographies in *PMLA* and *Shakespeare Quarterly* include almost all books and articles for the year, and the *Shakespeare Quarterly* listing is now conveniently indexed for "psychoanalysis." On the clinical side, the regular listings in *Psychological Abstracts* are valuable, as well as the new *Chicago Psychoanalytic Literature Index,* inaugurated by the Institute for Psychoanalysis in 1975.

I am grateful to my research assistants, Beatrice Stern and Rena Patterson, for their help in collecting material, and to my colleagues Murray Schwartz and Norman Holland for their advice and suggestions.

1. Aarons, Z. Alexander. "Normality and Abnormality in Adolescence, with a Digression on Prince Hal: 'The Sowing of Wild Oats.'" *The Psychoanalytic Study of the Child,* 25 (1970), 309-39.

2. Abrams, Richard. "*The Tempest* and the Concept of the Machiavellian Playwright." *English Literary Renaissance,* 8 (1978), 43-66.

3. Abrams, Samuel, and Leonard Shengold. "The Meaning of 'Nothing': (I) A Note on 'Nothing', (II) More About the Meaning of 'Nothing.'" *Psychoanalytic Quarterly,* 43 (1974), 115-19.

4. Adamowski, T. H. "The Aesthetic Attitude and Narcissism in *Othello.*" *Literature and Psychology,* 18 (1968), 73-81.

5. Adelman, Janet. "'Anger's My Meat': Feeding, Dependency, and Aggression in *Coriolanus.*" In *Shakespeare: Pattern of Excelling Nature.* Ed. David Bevington and Jay Halio. Newark: Univ. of Delaware Press, 1978, pp. 108-24. (See Chapter 7 in this book.)

6. ———. *The Common Liar: An Essay on "Antony and Cleopatra."* New Haven, Conn.: Yale Univ. Press, 1973.

7. ———. Introduction to *Twentieth-Century Interpretations of "King Lear."* Ed. Janet Adelman, Englewood Cliffs, N. J.: Prentice-Hall, 1978, p. 1-21.

8. Adler, Gerhard. Foreword to James Kirsch, *Shakespeare's Royal Self.* New York: Putnam, 1966.

9. Aldus, P. J. *Mousetrap: Structure and Meaning in "Hamlet."* Toronto: Univ. of Toronto Press, 1977.

10. Alexander, Nigel. *Poison, Play, and Duel: A Study in "Hamlet."* Lincoln: Univ. of Nebraska Press, 1971.

11. ———. *Shakespeare: "Measure for Measure."* Studies in English Literature, 57. London: Arnold, 1975.

12. Almeida, Lilian Pestre de. "Le jeu du monde dans *Une Tempête.*" *Revue de littérature comparée,* 51 (1977), 85-96.

13. Anderson, Peter S. "Shakespeare's *Caesar*: The Language of Sacrifice." *Comparative Drama*, 3 (1969), 3-26.

14. Andreasen, Nancy J. "The Artist as Scientist: Psychiatric Diagnosis in Shakespeare's Tragedies." *Journal of the American Medical Association*, 235 (April 1976), 1868-72.

15. Anonymous. "Commentary." *Times Literary Supplement* (London), 30 Jan. 1969, p. 108.

16. Ansari, Ansloob Ahmad. "Shakespeare's Allegory of Love." *Aligarh Journal of English Studies*, 3 (1978), 44-62.

17. Anthonisen, Niels L. "The Ghost in *Hamlet.*" *American Imago*, 22 (1966), 232-49.

18. Aring, Charles D. "Perception as a Moral Test." *Journal of Nervous and Mental Disease*, 144 (1968), 539-45.

19. Armens, Sven. *Archetypes of the Family in Literature*. Seattle: Univ. of Washington Press, 1966.

20. Aronson, Alex. *Psyche and Symbol in Shakespeare*. Bloomington, Ind.: Indiana Univ. Press, 1972.

21. Bachmann, Susan. "'Daggers in Men's Smiles': The 'Truest Issue' in *Macbeth.*" *International Review of Psycho-Analysis*, 5 (1978), 97-104.

22. Bandero, Cesáreo. "Literature and Desire: Poetic Frenzy and the Love Potion." *Mosaic*, 8 (1975), 33-52.

23. Barber, C. L. "On Christianity and the Family: Tragedy of the Sacred." In *Twentieth-Century Interpretations of "King Lear."* Ed. Janet Adelman. Englewood Cliffs, N.J.: Prentice-Hall, 1978, pp. 117-19.

24. ———. "Shakespearean Comedy: *The Comedy of Errors.*" *College English*, 25 (1964), 493-97.

25. ———. "'Thou that beget'st him that did thee beget': Transformation in *Pericles* and *The Winter's Tale.*" *Shakespeare Survey*, 22 (1969), 59-67.

26. Barkan, Leonard. *Nature's Work of Art: The Human Body as Image of the World*. New Haven: Yale Univ. Press, 1975.

27. Barnett, Joseph. "*Hamlet* and the Family Ideology." *Journal of the American Academy of Psychoanalysis*, 3 (1975), 405-17.

28. Barroll, J. Leeds. *Artificial Persons: The Formation of Character in the Tragedies of Shakespeare*. Columbia: Univ. of South Carolina Press, 1974.

29. Barron, Frank, and Marvin Rosenberg. "King Lear and His Fool: A Study of the Conception and Enactment of Dramatic Role in Relation to Self-Conception." *Educational Theatre Journal*, 22 (1970), 276-83.

30. Beauchamp, Gorman. "Falstaff and Civilization's Discontents." *College Literature*, 3 (1976), 94-101.

31. Beauregard, David N. "*Venus and Adonis*: Shakespeare's Representation of the Passions." *Shakespeare Studies*, 8 (1975), 83-98.

32. Berger, Harry, Jr. "Miraculous Harp: A Reading of Shakespeare's *Tempest.*" *Shakespeare Studies*, 5 (1970), 253-83.

33. ———. "Theater, Drama, and the Second World: A Prologue to Shakespeare." *Comparative Drama*, 2 (1968), 3-20.

34. ———. "*Troilus and Cressida*: The Observer as Basilisk." *Comparative Drama*, 2 (1968), 122-36.

35. Berman, Ronald. "Shakespearean Comedy and the Uses of Reason." *South Atlantic Quarterly*, 63 (1964), 1-9.

36. Berry, Ralph. "Language and Structure in *Measure for Measure*." *University of Toronto Quarterly*, 46 (1976), 147-61.

37. ———. "Sexual Imagery in *Coriolanus*." *Studies in English Literature*, 13 (1973), 301-16.

38. ———. *The Shakespearean Metaphor: Studies in Language and Form*. Totowa, N.J.: Rowman and Littlefield, 1978.

39. ———. "'To Say One': An Essay on *Hamlet*." *Shakespeare Survey*, 28 (1975), 107-15.

40. Besdine, Matthew. "The Jocasta Complex: Mothering and Genius." *Psychoanalytic Review*, 55 (1968-69), 259-77, 574-600. (See pp. 576-77).

41. Biggins, Dennis. "Sexuality, Witchcraft, and Violence in *Macbeth*." *Shakespeare Studies*, 8 (1975), 255-77.

42. Bird, Christine M. "Games Courtiers Play in *Love's Labor's Lost*." *Hartford Studies in Literature*, 11 (1979), 41-48.

43. Bishop, Sharon. "Another Look at Desdemona, Heroine of Dry Dreams." *Paunch* (State Univ. of New York at Buffalo), 23 (1965), 5-9.

44. Black, Michael. "*Othello*: A Study of the Self." In Black, *The Literature of Fidelity*. New York: Barnes and Noble, 1975, pp. 16-42.

45. Bond, Edward. "The Duke in *Measure for Measure*." *Gambit*, 17 (1970), 43-45.

46. Bongiorno, Dominic, et al. "Remarks on the Freud-Jones Theory of *Hamlet*." *Shakespeare Newsletter*, 17 (1967), 15, 36, 58.

47. Boose, Lynda E. "Othello's Handkerchief: 'The Recognizance and Pledge of Love.'"*English Literary Renaissance*, 5 (1975), 360-74.

48. Booth, Stephen, ed. *Shakespeare's Sonnets*. New Haven: Yale Univ. Press, 1977.

49. Bougnoux, Daniel. "Repétér Hamlet." *Silex*, 3 (1977), 51-63.

50. Bourg-Oulé, Anne Marie le. "*Le songe d'une nuit d'été*: Perspectives de la fête." In Françoise Charpentier, "Poétique et langage dramatique." *Revue de littérature comparée* (Paris), 202 (1977), 298-306.

51. Boyette, Purvis E. "Shakespeare's Sonnets: Homosexuality and the Critics." *Tulane Studies in English*, 21 (1975), 35-46.

52. Breuer, Horst. "Zur Methodik der *Hamlet*-Deutung von Ernest Jones." *Shakespeare Jahrbuch* (Heidelberg), (1973), 144-71.

53. Brody, Jules. "Freud, *Hamlet*, and the Metaphysics of Tragedy." *Language and Style*, 10 (1977), 248-61.

54. Brody, Paula. "Shylock's Omophagia: A Ritual Approach to *The Merchant of Venice*." *Literature and Psychology*, 17 (1967), 229-34.

55. Burge, Barbara. "*Hamlet*: The Search for Identity." *Review of English Literature*, 5 (1964), 58-71.

56. Burke, Kenneth. "*Coriolanus*—and the Delights of Faction." In Burke, *Language as Symbolic Action*. Berkeley: Univ. of California Press, 1966, pp. 81-97.

57. ———. "*King Lear*: Its Form and Psychosis." *Shenandoah*, 21 (1969), 3-18.

58. ———. "Shakespearean Persuasion: *Antony and Cleopatra*." In his *Language as Symbolic Action*, pp. 101-14.

59. ——. "*Timon of Athens* and Misanthropic Gold." In his *Language as Symbolic Action*, pp. 115-24.

60. Byles, Joan Mary. "The Basic Pattern of Psychological Conflict in Shakespearean Tragic Drama." *Hartford Studies in Literature*, 11 (1979), 58-71.

61. Calderwood, James L. "Styles of Knowing in *All's Well*." *Modern Language Quarterly*, 25 (1964), 272-94.

62. Calef, Victor. "Lady Macbeth and Infanticide, or 'How Many Children Had Lady Macbeth Murdered?'" *Journal of the American Psychoanalytic Association*, 17 (1969), 528-48.

63. Callahan, Robert D. "Shakespeare's *Troilus and Cressida*: Lechery as Warfare." *Paunch* (State Univ. of New York at Buffalo), 23 (1965), 57-67.

64. ——. "The Theme of 'Government' in *Measure for Measure*." *Paunch* (State Univ. of New York at Buffalo), 25 (1967), 31-52.

65. Campbell, K.T.S. "'The Phoenix and the Turtle' as a Signpost of Shakespeare's Development." *British Journal of Aesthetics*, 10 (1970), 169-79.

66. Carroll, William. *The Great Feast of Language in "Love's Labour's Lost."* Princeton, N.J.: Princeton Univ. Press, 1976.

67. ——. "'A Received Belief': Imagination in *The Merry Wives of Windsor*." *Studies in Philology*, 74 (1977), 186-215.

68. Cavell, Stanley. "The Avoidance of Love: A Reading of *King Lear*." In Cavell, *Must We Mean What We Say?* New York: Charles Scribner's Sons, 1969, pp. 267-353.

69. ——. *The Claim of Reason: Wittgenstein, Skepticism, Morality, and Tragedy.* London: Oxford Univ. Press, 1979.

70. ——. "Epistemology and Tragedy: A Reading of *Othello*." *Daedalus*, 108 (Summer 1979), 27-43.

71. Chaplin, William H. "Form and Psychology in King Lear." *Literature and Psychology*, 19 (1969), 31-46.

72. Cixous, Hélène. "*Jules César*: un repas sacré. Discours autour d'un meurtre ritual." *Les langues modernes*, 61 (1967), 53-55.

73. Clay, Charlotte N. *The Role of Anxiety in English Tragedy: 1580-1642.* Jacobean Drama Studies, 23. Salzburg: Institut für Englische Sprache und Literatur, 1974.

74. Colman, E.A.M. *The Dramatic Use of Bawdy in Shakespeare.* London, Longman, 1964.

75. Cook, Albert. *Shakespeare's Enactment: The Dynamics of Renaissance Theatre.* Chicago: Swallow Press, 1976.

76. Corrao, Francesco, "Psicoanalisi ed Arte," *Revista di Psicoanalisi*, 11 (1965), 234-45.

77. Cox, Marjorie K. "Adolescent Process in *Romeo and Juliet*." *Psychoanalytic Review*, 63 (1976), 379-92.

78. Crossley, Robert. "Education and Fantasy." *College English*, 37 (1975), 281-93. (See pp. 284-85).

79. Desai, Rupin W. "Freudian Undertones in the Isabella-Angelo Relationship of *Measure for Measure*," *Psychoanalytic Review*, 64 (1977), 487-94.

80. ——. "Interdisciplinary Approaches to Shakespeare in Twentieth-Century

America." In Desai, *Twentieth-Century American Criticism*. New Delhi: Arnold-Heinemann, 1977, p. 278-302.

81. Dettmering, Peter. *Dichtung und Psychoanalyse. II. Shakespeare—Goethe—Jean Paul—Doderer*. Sammlung Dialog, 73. Munchen: Nymphenburger Verlagsbuch, 1974.

82. Dickes, Robert. "Desdemona: An Innocent Victim?" *American Imago*, 27 (1970), 279-97.

83. Dracoulides, N. N. "Psychoanalytic Investigation of Shakespeare's *Hamlet*." *Transnational Mental Health Research Newsletter*, 19 (1977), 2-9.

84. Draper, John W. "Shattered Personality in Shakespeare's Antony." *Psychiatric Quarterly*, 39 (1965), 448-56.

85. Dundes, Alan. " 'To Love My Father All': A Psychoanalytic Study of the Folktale Source of *King Lear*." *Southern Folklore Quarterly*, 40 (1976), 353-66.

86. Durham, Mildred. "Drama of the Dying God in *Julius Caesar*." *Hartford Studies in Literature*, 11 (1979), 49-57.

87. Eagleton, Terence. *Shakespeare and Society: Critical Essays on Shakespearean Drama*. New York: Schocken Books, 1971.

88. Ebel, Henry. "Caesar's Wounds: A Study of William Shakespeare." *Psychoanalytic Review*, 62 (1975), 107-30.

89. Edgar, Irving I. *Shakespeare, Medicine and Psychiatry*. New York: Philosophical Library, 1970.

90. Egan, Robert. "His Hour Upon the Stage: Role-Playing in *Macbeth*." *Centennial Review*, 22 (1978), 327-45.

91. Eissler, K. R. *Discourse on Hamlet and "Hamlet": A Psychoanalytic Inquiry*. New York: International Universities Press, 1971.

92. ——. "Fortinbras and Hamlet." *American Imago*, 25 (1968), 199-222.

93. ——. "The Relationship of Explaining and Understanding in Psychoanalysis: Demonstrated by One Aspect of Freud's Approach to Literature." *The Psychoanalytic Study of the Child*, 23 (1968), 141-77.

94. Ellis, Herbert A. *Shakespeare's Lusty Punning in "Love's Labour's Lost"*. The Hague: Mouton, 1973.

95. Ellis, John. "Rooted Affection: The Genesis of Jealousy in *The Winter's Tale*." *College English*, 25 (1964), 545-47.

96. Erlich, Avi. *Hamlet's Absent Father*. Princeton, N. J.: Princeton Univ. Press, 1977.

97. Eychène, Christian. "Essai d'interpretation psychanalytique de *Roi Lear*." In *"Le Roi Lear" de William Shakespeare. Texte, analyses, mise en scène, études*. Comédie de Saint-Etienne: Centre Dramatique National et Centre d'Etudes et de Recherches Théâtricales, Université de Lyon II, 1976.

98. Faber, M. D. "The Adolescent Suicides of Romeo and Juliet." *Psychoanalytic Review*, 59 (1972), 169-81.

99. ——. "Falstaff Behind the Arras." *American Imago*, 27 (1970), 197-225.

100. ——. "Freud and Shakespeare's Mobs." *Literature and Psychology*, 15 (1965), 238-55.

101. ——. "Hamlet, Sarcasm, and Psychoanalysis." *Psychoanalytic Review*, 55 (1968), 79-90.

102. ——. "Hermia's Dream: Royal Road to *A Midsummer Night's Dream.*" *Literature and Psychology*, 22 (1972), 179-90.

103. ——. "Lord Brutus' Wife: A Modern View." *Psychoanalytic Review*, 52 (1965-66), 108-15.

104. ——. "Oedipal Patterns in *Henry IV.*" *Psychoanalytic Quarterly*, 36 (1967), 426-34. Reprinted in Faber, ed., *The Design Within*, pp. 430-38. (See Item 114 below.)

105. ——. "On Jacques: Psychological Remarks." *University Review*, 36 (1970), 179-82.

106. ——. "Ophelia's Doubtful Death." *Literature and Psychology*, 16 (1966), 103-08.

107. ——. "Othello: Symbolic Action, Ritual, and Myth." *American Imago*, 31 (1974), 159-205.

108. ——. "Othello: The Justice of It Pleases." *American Imago*, 28 (1971), 228-46.

109. ——. "Shakespeare's Ghosts." *American Notes & Queries*, 5 (1967), 131-32.

110. ——. "Shakespeare's Suicides." In *Essays in Self-Destruction*. Ed. E. Shneidman. New York: Aronson, 1967, p. 30-58.

111. ——. "Some Remarks on the Suicide of King Lear's Eldest Daughter." *University Review*, 33 (1967), 313-17.

112. ——. "Two Studies in Self-Aggression in Shakespearean Tragedy: (I) The Conscience of the King: A Preliminary Investigation of Claudius' Self-Destructive Urges. (II) Suicidal Patterns in *Othello.*" *Literature and Psychology*, 14 (1964), 80-96.

113. ——. "The Victims and the Victimizers." *American Imago*, 29 (1972), 338-52.

114. Faber, M. D., ed. *The Design Within: Psychoanalytic Approaches to Shakespeare.* New York: Science House, 1970.

115. Faber, M. D., and A. F. Dilnot. "On a Line of Iago's." *American Imago*, 25 (1968), 86-90.

116. Fanchette, Jean. "*Hamlet*: au coeur de la catharsis Shakespearienne." *Annales médico-psychologiques*, 1 (1969), 369-74.

117. Farrell, Kirby. "Imitation and Identity: Shakespeare and the Imagination of His Culture." In *Shakespearean Metadrama*. Ed. John Blanpied. Rochester, N. Y.: Univ. of Rochester Department of English, 1977.

118. ——. *Shakespeare's Creation: The Language of Magic and Play.* Amherst, Mass.: Univ. of Massachusetts Press, 1976.

119. Feiner, Arthur H. "A Note on Ravich's 'Shakespeare and Psychiatry.' " *Literature and Psychology*, 15 (1965), 125-28. (See Item 322 below.)

120. Feinstein, Howard M. "Hamlet's Horatio and the Therapeutic Mode." *American Journal of Psychiatry*, 123 (1967), 803-09.

121. Fiedler, Leslie. *The Stranger in Shakespeare.* New York: Stein and Day, 1972.

122. Fineman, Joel. "Fratricide and Cuckoldry: Shakespeare's Doubles." *Psychoanalytic Review*, 64 (1977), 409-53. (See Chapter 5 in this book.)

123. Flaumenhaft, Mera J. "Begetting and Belonging in Shakespeare's *Othello.*" *Interpretation* (The Hague), 4 (1975), 197-216.

124. Fliess, Eleanor S., and Robert Fliess. "Shakespeare's Juliet and Her Nurse." *American Imago*, 33 (1976), 244-60.

125. Flynn, John T. "The Problem of the Prince." In Flynn, *Identification and Individuality*. New York: Beekman, 1970, p. 52-60.

126. Foakes, R. A. "What's New in Shakespeare Criticism." *English*, 23 (1974), 5-10.

127. Fraser, Duncan. "Much Virtue in 'Nothing': Cordelia's Part in the First Scene of *King Lear*." *The Cambridge Quarterly*, 8 (1978), 1-10.

128. Freeman, Derek. "Thunder, Blood, and the Nicknaming of God's Creatures." *Psychoanalytic Quarterly*, 37 (1969), 353-99. (See pp. 390-93.)

129. Freiman, Gwenne. "*Hamlet* as Theatre and as a Play." *American Imago*, 29 (1972), 377-83.

130. Frey, Charles. "Shakespeare's Imperiled and Chastening Daughters of Romance." *Shakespeare Association Bulletin*, 43 (November 1978), 125-40.

131. Fyler, Anson C., Jr. "Self-Unification: An Archetypal Analysis of Prospero in *The Tempest*." *Hartford Studies in Literature*, 3 (1971), 45-50.

132. Gagnebin, Murielle. "Poétique l'éros féminin: Variations sur Ophélie." *Silex*, 3 (1977), 78-83.

133. Gajdusek, R. E. "Death, Incest, and the Triple Bond in the Later Plays of Shakespeare." *American Imago*, 31 (1974), 109-58.

134. Ganim, Carole. "The Divided Self: Caliban from Shakespeare to Auden." *Kentucky Philological Association Bulletin* (1975), 9-15.

135. Garber, Marjorie. "Coming of Age in Shakespeare." *The Yale Review*, 66 (1977), 517-33.

136. ———. "*Cymbeline* and the Language of Myth." *Mosaic*, 10 (1977), 105-15.

137. ———. *Dream in Shakespeare: From Metaphor to Metamorphosis*. New Haven, Conn.: Yale Univ. Press, 1974.

138. Garner, Shirley N. "Shakespeare's Desdemona." *Shakespeare Studies*, 9 (1976), 233-52.

139. Gassenmeier, Michael. "Odi et Amo: Das Dilemma von Shakespeare's Coriolan." *Anglia*, 93 (1975), 70-110.

140. Gedo, John E. "Caviare to the General." *American Imago*, 29 (1972), 293-317.

141. Gerenday, Lynn de. "Play, Ritualization, and Ambivalence in *Julius Caesar*." *Literature and Psychology*, 24 (1974), 24-33.

142. Girard, René. "Lévi-Strauss, Frye, Derrida, and Shakespearean Criticism." *Diacrtitics*, 3 (1973), 34-38.

143. ———. *Violence and the Sacred*. Trans. Patrick Gregory. Baltimore: Johns Hopkins Univ. Press, 1977.

144. Goldstein, Melvin. "Identity Crises in a Midsummer Nightmare: Comedy as Terror in Disguise." *Psychoanalytic Review*, 60 (1973), 169-204.

145. Gordon, David J. *Literary Art and the Unconscious*. Baton Rouge, La.: Louisiana State Univ. Press, 1976.

146. Gottschalk, Paul. *The Meaning of "Hamlet": Modes of Literary Interpretation since Bradley*. Albuquerque: Univ. of New Mexico Press, 1972.

147. ———. "The Universe of Madness in *King Lear*." *Bucknell Review*, 19 (1971), 51-68.

148. Green, André. "*Othello*: une tragédie de la conversion." In Green, *Un oeil en trop: Le complex d'Oedipe dans la tragédie*. Paris: Editions de minuit, 1969, pp. 109-64.

149. ——. "Shakespeare, Freud, et le parricide." *La nef*, 31 (1967), 64–82.

150. ——. *The Tragic Effect: The Oedipus Complex in Tragedy*. Trans. Alan Sheridan. New York: Cambridge Univ. Press, 1979. (See item 148 above.)

151. Green, Martin B. *The Labyrinth of Shakespeare's Sonnets: An Examination of Sexual Elements in Shakespeare's Language*. London: Charles Skilton, 1974.

152. Greenberg, Bette, and Albert Rothenberg. "William Shakespeare (1564–1616): Medico-Psychological and Psychoanalytic Studies on His Life and Works: A Bibliography." *International Review of Psycho-Analysis*, 1 (1974), 245–56. (See also Item 354 below.)

153. Grinstein, Alexander. "King Lear's Impending Death." *American Imago*, 30 (1973), 121–41.

154. Groen, Jan. "Cordelia, dochter von Lear." *De Gids*, 140 (1977), 326–37.

155. Grotjahn, Martin. *The Voice of the Symbol*. Los Angeles: Mara Books, 1971.

156. Gurewitch, Morton. *Comedy: The Irrational Vision*. Ithaca, New York: Cornell Univ. Press, 1975.

157. Haefner, Gerhard. "Die Rede des Brutus—Psychologie der Masse und ihrer Fuhrer. Ein Beitrag zur politischen Rede (Shakespeare, *Julius Caesar*, III.2)." *Praxis des neusprachlichen*, 18 (1971), 266–69.

158. Halio, Jay L. "Anxiety in *Othello*." *Costerus*, 1 (1972), 123–31.

159. Hammersmith, James P. "*Hamlet* and the Myth of Memory." *ELH*, 45 (1978), 597–605.

160. Hammerström, Eckhardt. *Narzisstische Figuren in elisabethanischen Tragödien*. Salzburg: Institut für Englische Sprache und Literatur, 1976. See pp. 176–235.

161. Harding, D. W. "Women's Fantasy of Manhood." *Shakespeare Quarterly*, 20 (1969), 245–53.

162. Harding, F.J.W. "Fantasy, Imagination, and Shakespeare." *British Journal of Aesthetics*, 4 (1964), 305–20.

163. Hawkins, Harriett. " 'The Devil's Party': Virtue and Vices in *Measure for Measure*." *Shakespeare Survey*, 31 (1978), 105–13.

164. Heilbrun, Carolyn G. *Toward a Recognition of Androgyny*. New York: Harper, 1973. (See pp. 28–34.)

165. Helgerson, Richard. "What Hamlet Remembers." *Shakespeare Studies*, 10 (1977), 67–97.

166. Henderson, Archibald. "Coriolanus and the Grief of Shakespeare." In *Shakespeare in the Southwest: Some New Directions*. Ed. T. J. Stafford, Austin, Tex.: Univ. of Texas Press, 1969, pp. 71–79.

167. Henke, James T. *The Ego-King: An Archetype Approach to Elizabethan Political Thought and Shakespeare's Henry VI Plays*. Salzburg: Institut für Englische Sprache und Literatur, 1977.

168. Hennessey, Michael. " 'Had I Kingdoms to Give': Place in *As You Like It*." *Essays in Literature*, 4 (1977), 143–51.

169. Hepburn, James G. "A Dream That Hath No Bottom." *Literature and Psychology*, 14 (1964), 3–6. (See also Item 186 below.)

170. Herbert, Edward T. "Myth and Archetype in *Julius Caesar*." *Psychoanalytic Review*, 57 (1970), 303–08.

171. Herz, Judith Scherer. "Play World and Real World: Dramatic Illusion and the

Dream Metaphor." *English Studies in Canada* (Toronto), 3 (1977), 386–400.

172. Hofling, Charles K. "Notes on Shakespeare's *Cymbeline.*" *Shakespeare Studies*, 1 (1965), 118–36.

173. ——. "Notes on Shakespeare's *Winter's Tale.*" *Psychoanalytic Review*, 58 (1971), 90–110.

174. ——. "Psychoanalytic Aspects of Shakespeare's *Tempest.*" *Psychoanalytic Review*, 61 (1974), 375–95.

175. Holland, Norman N. "Caliban's Dream." *Psychoanalytic Quarterly*, 37 (1968), 114–25. Reprinted in Faber, ed., *The Design Within*, pp. 522–33.

176. ——. *The Dynamics of Literary Response.* London: Oxford Univ. Press, 1968.

177. ——. *Five Readers Reading.* New Haven, Conn.: Yale Univ. Press, 1975.

178. ——. "Freud and the Poet's Eye." In *Hidden Patterns: Studies in Psychoanalytic Criticism.* Ed. Leonard and Eleanor Manheim. New York: Macmillan, 1966, p. 151–70.

179. ——. "Freud on Shakespeare." *Show* (February 1964), 86, 108.

180. ——. "Hamlet–My Greatest Creation." *Journal of the American Academy of Psychoanalysis*, 3 (1975), 419–27.

181. ——. "How Can Dr. Johnson's Remarks on Cordelia's Death Add to My Own Response?" In *Psychoanalysis and the Question of the Text.* Selected Papers from the English Institute, 1976–77, new series, no. 2. Ed. Geoffrey Hartman. Baltimore: Johns Hopkins Univ. Press, 1978, p. 18–44.

182. ——. Introduction to the New American Library edition of *Henry IV, Part Two.* New York: New American Library, 1965. Reprinted in Faber, ed., *The Design Within*, pp. 411–28.

183. ——. "Mercutio, mine own son the dentist." In *Essays on Shakespeare.* Ed. Gordon Ross Smith. Pennsylvania State Univ. Press, 1965, pp. 3–14.

184. ——. *Psychoanalysis and Shakespeare.* New York: Octagon Books, 1976.

185. ——. "Psychology on Shakespeare: 1897-2064." *The Shakespeare Newsletter*, 14 (1964), 2–3, 27.

186. ——. Reply to J. G. Hepburn, "A Dream That Hath No Bottom." *Literature and Psychology*, 14 (1964), 6. (See Item 169 above.)

187. ——. *The Shakespearean Imagination.* Bloomington, Ind.: Indiana Univ. Press, 1964.

188. ——. "Shakespeare's Mercutio and Ours." *Michigan Quarterly*, 5 (1966), 115–23.

189. ——. "A Touching of Literary and Psychiatric Education." *Seminars in Psychiatry*, 5 (1973), 287–99.

190. ——. "Towards a Psychoanalysis of Poetic Form: Some Mixed Metaphors Unmixed." *Literature and Psychology*, 15 (1965), 79–91.

191. ——. "Transactive Teaching: Cordelia's Death." *College English*, 39 (1977), 276–85.

192. Homan, Sidney R. "The Single World of *A Midsummer Night's Dream.*" *Bucknell Review*, 17 (1969), 72–84.

193. Horowitz, David. *Shakespeare: An Existential View.* London: Tavistock, 1965.

194. Horwich, Richard. "Integrity in *Macbeth*: The Search for the 'Single State of Man.'" *Shakespeare Quarterly*, 29 (1978), 365–73.

195. Hoy, Cyrus. "Fathers and Daughters in Shakespeare's Romances." In *Shakespeare's Romances Reconsidered*. Ed. Carol M. Kay and Henry E. Jacobs. Lincoln: Univ. of Nebraska Press, 1978, pp. 77–90.

196. Hulme, Hilda M. *Explorations in Shakespeare's Language*. London: Longman, 1977.

197. Huston, J. Dennis. "'When I Come to Man's Estate': *Twlefth Night* and Problems of Identity." *Modern Language Quarterly*, 33 (1972), 274–88.

198. Hutter, Albert D. "The Language of Hamlet." *Journal of the American Academy of Psychoanalysis*, 3 (1975), 429–38.

199. Hyman, Stanley Edgar. "Iago Psychoanalytically Motivated." *Centennial Review*, 14 (1970), 369–84.

200. ——. *Iago: Some Approaches to the Illusion of His Motivation*. New York: Atheneum, 1970.

201. ——. "Portraits of the Artist: Iago and Prospero." *Shenandoah*, 21 (1970), 18–42.

202. ——. "Untuning the Othello Music: Iago as Stage Villain." In *The Rarer Action: Essays in Honor of Francis Fergusson*. Ed. Alan Cheuse and Richard Koffler. New Brunswick: Rutgers Univ. Press, 1970, pp. 55–67.

203. Ide, Richard S. "The Theatre of the Mind: An Essay on *Macbeth*." *ELH (English Literary History)*, 42 (1975), 338–61.

204. Jaarsma, Richard J. "The 'Lear Complex' in *The Two Gentlemen of Verona*." *Literature and Psychology*, 22 (1972), 199–202.

205. ——. "The Tragedy of Banquo." *Literature and Psychology*, 17 (1967), 87–94.

206. Jagendorf, Zvi. "The Life of Memory: The Experience of the Past in Shakespeare's History Plays." *Hebrew Univ. Studies in Literature*, 4 (1976), 138–53.

207. Janton, Pierre, "Othello's 'Weak Function,'" *Cahiers élisabéthains*, 7 (1975), 43–50.

208. Jiji, Vera M. "Portia Revisited: The Influence of Unconscious Factors upon Theme and Characterization in *The Merchant of Venice*." *Literature and Psychology*, 26 (1976), 5–15.

209. Jorgensen, Paul A. "Hamlet's Therapy." *Huntington Library Quarterly*, 27 (1964), 239–58.

210. ——. *Lear's Self-Discovery*. Berkeley: Univ. California Press, 1967.

211. Kahn, Coppélia. "Coming of Age in Verona." *Modern Language Studies*, 8 (1977–78), 5–22.

212. ——. "Self and Eros in *Venus and Adonis*." *Centennial Review*, 20 (1976), 351–71.

213. ——. "The Rape in Shakespeare's *Lucrece*." *Shakespeare Studies*, 9 (1976), 45–72.

214. Kanter, Victor. "Freud and Shakespeare." *Times Literary Supplement*, 27 Feb. 1969, pp. 210–11. (Reply to *TLS* "Commentary," 30 Jan. 1969).

215. ——. "Freud's Reading of Shakespeare." *Bulletin of the British Psychological Association*, 22 (1969), 225–26.

216. Kanzer, Mark. "Imagery in *King Lear.*" *American Imago*, 22 (1965), 3–13. Reprinted in Faber, ed., *The Design Within*, pp. 221–31.

217. Kaplan, Bert. "On Reason in Madness in *King Lear*," In *Challenges of Humanistic Psychology*. Ed. James Bugental. New York: McGraw-Hill, 1967, pp. 313–18.

218. Kaplan, Donald M. "Reflections on Eissler's Concept of the Doxalethic Function." *American Imago*, 29 (1972), 353–76.

219. Kaplan, Morton. "Fantasy of the Family Romance: Shakespeare's *The Tempest.*" In *The Unspoken Motive: A Guide to Psychoanalytic Literary Criticism*. Ed. Morton Kaplan and Robert Kloss. New York: Free Press, 1973, pp. 88–104.

220. Kaplan, Morton, and Robert Kloss. *The Unspoken Motive*, passim.

221. Kirsch, Arthur C. "The Polarization of Erotic Love in *Othello.*" *Modern Language Review*, 73 (1978), 721–40.

222. Kirsch, James. *Shakespeare's Royal Self.* New York: Putnam, 1966.

223. Knight, W. Nicholas. "Patrimony and Shakespeare's Daughters." *University of Hartford Studies in Literature*, 9 (1977), 175–86.

224. Kott, Jan. "The Sexual Triangle." Trans. Mark Rosenzweig. *Partisan Review*, (1977), 584–90.

225. Kovel, Joel. "Othello." *American Imago*, 35 (1978); 113–19.

226. Kuhn, Reinhard. *The Demon of Noontide: Ennui in Western Literature.* Princeton, 1976. (See esp. pp. 89–127.)

227. Kuriyama, Constance Brown. "The Mother of the World: A Psychoanalytic Interpretation of Shakespeare's *Antony and Cleopatra.*" *English Literary Renaissance*, 7 (1977), 324–51.

228. Labriola, Albert C. " 'This Sceptred Isle': Kingship and the Body Politic in the Lancastrian Tetralogy." In *Shakespeare and English History: Interdisciplinary Perspectives*. Ed. Ronald G. Shafer. Indiana, Pa.: Indiana Univ. of Pennsylvania, 1976, pp. 45–64.

229. Lacan, Jacques. "Desire and the Interpretation of Desire in *Hamlet.*" Trans. James Hulbert. *Yale French Studies*, 55–56 (1977), 36–66.

230. Latham, Jacqueline E. M. "Unconscious Self-Revelation by Goneril and Regan." *Shakespeare-Jahrbuch* (Weimar), 113 (1977), 164–67.

231. Leite, Dante Moreira. "Hamlet visto por Freud." *Occidente* (Lisboa) (September 1964), 127–31.

232. Lesser, Simon. "Act One, Scene One, of *Lear.*" *College English*, 32 (1970), 155–71. Reprinted in *The Whispered Meanings: Selected Essays of Simon O. Lesser*. Ed. R. Sprich and R. Noland. Amherst: Univ. of Massachusetts Press, 1977, pp. 181–202.

233. ——. "*Macbeth*: Drama and Dream." In *Literary Criticism and Psychology*. Ed. J. P. Strelka. University Park: Pennsylvania State Univ. Press, 1976. Reprinted in Sprich and Noland, eds., *Whispered Meanings*, pp. 212–34.

234. Leverenz, David. "The Woman in Hamlet: An Interpersonal View." *Signs*, 4 (1978), 291–308. (See Chapter 6 in this book.)

235. Lewis, Allan. "*A Midsummer Night's Dream*: Fairy Fantasy or Erotic Nightmare?" *Educational Theater Journal*, 21 (1969), 251–58.

236. Lewis, Anthony J. "Interdisciplinary Approaches to Shakespeare Studies." *Shakespeare Research Opportunities*, 7-8 (1975), 53-60.

237. Lewis, Aubrey. "The Psychology of Shakespeare." In Lewis, *The State of Psychiatry*. New York: Science House, 1967, pp. 295-98.

238. Lichtenberg, J. D., and C. Lichtenberg. "Prince Hal's Conflict: Adolescent Idealism and Buffoonery." *Journal of the American Psychoanalytic Association*, 17 (1969), 873-87.

239. Lickorish, John R. "The Casket Scenes from *The Merchant of Venice*: Symbolism of Life Style." *Journal of Individual Psychology*, 25 (1969), 3-9.

240. Lidz, Theodore. *Hamlet's Enemy: Madness and Myth in "Hamlet."* New York: Basic Books, 1975.

241. Lindauer, M. S. "Quantitative Analyses of Psychoanalytic Studies of Shakespeare." *Journal of Psychology*, 72 (1969), 3-9.

242. Llorca, Raymond L. "*Macbeth* and the Use of Appetite in Tragedy." *Silliman Journal*, 15 (1968), 151-89.

243. Long, Michael. *The Unnatural Scene: A Study in Shakespearean Tragedy*. London: Methuen, 1976.

244. Lyman, Stanford M., and Marvin B. Scott. *The Drama of Social Reality*. New York: Oxford, 1976.

245. Lynch, William. "The Imagination of the Drama." *Review of Existential Psychology and Psychiatry*, 14 (1975-76), 1-10.

246. Lyons, Charles R. "Some Variations of *Kindermord* as Dramatic Archetype." *Comparative Drama*, 1 (1967), 56-70.

247. Lyons, Clifford. "The Complex Oedipus Complex of Shakespeare's Plays." *The Shakespeare Newsletter*, 18 (1968), 40-41.

248. Lyotard, Jean-François. "Oedipe juif." *Critique* (Paris), 26 (1970), 530-45.

249. Maguin, Jean-Marie. "Imagination and Image Types in *King Lear*." *Cahiers élisabéthains*, 9 (1976), 9-28.

250. Mairet, Philip. "*Hamlet* as a Study in Individual Psychology." *Journal of Individual Psychology*, 25 (1969), 71-88.

251. Maitra, Sitansu. *Psychological Realism and Archetypes: The Trickster in Shakespeare*. Calcutta: Bookland, 1967.

252. Manheim, Leonard F. "The Mythical Joys of Shakespeare: Or, What You Will." In *Shakespeare Encomium*. Ed. Anne Paolucci. New York: City College of City Univ., 1964. Reprinted in Faber, ed., *The Design Within*, pp. 465-78.

253. Manheim, Leonard F., M. D. Faber, and Harvey Resnick. Introduction to a special issue entitled *A New Anatomy of Melancholy*. *University of Hartford Studies in Literature*, 10 (1978), 1-13.

254. Manocchio, Tony, and William Petitt. *Families Under Stress: A Psychological Interpretation*. London: Routledge and Kegan Paul, 1975.

255. Margoshes, A. "Projective Imagery in Shakespeare." *Journal of Projective Techniques and Personality Assessment*, 30 (1966), 290-92.

256. Maruta, Kei. "The Necessary Question of the Play." *Bungei to Shiso* (Fukuoka Women's College), 41 (1977), 1-41.

257. Matchett, William H. "Shylock, Iago, and *Sir Thomas More*: With Some Further Discussion of Shakespeare's Imagination." *PMLA*, 92 (1977), 217-30.

258. Mathieu, Gisèle. "Mythes, symboles, signes." *Revue de littérature comparée* (Paris), 202 (1977), 287-98.

259. McCall, John J., *William Shakespeare: Spacious in the Possession of Dirt.* Washington: Univ. Press of America, 1977.

260. McCurdy, H. "Shakespeare: King of Infinite Space." *Psychology Today*, April 1968, pp. 39-41, 66-69.

261. McEwan, Neil. "The Lost Childhood of Lear's Fool." *Essays in Criticism*, 26 (1976), 209-17.

262. McLaughlin, Anne L. "The Journeys in *King Lear*." *American Imago*, 29 (1972), 384-99.

263. McLaughlin, John J. "The Dynamics of Power in *King Lear*: An Adlerian Interpretation." *Shakespeare Quarterly*, 29 (1978), 37-43.

264. McMahon, Carol E. "Psychosomatic Concepts in the Works of Shakespeare." *Journal of the History of the Behavioral Sciences*, 12 (July 1976), 275-82.

265. Melon, J. "A Study of the Psychopathology of Inter-racial Marriage." *Feuillets psychiatriques de Liège*, 5 (1972), 5-14.

266. Mendel, Sydney. "The Revolt against the Father: The Adolescent Hero in *Hamlet* and *The Wild Duck*." *Essays in Criticism*, 14 (1964), 171-78.

267. Mills, Gordon. *Hamlet's Castle: The Study of Literature as a Social Experience.* Austin: Univ. of Texas Press, 1976.

268. Mirek, Roman. "*Burza* Szekspira dramatem osobowosi (Shakespeare's *Tempest*: A Drama of Personality)." *Przeglad Lekarski*, 24 (1968), 721-25.

269. ———. "Erotyka w komediach Szekspira. *Sen nocy letniej. Wieczor Trzech Kroli. Jak qam sie podoba* (Eroticism in Shakespeare's Comedies: *A Midsummer Night's Dream. Twelfth Night. As You Like It*)." *Przeglad Lekarski*, 25 (1969), 391-95.

270. ———. "Kroniki dramatyczne Szekspira w ocenie psychiatrycznej. II. *Tragedia Ryszarda 3. Zycie e smierc krola Jana. Slawna historia zycia Henryka 8* (Dramatic Chronicles of Shakespeare in Psychiatric Evaluation. II. *Tragedy of Richard III. Life and Death of King John. Famous History of the Life of Henry VIII*)." *Przeglad Lekarski*, 23 (1967), 861-64.

271. ———. "Kroniki i tragedie Szekspira w swietle psychiatrii sadowei (Shakespeare's Chronicles and Tragedies in the Light of Forensic Psychiatry)." *Przeglad Lekarski*, 25 (1969), 331-33.

272. ———. "(The Personality of William Shakespeare)." *Przeglad Lekarski*, 25 (1969), 556-58.

273. ———. "(Psychiatric Problems in Shakespeare's Sonnets)." *Przeglad Lekarski*, 24 (1968), 885-86.

274. ———. "Spojrzenis psychiatry na komedia Szekspira. I. *Wesole kumoszki z Windsoru. Kupiec weneski. Miaraka za miarke. Uglaskanie sekutnicy* (Psychiatric Insight into Shakespeare's Comedies. I. *The Merry Wives of Windsor. The Merchant of Venice. Measure for Measure. The Taming of the Shrew*)." *Przeglad Lekarski*, 24 (1968), 498-502.

275. ———. "Sylwetki osobowosciowe postaci Szekspirowskich tragedii. I. *Krol Lir* i *Otello* (Sketches of the Personalities of Characters in Shakespeare's Tragedies. I. *King Lear* and *Othello*)." *Przeglad Lekarski*, 22 (1966), 557-61.

276. ———. "Sylwetki osobowosciowe postaci Szekspirowskich tragedii. *Troilus i*

Kresyda. Koriolan. Tymon Atenczyk. Perykles. Tytus Andronikus. Cymbelin. Romeo i Julia (Sketches of the Personalities of Characters in Shakespeare's Tragedies: *Troilus and Cressida. Coriolanus. Timon of Athens. Pericles. Titus Andronicus. Cymbeline. Romeo and Juliet*)." *Przeglad Lekarski*, 23 (1967), 477-80.

277. ——. "Sylwetki osobowosciowe postaci tragedii Szekspirowskich (Sketches of the Personalities of Characters in Shakespeare's Plays)." *Przeglad Lekarski*, 23 (1967), 415-18.

278. ——. "Szekspirowski *Hamlet* w swietle badan literackich i wspolczesnej psychiatrii (Shakespeare's *Hamlet* in the Light of Literary Research and Modern Psychiatry)." *Przeglad Lekarski*, 22 (1966), 761-65.

279. ——. "William Szekspir dramturg chorej psychiki (William Shakespeare: Dramatist of the Sick Psyche)." *Przeglad Lekarski*, 25 (1969), 445-48.

280. Mise, Raymond S. "Motivation and Ritual Again in *Julius Caesar*." *Paunch* (State Univ. of New York at Buffalo), 23 (1965), 45-57.

281. Moglen, Helene. "Disguise and Development: The Self and Society in *Twelfth Night*." *Literature and Psychology*, 23 (1973), 13-20.

282. Monterde, Francisco. "Un Arquetipo: El Otelo de Shakespeare." *Cuadernos de bellas artes* (April 1964), 24-27.

283. Mukherjee, Ashim Kumar. "The 'Blissfully Unconscious' and the 'Careful Observer': A Jungian Interpretation of *Othello*." *Literary Criterion* (Univ. of Mysore), 13 (1978), 1-16.

284. Nardo, A. K. "Romeo and Juliet Up against the Wall." *Paunch* (State Univ. of New York at Buffalo), 48-49 (1977), 126-32.

285. Narkin, Anthony P. "Day-Residue and Christian References in Clarence's Dream." *Texas Studies in Literature and Language*, 9 (1967), 147-50.

286. Neely, Carol Thomas. "Detachment and Engagement in Shakespeare's Sonnets: 94, 116, and 129." *PMLA*, 92 (1977), 83-95.

287. ——. "Women and Men in *Othello*: 'What should such a fool/Do with so good a woman?'" *Shakespeare Studies*, 10 (1977), 133-58.

288. Neiditz, Minerva. "Primary Process Mentation and the Structure of *Timon of Athens*." *Hartford Studies in Literature*, 11 (1979), 24-35.

289. Neill, Michael. "Shakespeare's Hall of Mirrors: Play, Politics, and Psychology in *Richard III*." *Shakespeare Studies*, 8 (1975), 99-129.

290. Nelson, Cary. "Prospero's Island: The Visionary Body of *The Tempest*." In Nelson, *The Incarnate Word: Literature as Verbal Space*. Urbana: Univ. of Illinois Press, 1973, pp. 53-75.

291. Noland, Richard W. "Psychoanalysis and *Hamlet*." *Hartford Studies in Literature*, 6 (1974), 268-81.

292. Norton, Rictor H. *The Homosexual Literary Tradition: An Interpretation*. New York: Revisionist Press, 1974. (See pp. 242-58, 264-70.)

293. Novy, Marianne L. "'And You Smile Not, He's Gagged': Mutuality in Shakespearean Comedy." *Philological Quarterly*, 55 (1976), 178-94.

294. ——. "Patriarchy and Play in *The Taming of the Shrew*." *English Literary Renaissance*, 9 (1979), 264-80.

295. Orbison, Tucker. "'This Distracted Globe': Self in *Hamlet*." In *Perspectives*

on "Hamlet". Ed. W. G. Holzberger and P. B. Waldeck. Lewisburg, Pa.: Bucknell Univ. Press, 1975, pp. 112-41.

296. Orgel, Shelley. "Iago." *American Imago*, 25 (1968), 258-73.

297. Ota, Kazuaki. "On *Richard III.* Act One, Scene Two." *Cairn* (Kyushu University), 21 (1978), 48-60.

298. Otsuki, Kenju. *Psychoanalytic Insight of the Poet Shakespeare: Analytic Appreciation of His Five Great Tragedies* (in Japanese, summary in English). Tokyo, 1974.

299. Otten, Terry. "*Woyzeck* and *Othello*: The Dimensions of Melodrama." *Comparative Drama*, 12 (1978), 123-36.

300. Padel, J. H. "'That the Thought of Hearts Can Mend': An Introduction to Shakespeare's Sonnets for Psychotherapists and Others." *Times Literary Supplement* (London), 19 Dec. 1975, pp. 1519-21.

301. Paris, Bernard J. "Hamlet and His Problems: A Horneyan Analysis." *Centennial Review*, 21 (1977), 36-66.

302. Partridge, Eric. *Shakespeare's Bawdy: A Literary and Psychological Essay and a Comprehensive Glossary*. Revised and enlarged. London: Routledge and Kegan Paul, 1968.

303. Payne, Michael. "What's the Matter with Hamlet?" In Holzberger and Waldeck, eds., *Perspectives on "Hamlet,"* p. 100-11.

304. ———. "Phenomenological Criticism of Shakespeare." *Shakespeare Research Opportunities*, 7-8 (1975), 75-77.

305. Pearlman, E. "Shakespeare, Freud, and the Two Usuries, or, Money's a Meddler." *English Literary Renaissance*, 2 (1972), 217-36.

306. Pedrini, Duilio T., and Lura N. Gregory. "Hamlet's Character: The Quest of Literary Analysis." *Journal of the American Academy of Psychoanalysis*, 1 (1973), 417-27.

307. Perloff, Evelyn. *A Selected Bibliography on Psychology and Literature: "Psychological Abstracts" 1960-1969. Catalog of Selected Documents in Psychology*, vol. 4, no. 68-69 (Summer 1974). MS. 661.

308. Perret, Marion. "'A Hair of the Shrew . . .'" *Hartford Studies in Literature*, 11 (1979), 36-41.

309. Perrot, Jean. "Nativités et paques gémellaires: La magie du quatuor shakespearien." *Mythe et littérature sous le signe des Jumeaux*. Paris: Presses Univ. de France, 1976, pp. 73-143.

310. Pinder, Donna. "The Normalcy of Suffering and Artistic Survival." *Paunch* (State Univ. of New York at Buffalo), 38 (1974), 66-78.

311. Plank, Robert. "Hamlet and Prospero: Father Figures." In Plank, *The Emotional Significance of Imaginary Beings*. Springfield, Ill.: Thomas Press, 1968, pp. 147-71.

312. Pönitz, K. "Shakespeare und die Psychiatrie." *Therapie der Gegenwart* (Berlin), 103 (1964), 1463-78.

313. Proser, Matthew. "Hamlet and the Name of Action." In *Essays on Shakespeare*. Ed. G. R. Smith. University Park, Pa.: Pennsylvania State Univ. Press, 1965, pp. 84-114.

314. ———. *The Heroic Image in Five Shakespearean Tragedies*. Princeton, N.J.: Princeton Univ. Press, 1965.

315. ——. "Shakespeare of the Sonnets." *The Critical Survey*, 5 (1971), 243-54.
316. Pryse, Marjorie. "Lust for Audience: An Interpretation of *Othello*." *ELH*, 43 (1976), 461-78.
317. Quijano, Margarita. "La Tortura de Macbeth." *Cuadernos Americanos* (Mexico), (July-August 1964), 243-61.
318. Rabkin, Leslie Y. *Psychopathology and Literature*. San Francisco: Chandler, 1960.
319. Rabkin, Leslie Y., and Jeffrey Brown. "Some Monster in His Thought: Sadism and Tragedy in *Othello*." *Literature and Psychology*, 23 (1973), 59-67.
320. Ramnoux, Clemence. "Mythe, conte et tragédie: une interpretation Freudienne du *Roi Lear*." *La revue d'esthétique*, 21 (1968), 1-25.
321. Ravich, Robert A. "A Psychoanalytic Study of Shakespeare's Early Plays." *Psychoanalytic Quarterly*, 33 (1964), 388-410.
322. ——. "Shakespeare and Psychiatry." *Literature and Psychology*, 14 (1964), 97-105.
323. ——. "'Such seething brains, such shaping fantasies.'" *Abbottempo*, 2 (19 Aug. 1964), 28-35.
324. Reed, Robert R., Jr. "Richard II: Portrait of a Psychotic." *JGE: The Journal of General Education*, 16 (1964), 55-67.
325. Reid, Stephen. "Desdemona's Guilt." *American Imago*, 27 (1970), 245-62.
326. ——. "Hamlet's Melancholia." *American Imago*, 31 (1974), 378-400.
327. ——. "'I am misanthropos': A Psychoanalytic Reading of Shakespeare's *Timon of Athens*." *Psychoanalytic Review*, 56 (1969), 442-52.
328. ——. "In Defence of Goneril and Regan." *American Imago*, 27 (1970), 226-44.
329. ——. "Othello's Jealousy." *American Imago*, 25 (1968), 274-93.
330. ——. "Othello's Occupation: Beyond the Pleasure Principle." *Psychoanalytic Review*, 63 (1976-77), 555-70.
331. ——. "A Psychoanalytic Reading of *Troilus and Cressida* and *Measure for Measure*." *Psychoanalytic Review*, 57 (1970), 263-82.
332. ——. "*The Winter's Tale*." *American Imago*, 27 (1970), 262-78.
333. Ricciardelli, Rachel M. "*King Lear* and the Theory of Disengagement." *Gerontologist*, 13 (1973), 148-52.
334. Riemer, Andrew. "*King Lear* and the Egocentric Universe." *Balcony: The Sidney Review*, 5 (1966), 33-42.
335. Riklin, Franz. "Shakespeare's *A Midsummer Night's Dream*: ein Beitrag zum Individuationprozess." In *The Reality of the Psyche: The Proceedings of the Third International Congress for Analytic Psychology*. Ed. Joseph B. Wheelwright. New York: G. P. Putnam's Sons, 1968, pp. 262-77.
336. Roberts, Jeanne A. "Shakespeare's Forests and Trees." *Southern Humanities Review*, 11 (1977), 108-25.
337. Roberts, Patrick. *The Psychology of Tragic Drama*. London, Routledge and Kegan Paul, 1975.
338. Robertson, P. L. "The Role of the Political Usurper: Macbeth and Boris Godounov." *American Imago*, 23 (1966), 95-109.
339. Rogers, Robert. "The Dynamics of Metaphor: Modes of Mentation in Poetry." *Hartford Studies in Literature*, 3 (1971), 157-90. (See pp. 172-73.)

340. ——. "Endopsychic Drama in *Othello.*" *Shakespeare Quarterly*, 20 (1969), 205–15.

341. ——. *Metaphor: A Psychoanalytic View*, Berkeley: Univ. of California Press, 1978.

342. ——. "On the Metapsychology of Poetic Language: Modal Ambiguity." *International Journal of Psycho-Analysis*, 54 (1973), 61–74. (See pp. 5–6.)

343. ——. *A Psychoanalytic Study of the Double in Literature*. Detroit: Wayne State Univ. Press, 1970.

344. Rollin, Henry R. "Psychiatry and Shakespeare." *University of Leeds Review*, 9 (1964), 136–47.

345. Rose, G. J. "*King Lear* and the Use of Humor in Treatment." *Journal of the American Psychoanalytic Association*, 17 (1969), 927–40.

346. Rosenberg, Marvin. *The Masks of King Lear.* Berkeley: Univ. of California Press, 1972.

347. ——. *The Masks of Macbeth.* Berkeley: Univ. of California Press, 1978.

348. ——. "Shakespeare's Fantastic Trick: *Measure for Measure.*" *Sewanee Review*, 80 (1972), 51–72.

349. Ross, Frank. "'Once More unto the Breach, Dear Friends. . . .'" *Paunch* (State Univ. of New York at Buffalo), 23 (1965), 36–45.

350. Rothenberg, Alan B. "Infantile Fantasies in Shakespearean Metaphor: (I) The Fear of Being Smothered." *Psychoanalytic Review*, 60 (1973), 205–22.

351. ——. "Infantile Fantasies in Shakespearean Metaphor: (II) Scopophilia and Fears of Ocular Rape and Castration." *Psychoanalytic Review*, 60 (1973–74), 533–56.

352. ——. "Infantile Fantasies in Shakespearean Metaphor: (III) Photophobia, Love of Darkness, and 'Black' Complexions." *Psychoanalytic Review*, 64 (1977), 173–202.

353. ——. "The Oral Rape Fantasy and Rejection of Mother in the Imagery of Shakespeare's *Venus and Adonis.*" *Psychoanalytic Quarterly*, 40 (1971), 447–68.

354. Rothenberg, Albert, and Bette Greenberg. *The Index of Scientific Writings on Creativity: Creative Men and Women.* Hamden, Conn.: Shoe String Press, 1974.

355. Roy, Emil. "War and Manliness in Shakespeare's *Troilus and Cressida,*" *Comparative Drama*, 7 (1973), 107–20.

356. Rubin, Samuel S. "*Hamlet*: A Psychoanalytic Re-interpretation." *Psychoanalytic Review*, 57 (1971), 660–70.

357. Saagpakk, Paul F. "A Survey of Psychopathology in British Literature from Shakespeare to Hardy." *Literature and Psychology*, 18 (1968), 135–65. (See pp. 140–42.)

358. Sanders, Kenneth. "Shakespeare's *The Winter's Tale*—and Some Notes on the Analysis of a Present-Day Leontes." *International Review of Psycho-analysis*, 5 (1978), 175–78.

359. Sasaki, M. S. "Influence Structure of *Julius Caesar.*" *Psychological Reports*, 39 (1976), 1191–95.

360. Sasayama, Takashi. "Ishiki Kozo to Drama no Keitai: Genshogaku-teki Shakespeare Josetsu" ("Structure of Consciousness and Form of Drama:

A Phenomenological Introduction to Shakespeare"). In *Shakespeare no Engekiteki Fudo* (*Dramatic Climate of Shakespeare*). Ed. Nihon Shakespeare Kyokai. Tokyo: Kenkyusha, 1977, pp. 2-22.

361. Saul, L. J. "*Othello:* Projection in Art." *Journal of the American Medical Association*, 200 (3 April 1967), 39-40.

362. Scheff, Thomas J. "Audience Awareness and Catharsis in Drama." *Psychoanalytic Review*, 63 (1976-77), 529-54.

363. Schlosser, Anselm. "Das Motiv der Entfremdung in der *Komedie der Irrungen.*" *Shakespeare Jahrbuch* (Weimar), 100-01 (1965), 57-71.

364. Schmidl, Fritz, "Problems of Method in Applied Psychoanalysis." *Psychoanalytic Quarterly*, 41 (1972), 402-19.

365. Schneiderman, Stuart Allen. "The Saying of Hamlet." *Sub-stance*, 8 (1974), 77-88.

366. Schwartz, Murray M. "Between Fantasy and Imagination: A Psychological Exploration of *Cymbeline.*" In *Psychoanalysis and Literary Process*. Ed. Frederick Crews. Cambridge, Mass. Winthrop Publishers, 1970, pp. 219-83.

367. ———. "Critic, Define Thyself." In Hartman, ed., *Psychoanalysis and the Question of the Text*, pp. 1-17.

368. ———. "Leontes' Jealousy in *The Winter's Tale.*" *American Imago*, 30 (1973), 250-73.

369. ———. "Shakespeare Through Contemporary Psychoanalysis." *Hebrew University Studies in Literature*, 5 (1977), 182-98. (See Chapter 2 in this book.)

370. ———. *A Thematic Introduction to Shakespeare*. Saratoga Springs, N.Y.: Empire State College, State Univ. of New York, 1974.

371. ———. "*The Winter's Tale*: Loss and Transformation." *American Imago*, 32 (1975), 145-99.

372. Searles, Harold. "The Psychodynamics of Vengefulness." In Searles, *Collected Papers on Schizophrenia and Related Subjects*. New York: International Univ. Press, 1965, pp. 177-91. (See espec. pp. 190-91.)

373. Seidenberg, Robert. "Fidelity and Jealousy: Socio-Cultural Considerations." *Psychoanalytic Review*, 54 (1967), 27-52.

374. Serpieri, Alessandro. *Othello, l'Eros Negato: Psicoanalisi di una proiezione distruttiva*. Milano: Il Formichiere, 1978.

375. Servadio, Emilio. "Critica y psicoanalisis." *Archivos Panameños de psicologia*, 1 (1965), 164-69.

376. Seward, T. C., and M. D. Faber. "A Note on Stephen Reid's Essay, 'I am misanthropos': A Psychoanalytic Reading of Shakespeare's *Timon of Athens.*" *Psychoanalytic Review*, 58 (1971), 617-23. (See Item 327 above.)

377. Seymour-Smith, Martin. "Shakespeare's Sonnets 1-42: A Psychological Reading." In *New Essays on Shakespeare's Sonnets*. Ed. Milton Landry. New York: AMS Press, 1976, pp. 21-39.

378. Shainess, Natalie. "*Hamlet*: The Coup that Failed." *Journal of the American Academy of Psychoanalysis*, 3 (1975), 383-403.

379. Shapiro, Stephen A. "Othello's Desdemona." *Literature and Psychology*, 14 (1964), 56-61. Reprinted in Faber, ed., *The Design Within*, pp. 185-92.

380. ———. "*Romeo and Juliet*: Reversals, Contraries, Transformations, and Ambivalence." *College English*, 25 (1964), 498-501.

381. ——. "The Varying Shore of the World" Ambivalence in *Antony and Cleopatra*." *Modern Language Quarterly*, 27 (1966), 18–32.

382. Shupe, Donald R. "The Wooing of Lady Anne: A Psychological Inquiry." *Shakespeare Quarterly*, 29 (1978), 28–36.

383. Sibony, Daniel. "*Hamlet*: A Writing-Effect." Trans. James Hulbert and Joshua Wilner. *Yale French Studies*, 55–56 (1977), 53–93.

384. Silhol, Robert. "Magie et utopie dans *La Tempête*." *Etudes Anglaises*, 17 (1964), 447–56.

385. Simon, Alfred. "Les masques de la violence." *Esprit*, 11 (1973), 515–27.

386. Simons, Richard C. "The Clown as a Father Figure." *Psychoanalytic Review*, 52 (Summer 1965), 75–91.

387. Sinfield, Alan. "Lear and Laing." *Essays in Criticism*, 26 (1976), 1–16.

388. Singh, Ram Sewak. "A Psychological Approach to Shakespeare." *Vidya* (Journal of Gujrat Univ.), 8 (1965), 81–98.

389. Skura, Meredith. "New Interpretations for Interpretation in *Measure for Measure*." *Boundary 2*, 7 (Winter 1979), 39–59.

390. Slochower, Harry. *Mythopoesis: Mythic Patterns in the Literary Classics*. Detroit: Wayne State Univ. Press, 1970.

391. ——. "Suicides in Literature: Their Ego Function." *American Imago*, 32 (1975), 389–416. (See "A Note on Ophelia," pp. 403–04.)

392. Smith, Gordon Ross. "The Balance of Themes in *Romeo and Juliet*." In *Essays on Shakespeare*. Ed. G. R. Smith. Pennsylvania State Univ. Press, 1965, pp. 15–66. (See esp. pp. 56–63.)

393. ——. "Negative and Positive upon the Psychology of Shakespearean Theater and Audiences." *College Literature*, 5 (1978), 94–100. (See Item 411 below.)

394. Smith, Stephen L. "*A Midsummer Night's Dream*: Shakespeare, Play, and Metaplay." *Centennial Review*, 21 (1977), 194–209.

395. Smith, Warren D. "Romeo's Final Dream." *Modern Language Review*, 62 (1967), 579–83.

396. Snodgrass, W. D. "Moonshine and Sunny Beams: Ruminations on *A Midsummer Night's Dream*." In Snodgrass, *In Radical Pursuit: Critical Essays and Lectures*. New York: Harper and Row, 1975, pp. 203–40.

397. Spevack, Marvin. "Hamlet and Imagery: The Mind's Eye." *Die Neueren Sprachen* (May 1966), 203–13.

398. Staebler, Warren. "The Sexual Nihilism of Iago." *Sewanee Review*, 83 (1975), 284–304.

399. Stampfer, Judah. *The Tragic Engagement: A Study of Shakespeare's Classical Tragedies*. New York: Funk & Wagnalls, 1968.

400. Stanton, R. G. "*A Midsummer Night's Dream*: A Structural Study." *Psychological Reports*, 20 (1967), 657–58.

401. Stanzel, F. K. "Hamlet—psychologisches oder literarhistorisches Problem?" In *Gestalt und Wirklichkeit. Festgabe für Ferdinand Weinhandl*. Ed. R. Muhler and J. Fischl. Berlin: Duncker und Humblot, 1967, pp. 397–409.

402. Starobinski, Jean. Preface to Ernest Jones, *Hamlet et Oedipe*. Trans. Anne-Marie Le Gall. Paris: Gallimard, 1967.

403. Steig, Michael. "The Grotesque and the Aesthetic Response in Shakespeare, Dickens, and Gunther Grass." *Comparative Literary Studies*, 6 (1969), 167–81.

404. Stephenson, William E. "The Adolescent Dream-World of *The Two Gentlemen of Verona.*" *Shakespeare Quarterly*, 17 (1966), 165-68.

405. Stetner, S.C.V. "Baptista and His Daughters." *Psychoanalytic Review*, 60 (1973), 233-37.

406. ——. "The Bawdy Bard (I). Shakespeare and the Devil, an Exploration in Subliminal Obscenity." *Fragments* (New York), 3 (1971), 11-19.

407. Stetner, S.C.V., and Oscar B. Goodman. "Lear's Darker Purpose." *Literature and Psychology*, 18 (1968), 82-90.

408. Stockholder, Katherine. "Fictions, Phantasies, and 'Reality': A Re-evaluation." *Literature and Psychology*, 26 (1976), 17-30.

409. ——. "Hamlet: Between Night and Day." *Literature and Psychology*, 21 (1971), 7-20.

410. Stoller, Robert J. "Shakespearean Tragedy: *Coriolanus.*" *Psychoanalytic Quarterly*, 35 (1966), 263-74. Reprinted in Faber, ed., *The Design Within*, pp. 329-39.

411. Styan, J. L. "Psychology in the Study of Drama: The Negative and the Positive." *College Literature*, 5 (1978), 77-93. (See Item 393 above.)

412. Summers, Joseph H. "The Anger of Prospero." *Michigan Quarterly Review*, 12 (1973), 116-35.

413. Tennenhouse, Leonard. "*Coriolanus*: History and the Crisis of Semantic Order." *Comparative Drama*, 10 (1976), 328-46.

414. Tennenhouse, Leonard, ed. *The Practice of Psychoanalytic Criticism*. Detroit: Wayne State Univ. Press, 1976.

415. Teplitz, Zelda. "*King Lear* and *Macbeth* in Relation to Shakespeare." *Bulletin of the Philadelphia Association for Psychoanalysis*, 20 (1970), 196-211.

416. Tomieic, Zlatko. "Otac i sin, glavni eticki problem Shakespeare ovog *Hamletu.*" *Marvlic* (Zagreb), 1 (1968), 64-71.

417. Toole, William B., III. "'Iagothello': Psychological Action and the Theme of Transformation in *Othello.*" *South Atlantic Bulletin*, 41 (1976), 71-77.

418. ——. "Psychological Action and Structure in *Richard II.*" *Journal of General Education*, 30 (1978), 165-84.

419. Trachtenberg, Stanley. "The Economy of Comedy." *Psychoanalytic Review*, 62 (1975-76), 557-78.

420. Traci, Philip J. "Suggestions About the Bawdry in *Romeo and Juliet.*" *South Atlantic Quarterly*, 71 (1972), 573-86.

421. Tricomi, Albert H. "The Aesthetics of Mutilation in *Titus Andronicus.*" *Shakespeare Survey*, 27 (1974), 11-19.

422. ——. "The Mutilated Garden in *Titus Andronicus.*" *Shakespeare Studies*, 9 (1976), 89-106.

423. Trosman, H. "Freud and the Controversy over Shakespearean Authorship." *Journal of the American Psychological Association*, 13 (1965), 475-98.

424. Vaidyanathan, T. G. "The Psychological Interpretation of *Hamlet.*" *Osmania Journal of English Studies*, 4 (1964), 67-76.

425. Valesio, Paolo. "'That Glib and Oylie Art': Cordelia and the Rhetoric of Antirhetoric." *Versus: Quaderni di studi semiotici* (Milano), 16 (1977), 91-117.

426. Van Kaam, Adrian, and Kathleen Healy. "Angelo in Shakespeare's *Measure for Measure.*" In Van Kaam and Healy, *The Demon and the Dove: Personality Growth through Literature.* Pittsburgh: Duquesne Univ. Press, 1967, pp. 139-67.

427. Varga, Laszlo, and Bonnieta Fye. "Ghost and Antic Disposition: An Existential and Psychoanalytic Interpretation of Shakespeare's *Hamlet.*" *Psychiatric Quarterly,* 40 (1966), 607-27.

428. Vesny-Wagner, L. "*Macbeth*: 'Fair is Foul and Foul is Fair.'" *American Imago,* 25 (1968), 242-57.

429. Von Stockert, F. G. "(Shakespeare and Modern Psychiatry)." *Jahrbuch für Psychologie und Psychotherapie,* 11 (1964), 42-50.

430. Vygotsky, Lev Semenovich. *The Psychology of Art.* Trans. A. N. Leontiev, Cambridge, Mass.: M.I.T. Press, 1971. (See pp. 166-96.)

431. Waldeck, Peter B. "Anxiety, Tragedy, and Hamlet's Delay." In Holzberger and Waldeck, eds., *Perspectives on "Hamlet,"* pp. 142-62.

432. Wall, John N., Jr. "Suffering and Charity: Similarities between Rank's View of Illness and Shakespeare's Christian Humanism." *Journal of the Otto Rank Association,* 11 (1976), 29-32.

433. Wangh, Martin. "A Psychoanalytic Commentary on Shakespeare's *The Tragedie of King Richard the Second.*" *Psychoanalytic Quarterly,* 37 (1968), 212-38.

434. Warnken, Henry L. "Iago as a Projection of Othello." In Paolucci, ed. *Shakespeare Encomium,* pp. 1-15.

435. Webber, Joan. "*Hamlet* and the Freeing of the Mind." In *English Renaissance Drama: Essays in Honor of Madeleine Doran and Mark Eccles.* Ed. Standish Henning, Robert Kimbrough, and Richard Knowles. Carbondale, Ill.: Univ. of Illinois Press, 1976, pp. 76-99.

436. Weigard, Hermann J. "Hamlet's Consistent Inconsistency." In *The Persistence of Shakespeare Idolatry.* Ed. Herbert Schueller. Detroit: Wayne State Univ. Press, 1964, pp. 135-72.

437. Weisberg, Richard. "Hamlet and *Ressentiment.*" *American Imago,* 29 (1971), 318-37.

438. Weissman, Philip. *Creativity in the Theater: A Psychoanalytic Study.* New York: Basic Books, 1965.

439. Welsh, Alexander. "The Loss of Men and Getting of Children: *All's Well That Ends Well* and *Measure for Measure.*" *Modern Language Review,* 73 (1978), 17-28.

440. West, Fred. "Iago the Psychopath." *Shakespeare Association Bulletin,* 43 (1978), 27-35.

441. West, L. J. "The Othello Syndrome." *Contemporary Psychoanalysis,* 4 (1968), 103-10.

442. Westlund, Joseph. "Ambivalence in the Player's Speech in *Hamlet.*" *Studies in English Literature,* 18 (1978), 245-56.

443. Wheeler, Richard P. "History, Character, and Conscience in *Richard III.*" *Comparative Drama,* 5 (1971-72), 301-21.

444. ——. "The King and the Physician's Daughter: *All's Well That Ends Well* and the Late Romances." *Comparative Drama,* 8 (1974-75), 311-27.

445. ——. "Marriage and Manhood in *All's Well That Ends Well*." *Bucknell Review*, 21 (1973), 103-24.

446. ——. "Poetry and Fantasy in Shakespeare's Sonnets 88-96." *Literature and Psychology*, 22 (1972), 151-62.

447. White, R. S. "The Tragedy of Ophelia." *Ariel: A Review of International English Literature*, 9 (April 1978), 41-53.

448. White, Sydney Howard. "What Freudian Death-Wish in the Crown 'Borrowing' in *2 Henry IV?*" *Ball State Teachers College Forum* (Autumn 1964), 42-44.

449. Wilkinson, Andrew M. "A Psychological Approach to *Julius Caesar*." *Review of English Literature*, 7 (1966), 65-78. Reprinted in Faber, ed., *The Design Within*, pp. 65-78.

450. Willbern, David. "Malvolio's Fall." *Shakespeare Quarterly*, 29 (1978), 85-90.

451. ——. "Paranoia, Criticism, and Malvolio." *Hartford Studies in Literature*, 11 (1979), 1-23.

452. ——. "Rape and Revenge in *Titus Andronicus*." *English Literary Renaissance*, 8 (1978), 159-82.

453. ——. "William Shakespeare: A Bibliography of Psychoanalytic and Psychological Criticism, 1964-1975." *International Review of Psycho-Analysis*, 5 (1978), 361-72.

454. Williams, George W. "The Complex Oedipus Complex: Claudius, the Rat." *The Shakespeare Newsletter*, 18 (1968), 12.

455. Williams, Gwyn. "*The Comedy of Errors* Rescued from Tragedy." *Review of English Literature*, 5 (1964), 63-71.

456. Williamson, Marilyn L. "Oedipal Fantasies in *Measure for Measure*." *Michigan Academician*, 9 (1976), 173-84.

457. Wilson, Emmett, Jr. "*Coriolanus*: The Anxious Bridegroom." *American Imago*, 25 (1968), 224-41.

458. Wolff, Reinhold. *Psychoanalytische Literaturkritik*. Munich: Fink, 1975.

459. Wolfinger, W. O. "The Seven Deaths in *Hamlet*." *Cresset* (Valparaiso), 28 (1965), 7-12.

460. Zarlove, Jerald. "Romeo and Juliet: The Rites of Disciplined Youth." *Paunch* (State Univ. of New York at Buffalo), 23 (1965), 10-17.

461. Zweig, Paul. "The Sonnets of Shakespeare." *The Heresy of Self-Love: A Study of Subversive Individualism*. New York: Harper and Row, 1968, pp. 100-08.

Index to Bibliography

The numbers following each subject refer to items in the bibliography.

Contributors

(in the order in which their essays appear in the anthology)

NORMAN N. HOLLAND'S contributions to the psychoanalytic study of literature are wide-ranging and influential. They include *Psychoanalysis and Shakespeare* (New York: McGraw-Hill, 1964), *The Dynamics of Literary Response* (London: Oxford Univ. Press, 1968), *Poems in Persons* (New York: W. W. Norton, 1973), *5 Readers Reading* (New Haven, Conn.: Yale Univ. Press, 1975), and *Laughing*, just completed at this writing. Director from 1970 to 1979 of the Center for the Psychological Study of the Arts (which he also founded), he is currently the James H. McNulty Professor of English at the State University of New York at Buffalo. He is writing a book about "third-phase" psychoanalysis and the theory of identity.

MURRAY M. SCHWARTZ is professor of English at the State University of New York at Buffalo, Director of the Center for the Psychological Study of the Arts, and Dean of the Colleges. He has written on Shakespeare, psychoanalytic interpretation and theory, D. H. Lawrence, Pushkin, Sylvia Plath, and Erik Erikson. He is currently working on *Toward Shakespearean Identity*, a book about Shakespeare's representations of the self.

DAVID SUNDELSON, who teaches at the New York State University College at Geneseo, is completing a book on Shakespeare's use of the family as a metaphor for conflicts concerning political authority. He has also published articles on De Quincey, Conrad, and Alfred Hitchcock.

LEONARD TENNENHOUSE, associate professor of English at Wayne State University, edits *Criticism* and has published articles on *Beowulf*, *Coriolanus*, *Tamburlaine*, and Sir Walter Raleigh. He also edited *The Practice of Psychoanalytic Criticism* (Detroit: Wayne State Univ. Press, 1976).

JOEL FINEMAN is writing a book called *The Subject of Shakespeare*; it will be a psychoanalytic account of the development of Shakespeare's canon. He has published articles on gnosticism, psychoanalytic theories

289

of sexual identity, and literary theory, and is assistant professor of English at the University of California at Berkeley.

DAVID LEVERENZ, associate professor and chairman of the English department at Livingston College, Rutgers University, is the author of *The Language of Puritan Feeling: an Exploration in Literature, Psychology and Social History* (New Brunswick, N.J.: Rutgers Univ. Press, 1979). He is also the co-editor, with George Levine, of *Mindful Pleasures: Essays on Thomas Pynchon* (Boston: Little, Brown, 1976), and has written various essays on American literature.

JANET ADELMAN is the author of *The Common Liar: An Essay on "Antony and Cleopatra"* (New Haven, Conn.: Yale Univ. Press, 1973) and editor of *Twentieth-Century Interpretations of "King Lear"* (Englewood Cliffs, N.J.: Prentice-Hall, 1978). Associate professor of English at the University of California at Berkeley, she has also published articles on Shakespeare, Milton, and Chaucer.

RICHARD P. WHEELER, associate professor of English, teaches at the University of Illinois. He has written *Shakespeare's Development and the Problem Comedies: Turn and Counter-turn* (Berkeley: Univ. of California Press, 1980). He has also published articles on Shakespeare, Yeats, and D. H. Lawrence.

MADELON S. GOHLKE has published articles on Nashe, Spenser, and Lyly. She is associate professor of English at the University of Minnesota and is writing a book on Shakespeare's language of masculine and feminine identity.

C. L. BARBER'S book on *Shakespeare's Festive Comedy* (Princeton, N.J.: Princeton Univ. Press, 1959) has been widely influential. He was professor of literature at the University of California at Santa Cruz and, at the time of his death, was completing a book on Shakespeare's development as it gives dramatic form to family relations.

MEREDITH SKURA has written *The Critic and the Psychoanalyst: Literary Uses of the Psychoanalytic Process* (New Haven, Conn.: Yale Univ. Press, 1980). She is associate professor of English at Rice University and has published articles on Shakespeare and psychoanalytic interpretation.

COPPÉLIA KAHN is associate professor of English at Wesleyan University and author of *Man's Estate: Masculine Identity in Shakespeare* (Berkeley: Univ. of California Press, 1980). She has also published several articles on Shakespeare.

DAVID WILLBERN has published articles on Kyd, Shakespeare, D. H. Lawrence, and Freud. An associate professor of English at the State University of New York at Buffalo, he is now completing a psychoanalytic study of the revenge play.

Index